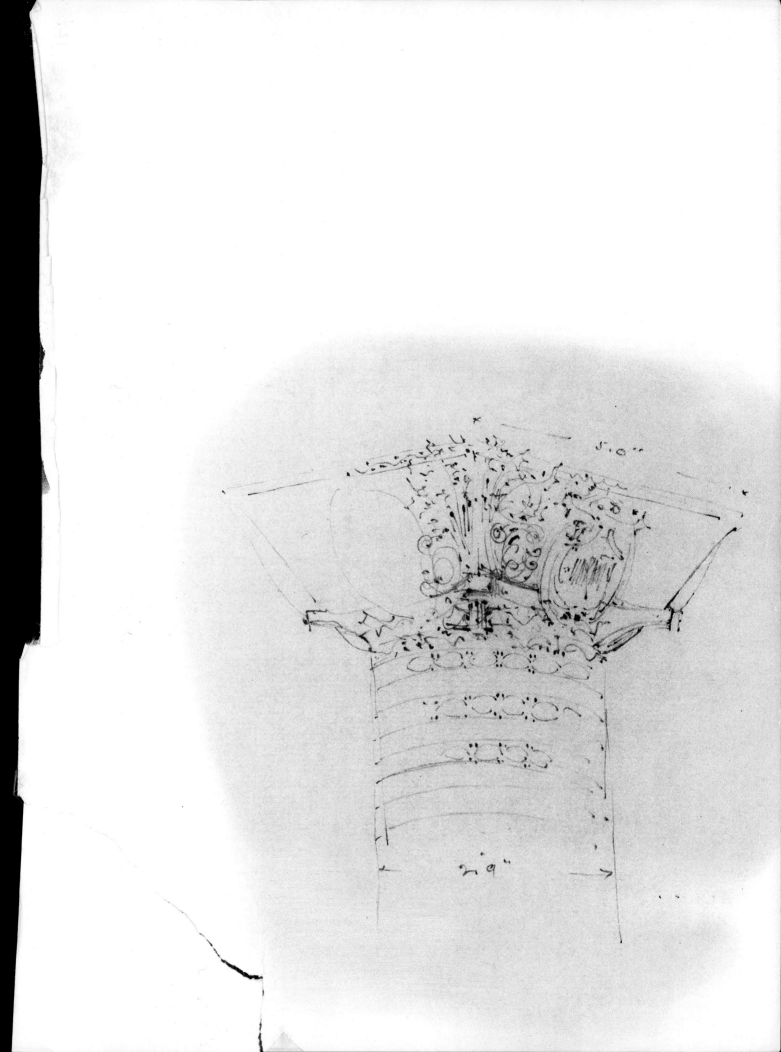

THREE CENTURIES OF
NOTABLE AMERICAN ARCHITECTS

Edited by JOSEPH J. THORNDIKE, JR.

Book Trade Distribution by Charles Scribner's Sons
Published by AMERICAN HERITAGE PUBLISHING CO., INC., New York

CONTENTS

Library of Congress Cataloging in Publication Data
Main entry under title:
Three centuries of notable American architects.
    Includes index.
    1. Architecture—United States—Addresses, essays, lectures. 2. Architects—United States—Addresses, essays, lectures. I. Thorndike, Joseph Jacobs, 1913—
NA705.T5 720'.92'2 [B] 81-7968
ISBN 0-8281-1157-X   AACR2
ISBN 0-8281-1158-8 (deluxe)

EDITOR
Joseph J. Thorndike, Jr.

ASSOCIATE EDITOR
Constance R. Roosevelt

ART DIRECTOR
Marleen Adlerblum

MANAGING EDITOR
Brenda Niemand

PICTURE RESEARCHER
Lucia Scala

ARCHITECTURAL CONSULTANT
William Marlin

ASSISTANT EDITOR
Donna Whiteman

RESEARCH LIBRARIANS
Laura Lane
Deborah Rogers

OPPOSITE PAGE: *A detail of Henry Hobson Richardson's Town Hall in North Easton, Massachusetts (David Plowden).* END PAPERS: *Detail of the cast-iron ornament designed by Louis Sullivan for the Carson, Pirie, Scott store (Kidder Smith).* HALF-TITLE PAGE: *Sullivan's sketch for a capital for the Prudential Building, Buffalo, New York (Avery Library, Columbia University).* TITLE PAGE: *Frank Lloyd Wright in his studio at Taliesin West (Mildred Schmertz).*

Introduction

The publication of this collection of biographical essays attests to the popularity of the architectural profession in the United States and suggests some questions regarding biography as a historical method. It is true that history resolves itself into the actions of individual human beings, but history told purely as biography is not history entire—or even quite history itself. This is especially the case with the history of art, where the major relevant data are not human thoughts or actions but the results of those activities, i.e., works of art. The human intentions that give rise to works of art are transformed by the process of art itself; they result in objects which are in no way the simple sum of those intentions, and whose effects, as works of art, go on and on in chain after incalculable chain.

Works of art are the most protean of documents. Each generation perceives them in new ways. They have as many meanings as those who experience them can bring to them and draw from them. They are bound into the culture which produced them, but if they are in some way enduring works of art, they will eventually outlive the codes of that culture and suggest new meanings and ways of seeing not imagined when they were made.

This has most markedly been the case with American architecture, whose forms have changed the world. No collection of essays, however able or charming, which focuses upon the personalities of its makers can trace that architecture's complex development in any entirely satisfactory way. It is always a mistake to forsake the art for its makers. It is in their art, not in themselves, that artists are at their most human. In it they transcend the littleness of humanity and magnify its grandeur. It is therefore only through art of one kind or another, and perhaps through architecture most of all, that the shape of a larger humanity can be suggested, imaged, or perceived.

For that reason it is in a sense not too important to ask who is and who is not represented in these essays. The choice is unexceptionable on the whole—and generally a conservative one. It is interesting to note that Raymond Hood would have been on the list fifty years ago but not twenty years ago, and probably not Richard Morris Hunt either. Forty years ago Maybeck would not have been included, and reactionaries would have squabbled over Frank Lloyd Wright, while Mies's work in America had only just begun and Eero Saarinen had hardly gotten started. It is true that one must regret the absence of Frank Furness, without whose inimitable buildings no feeling for all that was strongest in the nineteenth century can be gained. One might also question the capping off of the structure with a general essay on living architects. If there is validity in the decision to tell the story in terms of persons, then it is an existential responsibility to make a choice among living persons as well. Given that challenge, I would choose Robert Venturi, whose writings and buildings have turned architecture wholly around, and, rather to my surprise, Philip Johnson, who throughout a long lifetime has never given up in his search for new and significant forms. It goes without saying that other historians might make other choices.

But the central issue is a different one. It involves a need to fill out the history of American architecture in some of the ways that biography cannot do. This is especially so when a major part of that history must be based on typology, since it has to do largely with the development of two building types: the single-family suburban house and the center-city office building. It is with these two kinds of buildings that America has most shaped her own environment and affected that of the rest of the world. The history of the house in particular leads us at first to an architecture without names and to a period in time further back than that at which our biographies begin. The creation of the American domestic vernacular is largely a colonial product—whether the mother country was England, Holland, France, or Spain. In each case, and in their different sections of the continent, the parent European forms were simplified, regularized, and adapted to local conditions, so that true, preindustrial American vernaculars came to be formed. In the nineteenth century, above and beyond minor variations in style, those vernaculars were modernized and expanded in size and complexity to serve a more pluralistic kind of life and to accommodate technological developments such as central heating.

Those developments were particularly striking in relation to the New England vernacular, out of whose revival, after the Civil War, the Shingle style of the 1880's took shape. Frank Lloyd Wright's work grew directly out of that style; it was the tradition upon which his earliest experiments were based. Its program of the suburban house was his program, and he made its major feature, the open plan with horizontally continuous space, entirely his own. Out of these elements Wright created the most original monuments of the American domestic tradition, and in those great years from the nineties to World War I, other architects around the country were doing work of at least comparable stature—much of it derived in large part from the Shingle style tradition as well. Maybeck in San Francisco and Greene and Greene in Pasadena come especially to mind, while Irving Gill in San Diego was working out his own modernization of the Spanish Colonial tradition. Those years were perhaps the richest architecturally that America has ever known.

In the meantime, the influence of Wright's early work was playing a part in creating what Europeans called the Modern movement but which Americans tended to define more exactly as the International style. Its purest monument in American domestic architecture is surely Philip Johnson's Glass House of 1949. It is the ultimate International type, in which architecture, plugged into the existing (and then abundant) sources of energy, dissolves into nature through sheets of glass.

Yet the most important development in American architecture since that time has been a concerted reaction against the hermetic abstraction of the International style, which by the late sixties had shown itself to be especially destructive in terms of city planning and redevelopment. Once again the vernacular, as modernized by the Shingle style of the nineteenth century, lay ready to hand. Venturi's Beach House project of 1959, which was based upon McKim, Mead and White's Low house of 1887, was the first gun of its revival. Since that time any number of architects, from Venturi and Charles

Moore and their students to Johnson himself, have participated in that movement. It involves not only the shape and character of individual houses but also a renewed respect for the vernacular order of the traditional city, which the architects and planners of the International style had so unswervingly despised and had gone so far toward destroying.

The events of those years, when our cities were changed beyond recognition, force us to consider the other peculiarly American architectural form: the office building, out of which the skyscraper, the eighth wonder of the world, was born. Of all modern architectural types the skyscraper would seem in one sense the most modern of all, the least based on traditional programs or forms. But the history of the skyscraper, which is told in these pages largely through the biographies of Louis Sullivan and Raymond Hood, shows that the reality of its development was somewhat more complex. That is to say, Sullivan's forms, generally taken to be prototypical of antihistorical "modern" architecture, are in fact closely based on European *palazzo* precedent. His greatest skyscrapers, such as the Wainwright in Saint Louis and the Guaranty in Buffalo, are in fact not so very tall and are conceived as classical Renaissance palaces, behind which stands the further model of Sullivan's classical order, with its base, shaft, and cornice. Sullivan's buildings are thus solid blocks conforming to the shape of the traditional street, and the major difference from their predecessors in Florence, Rome, and Vicenza is the expression of the skeletal quality of their steel frames and the purely repetitive character of their office spaces. But for all that, they are treated as dense blocks in traditionally solid urban groupings. It is this solution that Mies van der Rohe adapts later, though he thins his buildings toward a more purely skeletal expression and opens out their groupings with less respect for the street. He still remains concerned, nevertheless, with the moderate scale of a classically traditional urban form.

It was in fact not in Chicago but in New York that the skyscraper literally burst free. Starting with Richard Morris Hunt's Tribune Building of 1873–75, its whole intention was to leap upward. The solidity of its lower floors still respected the integrity of the urban fabric and the clear definitions of the street, but as it rose into the upper air its model became not the *palazzo* block but the church steeple, the bell tower, the spire. So from the first it was determined, as the Chicago skyscrapers were not, to reach up and scrape the sky. That instinct culminated in the great group of Beaux-Arts skyscrapers which is defined chronologically by Cass Gilbert's Woolworth Building of 1913 and Shreve, Lamb and Harmon's Empire State Building and William Van Alen's Chrysler Building of the early thirties. In between, however, another image had been woven into the spire: the image of the mountain, encouraged by New York's zoning laws of the teens and finding its most beautiful early formulation in Eliel Saarinen's entry in the Chicago Tribune competition of 1922. Hood's work of the twenties, from his exquisite American Radiator Building onward, takes up the double challenge of spire and mountain, and in the end it compresses the two into the incomparable, space-making slabs of Rockefeller Center, the finest urban grouping of skyscrapers so far achieved

in the modern world. Its lessons, like those of the vernacular in domestic architecture, are now being learned again by a generation of architects in revolt against the destruction of urban space through the cataclysmic planning practices of the International style. Johnson's AT&T is a delightfully controversial attempt to put Hood's lessons to use and to define, rather than to destroy, the traditional street once again.

Whatever may come of that development, it is obvious that American cities from Maine to California— but especially in the Sun Belt areas—have continued to define themselves in terms of the same two complementary building types, the suburban houses where the office force lives and the center-city skyscrapers where it mans its computers. The pattern is now so clear and inflexible in prosperous cities like Houston that it approaches a state of parody. The skyscrapers in the center are as scaleless as models, and as empty as models half the day, while the suburbs stretch out forever, across featureless landscapes, coagulating at intervals into little ersatz towns around their shopping centers. On this model, grand old cities like downtown Denver are now being destroyed.

Another fact which is clear enough is that the twin poles of suburban house and city office, along with the very size of the continent itself, have created a third uniquely American architectural type: the modern road, whether multilane highway or commercial strip. The road in all its forms is, after all, much more of a work of architecture than any individual building can be, because it does more than any individual building can do to shape the entire environment and to mold a way of life. Architects like Venturi—and he certainly most of all—have learned how to draw architectural lessons from the road and its furniture, such as its beckoning signs. This phenomenon, if it may come to include mass transit, suggests that the American road may someday be integrated into a more stable structure of life as a whole, without losing those special qualities of drama and release which are unique to it.

The demands of energy may also work toward a similar end. Passive solar design, for example, as it is now being practiced by a rapidly increasing number of young architects, has as its objective a way of living which is fundamentally in tune with nature rather than in opposition to it—but also thrifty, spare, and self-reliant, in the mythic American way. Hence the solar house, in whatever section of the country, tends to resemble the vernacular of that region—which, by definition, was always energy efficient in relation to its climate. In this way, too, the demands of contemporary reality lead toward a vernacular revival. Where in the end that will leave the skyscraper and the suburban house we cannot yet foresee, just as we cannot yet determine how to cope with our larger dilemma, wherein our cities lie in ruins or are mushrooming in unhealthy growth, spurred by such a ruthless exploitation of our natural resources as to suggest that the momentum cannot long endure.

As this collection of essays suggests, the patterns of the future will be imagined by individuals, but their architectural implementation will be, as always, a collective art, bringing into form not buildings alone but all the physical elements that create our environment and go so far toward directing our lives. —Vincent Scully

7

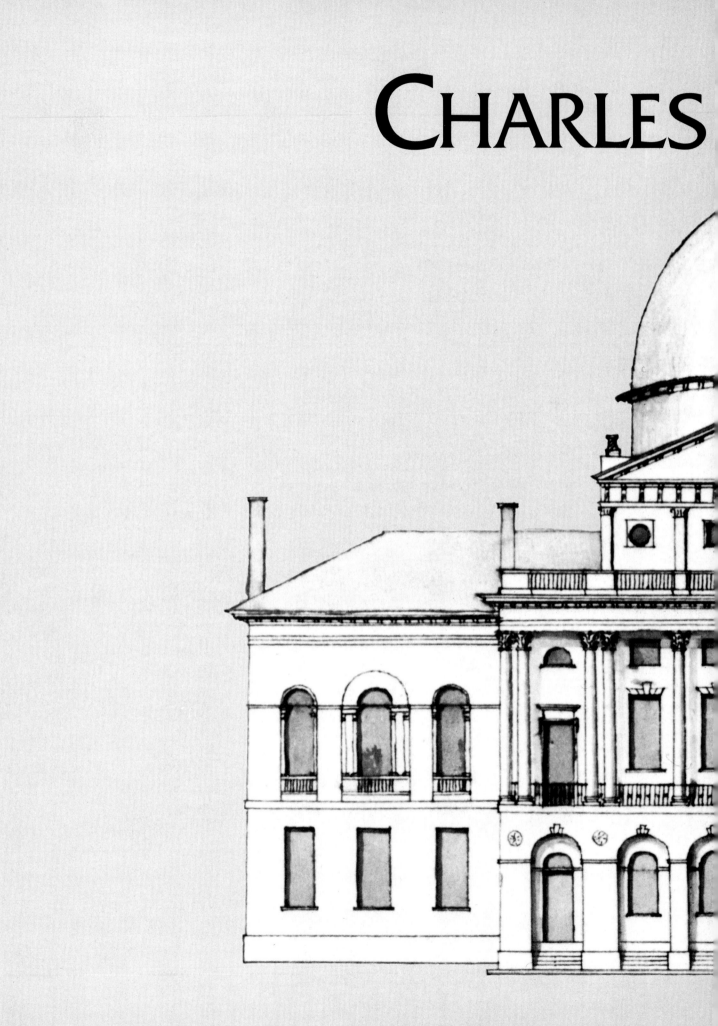

CHARLES

BULFINCH

Bulfinch's elevation of the Massachusetts State House, Boston, 1795–98

1763–1844

10

BY MARSHALL B. DAVIDSON

Charles Bulfinch was the first native-born professional architect in America. He emerged as such by accident and in spite of the fact that he was self-taught. Among his considerable accomplishments during a long, active, and varied career, he transformed Boston, his birthplace, from a provincial town into an orderly, elegant New England capital, a city with more harmonious architecture than any other in the land. With all the changes that have taken place in that city in the many years following his departure from the scene, providentially there still remain impressive evidences of his achievements.

Beyond that, the influence of his work spread over a large part of New England, in the buildings of his disciples and imitators as well as in his own widely scattered projects; and this significantly changed the architectural landscape of the whole region. This influence also extended as far south as Washington, D.C., where he spent a number of years completing the construction of the national Capitol.

To do the man full justice, his accomplishments should be measured against the earlier history of architecture in America and the special conditions under which he achieved what he did. They should also be considered along with his role as a dedicated public servant and a cultured gentleman in the finest Boston tradition. Those different aspects of his career brought him both unusual opportunities and at times grievous trials, as will be told. But they were inseparable parts of a singular personality.

Born in 1763, Bulfinch was a fourth-generation Bostonian. It is altogether unlikely that the word *architect* was even in the vocabulary of his first ancestors who arrived in America, and certainly it was not in common usage at the time. For many

In 1786, during his visit to London, Bulfinch commissioned his compatriot Mather Brown, who was living in England, to paint this portrait. The budding architect was then twenty-three.

years after the first colonies were settled, the building and most often the planning of even the most important structures were the province of more or less skilled housewrights who worked according to traditional, time-tested practices with little attention to matters of style. Basically, these men were accomplished carpenters and joiners. (The word *wright* was another name for *carpenter*.)

Around the year 1700, as transatlantic communications quickened, the more formal standards of design that had been developing in England for decades past began gradually to find their way to the New World. These newly fashionable patterns in building had their remote origins in ancient Roman precedents that had filtered down through the ages, principally in translations of the classical vocabulary that were made by architects of the Italian Renaissance. Of these, by far the most influential was Andrea Palladio. His published interpretation of the rules of architecture fired the imagination of builders and architects throughout the western world for years to come. This may well have been the most influential book on architecture ever written.

In eighteenth-century England "dear Impeccable Palladio's rule," as Lord Bristol referred to the matter, spread like a rash that covered the countryside with local and personal versions of the Italian master's style. English designers were quick to issue their own building guides and pattern books according to their individual and often very free interpretations of Palladian models. Mounting volumes of such publications soon found their way to the colonies and here, as in Britain, they played a leading role in the development of what has become known as the Georgian style.

It is safe to say that every house and public structure of any pretension built in America during the eighteenth century owed some debt to one or another of these publications. Such historic edifices as Independence Hall, Mount Vernon, Monticello, and the White House are merely the more eminent examples. With such guides in hand, large numbers of skilled American practitioners, some of them recent immigrants familiar at first hand with the latest English developments, filled the eastern coastal area with buildings reflecting the current style. Some of these were all but indistinguishable from English counterparts. Others were regional variants adapted to local circumstances, in which climate and available building materials were essential factors.

Bulfinch was born into such an architectural world. Few if any of the men responsible for the buildings constructed before he reached manhood had what today would be considered professional architectural training. More than a few, however,

11

Bulfinch's childish sketches of a Corinthian column and a capital of some indeterminate nature were made at age ten. They indicate that his interest in architecture had already been aroused.

designed and produced such distinguished structures that they might fairly be termed architects rather than mechanics. In 1749 one of them, a native-born Virginian named Richard Taliaferro (pronounced and sometimes written "Toliver,"), was in fact referred to by the acting governor of the colony as "our most skillful architect." If, as seems certain, he taught Thomas Jefferson the principles of architecture, he had by that token alone an indirect but important and lasting influence on the future of American architecture. It should be noted that Taliaferro was also a burgess, justice of the peace, sheriff, and assemblyman, an early example of the gentleman-amateur who studied architecture as an avocation, a type of cultivated person well known to the eighteenth century.

Peter Harrison, an English immigrant who settled in Newport, Rhode Island, and became a friend of Bulfinch's grandfather, has often been labeled the colonies' first true architect, although for him also architecture was neither a sole nor always a major interest. He was an active trader, a dealer in real estate, and, among other things, a farmer—all of them occupations that provided his main and ample source of income until the disruptions caused by the French and Indian War. Nevertheless, he also became the most versatile, the most masterly, and the most prolific of those who might reasonably be designated as architects. At one time or another during the pre-Revolutionary decades, Harrison was involved in the design and construction of everything from forts and lighthouses to churches, public markets, and private dwellings. His earliest effort, and among his most memorable achievements that still stand, is Newport's Redwood Library, a unique gem of colonial architecture that clearly reveals Harrison's devotion to Palladian principles. He received nothing for the design he provided (a strictly *non*professional way of operating). It was Bulfinch's grandfather, Charles Apthorp, who induced Harrison to design King's Chapel in Boston, the first sizable cut-stone structure in America. That, too, still stands, although after two and a quarter centuries Harrison's design has never been fully completed.

On one of his Atlantic crossings from England, Harrison brought with him a large assortment of books on architecture. Virtually every member of the educated colonial gentry professed an interest in architecture and had books on the subject in his library. Bulfinch's grandfather was no exception. This wealthy gentleman was once described by a contemporary as "very proficient in and a great admirer of the Fine Arts, especially . . . architecture." Apthorp's well-stocked library inevitably included books by Palladio and his interpreters—books which presumably were at the disposal of young Charles Bulfinch while he was growing up in Boston. Charles Ward Apthorp, an uncle, must also have contributed to his education, for this gentleman appears to have designed several much-admired prerevolutionary residences, notably one sterling example constructed in New York City.

With such a background Bulfinch was quite naturally attracted to architectural matters. In a childish pen-and-ink sketch that still survives, drawn when he was ten years old, he attempted a rendering of a classical column. It is the earliest evidence of an interest which would become first a pleasant diversion and then a commanding activity. After attending the Boston Latin School he entered Harvard College, from which institution he graduated in 1781 in a war-torn class of just twenty-one students, and from which he took a Master of Arts degree three years later. (He was too young to participate in the Revolution, although he watched the Battle of Bunker Hill from the roof of his parents' house.) While at Harvard he first became acquainted with fairly recently published books on classical archaeology, including at least one by the famous English architect and taste maker Robert Adam. Adam had toured Italy and Dalmatia and examined their classical ruins at first hand. He had also studied in Paris under the great classicist Charles Louis Clérisseau. Instead of relying on Renaissance transformations of classical architecture, Adam and some of his contemporaries and followers went straight to ancient models for their inspiration. The books in which he (and his brother James) explained and illustrated his explorations and studies had an "electric power," as one of his disciples later observed, that incited a revolution in the arts of his time. They sparked a fashion for neoclassicism that would be the rage for some years to come, as Palladianism had earlier been. Bulfinch was to be an heir to that revolution.

When he came of age he fell heir also to a bequest left to his parents by an uncle in England (an exiled Boston Tory) and given over by them to young Charles to advance his education. With that money in hand, in 1785 he took off for a grand tour of Europe, as was the wont of moneyed young aristocrats of his time. The grievous wounds that had been opened by the Revolutionary War, and the political independence America had so stubbornly gained, did not radically reduce the new nation's reliance upon England for cultural guidance. Ties of common ancestry, a common tongue, and, on the whole, a common way of life were too strong to be easily severed. Americans continued to go to England to enrich their experience and to buy that country's products. "I hardly know how to think myself out of my own country," wrote Abigail Adams from London shortly after the Revolution, "I see so many Americans about me." About the same time a New England merchant observed that "all who can cross the Atlantic seem determined to go and procure their goods from England." For most liberated Americans London remained the center of style and fashion, as Bulfinch quickly discovered when he got there. He was as well prepared to appreciate and learn from the architectural monuments of England and the Continent as any young American could be.

Thomas Jefferson was a supreme example of the gentleman-architect, well read in the practice and theory and sensitively alive to what he observed of past and present building as he traveled about. It was to Jefferson that Bulfinch turned for guidance when he arrived in Paris. Jefferson was then minister plenipotentiary to the court of Louis XVI, and Bulfinch stayed with him at his residence on the Champs Elysées, the Hôtel de Langeac, a house that had recently been designed according to the most enlightened neoclassical taste of the day. With Jefferson's benevolent counsel the young traveler formed an understanding of Parisian architecture to add to his experience in England. Following Jefferson's prescription, he proceeded from there on a pilgrimage through France and Italy to further widen his horizons. However, his stay in England, at a time when the influence of Adam and his followers was at its height, seems to have been the most memorable point in his travels.

He returned to Boston in 1787, undecided as to his future career but with a collection of architectural books and a portfolio of drawings. Born to ease, he was under no serious compulsion to earn his own living. Even when he took a temporary job in a counting house, he found ample leisure to improve his taste for architecture. He freely offered his advice to friends in the remodeling of their houses, many of which had become dilapidated during the course of the Revolutionary War. Also, as a commercial venture he bought shares in the ship *Columbia*, the first American vessel to circumnavigate the globe and a pioneer in the lucrative trade with China that was just opening to America. A year later he married his cousin, Hannah Apthorp, who observed that she had thus become "united to a man of high attainments, of strict moral worth . . . , his fortune equal to my own, and his family the same."

In the spring of 1789 the newlyweds journeyed to New York to witness the inauguration of George Washington as the nation's first president. The ceremonies took place on the balcony of Federal Hall, New York's second city hall, which had been modernized especially for the occasion by Pierre Charles L'Enfant, the French architect and veteran of the American Revolution. (Bulfinch made a drawing of the building, which was widely reproduced in engravings.) On the same trip the young couple visited Philadelphia, and while there, they attended the theater several times, as they had in New York. Bulfinch had also gone to the theater in Paris. His interest in the design of such structures would come into play when he returned to Boston.

Also while in Philadelphia the Bulfinches dined at the newly constructed town house of the enormously wealthy William Binghams. In this extravagant edifice, modeled on the duke of Manchester's London residence, the Binghams entertained at a level of luxury and urbanity hitherto unknown in America. With its white marble staircase, valuable paintings, rich furniture, and magnificent decorations, the building seemed to Bulfinch "far *too* rich for *any* man in this country."

That was the observation of a proper Bostonian. There was no house in Boston comparable to

13

The Three Houses of Harrison Gray Otis

The portraits by Gilbert Stuart at right show Harrison Gray Otis and his wife, Sally. During his career as a wealthy lawyer and political leader, Otis commissioned Bulfinch to build three dwellings at intervals of about five years. Bulfinch's elevation of the first (bottom) almost duplicates the drawing he had earlier made of William Bingham's house in Philadelphia (below).

The second Otis house (left) shows more of Bulfinch's own inventive talents in its design and his command of the neoclassical style. Plans for the first and second floors of the third Otis house (below) indicate Bulfinch's ingenuity in contriving a commodious, convenient, and fashionable residence on a relatively narrow urban plot on Beacon Hill. A water color (bottom) shows the building as it appeared about 1900.

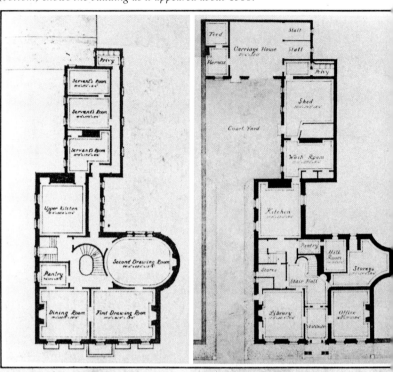

NICHOLAS DEAN, RIGHT: *GREAT GEORGIAN HOUSES IN AMERICA* (1933), BELOW: PRIVATE COLLECTION

Bingham's, and Bulfinch doubted there ever would be. Nevertheless, he made a drawing of the Bingham house for his portfolio and possible future reference. Philadelphia was then the most progressive city in the new nation; Boston may have been the most conservative. It was still essentially a colonial town when Bulfinch returned there from his *wanderjahr* in Europe. There had been little significant building there for decades. Its crooked streets and lanes contrasted remarkably with the regular pattern of Philadelphia's modern thoroughfares. In the game of counting heads and in the race for size, Boston was losing ground to other leading cities. But it was still the hub of New England, a region, claimed one of the Cabots in 1804, where there were among the people "more wisdom and virtues than in any other part of the world." And it was among the elite of this population that Bulfinch would find his most appreciative patrons and supporters as his architectural career developed.

Although not at such a giddy pace as New York or Philadelphia, Boston was nevertheless growing. Its population almost doubled between 1790 and 1810. Its merchant aristocracy was wealthy, if not spendthrift (in October 1791 it was reported that "upwards of seventy sail of vessels sailed from this port on Monday last, for various parts of the world"), and both the town and its leading citizens needed more and better accommodations. Immediately upon his return Bulfinch set about providing them in a wide variety of undertakings. It is not possible here to give more than a very partial list of the projects in Boston and elsewhere that are associated with his name. (Unfortunately, any list would be a doleful litany of demolished and sadly altered structures.) It is possible, however, to suggest the pace and nature of his activity. Within the first dozen years following his return home he had already designed two state capitols (Hartford and Boston), three churches, two public monuments, a theater, a hotel, and a good number of distinguished private houses.

Among the earliest of the houses, built in 1791 for John Joy, Jr., was a country place on Beacon Hill, a site then so remote from the center of town that Joy's wife was dismayed by its isolation. The hill (then twice its present height) was the highest of three rugged peaks overlooking the Common, which was used mainly as pasturage for cattle and horses. (The eminent colonial painter John Singleton Copley owned a few farmhouses in the area.) At about the same time, Bulfinch designed a house for Joseph Coolidge, Sr., to be built in Bowdoin Square, then a more acceptable social center, where Bulfinch himself had grown up. With this mansion the architect gave Boston its first taste of the neoclassic style. Its delicate Adamlike façade was inspired by the Royal Society of Arts building in the Adelphi section of London, an urban project promoted by Adam and much admired by Bulfinch. He had to tailor his design to the economic and cultural conservatism of his client, but the Adam influence is clearly revealed. Within the building he constructed one of the first geometrical staircases put up in America—a structural device such as he had discovered abroad that gave the illusion of a "free hung" flight of steps.

Bulfinch's impress on the city and its environs would now be increasingly felt. In quick succession he became responsible for other buildings of different types that reshaped the taste of his fellow Bostonians. In 1792 he conceived a house for Joseph Barrell, in Somerville, which it was confidently predicted by one of the architect's acquaintances would be "infinitely the most elegant dwelling house in New England." From surviving descriptions this it may well have been, for it became the most talked-of property of the area. Samuel McIntire, the master builder and carver of Salem, traveled to Somerville to see it, made a sketch of it, and subsequently incorporated some of its sophistications in structures he planned for the gentry of his own town and neighborhood.

Here Bulfinch turned away from all vestiges of colonial tradition and designed a house such as he had come to know in Europe, its rooms freely planned in different shapes and sizes to serve both comfort and convenience. Its most conspicuous feature was a large oval salon "fronting the town," a fashionable innovation new to New England but one that would become a characteristic grace of many of the best Federal architectural interiors, including that of the White House. A spacious dining room adjoined the salon, also facing the street. During the Federal period, dining rooms assumed an increasingly important role in social life. In the words of Robert Adam, they had become "apartments of conversation" and were equipped with such relatively novel gear as sideboards, mixing tables, and cellarets for the storage and cooling of wines and spirits. Many of Bulfinch's houses were designed with this current modishness much in his mind.

In the course of a decade Bulfinch designed three separate houses for Harrison Gray Otis, his lifelong friend, a spellbinding politician (sometime mayor of Boston), and an aristocrat who made an art of social entertaining. All three houses are still standing, somewhat miraculously. The first, built in 1795–96 on Cambridge Street, was clearly designed with William Bingham's great Philadelphia mansion in mind, as can be seen by comparing

Bulfinch's drawing of that house with his elevation of the Otis house. The second was completed six years later on Mount Vernon Street. Otis finally settled down for the rest of his years in the third of the houses Bulfinch designed for him, at 45 Beacon Street, in 1805. Otis was immensely proud of his last dwelling. It was here that in 1817 President James Monroe attended a great ball, an elaborate social occasion at which it was said the "Era of Good Feelings" was introduced, as the once obdurate Boston Federalists danced in the company of the leader of the long-despised Republicans. This was the last great house Bulfinch designed in Boston: a handsome summary of the Federal style in residential architecture which he had so effectively advanced in the city.

As he was intermittently engaged in these important assignments, Bulfinch was designing other houses of hardly less elegance but of a different character on the outskirts of Boston, where there was more land to work on than in the crowding city. He has been credited (on uncertain evidence) with the very elegant mansion built at Dorchester about 1796 for Colonel James Swan, a Scotch-born veteran of the Battle of Bunker Hill who married a wealthy Boston heiress and left her at home to go to Europe and amass a fortune of his own (with the help of Lafayette and other Frenchmen he had met during the American Revolution). In the Dorchester house Swan got what he apparently wanted, a pavilion constructed in the French manner with a huge circular salon, such as both he and Bulfinch were probably familiar with from their stays in France, that was thirty-two feet in diameter and more than twenty-five feet high—a feature prominently projecting onto the façade of the building. (The dining room was about the same length.) Swan sent home magnificent French furnishings for his new establishment, some of which may now be seen in Boston's Museum of Fine Arts. He himself never did return. The last twenty-two years of his life were spent in a debtor's prison in Paris, refusing to have his debts paid because he thought that the charges against him were unjust. In 1825 Lafayette came to the Round House, as Swan's Dorchester home was actually called, to explain to his widow the circumstances that led to her husband's end.

In 1796 Bulfinch also built a hilltop house at Roxbury for Perez Morton, whose lovely wife (née Sarah Wentworth Apthorp) was known as the American Sappho because of her literary talents—and who carried on a titillating correspondence with the artist Gilbert Stuart, who painted her portrait and, in verse of his own, once wrote her, "T'was heaven itself that blended in thy face, the

lines of Reason with the lines of Grace." Inside and out the Morton house was a virtual catalogue of the stylistic features Bulfinch had learned to admire in the work of Adam. It, too, had an elliptical salon and was called "one of the finest interiors to be found in this part of the country." Both the Swan and Morton houses were destroyed about 1890.

During the years when Bulfinch was engaged in providing the New England gentry with such special and elegant accommodations, he was also concerned with a wide variety of other matters that played an even more important part in his professional and personal fortune. Most crucial of these was a plan he undertook in 1793 to build two crescent-shaped rows of connected houses, three stories high and uniform in design, on either side of an enclosed park in Franklin Place. Bulfinch had seen examples of such solid blocks of urban dwellings by the Adam brothers and others in England, notably the Adelphi Terrace in London and the famous crescent at Bath, and these had stirred his imagination and clung to his memory. To add further distinction to that Franklin Place area, Bulfinch had already designed "an elegant *House* for Theatrical Exhibitions" (to counter a strong local prejudice against such forms of entertainment, it was originally proposed as a "New Exhibition Room," where points of morality and virtue could be dramatically demonstrated). Nearby he also helped to create Boston's first Catholic church for his friend Bishop Jean Louis Lefebvre de Cheverus (without a fee). In recognition of the first of these services he was awarded a gold medal and a seat in the theater "for life"; for the second he received a silver tea urn—other examples of nonprofessional architectural practice but a tribute to his public spirit and good will.

The so-called Tontine Crescent was a bold and, as it turned out, a rash enterprise. Bulfinch planned to break the crescent at the center, where another street entered Franklin Place. Over this break he would arch a library faced by classical columns, a Venetian window, and a pedimented attic story that agreeably broke the pattern of the flanking rows of identical buildings. (He freely donated the space reserved for the library to the Boston Library Society, which he had helped organize in 1792, and, in association with his friends, to the newly founded Massachusetts Historical Society—further examples of his irrepressible public spirit.) It was called the Tontine Crescent after its method of financing, originated by the Italian banker Lorenzo Tonti. This amounted essentially to a mutual assurance pact in which the shares of each participant upon his death were passed on to the remaining shareholders until the final survivor held all the shares. *Text continues on page 20*

Unable to complete his plans for the Tontine Crescent, Bulfinch designed four double houses on the site where originally he had intended to erect the northern half of a double crescent. One of them is pictured above as it appeared about 1850, facing the completed southern half of the crescent on Franklin Place. Bulfinch's plan and elevation for the latter (opposite, bottom) was engraved in 1794 for the Massachusetts Magazine. As announced in a prospectus for the crescent published in 1793 it was to consist of "a number of convenient, and elegant HOUSES, in a central situation." Some idea of that elegance can be had from the painting by Henry Sargent showing a convivial stag party in a dining room of one of the row of buildings. One architectural critic was especially impressed by the spaciousness of the rooms and the care given to household conveniences.

The Tontine Crescent

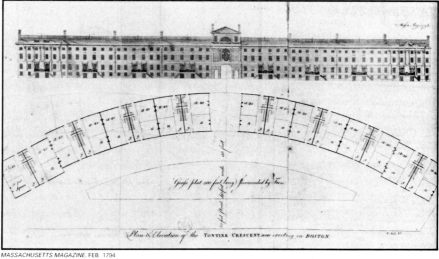

Plan & Elevation of the TONTINE CRESCENT *now erecting in* BOSTON

Unfortunately, the project was started in the midst of an economic recession. In 1793, with most of Europe at war, America remained the only important trading neutral in the world. Differences with France had developed into what was in effect a cold war, which created hazards and difficulties for Boston's merchant fleet.

Participant financiers of the Tontine plan dropped out, leaving Bulfinch with the entire cost. By 1794 only the southern crescent of the great ellipse was completed, and the architect abandoned thoughts of its further development. In the enterprise he had sacrificed both his wife's fortune and his own. He was bankrupt.

This serious blow to his fortunes, however, proved to be a catalyst to his professional career. Contrary to all his earlier expectations he was now obliged to renounce his amateur status and work for his living. As his wife succinctly put it, "My husband made Architecture his business, as it had been his pleasure." Bulfinch adjusted to his drastically reduced circumstances by moving from the fine home he had built for his family in Bulfinch Place, just a year or so before his bankruptcy, to much more modest quarters.

From the beginning, Bulfinch always had a number of projects in hand and in his mind at the same time. He had returned to America in 1787 filled with aspirations and inspirations. He was well aware that the historic old State House, built in 1748 at the head of State Street to house the colonial government, was no longer adequate to serve its purposes. He immediately proposed a design for a new building that would accommodate the more pressing demands of the time and would give the city a new vision of the up-to-date styles he had so studiously observed in London. His proposal took eight years to materialize, but in 1795 eight thousand pounds were appropriated for the building of such a structure on Beacon Hill, after one of his designs.

This would be, Bulfinch wrote, "in the stile of a building celebrated all over Europe." Here he referred to Somerset House, the great neoclassical government building that had just been completed by Sir William Chambers in London. On the Fourth of July, 1795, those two celebrated patriots, Samuel Adams and Paul Revere, laid the cornerstone of the new building. When it was completed two and a half years later Bulfinch had given the nation what is today the most conspicuous remaining example of his work. The result was considerably less magnificent than Somerset House. (In none of his projects did Bulfinch command the huge resources available to Europe's great builders.) But the main colonnade of its façade clearly reflects the central

pavilion of Chambers's huge building on the Thames. For the rest, the State House's delicate details and almost austere elegance also clearly reflect a typical Yankee reticence. On its high site, with its bold timber dome—"a grand dominating hemisphere" that in 1802 was sheathed in copper rolled at the mill of Paul Revere and Son (and almost sixty years later was covered with the gold leaf it now displays)—it became and remains the architectural symbol of the Bay State. And it bears Bulfinch's indelible signature. A group of early visitors from the South pronounced it "the most magnificent building in the Union." (Following a pattern still familiar to government builders, the actual construction cost four times the original estimate, as Bulfinch himself had warned it might.) For his own services as resident architect of the State House, Bulfinch received just over six hundred dollars, hardly enough to measurably alleviate his debt-ridden condition.

Then, a year after the building was completed, the circumstances of the architect's life changed dramatically. In 1791 he had been elected to Boston's board of selectmen, a body that administered the city's affairs (until years later a mayor was installed to attend to such matters). Under the stress of his personal affairs he had resigned from that post. However, in 1799 he returned to the board and was unanimously chosen as its chairman, a position he held for the next nineteen years. As such, he was Boston's chief administrator. At the same time he was appointed superintendent of police at a salary of six hundred dollars a year (later raised to one thousand). During those years this was his only steady source of income. And during those same years, thanks to his public offices, almost every problem concerned with the community's welfare and general appearance crossed his desk. The planning and renovation of public buildings called for his attention, as did the laying out of new streets and malls, and the building of new bridges to facilitate the city's communications with its environs. Land shoveled off the crest of Beacon Hill was used to fill Mill Pond to create much-needed new ground for building. The most ambitious example of harbor development in America came about with Bulfinch's design for the brick block of thirty-two stores, with warehouses or counting rooms above them, designed for the new India Wharf, where tall sailing ships clustered before and after their ventures overseas. He oversaw the repairing and enlarging of such old buildings as Christ Church and Faneuil Hall with sensitive respect for their essential character. (One day in 1813 he slipped on an icy step of Faneuil Hall and fractured his leg. The accident left him lame for the rest of his life.) And all the time Bulfinch punctiliously fulfilled his other civic chores, dealing with vagrants, malefactors, and the penniless.

Most of these matters concerned him both as an architect and designer and as an administrator and civic planner. Those dual roles sometimes opened the doors to unusual professional opportunities but at other times led to conflicts of interest and embarrassments. The fact that he survived so long and so successfully on that uneasy, if not precarious, perch was a tribute to his character and his capabilities, and to the esteem in which he was held as an honorable gentleman, a skilled professional, and a faithful public servant.

Within the course of the quarter century of Bulfinch's activities in Boston, the city was practically rebuilt. In 1808, upon a return visit, one Boston Loyalist who had fled the country during the Revolution remarked with astonishment "the great number of new and elegant buildings" that had been erected during his absence. Much of this distinction, and further similar developments in the years immediately following, has to be attributed to Bulfinch and those other builders whose work he influenced. "Boston was a child of my father's," one of his sons recalled, "and he did pretty much what he pleased with it." It was in good measure his accomplishment that turned all eyes to fashionable Beacon Hill, so few years earlier a virtual wilderness. It was under his administration of public affairs that the Common was transformed from a neglected pasture into the finest urban park in post-Revolutionary America.

Shortly after he became chief officer of the selectmen, this group approved the removal of the decrepit old almshouse that had long stood near the northeast corner of the Common, at the top of Park and Beacon streets. A new and much larger facility was immediately begun some distance away to the east on Leverett Street. Two important results followed this action. Park Street was now opened to urban development, and the site was quickly filled with a row of distinguished town houses, which still stand, designed by Bulfinch. The second was the erection of the new almshouse, most probably also designed by Bulfinch, which most of his contemporaries considered second in distinction only to the State House—"a noble monument to the munificence of the town," as one of them termed it. Sad to report, that handsome structure was demolished within twenty-five years.

To finance the construction of the almshouse, the town's selectmen sold some blocks of land across from the east boundary of the Common. Here, under Bulfinch's direction, was erected a row of nineteen brick dwellings which in their quality rivaled those he had completed on Park Street and which were together known as the Colonnade. It was Bulfinch's last—and admirable—effort to enhance the surroundings of the Common. One contemporary wrote without reservation that the appearance of the whole was "grand, uniform and chaste, and is surpassed by nothing of the kind . . . in the United States." Indeed, it has been further

A view of Boston was engraved in 1790 when Bulfinch was just starting his architectural practice. It was still essentially a colonial town at the center of a predominantly rural area.

Boston After Bulfinch

The dramatic changes in Boston's cityscape during the course of Bulfinch's lifetime are shown in a bird's-eye view made around 1850, a very few years after his death. As they had in the long past, the masts of ships that ringed the shore line still resembled "a kind of wood of trees." In part due to Bulfinch's activities the shore line had been pushed out into the bay. (The Back Bay had not yet been filled in, as it would be in time.) The general plan of the city's core reflects his influence, and this panorama is dotted with eminent structures for which he was entirely or chiefly responsible. Five of these, a small but significant selection, are reproduced in the surrounding illustrations on these pages.

CALEB SNOW, *A HISTORY OF BOSTON* (1825)

1.
Bulfinch's Boston Theater on Federal Street, replacing an earlier burnt-out structure that was also his work, was hailed as "perfectly *brilliant* in its *effect*, yet perfectly simple in its *design*" when it was completed in 1798. It was demolished in 1852.

2.
The Colonnade, a row of nineteen houses fronting on the Common (below), was completed by Bulfinch in 1812 along what is now Tremont Street. One contemporary reporter observed that this building complex was "surpassed by nothing of the kind in the United States."

BOSTONIAN SOCIETY

5

BOSTONIAN SOCIETY

4. In its time the New South Church built by Bulfinch in 1814 on Church Green at Summer and Bedford streets was considered one of his finest ecclesiastical buildings. His elevation barely suggests the especially attractive character of the completed masonry construction—which was demolished in 1868.

3. India Wharf consisted of more than a half mile of wharves, warehouses, and stores—a block of thirty-two associated buildings that was one of Bulfinch's major accomplishments. He drew the plans, designed the structures, and laid out the new streets required for the operations of this mercantile center. None of it stands today.

ROTCH LIBRARY, M.I.T.

5.
An elevation of the south front of the Massachusetts General Hospital is very close to the building's appearance as it was constructed after Bulfinch left Boston to work on the national Capitol. He was gratified that his plan had been accepted as his "last act for Boston," although he could not remain to see the job through.

claimed that this civic improvement vied with anything of the kind that had been achieved in Europe. And, tragically, the Colonnade was demolished within forty-five years. The tragedy is underlined by the character of the structures that replaced that once handsome prospect along what is now known as Tremont Street.

In spite of all these wide-ranging accomplishments and unmentioned others, Bulfinch did not flourish financially. Indeed, at one point he was briefly imprisoned as a debtor, although he was chief of police at the time. A decisive change in his affairs took place in 1817 when President James Monroe visited Boston. As earlier told, it was on that occasion that Harrison Gray Otis entertained the distinguished guest in his Bulfinch-designed residence on Beacon Hill. In his official capacity, Bulfinch, it seems certain, led the president on a tour of the city. Monroe, whom Bulfinch already knew, was apparently very pleasantly impressed by the public buildings he was shown and delighted to learn that his guide was their principal architect. Within a year of that episode Bulfinch was appointed to the job of finishing the United States Capitol in Washington, following the resignation of Benjamin Henry Latrobe from that post. His salary was to be $2,500 a year, with moving expenses and other perquisites added; his insolvency was ended.

He passed twelve years in Washington, years which he later recalled were among the happiest years of his life and where, as he wrote, "my labors were well received." Concerning his work on the Capitol he wrote, "I shall not have credit for invention, but must be content to follow in a prescribed path." Nevertheless, this commission marked the climax of his career as an architect. (The late great historian Samuel Eliot Morison went so far as to say that no American save Stanford White ever surpassed Bulfinch as an architect of public buildings.) He undertook few other projects of consequence, either in Washington or upon his return to Boston in 1830.

It would be hard to deny that this man of so many accomplishments was a professional architect, even though he had no formal training in the profession. He was among the earliest Americans—if not the first—to employ perspective drawings to visualize the spatial qualities of his proposed structures. Had he worked in a less frugal and less conservative environment he might have created greater and more splendid buildings. But that does not rob him of the esteem in which he was held by his countrymen. He filled the needs of his time and his place with unforgettable grace.

After his return from Washington, he lived in virtual retirement until his death in 1844. Once he was asked whether he had trained any of his sons to follow in his footsteps, and he answered quite simply that he thought there was little left to do. (One of them, Thomas Bulfinch, in an otherwise undistinguished career, took to writing and produced those two well-remembered books *The Age of Fable* [1855] and *The Age of Chivalry* [1858].) Yet he remained always a gentleman, modest almost to the point of diffidence. A friend once wrote of him

A wonder in our days, my friend—
An artist I have known,
Who never slandered others' works,
Nor ever praised his own.

Shortly before his death, Josiah Quincy, once mayor of Boston, added to that tribute, "Few men deserve to be held by the citizens of Boston in more grateful remembrance. . . . During the many years he presided over the town's government he improved its finances, executed the law with firmness, and was distinguished for gentleness and urbanity of manners, integrity and purity of character." Few architects have ever been so fondly remembered and for such good reasons.

Ever a tactful gentleman and a resourceful architect, Bulfinch in finishing the Washington Capitol raised the height of the central dome, against his inclinations, to accommodate the preferences of certain Cabinet members. That original dome, completed in 1827, appears in this painting of about 1845.

BENJAMIN

Section of the Cathedral of Baltimore...

...In the ground plan which accompanies the Section here is an alteration...

HENRY LATROBE

Latrobe's cross-sectional drawing of the Baltimore Cathedral

1764–1820

BY MARSHALL B. DAVIDSON

Benjamin Henry Latrobe was a man of the world who chose to live in the United States. That choice, made in 1796 when he was thirty-two years old and on the brink of what could have become an eminent architectural career in his native England, was a fortunate one for his chosen land. He arrived in America at a critical point in the formative years of the new republic and lived here for the remainder of his life, until his sudden and premature death in 1820. At that tragic moment when he was stricken with yellow fever, he was still actively pursuing the many-faceted career that had long since won him an outstanding position in American life.

For Latrobe was more than a superb architect. He was also an engineer, whose proficiency as such played a vital part in his building practices; this at a time when such a combination of skills in one individual was all but unheard of in America. As late as 1812 he wrote to a Philadelphia publisher, "Here I am the only successful Architect & Engineer." He was as well a compulsive artist, whose innumerable drawings and paintings, although not major accomplishments, evince that continuously creative spirit that informed his architectural designs. In addition he was a town planner, an environmentalist and preservationist of sorts, something of a naturalist and geologist, a performing musician, an occasional poet, and a highly articulate writer. He was widely read in a half dozen languages, including Greek and Latin. He once reminded his son, paraphrasing an observation attributed to the emperor Charles V, that "a man's powers & existence is multiplied in proportion to the number of languages he speaks," a counsel to which his own career lent credence.

With such a wide variety of skills and interests, Latrobe quite naturally became intimately associ-

Charles Willson Peale, that very versatile artist, craftsman, and Jack-of-all-trades, probably painted this portrait of Latrobe shortly after the architect's marriage in Philadelphia.

ated with many leaders of the political, economic, and social affairs of the nation. George Washington and Thomas Jefferson were just two such prominent personages who early welcomed this tall, attractive, and gifted newcomer to their midst. Like Jefferson, Latrobe was both deeply philosophical by nature and immersed in the study of architecture, and although the two men did not always agree, they enjoyed a mutually respectful and rewarding relationship.

In spite of the many other pursuits into which his inventive mind led him, Latrobe remained a practicing architect until, quite literally, his dying day. It would be extravagant to claim that he changed the architectural scene of America in his lifetime, but he made enduring contributions to that scene. The most dramatic and significant symbol of these is the United States Capitol, which as it stands today remains essentially Latrobe's creation. Many of the other major structures he designed and built have unhappily long since disappeared. But by his example and his precepts, he more than any other contemporary architect infused a new spirit into American architecture; and in the work of younger architects whom he helped to train—men such as Robert Mills and William Strickland—his influence was carried on into another generation or two.

Latrobe was but one of a number of professional European architects who, for the most part, were uprooted by the disorders attending the French Revolution and the Napoleonic Wars, and who turned to America for refuge and brighter chances to exercise their talents; but when he arrived he carried with him unexcelled credentials. He was born in Yorkshire, England, of a Pennsylvania-born mother and a father who may also have been born in America. Both were devout Moravians, and in accordance with an established custom of that international sect, their young son was shipped off to Germany to complete his education when he was twelve years old.

After eight years of intensive study, capped by a Continental tour that took him through France and Italy, he returned to England in 1784, a precocious young intellectual in search of a future. His parents' social circle included, among others, such intimate acquaintances as the eminent musician and musicologist Dr. Charles Burney and his daughter Fanny, a distinguished author, and the venerable Dr. Samuel Johnson. Their brilliant company must have excited young Benjamin's cultural aspirations.

For a while, Latrobe was apprenticed to John Smeaton, the engineer who rebuilt the famous Eddystone lighthouse and who became the first fully professional engineer of his time. He was also

29

engaged in at least one canal project. Then in 1787 or 1788 he began work in the office of Samuel Pepys Cockerell, a highly successful London architect at a time when buildings of all description were rising in that rapidly growing city. Here Latrobe's obvious brilliance quickly won him a favored position on the busy staff, and here he stayed for three or four years of invaluable experience. Then in 1791 he quit that firm to open his own office. In spite of the unsettled conditions caused by the recent outbreak of the French Revolution, Latrobe secured commissions for a number of domestic buildings, some of which still stand in and about London. He also served the government briefly as surveyor to the public offices, which he found a disenchanting job, although the work gave him experience in various types of construction work.

Meanwhile, Latrobe had married Lydia Sellon, a well-born young lady who had an informed and sympathetic interest in her husband's work. In quick succession she bore him a daughter, Lydia, and a son, Henry. Then tragedy struck. In 1793 Latrobe's devoted helpmate died in childbirth along with her third child. Latrobe's spirit was shattered; his professional work faltered. After two years of desperate grief and loneliness and nervous disorders, during which his two children were put in the custody of relatives, Latrobe made his large decision. He sailed for America and whatever fresh prospects it might provide.

From the start, everything about this strange new world attracted his interest. With inexhaustible curiosity he studied its history, its legends, the dress and manners of its people—and, of course, its architecture. He noted its varying patterns of speech, the particular character of the Negroes, Indians, and other races that he encountered. Geological formations, waterfalls, the courses of rivers, and the nature of the soil and terrain were all carefully observed and often recorded in his bulging sketchbooks. Every aspect of natural life, including snakes and insects, fascinated him and aroused his speculation. He admired the engineering skills of beavers as they built their dams, and he observed that these industrious creatures should be preserved rather than exterminated, as was happening.

His interest in such things was both academic and philosophical, as one of the entries in his notebook demonstrates:

See how the poor little fly struggles in the net, and with what savage activity and joy the spider weaves the web about him. He is yet too free, too unfettered to be safely attacked; he can move his wings, he can move his legs, he buzzes violently with his wings. Already the action of his wings is clogged. He sinks into the net that is every moment strengthened. Hold, I will relieve thee, little sufferer! But is this humanity? Art thou not truly destined for the food of spiders by the hand that created you both? Shall I interfere and, by saving a life half destroyed, rob another of its support? I will venture it.

For a man of his background and caliber, this strange new world offered the possibility of abundant rewards. It was a long, safe distance from the convulsions of the European wars—or so it seemed at first. In all too short a time Latrobe would learn how those conflicts would bring troubles to the American coast and thwart some of his own enterprises. However, in those early years of the republic, by natural growth and by reason of increasing immigration, the number of Americans was rapidly mounting. Construction was booming in every state of the federal union. Not only were many more houses needed to accommodate the rising population, but public buildings as well, to serve the new state and national governments. And in every part of the land the more distinguished structures that were rising reflected in one way or another a classical spirit that broke with colonial traditions and looked much further back in time for inspiration, to ancient Greek and Roman precedents. Latrobe was completely familiar with the vocabulary and idioms used to express this new spirit in architecture before he arrived in America: so familiar with such terms, indeed, that he used them with a freedom, originality, and even audacity that was not always easy for his American contemporaries to grasp.

More than new buildings were needed. As the disruptions caused by the American Revolution subsided, new problems arose that crucially affected the development of the nation. With the return of active overseas commerce (now extended as far as the Orient), internal commerce bred constantly heavier traffic between the major port cities. Urban centers, still relatively small but expanding and becoming more complex in their structure, needed solutions to pressing problems that had not before appeared urgent—providing adequate water supplies and other hygienic systems, plus transporting food supplies from the receding areas of farmland. These needs were elementary and vital for every city that hoped to survive and grow. Also, as both Benjamin Franklin and George Washington had foreseen, Americans

Two trompe l'oeil water colors by Latrobe are among the earliest examples of this genre produced in America. In the one at top of the opposite page he depicted two little landscapes and a ghostly head of George Washington placed on the manuscript of a poem. After his transatlantic crossing on the ship Eliza in 1796, he pictured his breakfast tray (bottom) superimposed on playing cards and other miscellany.

A Latrobe Sketchbook

Sketch at Norfolk.

Throughout his life Latrobe sketched everything that caught his attention. The examples on these two pages suggest the wide range of his interests: a landscape showing a section of divided highway between Newark and Paterson, New Jersey (above); the falls of the Passaic River (right); his cousin in a carriage (bottom, right); knee breeches designed to frustrate "muskitoes" (below); and a view of the Norfolk waterfront (opposite).

by My cousin enjoying the country air on the Frankfort road

One of the earliest sketches Latrobe made on his arrival in the United States pictured a ground squirrel (Tamias striatus), which he rendered in water color, pen, and ink in 1796.

were streaming westward at an unprecedented rate. To keep the social, economic, and political fabric of the nation intact under these circumstances called for improvements in communication and services that had not been very seriously considered in colonial times. "Open all the communications which nature has afforded between the Atlantic States and the Western Territory, and encourage the use of them to the utmost," Washington urged, ". . . sure I am there is no other way by which they will long form a link in the chain of the Federal Union."

In all these areas, Latrobe, with his singular combination of knowledge, experience, and creative imagination, could play an important role in the progress of his country. (Because of the American background of his mother and, quite probably, his father, he assumed American citizenship for himself at the start. Indeed, he claimed to be a fourth-generation American, and as the War of 1812 approached, his sympathies were altogether with this country against Britain.) Within a few months of his landing at Norfolk, Virginia, he received his first commission, a residence for William Pennock of that city. The house no longer

stands, but from Latrobe's surviving sketches it was a prophetic structure that embodied the basic principles he followed in his subsequent work.

Latrobe was keenly aware that in this country new standards of convenience, comfort, and privacy, features that had rarely been so carefully considered in earlier times, must be observed in his domestic designs without infringing on the architectural integrity of his buildings. With this in mind, in most of his private dwellings the main staircase, which had claimed a prominent place in the entrance hallways of the finest colonial houses, was moved to the side to discourage the casual caller from visiting the upper chambers, thus assuring an unwonted and welcome sense of privacy. With a similar objective in mind, a second, hidden or inconspicuous staircase was introduced for workaday household service. Circulation within the house became more agreeable and more efficient. To those same ends, in some of his houses he devised rotating servers by means of which food and drink could be delivered to important rooms without having servants enter at all. His up-to-date accommodations in some instances included indoor water closets—and in one case, at least, the rare luxury of a complete bathroom. It is a sad fact that few of Latrobe's private houses still stand in anything like their original state. It is a much happier circumstance that many of his scrupulous drawings (many of them of projects never completed) have survived to remind us of the man's fertile genius.

Latrobe seems never to have had less than a half dozen projects in his mind or on his drawing board at the same time. His work on the Pennock house was not completed before he made a trip to assay the merits of a proposed canal to improve the channels of the James River and its tributaries, particularly the Appomattox. In the course of that survey he spent some time in Richmond, where he met a group of English actors, to whom he was immediately attracted, playing their parts in the ramshackle local theater. This congenial association inspired Latrobe to design for the little city a new theater, in combination with assembly rooms and a hotel. If one can judge from his preparatory drawings, his plan, had it been consummated, would have produced one of the most distinguished architectural complexes of the sort anywhere in America or Europe.

Betimes, on commission from the state of Virginia, he designed and supervised the construction of the Richmond penitentiary. The massive stone entrance arch, symbolic of the building's security purpose, anticipated the designs so successfully used by H. H. Richardson some eighty years later. Latrobe put a primitive water closet in each cell. Both in its architectural conception and in its recognition of advanced notions of humane penology, Latrobe's first public building in America had made a unique and positive contribution to his chosen country. It was not achieved without interference and harassment by state officialdom. With such obstacles he would become increasingly concerned, as his career advanced, almost to the point of complete frustration.

Within another year Latrobe had moved to Philadelphia, then the nation's largest city, its most important cultural center, and until recently its capital. It had been and it remained the seat of the "republican court" and the center of fashion. Latrobe immediately became a familiar figure in that brilliant society. Here he met on easy terms not only the wealthy and influential but as well the leading savants and scholars, the artists and scientists who contributed so much to the tone and prestige of the city. "Ben. Henry Latrobe, Engineer" was soon elected to full membership in the American Philosophical Society, the country's first and most important learned society. Philadelphia at the time was also a favored retreat of refugees from the French Revolution, and here Latrobe met such men as Constantin Volney, the distinguished author who before the Terror had been a member of the States-General and the National Assembly, and Moreau de Saint-Mery, whose famous Philadelphia bookshop was a favorite gathering place of the refugees.

That point is worth a note in passing, for Latrobe's sympathetic associations with these liberal-minded foreigners, together with his own French name, branded him as a man of democratic principles. This won him the hostility of the Federalists, then in power under John Adams's presidency, to whom Frenchmen of any stripe were dangerous liberals and all liberals were suspect, as the Alien and Sedition Laws passed in 1798 made clear. Even such eminent patriots as Thomas Jefferson and Albert Gallatin, both Francophiles and democrats, were scurrilously attacked by the Federalist press. This sort of hysterical prejudice would hamper Latrobe's progress at various points in his career.

However, it was Philadelphia that gave Latrobe the opportunity to create two of his most memorable masterpieces—the Bank of Pennsylvania and the city's new waterworks. In neither case was there an American precedent for what he accomplished with these commissions. Latrobe has commonly been considered the originator of the Greek Revival style in American architecture, a style that in its long sway constituted an all but national style. Both the bank and the building that housed the waterworks clearly indicate his familiarity with and admiration of ancient Greek forms. But as in so many of Latrobe's other ventures, their over-all designs were dictated by strict regard for practical, efficient accommodation of the buildings' functions.

Latrobe once wrote Jefferson, "My principles of good taste are rigid in Greek architecture." But, he pointed out, ancient buildings, admirable as they were to contemplate, did not offer designs applicable to the objects and uses of current constructions. "Our religion requires a church wholly different from the temples, our legislative assemblies and our courts of justice, buildings of entirely different principles from their basilicas; and our amusements could not possibly be performed in their theaters & amphitheaters." And, he added, the American climate was an even more important reason for departing from the ancient models.

The Bank of Pennsylvania is often referred to as the first Greek Revival structure in America. It was more truly a modern building of the Federal period, and as such it was a monument unlike any other building then standing in America. For the first time in this country a masonry vault was used as an integral element in a total architectural concept. The large, circular space that served as the main banking room was lighted by a glazed cupola surmounting the soaring central dome. Elsewhere in the structure all the facilities required by the developing banking procedures of the time—fireproof vaults, stockholders' room, directors' room, and sundry offices for clerks and other personnel—were given suitable space, appropriate shapes, and convenient locations. Elements of the interior were sensitively colored to emphasize their various agreeable patterns. The total effect must have been one of airy grace and beauty that we can only imagine.

This highly coherent interior was very sensibly and directly expressed by the bank's exterior. In spite of its two pedimented end porticoes in the Greek Ionic style (the first use of this style in America), which alluded to an ancient temple, the bank's functions were otherwise enclosed in a design of almost geometric simplicity. Many years later Latrobe recalled having overheard a French officer standing before the bank and remarking to a companion, "C'est si beau, et si simple." It was indeed both beautiful and simple, and it remained a distinguished landmark until it was destroyed in the 1860's.

The next test of Latrobe's architectural and engineering skills came when he was commissioned to devise a system to provide Philadelphia with an adequate supply of clean water for private and civic uses. It was the first time a major American city had undertaken such a challenging enterprise. Latrobe proposed to tap the Schuylkill River as it flowed through the city and to raise the water by steam power to a central storage tank, whence it could be distributed through the city by gravity.

Critics decried such a hopelessly visionary scheme. But on the morning of January 27, 1801, after Latrobe and his helpers had feverishly and anxiously worked throughout the night firing the boilers, the city awoke to find clear water abundantly flowing from the new hydrants, which Latrobe had ordered to be kept open to dramatize the successful completion of the operation. It had taken the "damned Frenchman," as some persons referred to Latrobe, less than two years to accomplish this singular, path-breaking feat. His reputation as an engineer was immediately established. The popular success of this innovation in public service is suggested in a report stating that by 1815 no fewer than 228 bathrooms had been installed in Philadelphia. What had earlier been a rare convenience was becoming a practical necessity. (Forty years later Charles Dickens was surprised at the fresh water that was "showered and jerked about and turned on, and poured off," everywhere in Philadelphia.)

The structure that Latrobe erected in Center

Square to house the pumping machinery and attendant offices was in itself an architectural gem. Like the bank building, it was designed to serve its essential purposes in the most straightforward manner, again alluding to ancient Greek modes but subjecting these to a total plan that was highly articulate in functional terms, monumental in its expression, and, again, of geometric simplicity. As he once wrote Jefferson of his driving motivation in architectural composition, "It is not the *ornament*, it is the use that I want." He was the first in the United States to provide a neat solution to a problem that would grow larger with time—how to accommodate the discipline of the new machinery to the discipline of architecture.

With these two creations, both finished the same year, Latrobe issued a sharp challenge to the traditional American architectural procedures that still largely prevailed in the country. As he complained in reciting some of the difficulties he faced, the "profession" of architecture was, as it had long been, in the hands of two disparate sets of men; on the one hand there were well-to-do gentlemen who had learned what they knew of the theory of architecture from traveling and consulting books, and on the other hand, mechanics who knew nothing but the practice of building. As a truly professional architect who concerned himself with all details of design and construction, Latrobe often found it hard to win recognition of this role of complete authority in his projects.

Meanwhile, Latrobe had designed a suburban retreat called Sedgeley on the banks of the Schuylkill for William Crammond, a Philadelphia merchant. It was his first private commission in that area and was as revolutionary in its entirely different way as the bank and the pumping station were to be, for it was possibly the first example of the Gothic Revival style to be built in America. Basically Sedgeley was a conventional dwelling, but Latrobe encircled it with a picturesque colonnade featuring pointed arches in the Gothic manner. These alone were enough to evoke romantic associations with the remote, dimly perceived medieval past. When it was completed in 1799 Sedgeley excited some wonderment and interest because of its novelty—a type of novelty that in a coming generation, as subsequent chapters in this book will explain, became a very popular style of building in the United States.

In 1800 Latrobe had married Mary Elizabeth Hazlehurst, a charming and witty Philadelphia socialite, who for the rest of his days proved a perfect wife and companion. Generously and affectionately, Mary made it a condition of their marriage that her husband have Lydia and Henry,

The Bank of Pennsylvania, completed in Philadelphia in 1800, was the earliest Greek Revival structure in America and Latrobe's first great success in this country.

the children of his first marriage, brought over from England to join their father's new ménage. This happy reunion with his daughter and son brought Latrobe a further, deep satisfaction with his prospects for a future in America. Henry was to prove a great aid to his father in years to come. Lydia would marry one of Latrobe's close associates in his later enterprises.

As a family man he bore heavier responsibilities than he had known as a bachelor. The completion of the bank and waterworks left him with no other jobs on hand, and work must be found. His active imagination continued to lead in many different directions at once. Within a few months, by the fall of 1801, he was engaged to supervise the improvement of the Susquehanna River, clearing the channel for downstream navigation from Columbia, near Lancaster, Pennsylvania, to tidewater. He soon completed his part in this operation and after some months received a welcome $1,000 fee.

About this time he also undertook a radical renovation of the Chestnut Street Theater in Philadelphia, which had already outgrown its facilities although it was but ten years old. Among other changes, he altered the outmoded façade, adding a classical colonnade of the Corinthian order and new end wings. The latter he adorned with sculptured panels that harmonized with the old niches where the wooden figures of Comedy and Tragedy, carved by William Rush, were displayed.

The theater's boxes were "lined with pink colored paper, with small dark spots," according to a report in *The New-York Magazine*, "and supported by pillars representing bundles of reeds (gilt) bound with red fillets . . . festoons of crimson curtains, with tassels intervening, and a profusion of glass chandeliers." For some years after the Revolution, as in colonial days, theatrical performances had been frowned upon in America. They were variously considered impious, immoral, extravagant, and distractions from industry. Playgoing, warned the eminent clergyman and sometime president of Yale College, Timothy Dwight, endangered "that most valuable treasure the immortal soul." However, there were more liberal attitudes, and the Chestnut Street Theater became a fashionable resort, to the great advantage of those who staged entertainments there. Philadelphia was now the drama capital of the country.

In 1804 Latrobe made preliminary estimates for a bridge that would ease the growing flow of traffic from New York to Long Island by way of Blackwell's Island. The scheme came to nothing, largely because Latrobe's insistence on solid stone arches would have incurred expenses far greater than available resources could meet. Here again he was at odds with traditional American experience. In this country capital resources were still relatively limited, and construction had to be speedy to satisfy the temper of the people as well as their rapidly growing needs; it seemed that there was never time to lose, and much ground had to be covered. Hasty contrivances would suffice for the quickly passing time. Such an attitude was anathema to Latrobe, who wanted to build for the ages. Only solid, permanent construction would satisfy him. At times even Jefferson found Latrobe too demanding in this viewpoint.

A crucial point in Latrobe's career came in 1803, when President Jefferson appointed him surveyor of the public buildings of the United States, the most important architectural position in the country. (The two men had dined together at the White House late the previous year and talked of architecture, among many other matters of scientific and professional interest.) For the next eight years Latrobe would be concerned with the completion of the Capitol.

These were years filled with heavy responsibilities, maddening frustrations, and very considerable achievements. At the start he had been instructed to follow the plans for the Capitol drawn up by a gentleman-architect, Dr. William Thornton, a young physician from the Virgin Islands. These had won President Washington's approval in a competition for the award. Only the north wing had thus far been raised, and at first glance Latrobe considered it functionally inadequate, badly constructed, and aesthetically deficient. As to the south wing, and the main, central structure that remained to be built, there was little exact evidence of what Thornton had in mind, and he was contemptuously unresponsive to Latrobe's questions to him on the matter.

That Latrobe completed the job at all is a tribute to his stubborn persistence in the face of shortages of labor and materials, official interference, and often vicious public criticism by Thornton and others. (In time Thornton's criticism became so slanderous that Latrobe felt obliged to sue him for libel. He won the case.) Even Jefferson presented difficulties for the architect, with his contrary suggestions and instructions. At one point, when Congress was impatient with the slow progress and the rising costs of the building, the president recommended wooden columns for the House of Representatives to save both time and money. But this Latrobe adamantly refused to consider. "I will give up my office," he wrote, "sooner than build a temple of disgrace to myself and Mr. Jefferson." The building must be an enduring and monumental symbol of the nation's great destiny and a point of pride for all Americans.

The different viewpoints of the two men bring to mind two points of interest. From Jefferson's various suggestions it seems apparent that he could not always grasp the full significance of Latrobe's concept of architecture—the complete integration of construction, function, appearance, and lasting qualities that comprised his professional ideals in building. This in turn leads to the larger point, already alluded to, that Latrobe's approach to architecture went against the grain of typical American thinking. As Alexis de Tocqueville, one of the most perceptive critics of America democracy, long ago observed, this country's faith in immediate growth and endless progress left it with a prevailing belief that anything accomplished today would in short time prove obsolescent and would be replaced by something newer and better. (In 1845 Walt Whitman referred to this characteristic strain in American experience as the "pull-down-and-build-over-again spirit.") That underlines the fact reported by Talbot Hamlin, Latrobe's biographer, that most of Latrobe's English buildings remain standing—or at least did until the bombings of World War II—whereas, aside from the Capitol and the Baltimore Cathedral, few of his buildings in this country have survived.

For eight years preceding the War of 1812 Latrobe was also responsible for the continuing work on the President's House, including its interior decoration. Latrobe never did approve of the building as designed by James Hoban, an Irish-born immigrant. He called the plan, which had been accepted for the structure in a competition (in which Jefferson was an anonymous participant), "all stomach," and said that it was "a mutilated copy of a badly designed building near Dublin." Here he was unusually hypercritical, for some reason. However, when James Madison succeeded Jefferson as president in 1809, Latrobe worked closely with Dolley Madison, selecting the carpets, silverware, lighting fixtures, and draperies that would complete "the domestic arrangements of the house." He designed the chairs and sofas for "Queen Dolley's" drawing room in the Greek manner. It was a very sympathetic relationship, for Mary Latrobe was a childhood friend and intimate of the First Lady. Latrobe's efforts resulted in what Washington Irving described in 1811 as a room of "blazing splendor," an unfortunately apt phrase, for all those appointments went up in flames just three years later. It is to Latrobe's designs that we owe the porticoes (constructed later), which are such impressive features of the building as it stands today.

Even while he was concerned with these important matters, Latrobe undertook a variety of other public and private architectural and engineering enterprises. Among the most ambitious and successful of them was the designing and building of the Roman Catholic cathedral in Baltimore. He offered to design the structure free of charge, as he did in other cases that involved religious or academic edifices, and in 1804 his offer was quickly accepted. In John Carroll, the first Catholic bishop in the United States, Latrobe found an understanding and co-operative patron. Here, at last, the architect was free of nagging interference in the development of his ideas. As a result, when it was completed about 1818, the church stood as perhaps the most significant monument to Latrobe's architectural genius.

At the beginning Latrobe had offered the churchmen a choice of styles for the proposed building—one Gothic, the other classical. This was a somewhat singular gesture, testifying to his abiding conviction that style as such was a less important consideration than serviceability, and to his confidence that he could achieve this in either case. Fortunately, the classical scheme was the one selected.

Only a qualified engineer would have attempted what Latrobe in fact finally accomplished: a large masonry construction in the form of a Greek cross, with a daringly complex system of interrelated vaults that reached a climax in the spacious central crossing, which was topped by a lofty dome more than sixty feet in diameter. In concept and execution it was a much bolder expression of his vision and ability than even the Bank of Pennsylvania had been. But once again the essential character of this greater accomplishment, inside and out, creates an impression of geometric simplicity; once again it was a unique contribution to the history of American architecture. And in all this he was a generation ahead of his time.

In spite of his very real successes, Latrobe's fortunes during the last fifteen years of his life were often in a most precarious balance. When he did not offer his services free of charge, he often had to wait interminably for payments that were due him, and some of these never did materialize because of legal complications he could not master. Among other resulting difficulties, he often signed notes for trusted but irresponsible friends and acquaintances who failed to make good on their obligations. Eventually this brought him to actual bankruptcy. Before that came about, the various endeavors he made to stay financially afloat—and to pursue his many different interests—comprised a long and complicated list of ventures and adventures.

He had already (without fee) advised Princeton College in the renovation of Nassau Hall—where Congress had once held its sessions during the dark days of the Revolution—after it suffered serious damage from fire in 1802. The next year he designed a building (again without charge) for Dickinson College, a Presbyterian institution at Carlisle, Pennsylvania. Latrobe's counsel included almost every aspect of a well-considered program—planning the building in relation to the climate, prevailing winds, and other environmental factors; the disposition of various accommodations according to necessary conveniences and separate functions; matters of ventilation and outlook; materials to be used in construction; and the design and decorative details of the building. It was probably the most thoroughly thought-out and subtly designed of all early American academic facilities, and another tribute to Latrobe's wide-ranging concept of architectural theory.

He also renovated the great house formerly occupied by George Washington in Philadelphia to serve as the chief building of the University of Pennsylvania. A few years later he designed an entirely new wing for that institution's medical school and a new hall for his brother Masons. During these years Latrobe also built the short-lived Bank of Philadelphia and Christ Church, which still stands in Washington. Both were in the Gothic style, and neither added substantially to his reputation or his means.

More rewarding was his commission to build a large house in Philadelphia for William Waln, a prosperous merchant in the China trade and husband of one of Mary Latrobe's dearest friends. The architect wrote several long letters explaining his approach to this assignment. The basic requirement of such a house, he observed, was "the greatest possible compactness, & convenience for the family, expressed in the very comprehensive word *comfort*, and moderate means of entertaining company." It must have a bathroom and water closet as well as a separate service stair for the sake of privacy. And he insisted that he should supervise every aspect of the construction, lest his specifications not be perfectly construed. Further, he designed all the furniture; dictated the wall decorations, including scenes from the *Iliad* and the *Odyssey* painted in "Etruscan colors"; and advised on the landscaping of the grounds. In these matters he had the assistance of his young associate Robert Mills. Apparently Latrobe was pleased with the final results, which we can visualize from a water color of the site painted before the house was converted into a public bath.

During their residence in Washington the Latrobes enjoyed a gracious and pleasant social life. They numbered among their good friends Dolley Madison and her husband, and the Joel Barlows, for whom Latrobe did some work on Kalorama, the Barlows's nearby residence. Washington Irving and Robert Fulton were but two of the day's other celebrities who came to dine with the Latrobes. Many prominent members of the Washington diplomatic corps also came to visit, as frequently

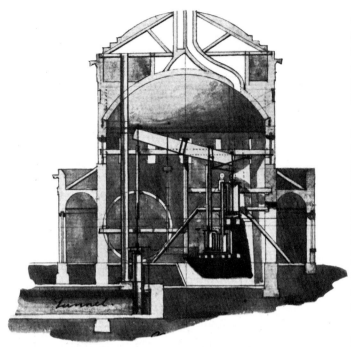

In 1819 John Lewis Krimmel depicted a Fourth of July celebration in Philadelphia's Center Square in front of the pump house that Latrobe had designed for the city's waterworks (opposite). Latrobe himself drew cross-sectional views of the wonder-working mechanisms he had installed within that structure (above) and of the settling basins for water from the Schuylkill River, which he had engineered (below).

did Paul Svinin, secretary of the Russian legation and also an artist. For a year another artist, the witty, bibulous, and celebrated Gilbert Stuart, occupied an atelier found for him by Latrobe. (Characteristically, Stuart neglected to pay the rent for these accommodations.)

Had Latrobe depended entirely upon his architectural commissions and upon the monies due him from his debtors, he would have been hard put to meet his expenses. He turned hopefully to his engineering skills for further income, working on several canal projects, among others. For several years he was concerned with an unsuccessful scheme for a Chesapeake and Delaware canal. His participation in this undertaking ultimately left him holding a bundle of worthless stock and only deeper in debt, although it left us in *his* debt for a series of delightful water colors that he made on his surveying trips.

Latrobe's association with that abortive enterprise did, however, lead to other opportunities. In 1806 he was commissioned to make a survey of the town of Newcastle, Delaware. This he did in his usual fashion as both architect and engineer, with a broad and comprehensive consideration of the total problems no less than with very specific details. He brought into view questions of hygiene, the orientation of streets to suit the town's geography, the elevation of its existing buildings, the tradition-

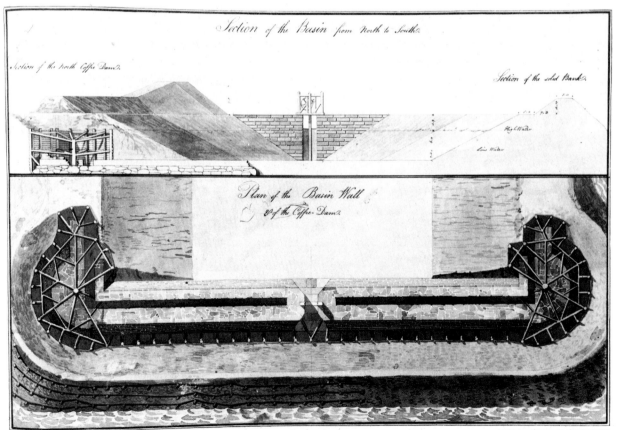

al architecture that gave the town its established character, and the designs of buildings to be erected. Such careful thought of the future, as well as the present, was one of the qualities that made Latrobe a prophetic critic of the careless, scrambling, impatient growth so characteristic of the American scene then and for years to come.

In 1809 Latrobe's interest and imagination were immediately fired by a letter from his good friend Albert Gallatin, then secretary of the treasury, asking for help in preparing a report to Congress concerning internal developments of the nation. The results of the Embargo and the Non-Intercourse acts, and especially the growing threat of war and interference with American shipping, made the need for more and better canals and roads increasingly evident. Even without those extraneous factors, the need was apparent enough when, for example, it cost as much to cart a ton of merchandise barely thirty miles overland in America as it did to ship an equivalent cargo from England.

Latrobe's recommendations were typically both exhaustive and detailed. Among them was support for a plan to connect the Great Lakes (and thus the entire Midwest) with the Hudson River by means of a long canal. (On this point even Thomas Jefferson remarked that the "talk of making a canal *three hundred and fifty miles* through the wilderness" was "little short of madness.") Once again however, Latrobe proved himself a man ahead of his time. What he himself referred to as part of a "Utopian" scheme was actually realized with the completion of the Erie Canal sixteen years later. But Gallatin's grand concept of a national system of roads and canals got nowhere.

With the outbreak of war in 1812 Latrobe's prospects in the East all but vanished. He was in fact close to destitution. For years he had been associated with Nicholas Roosevelt, the engineer who supplied the steam machinery for the Philadelphia waterworks. Roosevelt had in 1808 married the Latrobes' young daughter, albeit he was old enough to be her father. Roosevelt was speculative by nature, and more than once Latrobe signed notes of his that proved worthless, and joined him in deals that went awry. In 1809 Roosevelt had joined with Robert Fulton and his patron Robert Livingston as a founder of the Mississippi Steamboat Navigation Company, with operational headquarters in Pittsburgh. In that city Roosevelt built the *New Orleans,* in which he successfully made a run down the river to New

41

Orleans. It was the first steam vessel to complete that long and difficult passage, and the event created a sensation, as well it might have. From this time the commerce of the whole Mississippi River basin would be revolutionized.

To take further advantage of this growing possibility, Fulton and his associates formed a new company, the Ohio Steamboat Navigation Company. In 1813, with most of his Washington affairs stalled, Latrobe took his family off to Pittsburgh to serve as the company's operating agent with a promised salary and a one-third interest in the company. America's most creative and advanced architect was obliged to make his living by building steamboats. "I am going to be a blacksmith at Pittsburgh," he wrote to a friend, with unconcealed chagrin. (They set off for the West in what appears to have been one of the most ingeniously contrived vehicles yet to be seen, a wagon designed by Latrobe himself, of course, to accommodate every contingency that might cause discomfort or inconvenience on the long, rough, overland trip.)

Latrobe's nearly two years as a Pittsburgh "blacksmith" developed into a nightmare of frustrations. There is little reason here to detail the web of circumstances that brought him to the point of despair. As in the past, his relationship with his son-in-law, Roosevelt, again added complications to his life. Business dealings with Fulton's group in New York deteriorated until they altogether collapsed. For all his earnest, industrious, and thoughtful efforts to do the job assigned to him, he was virtually abandoned to face alone the obligations that he had assumed in what he considered to be his partners' interest. With or without good reasons, Fulton wrote that he was "tired of distant operations" and that his Ohio company was "alarmed and disgusted with the expenses and the state of their affairs."

During the course of this unhappy association Latrobe assumed a number of architectural commissions in the western city. In order to accommodate to local circumstances, in a number of cases he put aside his pride and worked as a contractor. He exultantly noted that the buildings he raised were finished much more quickly than those put up by mere mechanics. The most important of his assignments was the great United States arsenal, which was not completed until long after his return to the East and only parts of which remain standing. He also wrote an essay on acoustics for publication. It was a study that particularly concerned him in the planning of public buildings. For another publication he wrote a report on turnpikes, exchanging learned puns in Greek and Latin in the correspondence with his editor (along with knowledgeable comments on the art of cooking and gas lighting, among other matters). As further evidence of his vision and of his driving pursuit of engineering questions, at a somewhat later date he outlined the advantages of mass manufacture by the use of accurately tooled, identical, interchangeable parts.

He may have been aware of Eli Whitney's successes in operating by such a system.

After a bout of serious illness and of deep depression, he quit Pittsburgh in 1815. Financially he was practically ruined, but he left armed with a letter from President Madison (secured partly by the connivance of Mrs. Latrobe and Dolley Madison) recalling him to Washington to oversee the reconstruction of the Capitol. This, he wrote Jefferson, he found "a most magnificent ruin." Demolition by the British troops had been thoroughly accomplished (although one officer in charge of the destruction is said to have remarked that "it was a pity to burn anything so beautiful").

In the reconstruction Latrobe enjoyed somewhat more freedom than he had known when he inherited the supervision of the original building. Singlehandedly he drew up all the plans for the reconstruction. He proposed many changes in the old plans and designs. Of these Madison approved, and the large job was started. In the small rotunda of the old Senate wing he devised columns in the classical spirit but topped by capitals representing leaves of the America tobacco plant (in his earlier work on the Capitol he had used capitals with a corn plant motif). He found and developed new quarries to provide better stone for the construction. Understaffed as he was, and bedeviled by labor problems, he completed much of the work in twenty-nine months. Even so, he suffered repeated stings from an officialdom that was outraged by

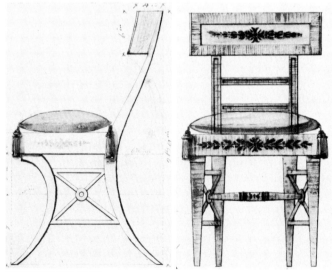

In 1807 Latrobe did the water color at left, showing the White House with the addition of the north and south porticoes, which he designed. When Madison succeeded Jefferson as president in 1809, the architect helped Dolley Madison in decorating the mansion. He designed suites of furniture, including a mantel-piece and an overmantel mirror (left, above) and chairs in the Greek manner (above), all of which went up in flames in 1814.

43

TO THOMAS JEFFERSON Prᵗᵗ U.S.
B.H.LATROBE. 1806.

44

A pencil portrait of Thomas Jefferson from about 1799 (left) was probably drawn by Latrobe. In 1806 the architect delivered to the president a signed drawing of the Capitol (bottom, left), showing the building as it would have looked if completed according to the original Thornton design with Latrobe's revisions. Latrobe's designs for the innovative corn and tobacco capitals installed in the Capitol are reproduced below.

This view of the Capitol, attributed to Latrobe, shows it as it looked from Pennsylvania Avenue in 1819 with the north and south wings built according to Latrobe's design. The central section and dome were completed by Bulfinch (see page 24).

45

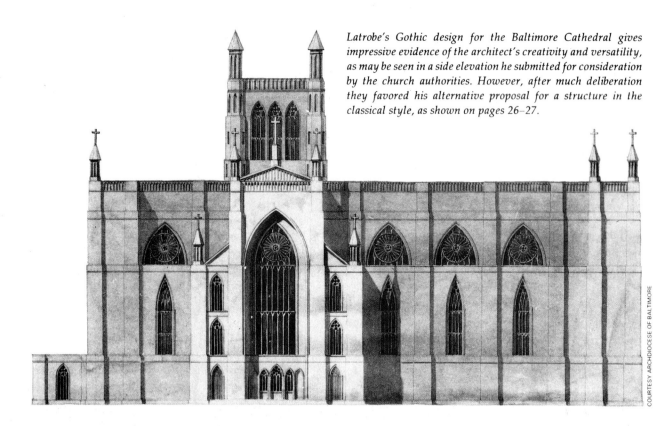

Latrobe's Gothic design for the Baltimore Cathedral gives impressive evidence of the architect's creativity and versatility, as may be seen in a side elevation he submitted for consideration by the church authorities. However, after much deliberation they favored his alternative proposal for a structure in the classical style, as shown on pages 26–27.

what it considered slow progress and excessive costs. President Monroe was now in office, and neither he nor some of his close and often malicious advisers could or would try to understand Latrobe's problems. Neither did they acknowledge his amazing accomplishments. Even his workmen complained of the deliberate and sometimes time-consuming care he took with the realization of his plans. "Every carpenter and mason thinks he knows more than Latrobe," wrote one understanding friend of the architect, "and such men have got on so fast last year with the President's House (a mere lathing-and-plastering job) that they have the audacity to think they ought to have the finishing of the Capitol, a thing they are totally unfit for. . . ." Finally, stung beyond endurance by such interference and hostile criticism, Latrobe submitted his resignation in 1817.

Charles Bulfinch, the eminently capable Boston architect, finished the job over the next eleven years. Fortunately, in the end he did very little to alter Latrobe's work. Even Mrs. Trollope, that usually caustic critic of the American scene, was struck with surprise and admiration when some years later she viewed such a magnificent structure rising out of the landscape of what was still a very raw young city.

In the meantime, Latrobe had completed—as always, among still other projects—houses in Washington for the Casanove family, General J. P. Van Ness, and Stephen Decatur. (Only the Decatur house still stands.) These he himself called the "three finest houses in Washington," although he conceded this might not be saying very much, such was the state of domestic architecture in the city. The Van Ness house in particular was nevertheless probably the most impressive of all the dwellings Latrobe designed. His success here was made possible in good part by the understanding indulgence of a wealthy client. In its size, but more importantly in the elegance and the functional perfection of its interior appointments, this was truly a "great" house, fully worthy of the admiration it excited in Washington society.

He also had designed Saint John's Church. He was so proud of this architectural gem that he wrote his son Henry that it brought religion to many otherwise diffident or indifferent Washingtonians. The structure still stands on Lafayette Square. It has an extra association with Latrobe, for here he served for a time as organist and choirmaster.

However, with the cessation of his government contract Latrobe's finances worsened to the point that in December 1817 he filed a plea of bankruptcy. He sold off furniture and other goods to help repay some of his debts and in January moved his family to Baltimore. There his largest commission, the Baltimore Exchange, awaited completion, as did the Baltimore Cathedral. The Exchange was a huge, complicated, and elaborate masonry construction that called for daring and skills which at that time only Latrobe could command. It was in this building, according to the architect's most informed biographer, that "his integration of use, construction, and beauty received its most perfect expression." Over the years following its completion the building was variously deformed and was finally torn down in 1904. The cathedral remains very much as Latrobe designed it.

From time to time Latrobe had under his wing assistants and associates who went on to eminent and independent careers. Especially in the work of Robert Mills and William Strickland, his influence was carried on into another generation. Mills, a native of Charleston, South Carolina, came to work in Latrobe's office in 1803 after having served two years as Jefferson's draftsman at Monticello. Under Latrobe's supervision he became the first professionally trained American-born architect. Among his many and varied later accomplishments, ranging from great bridges to private houses, in 1836 he designed the Washington Monument, at the time the tallest building in the world. Under President Andrew Jackson, Mills became architect of public buildings for the government, and as such he set the style for such structures for future decades. Much of his work was in the Greek Revival mode, a vogue that remained widely popular until his death in 1855.

Strickland, the son of a Philadelphia carpenter, was apprenticed to Latrobe the same year as Mills. But because of his indolence and undependability, he was fired two years later, in 1805. Like Mills, he worked mainly in the Greek Revival style, and his important structures were scattered across the country, from Philadelphia and Providence, Rhode Island, to New Orleans and Nashville, Tennessee. One of his most memorable achievements was the famous Philadelphia Exchange, built in the early 1830's. His influence was further felt through his participation in the planning of canals, railroads, and turnpikes.

Another protégé who might have gone on to a notable career was Latrobe's son Henry. With his father's guidance, plus several years of study at West Point, which was then primarily an engineering school, young Henry had already developed at the age of eighteen into a highly competent architect-engineer. In 1811 Latrobe sent him to New Orleans to commence work on a scheme for providing that city with desperately needed fresh water. This was Latrobe's private undertaking, but

it was interrupted by the War of 1812. In that conflict Henry won the commendation of General Andrew Jackson for his services at the Battle of New Orleans. Then, with work resumed, Henry suddenly died of yellow fever, a tragedy that deeply affected his father. It also brought the water-supply operation almost to a halt.

In Baltimore the elder Latrobe submitted a design for the proposed new Bank of the United States in Philadelphia. The terms of the competition called for a design that would "imitate the Greek" in its simplest and least expensive form. In submitting his own proposal Latrobe pointed out to the judges that the "necessary arrangement of a house of business—requiring a multitude of apartments and abundant light—is so contrary to that of a Temple . . . that nothing but the general character and style of the best Grecian architecture can ever be preserved in such a design." This reflected the approach he had earlier used in designing the Bank of Pennsylvania, a basic principle he observed in all his designs. But his proposal was rejected in favor of one by his erstwhile pupil William Strickland (who Latrobe believed had stolen his own plan).

With this bitter disappointment added to his grief, Latrobe shipped off to New Orleans to finish the job Henry had so competently carried on until his death. En route the architect, with time on his hands, filled his sketchbook with pictures of life at sea. Once arrived at his destination, he was fascinated by everything about life in the exotic city, so completely different from anything he had previously known. His notebooks and sketchbooks continued to abound with speculations and drawings concerning the local scene—not neglecting a study of the various types of mosquitoes that infested the area.

Within less than two years those mosquitoes did him in. On September 3, 1820, he himself succumbed to yellow fever, his work unfinished, a memorable if erratic career brought to a premature end. In his lifetime, by his stubborn insistence, he had established a strong image of the professional architect that would helpfully serve the development of that profession in this country in years to come. He had also provided a rational basis for the neoclassical style that was to be such a prominent aspect of the American scene until long after his death.

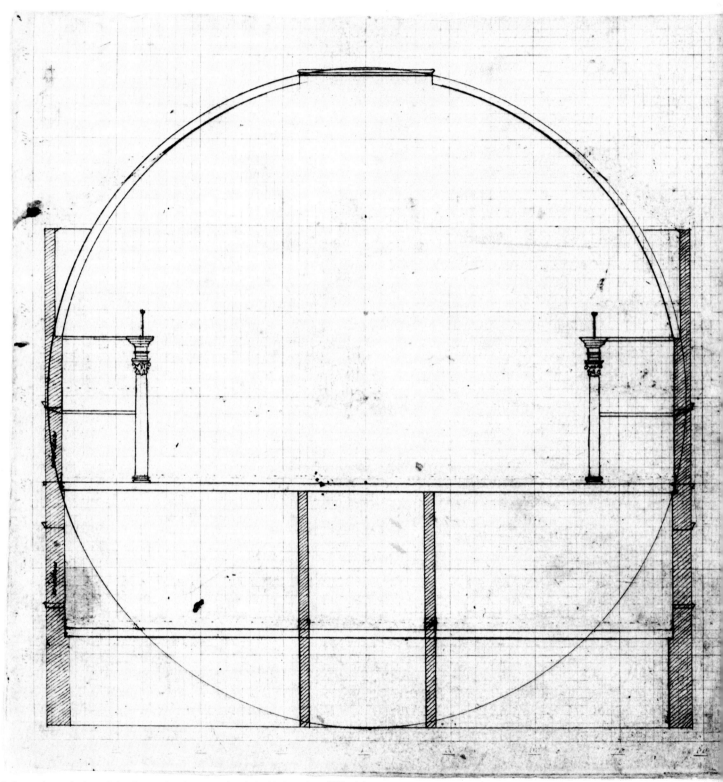

Jefferson's rendering of the design for the rotunda of the University of Virginia

THOMAS JEFFERSON

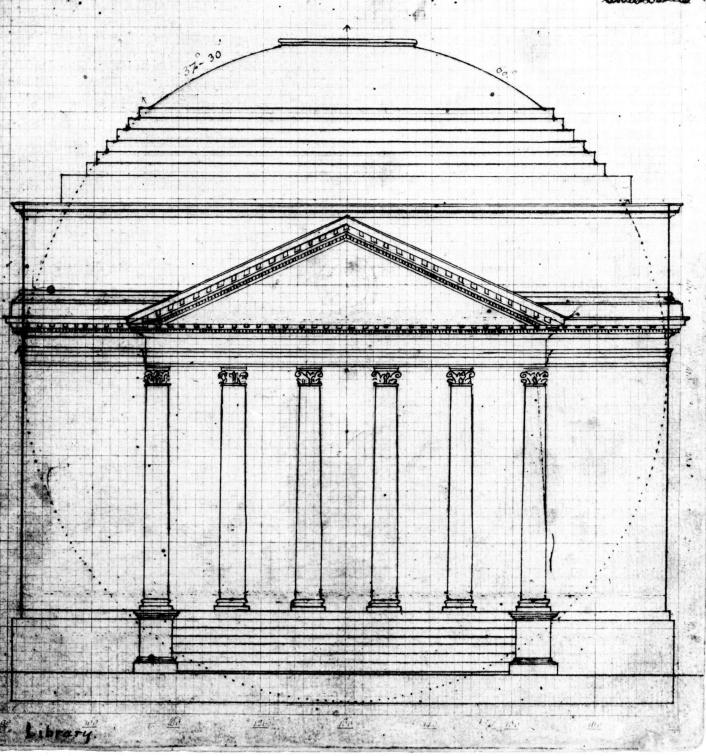

50

1743–1826

BY MARSHALL B. DAVIDSON

Before Thomas Jefferson died on the Fourth of July, 1826, precisely fifty years after the Declaration of Independence, he had long since composed the epitaph that would be inscribed on the simple granite shaft of his own design that would be raised over his grave:

Here was buried
THOMAS JEFFERSON
Author of the Declaration of American Independence,
Of the Statutes of Virginia for Religious Freedom,
And Father of the University of Virginia.

The last of these memorable achievements was the final project of his old age. As he designed and planned the university's buildings and campus, Jefferson's lifelong preoccupation with architecture found its most mature and sophisticated expression. Had he created no other structures, his lasting reputation would be secured by this single accomplishment. Yet, as his epitaph implies, it was more than an architectural triumph. It was a material extension of his deepest personal convictions, of his vision of the future as it might be realized in this land of freedom. "This institution of my native state," he once wrote with pride, "the hobby of my old age, will be based on the illimitable freedom of the human mind to explore and expose every subject susceptible of its contemplation."

Such an ambitious and liberal program summarized the principles that had guided Jefferson's approach to life over all the years since his youth. In the course of this nation's history, few of his countrymen have matched the intense, informed, and varied interests with which he pondered the nature and meaning of the world he lived in; none, at least, who at one time or another has enjoyed the prestige and the authority of the presidency of the United States and the influence this distinction bestowed upon them.

Charles Willson Peale painted this portrait from life in 1791, when Jefferson was serving as secretary of state.

Among the wide-ranging concerns that occupied Jefferson's mind throughout his career, his interest in the arts played a prominent role. "I am an enthusiast on the subject of the arts," he wrote his friend James Madison. "But it is an enthusiasm of which I am not ashamed, as its object is to improve the taste of my countrymen, to increase their reputation, to reconcile to them the respect of the world, and to procure them its praise." This in fair measure he succeeded in doing, both directly and indirectly, and both through his official acts and his private enterprises.

His enthusiasm embraced virtually all the arts—music, sculpture, and painting, among them. As his kinsman Edmund Randolph observed, Jefferson "panted after the fine arts and discovered a taste in them not easily satisfied with such scanty means as existed in a colony, for it was a part of Mr. Jefferson's pride to run before the times in which he lived." It was the most practical of all the arts, architecture, that remained his main, abiding preoccupation. The marquis de Chastellux, who had served as a major general in Rochambeau's army during the American Revolution and who visited Jefferson at Monticello in 1782, concluded that (although the building was then far from completed) Jefferson was "the first American who has consulted the Fine Arts to know how he should shelter himself from the weather." Here he was implying that Jefferson's planned home was the first he had seen in the new republic that paid high and strict regard to the "rules" of architecture as these had been laid down by the Renaissance interpreters of the classical styles.

Jefferson himself took a dim view of the freedom with which colonial builders in various parts of the country had construed and applied those rules. The William and Mary College at Williamsburg, Virginia, he termed a "rude, mis-shapen" pile that might have been taken for a brickkiln, except that it had a roof. "The genius of architecture seems to have shed its maledictions over this land," he wrote in his *Notes on the State of Virginia*, ". . . the first principles of the art are unknown, and there exists scarcely a model among us sufficiently chaste to give an idea of them."

Not many of his contemporaries would have agreed with such an appraisal. But as Randolph had observed, Jefferson was running before the times. Although today we admire many of the colonial structures that he considered to be of indifferent character, Jefferson's vision led him both back and forward in time; back to models of the classical past, and forward to the day when the principles that had inspirited such ancient buildings could be transplanted in the New World to find fresh life in this remote western margin of civilization.

Jefferson had given thought to such a classical revival years before Latrobe arrived in America with similar thoughts of his own. It was probably before he drafted the Declaration of Independence that Jefferson drew up measured plans to remodel the governor's palace at Williamsburg into a structure that, had his studies materialized, would have resulted in the first temple-form house in the neoclassical spirit anywhere. With the palace in mind as it now stands, impressively restored to its original appearance, we cannot easily conclude how much might have been gained or lost had Jefferson's project got off the drawing board. It poses a large question that continues to plague us today—architects, planners, and public alike—in contemplating the fate of our historic architectural landmarks.

For all his knowledge of the subject and the many architectural ventures with which he was intimately involved, Jefferson was never a professional practitioner in this field. He was the quintessential American gentleman-architect of

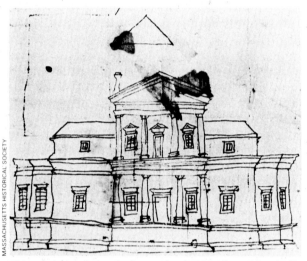

This rough pencil sketch, drawn about 1770, shows Monticello as Jefferson first conceived it. OPPOSITE: An aerial view of Monticello's site with its commanding views reveals how admirably Jefferson realized his vision of an "elevated" setting for his estate, as recommended by Palladio.

his time. His interest in the subject was awakened at an early age and continued unabated until his death. He is said to have remarked to one visitor to Monticello, "Architecture is my delight, and putting up, and pulling down, one of my favorite amusements." And to such operations he gave abundant energy and passionate thoughtfulness. His advice in these matters was constantly solicited by friends, architects, the Congress of the United States, and other official public bodies.

The number of houses he is said to have designed for friends, relatives, and acquaintances is no doubt swollen by legend. But there is ample evidence that he provided plans for a variety of buildings in Virginia—residences, churches, and courthouses—a number of which still stand, bearing the imprint of his particular taste. Compared to his major contributions, they are for the most part relatively modest examples of his enterprising skill. Nevertheless, they suggest the disciplined attention he paid to problems of accommodation and style that arose at every level of building in which he was engaged.

One example of the projects in which he served the interests of his friends, Belle Grove in Middletown, Virginia, must suffice to indicate Jefferson's role in such matters. In 1794 the future president James Madison wrote Jefferson of a plan his brother-in-law had in mind to build a new residence, and requested Jefferson's counsel in designing the house. "In general," he wrote, "any hints which may occur to you for improving the place will be thankfully accepted. I beg pardon for being the occasion of this trouble to you, but your goodness has always so readily answered such draughts on it, that I have been tempted to make this additional one." Madison sent the builder of the house to Monticello, "not only to profit of examples before his eyes, but to ask the favor of your advice on the plan of the House." The house still stands, one of the properties of the National Trust for Historic Preservation.

But Jefferson's prominence in the history of American architecture rests more securely on the influence he exercised on the development of the national capital during his years in office and his later years as an elder statesman; on his part in the design of the Virginia State Capitol; on the ultimate completion of Monticello, the aerie he built for himself overlooking Charlottesville; and on the University of Virginia, a view of which he could contemplate in his later years from his mountain-top home. These four monumental achievements marked climatic passages in a career that had no really close parallel in our American cultural heritage.

Throughout his mature life Jefferson's most intimate architectural concern was with the evolution of Monticello into the home of his dreams—dreams that changed as his experience broadened and his circumstances changed. His first studies for a perch on that high site were undertaken in 1767 when he was twenty-four, and he continued "putting up, and pulling down," practically until his death almost sixty years later at the age of eighty-three. At Monticello, as with every other house he ever lived in (including the White House and his diplomatic headquarters in Paris) Jefferson designed or planned changes to keep pace with the

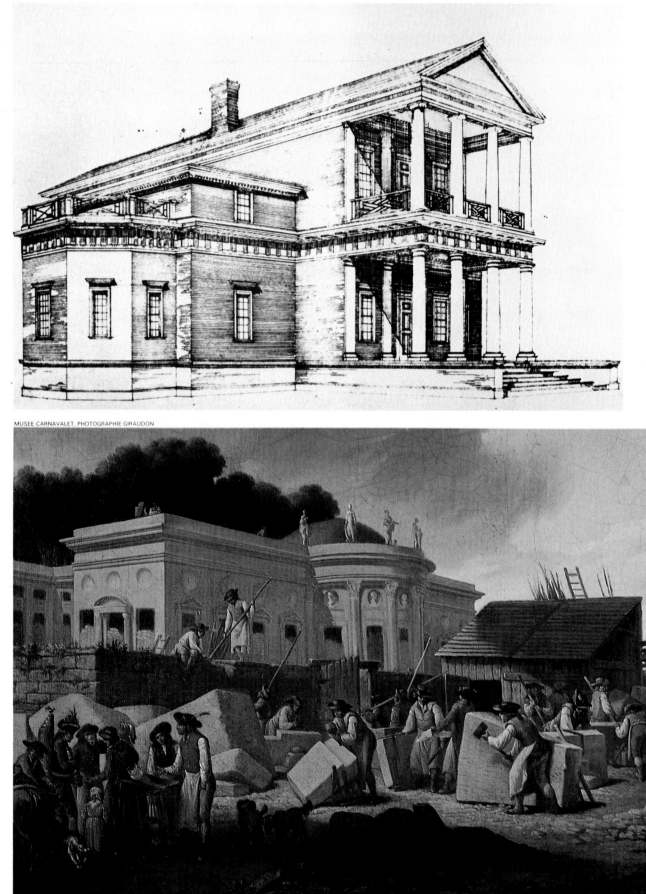

54

The drawing of Monticello at the top of the
opposite page, based on Jefferson's own drawings
and manuscripts, recreates the building as it must
have appeared in the 1780's when the Marquis de
Chastellux saw it. During the following years,
Jefferson's architectural taste was changed by
what he saw in France, and especially by the Hôtel
de Salm, shown during construction at left. He was
"violently smitten" with the design of this
residence as he saw it rising in the course of his
almost daily visits to the scene. When he returned
to Monticello he had the second-story colonnaded
porch torn down and replaced by a dome. The
water color above, painted in 1825, the year before
his death, depicts the west front of the house. Three
of his grandchildren appear on the spacious lawn
amid the various flowering plants and bordering
shrubs meticulously selected and placed by Jefferson to ornament the grounds.

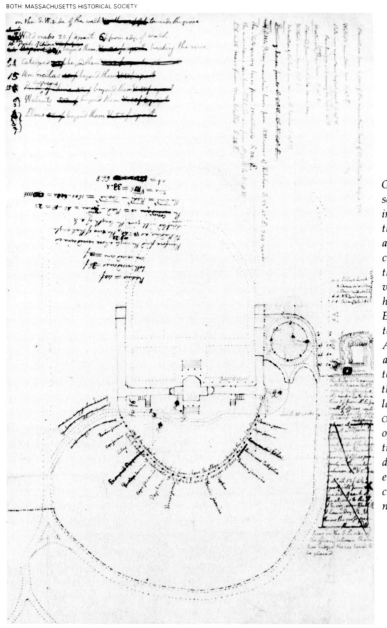

Gardening was one of Jefferson's lifelong and passionate interests. His early plans for the planting and landscaping about Monticello are recorded in a drawing (left) that dates from 1772. He revised his formal layout after he returned from his stay in Europe, where during a brief tour of England with John Adams in 1786, he became an enthusiastic convert to the idea that nature is the best model for the landscape gardener.
OPPOSITE: *About 1771, in one of his relatively few architectural renderings, Jefferson designed an observation tower for his gardens at Monticello. This ambitious project never materialized.*

fresh knowledge and understanding that he incessantly acquired.

He had graduated from William and Mary College in 1762. While he was there, Dr. William Small aroused in the youth scientific interests that Jefferson pursued all his life. Small introduced Jefferson to the "familiar table" of the colonial governor, Francis Fauquier, and to George Wythe, Virginia's most noted teacher of law. About that table the four men often dined and talked. "At these dinners," Jefferson recalled, "I have heard more good sense, more rational and philosophical conversations, than in all my life besides." He was also invited to play the violin in string concerts at the governor's palace in the company of Fauquier, who shared Jefferson's passion for music. And he studied law with Wythe, a man he described

variously as "the Cato of his country," "my second father," and "my antient master, my earliest & best friend."

Jefferson's true father, Peter Jefferson, a classic self-made Virginia frontiersman, died when the lad was fourteen, leaving a fairly substantial estate, a share of which eventually fell to Tom. In 1772, when he was twenty-nine years old, he married Martha Wayles Skelton, a widow whom he took home to Monticello, then the bare beginning of a building. Just a year earlier he had written a friend, "I have but one room, which like the coblers, serves me for parlor, for kitchen and hall. I may add, for bedchamber and study too. . . . I have hopes, however, of getting more elbow room this summer." In the next ten years Martha bore six children, only two of whom, both daughters,

reached maturity. She died in 1782, long before Jefferson had completed their mountaintop home.

The most important books in Jefferson's architectural library were Leoni's *Architecture of A. Palladio* in four volumes. He may have been the first colonist to acquire these seminal books, and they remained his most prized references as he built and rebuilt Monticello over the years. Most of the important Virginia plantation houses were built along the rivers, where the land was flat and fertile and where easy transportation by water routes was accessible. To erect such a structure on a height was virtually unprecedented in Jefferson's time, and not altogether reasonable for a practicing farmer, which he was. However, he must have read Palladio's advice that country houses should be built "in elevated and agreeable places . . . upon an eminence," and with this suggestion Jefferson's own romantic outlook was in complete sympathy, as his correspondence repeatedly observed. In reply to one of his letters to a Williamsburg friend describing the satisfaction he found in his location, she wrote, "I shal' think, Spirits of an higher order inhabits Yr. Aerey Mountains."

Work on Monticello came practically to a standstill when in 1784 Congress sent Jefferson to Paris to join Benjamin Franklin and John Adams in negotiating treaties with the various European powers. With those problems resolved, he stayed on for another three years, succeeding Franklin as the American minister to France. These five years on what he referred to as "the vaunted scene of Europe!" enriched his life and fired his imagination in all directions. As ever, architecture was a central focus of his attention to that scene. As he wrote a friend in Paris, he "fell in love" with one fine example after another—with the Hôtel de Salm in Paris, as he watched it being built across the Seine from the Tuileries; with the city gates designed by the classicist Claude Nicolas Ledoux; and with, among many others, the Maison Carrée at Nîmes, the best-preserved Roman temple in existence. His admiration for the Hôtel de Salm led him to modify his plans for Monticello upon his return to America, and he suggested it as one model for the building of the President's House in Washington. His respect for Ledoux's works was reflected in elements of the architecture at the University of Virginia.

Everywhere in France he was "nourished" by the remains of Roman grandeur. In that ancient structure at Nîmes he saw a precious and perfect exemplar of the true classical spirit, "noble beyond expression." He confessed to one intimate friend that he would gaze at it for hours at a time, "like a

57

lover at his mistress." It was with this vision in his mind's eye that he designed, or rather redesigned, the Virginia State Capitol at Richmond, a project in which he sought the advice of the French architect Charles Louis Clérisseau, whose *Monuments de Nîmes* had directed Jefferson's attention to the Maison Carrée in the first place.

In transmitting his proposed design to Virginia he wrote in an accompanying letter that he considered it "simple and sublime . . . copied from the most perfect model of antient architecture remaining on earth; one which has received the approbation of near 2,000 years." Conceding the justness of that appraisal, Jefferson had fair reason to be proud of what he had done. One of his proposed objectives as a founding father of the new republic was to ensure that the public buildings would present models of good taste for study and emulation. With its completion in 1789, the Virginia capitol became just that, much admired and much copied. It was the principal precursor of the classical revival style in the United States.

In all these years Jefferson was, to be sure, much more than a passionate devotee of architecture. He was an active statesman in the service of his state and country. He was a tireless and interested observer of the scene about him in all its aspects. He carefully noted novel developments in plows, steam engines, and water pumps. He collected seeds and plants of different sorts that he thought could be advantageously grown in America. He was an unremitting student of political thought and history. It was in Paris that he completed his *Notes on Virginia*, written for the instruction of the secretary of the French legation, which was immediately acclaimed as a classic study of its kind. And he ever remained a humanitarian philosopher of idealistic bent. All these various facets of his career and personality were tightly integrated in this one individual. It is practically impossible to separate Jefferson the architect from Jefferson the political activist, the planner of the University of Virginia from the author of the Declaration of Independence.

Jefferson returned to America in the autumn of 1789 and almost immediately was offered by President Washington the secretaryship of state, a post he accepted with some reservation. It was in that post that he provided the leadership and the knowledge that led ultimately to the planning and building of the new national capital in the District of Columbia. No American—no individual—of his times better understood the vital function that architecture might play in the political and social aspirations of the infant republic.

Washington himself had chosen the site along the Potomac for the permanent seat of the new government. Washington also chose Major Pierre Charles L'Enfant, a French architect, engineer, and veteran of the American Revolution, to lay out plans for the new capital city. To aid him in converting this barren ten-mile-square area into a well-organized pattern that would serve the country for time to come, Jefferson assembled what he considered the best city plans of Europe. L'Enfant was also to have designed the principal government buildings, but in 1792 he was dismissed because of a conflict with the commissioners who were overseeing the program. Nevertheless, with the guidance of Jefferson and Washington, the Frenchman had envisioned an over-all city plan, with anticipation of an executive residence and a complex of legislative buildings, which has continued to function with reasonable success through all the changes and growth that have taken place for almost two hundred years.

A year before L'Enfant's dismissal, Jefferson had suggested holding a competition for the actual design and construction of the President's House and a capitol building for Congress, a suggestion which was readily accepted by Washington and the three commissioners. These were the first important architectural competitions to be held in the United States. Here, as in so many other situations, Jefferson served not so much as a practicing architect but as a catalytic agent, setting standards of quality and performance that others would consult and profit from, and advising and guiding from his own rich experience and his understanding of the basic issues at stake.

In the competition for the design of the President's House, he submitted an anonymous design of his own, signed with the initials A. Z., which was not accepted. (Jefferson absented himself from the deliberations of the commission, for understandable reasons.) The final award was given to the Irish-born architect and builder James Hoban, described by one contemporary as "a very ingeniuous Mechanic & Draftsman," then operating out of Charleston, South Carolina. That the choice was a good one is indicated by the fact that Hoban was the only person connected with the construction of the capital who remained identified with it for the next three decades. Although there was nothing strikingly original in his design for the President's House (it was derived from typical mid-eighteenth-century English mansions such as were illustrated in James Gibbs's *Book of Architecture* published in 1728), it was unlike anything then standing in the United States. Beyond that, it conformed to the president's own somewhat austere notion of an appropriate executive mansion. No house in the nation has had such a continuous succession of residents of such differing tastes. Inside and out, the building has been subject to frequent alterations and enlargements to suit the needs and tastes of its many occupants. It has twice been damaged by fire and substantially rebuilt. Yet the White House today still recalls Hoban's original structure.

When Jefferson moved into the White House as president in 1805, he found it "big enough for two emperors, one Pope and the grand lamma," and proceeded to improve its accommodations. He had brought with him upon his return from Europe eighty-six cases of French furniture for his own use, some of which he installed in his presidential residence. However, whatever French accent he added to the decoration and equipment of the building can never be known, since the fire of 1814 destroyed the evidence. It would seem that the interior was taking on an unprecedented air of refinement. "This furniture is elegant," the financier Robert Morris advised him, "and well suited to your apartments, perhaps better than any other in America."

During his two terms in office, Jefferson also spent more than ten thousand dollars on French wines to be served at his table. He employed a French chef and steward, which, together with such epicurean delights as macaroni in the Italian manner, led Patrick Henry to label him as "a man unfaithful to his native victuals."

The competition for the Capitol was won by Dr. William Thornton, a young physician from the Virgin Islands and another typical eighteenth-century gentleman-architect. The original drawing has not survived, but Jefferson (who did not submit a plan in this competition) thought it "simple, noble, beautiful, excellently distributed, and moderate in size," and heartily recommended it to the commissioners.

As already told, the actual construction and completion of this building was beset with difficulties over the years, and as president, Jefferson became deeply involved in these and other architectural matters concerning the government. His appointment of Latrobe as the first surveyor of public buildings in the nation's capital was typical of the informed interest and good judgment he displayed in his executive office in those formative years of the city's development. He expressed his concern with the quality of the new government constructions in his remark that "when buildings are of durable materials, every new edifice is an actual and permanent acquisition to the State, adding to its value as well as to its ornament." Without such well-directed judgment exercised with presidential authority, Washington, D.C.,

might have become a quite different and a less impressive expression of national pride, a pride that sorely wanted bolstering as in its infancy the new republic struggled to prove itself to the world.

When Jefferson's presidency ended in 1809 he retired to his beloved Monticello exhausted by his public services. He had neglected his property, his lands, his crops, and to a considerable degree his home, in his labors to build a republican system of government. He was sixty-five years old, but there remained much for him to do. The completion of Monticello was a constant obsession. In 1787, twenty-two years earlier, he had written a friend, "All my wishes end where I hope my days will end, at Monticello," and thus it would be.

Changes and additions in the actual building and the grounds there continued, as they had from his first studies, virtually until his death. Such incessant reconstruction was not without its perils. Early on, in 1797, his younger daughter fell through one of the floors of the building and landed in the cellar. Shortly thereafter she fell out of an unprotected doorway. She suffered no serious harm in either case, but these episodes point up the frequent disruption of the house as Jefferson obstinately pursued his ever-changing notion of what in the end the house must be.

At best he was apparently somewhat less than perfect as a housekeeper. In 1815, when a visitor from Boston came to Monticello, he noted "chairs with leather bottoms stuffed with hair, but the bottoms were completely worn through and the hair sticking out in all directions." One broken pane of glass in a door was being replaced with a wooden panel, he continued, because the glass which had been procured from Bohemia was of a larger size than was available in the vicinity of Virginia. All this was in general accordance with the impression Jefferson often made on most distinguished visitors because of his own casual attire and his indifference to sophisticated politesse on even the most formal introductions. There will always remain something enigmatic about this man who paid such scrupulous attention to other details of his diverse architectural projects and their surroundings.

His ultimate plan, he once wrote the duc de La Rochefoucauld-Liancourt, was to have Monticello appear on the exterior as a one-story house "crowned with a balustrade and a dome," and that in the formation of that plan "the tastes and the arts of Europe have been consulted." His bible remained Palladio, but he used that reference creatively and in the light of his other studies and experience. Many of the features of Monticello, such as its octagonal projections, were all but

revolutionary at the time, and there was no close precedent for the interior plan as it finally evolved.

To achieve that one-story appearance, as well as to hide from view the service system of the house, he suppressed such functional elements below the main living floor at the rear. The various offices—kitchen, smokehouse, dairy, laundry, servants' quarters, and the like—were connected by colonnaded passages that protected the servants from inclement weather as they went about their rounds. On the front façade the existence of the second floor is partially disguised by the entablature that crowns the tops of the first-floor windows and by the balustrade that surmounts the cornices of the façade.

Like Mount Vernon, the White House, and other national shrines, Monticello is so rich in historical association that it is almost impossible to judge it as architecture. It is a symbolic monument. However, it is possible to distinguish it from these others by the ingenious devices that Jefferson contrived to suit his fancy and his convenience—its double doors that worked simultaneously, the concealed staircases; the dumbwaiters that further protected his privacy while dining; the bed alcoves, such as his own that was open at either side (like those he had seen in France) to permit him to retire

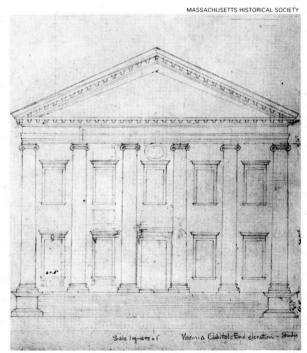

A dramatic nightime photograph (left) highlights the façade of the Virginia capitol in Richmond, as built to Jefferson's plan. Taking his design from the ancient Roman Maison Carrée at Nîmes, Jefferson had prepared the sketch above with the French architect Charles Louis Clérisseau. The finished building was the first important temple-form structure to be built in the United States and was widely copied.

61

An aerial view of the University of Virginia shows clearly how harmoniously Jefferson composed the elements of his over-all design of pavilions with their connecting colonnades, culminating in the central rotunda. The serpentine brick walls are a graceful feature of the superb campus landscape.

from and arise into either of two rooms; and endless other contrivances that contributed to the efficiency and comfort of his accommodations.

He felt a strong romantic attachment to this unique domestic establishment on its eminence, in the midst of an environment where, he exclaimed, nature had spread "so rich a mantle of mountains, forests, rocks, and rivers, under the eye." "With what majesty do we there ride above the storms!" he

wrote one correspondent. "How sublime to look down into the workhouse of nature, to see her clouds, hail, snow, rain, thunder, all fabricated at our feet! And the glorious Sun, when rising as if out of a distant water, just gilding the tops of the mountains, and giving life to all nature!" Rationalism, intellectualism, and romanticism were inseparable components of the man's character—a disparity he had once tried to reconcile in a memorable essay entitled "The Head and the Heart," which he addressed to a lady love in Paris in the 1780's.

Monticello looked out not only on the glories of nature but down upon the University of Virginia, his last and one of his most prestigious achievements, in which his architectural genius and his mature philosophy, his rationalism and his idealism, all merged in one triumphant creative act.

63

Jefferson not only designed this complex, he also charted the curriculum. On all counts the concept and the execution were alike revolutionary. Within the bounds of this campus, Jefferson wrote, "we are not afraid to follow the truth wherever it may lead or to tolerate any error so long as reason is left free to combat it." One critic has termed these buildings, so expressive of the intellectual activities they house, "one of the most modern works in the history of American architecture," a judgment with which it would be hard to find fault.

Jefferson had long been concerned for the need of just such an institution in his native state, one that would depart radically from existing American colleges, most of which had been founded by religious sects and, originally at least, were principally housed in single, all-purpose main buildings, with accretions of other separate structures as needs and resources made these essential and possible. At the University of Virginia, Jefferson wrote, the plan was

not to erect one single magnificent building to contain everybody and everything, but to make of it an academical village in which every professor should have his separate house (or "pavilion"), containing his lecture room with two or three or four rooms for his own accommodation according as he may have a family or no family, with kitchen, garden, etc.; distinct dormitories for the students, not more than two in a room; and separate boarding houses for dieting them by private housekeepers.

That he referred to his conception as a "village" shows how determined he was to organize the entire scheme into a unified whole, with respect for both symbolic function and human scale. To realize all this he sought the advice of William Thornton and Benjamin Latrobe, both of whom offered him helpful suggestions. He might also have been influenced by the roughly similar project earlier designed by the French émigré architect Jean Jacques Ramée for Union College in Schenectady, New York. It would seem, however, that Jefferson's basic scheme was in mind even before Ramée came to America. In the end the university remained true to Jefferson's basic principles and objectives and was his unique and probably most important architectural creation.

Jefferson's plan at the start of construction —the cornerstone for the first building was laid in 1817—consisted of a rectangular lawn bordered on three sides by academic buildings, with the fourth side left open to permit indefinite expansion of the facilities. At the center of the closed end he placed a large rotunda with a projection portico (as suggested by Latrobe) to serve as a focal point for the village. The rotunda contained the library, lecture room, and other common facilities, including the first planetarium in the United States. The central axis was flanked by two parallel ranges of colonnaded dormitories, behind which were gardens outlined by low, serpentine brick walls—walls low enough to provide vistas of the countryside beyond. The gardens in turn were bordered by an additional row of dormitories, parallel to the first. More than incidentally the serpentine garden walls had practical as well as aesthetic merits, for the undulations made it possible to build them one brick thick rather than the two that would have been required by a straight wall.

For the total design and the details of this extraordinary accomplishment he drew upon all his past experience both in America and, largely, in Europe. However, the refinements he introduced into the final result were distinctively drawn from his own personal vision, understanding, and imagination. Although the ten pavilions for the professors, placed at intervals along the dormitory rows, are coherently organized, each displays individual architectural features, most of them ultimately derived from different classical precedents. One pavilion, for example, has a Roman Doric order, another an Ionic order, and so on. "Now what we wish," Jefferson explained, "is that these pavilions, as they show themselves above the dormitories, shall be models of taste and good architecture, and of a variety of appearance, no two alike so as to serve as specimens for the architectural lectures." That he contained such diversity within a scheme of strictly organic character is just one more tribute to the man's special and very personal insights.

One of the refinements in Jefferson's plan, as William H. Pierson, Jr., has pointed out, is that the parallel rows of dormitories on the east side of the central lawn are considerably farther apart than the facing rows of the west side. Here—that is, on the east side—the land slopes downward more sharply than on the west, and rather than level it off for the sake of symmetry, Jefferson chose to allow the buildings to follow the natural rise and fall of the terrain. Here, as elsewhere in the university's design, there are subtleties demonstrating that in spite of his strong classic bent, he remained ever free from academic restraints, from set formulas and traditions. As had earlier been suggested, the university was in a real sense a biographical summary of the man in brick and mortar, in organization, in landscaping, and in all else that he had accomplished within that enclosure.

It should be recalled that in the years after Jefferson's death changes were made in his original design. In 1851 Robert Mills, a one-time protégé of

Benjamin Tanner's view of the University of Virginia, engraved in 1826, is considered the most accurate one of the buildings then completed. It was taken from the open end of the campus.

Jefferson, was commissioned to add an annex to the rotunda. Then, in 1895, this suffered a fire which spread to the rotunda itself. In the following reconstruction the eminent architect Stanford White introduced changes in the design which visibly altered the character of this very core of Jefferson's concept of the university. Fortunately, a careful restoration of the rotunda was completed in 1976, and the building as it stands today represents as nearly as possible Jefferson's original design.

Into his older age Jefferson continued to indulge his interest in architecture with other projects of a more or less private nature. As one example, in 1824 a plan for an episcopal church for Charlottesville was proposed by the first minister of the congregation. "I will forward you a plan for the building for your approbation as soon as it comes to hand," he wrote the former president, "but would prefer receiving from you a draft which our means would justify us in adopting." Jefferson not only provided a design but made a large contribution to its building and the support of its minister. The building was torn down in 1895, but its design influenced that of many other Virginia churches.

In spite of his overriding Francophilia, Jefferson preferred the informal style of English landscape gardening, which he had regarded with special pleasure during a visit to that country with John Adams in 1786 (although he was not impressed by the architecture he saw there). His romantic appreciation of the natural scene took deep root in a man familiar as Jefferson was with descriptions of the ideal landscape, as these appeared in works of the classical poets from Homer to Virgil. This appreciation appears to have been without precedent in America, and upon his return from Europe it was immediately reflected in his redesigning of the grounds about Monticello that from his vantage they might better accord with his prospect of all nature as a garden. Late in his life Jefferson remarked that he was an old man but still a young gardener. His study of and experiments with botany, like his curiosity about the natural world at large, were of passionate concern to him all his days.

Jefferson lived on to witness changes in the American scene that he had not anticipated. In some cases these were changes that had germinated in the light of his own genius and influence. He had long envisioned plans for a school devoted primarily to the study of architecture, where professionals of sound knowledge and technical competence would be trained. Such a college was not realized until 1866, forty years after his death. However, by his own teaching and example and by the encouragement he gave to aspiring architects, he helped immeasurably to bring about and elevate standards of professionalism in architectural practice that bore rich fruit in his own time and in time to come.

65

ALEXANDER

Davis's presentation drawing of the John Herrick mansion, Tarrytown, New York, 1855

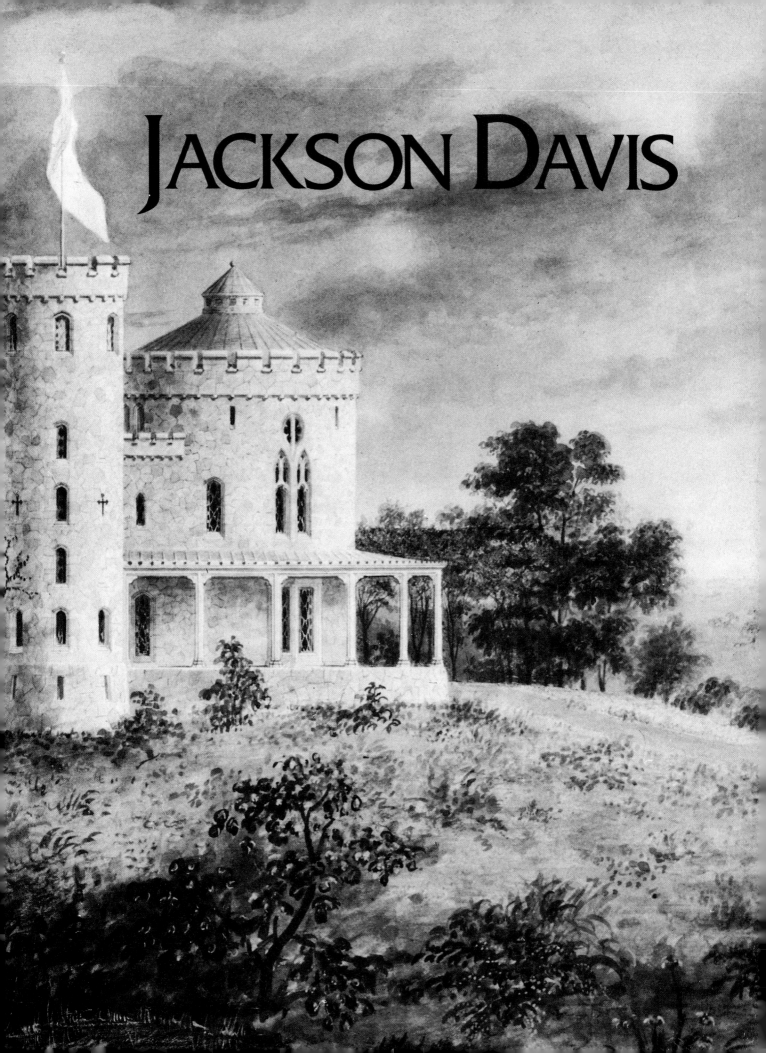

JACKSON DAVIS

Alex J. Davis.

1803–1892

BY JOSEPH KASTNER

There had not been an architect in America quite like Alexander Jackson Davis. In the 1830's he excelled in the dominant Greek Revival style: his State House in Raleigh, North Carolina, designed with his partner Ithiel Town, still stands as one of the finest examples of the mode. In the 1840's, with his collaborator, Andrew Jackson Downing, he pushed that staid classical style into limbo and brought in the exuberant Gothic Revival: it has no more lovely expression today than Lyndhurst mansion in Tarrytown, New York. Skilled in planning monumental structures, Davis had a hand in more important public buildings of his day than did any other architect. Imaginative in domesticating the Gothic, he built scores of picturesque mansions and rustic cottages.

But what set Davis apart from other architects of his time was his wide and varied clientele. He was something new, a popular—in fact, a mail-order—architect working for clients he never met on houses he never saw.

F. K. Hunt, a lawyer of Lexington, Kentucky, who had come into some money, addressed Davis: "Sir, I wish to build a mountain villa and having seen designs of one or two houses by you" ordered a plan for a home to cost $2,500. W. G. Jones of Auburn, New York, wrote: "Sir, I want to build a bold but simple little cottage. I am a labouring mechanic and cannot afford to pay a very high price," so would Davis please do "all you can for $15 or twenty dollars."

People in two dozen states, from Maine to Louisiana, consulted Davis by mail, and his approach brought a new Gothic look to America, reaching clear out to the wild Northwest. Where a Greek Revival building was symmetrical and plain, the Gothic was asymmetrical and picturesque. Its

Alexander Jackson Davis in 1852, about to turn fifty, was successful and self-assured. With no formal architectural training, he had generated the American Gothic Revival. With no formal education, he was one of New York's intellectual elite. And with no wife, he was a highly eligible bachelor.

roofs, instead of being flat or gently sloped, were steeply pitched. Instead of stately porticoes, it had deep, inviting verandas. Its surfaces were broken with bay windows and brackets, its roof lines, with gables and ornamented chimneys. It was restless, surprising, and suited to innovation—as Americans were. By 1850 it had entrenched itself as the most popular style of building in the country.

The classical style that preceded the Gothic had a strong philosophical grounding in American thought. The Founding Fathers had looked to Greece and Rome as political models for the new Republic and had thought it fitting to clothe their public institutions in neoclassical architecture. The Gothic style had no such credentials. It evoked the Dark Ages, the feudal antithesis of democracy, and to Calvinist Americans, any use of it in churches smacked of popery. When the style came into America, it came not through the faith of the Middle Ages but from the fancies of eighteenth-century England, where it began as an outsized whim.

Horace Walpole, the wit and writer, became enamored of the Middle Ages and around 1750 began embellishing his mansion at Strawberry Hill with fat turrets, conical spires, and crenelated parapets, like some medieval stronghold. Having put this playful façade on his home, Walpole proceeded to use it as a setting for his famous *Castle of Otranto*, the first of the Gothic novels. Just as Walpole's story became the model for an endless succession of tales of lurid crimes, dark-souled heroes, and supernatural happenings, so Strawberry Hill became the model for picturesque Gothic homes.

To sensible Americans, the pinnacles and oriels that were plastered on houses must have seemed as implausible as the goings-on in the novels. But they were just as fascinating. In a practical sense, the style was adapted to everyman's home. A Greek portico that suited a mansion would look silly on a plain man's house, but a bay window gave it a touch of class and a small tower added a bit of inexpensive ostentation. Besides, this was the era of Jacksonian democracy, when one man was told he was as good as any other, when a plumber was as free to consult his own tastes as a plutocrat was.

In a deeper sense, the Gothic appealed to the romanticism of Americans and to their new feeling for the wilderness. To the early American settlers, the wilderness was anathema, something to be pushed back for their own comfort and God's glory. Now the romantic writers and artists, who saw both beauty and God's handiwork in wildness, were making Americans proud of the picturesque glories of their land. And the same elements that defined the picturesque in the American landscape—

Davis spent boyhood hours sketching buildings, both real and fanciful. This drawing of a prison was done at age fifteen.

roughness, movement, irregularity, variety, intricacy—defined it in the new architecture.

Alexander Jackson Davis's mind was cast from boyhood in the Gothic, and he spent most of a long lifetime (1803–92) translating his youthful imaginings into shapes of wood and stone. "His earliest recollections," he wrote in a third-person autobiography, "was of hours spent puzzling over the plan of some ancient castle of romance, arranging the trap doors, subterraneous passages, and drawbridges." At sixteen, working as a typesetter for a newspaper in Alexandria, Virginia, he was "like another Franklin, strongly addicted to reading; being a quick compositor, he would fly to his books but not like Franklin to books of science and useful learning but to works of imagination." Joining a local acting troupe, he designed sets for Gothic dramas. "I do not trouble myself much about what business to follow," he wrote his family, "but jog along through the world without cares and at my ease. It's the best way!!!"

That was teen-age bravado. Coming back to New York, he chanced upon a camera obscura, a device painters used to sketch landscapes, and decided to become an artist. His first attempts gave a clue to the direction he would take: "designing streets in Venice, . . . planning interiors for churches, palaces, and prisons." Enrolling at an art academy, he was advised by his teacher, John Trumbull, to "devote himself to architecture, as a branch of art . . . for which, by the particular bent of his mind, he appeared to be well fitted."

There was no school to teach him architecture, so he taught himself in a practical and profitable way. Hired by a lithographer named A. T. Goodrich, who published views of New York and of other cities, he drew whole streets of buildings. A sure draftsman, meticulous in showing detail and instinctive in grasping the whole, he absorbed architecture by looking at it and setting it down. Going to Boston, where he got a course in architectural styles from the city's historic buildings, Davis made what he justifiably called "the finest examples of lithography in architecture done on this side of the Atlantic." Some of these examples were bought by a local potter to decorate his expensive chinaware.

Along the way, Davis worked in an architect's office, learning the mechanics of the craft, and in 1829 was given an enviable opportunity. Ithiel Town, who had employed him as an artist, wanted to take him in as a partner. Town, at forty-five, was nineteen years Davis's senior and one of the most respected and successful men in his profession. While making a name for himself as an architect, Town was making a comfortable fortune as inventor of the Town truss, a diagonal lattice of timbers which, used as a beam for bridges, could clear a span of 160 feet without supporting piers. The covered bridges of New England were mainly built on Town's truss, as were early railroad bridges. Traveling over the country to supervise installation of the truss and to collect fees from users, Town picked up architectural commissions that were executed in great part by his young partner.

Architecture at the time was still a haphazard practice. A young architect named Gallier, well known later for his work in New Orleans, wrote that when he came to New York in 1832 looking for work, most people did not know what was meant by *professional architect*. If a man wanted to build a house he called a carpenter or mason, asked to look at some plans, or, more likely, simply ordered the duplicate of a house that he had seen and liked. "There was, properly speaking," Gallier observed, "only one architect's office in New York, kept by Town and Davis." Here the client's special needs and means were consulted, plans done especially for him, specifications given the builder.

Town worked largely in Greek Revival, so Davis also did. They designed state houses in Indianapolis and Raleigh and the Custom House in New York, later the Subtreasury. They did mansions for Eli Whitney and other wealthy men in New Haven. On a row of houses on Lafayette Street in New York they set a superb façade of Corinthian columns—it is still known as Colonnade Row.

In 1832 Davis got a chance to let out all the Gothic feeling he had stored up. A wealthy young Marylander named Robert Gilmore had gone on a pilgrimage to Abbotsford, Sir Walter Scott's home in Scotland, where the novelist had built himself a towered and turreted castle glorifying the age of chivalry he so vividly exploited. (James Fenimore Cooper had come back from Abbotsford and put a battlemented roof on his Cooperstown farmhouse—and found that the flat roof leaked badly under the heavy snows.) Gilmore came home, eager to build a castle for his bride. Town was not comfortable in the Gothic, but Gilmore, abetted by Davis, forced irregularities on his symmetrical plan, and then Davis lavished Gothic details on the exterior—elaborate traceries and crenelations, an impressive porch, and huge oriels.

Other architects had already dipped into the Gothic in designing mansions. Latrobe, in 1799, had given a Gothic air to a Philadelphia mansion, Sedgeley, and Davis himself had done a Gothic house in Brooklyn. But nothing had been so impressive or influential as Gilmore's Glen Ellen.

Town let more and more work fall on Davis and, in 1835, retired from the firm and devoted himself to collecting the finest library on architecture in the country. Davis, freed of Town's restraint, gave himself over to the Gothic. Adventurous in his ideas and ingenious in executing them, he remodeled a house for Robert Donaldson in Barrytown,

Davis filled his sketchbooks with vignettes that were sometimes used later to enliven his architectural renderings.

New York, introducing one of his major contributions to Gothic Revival: a broad veranda that served to connect the house to the landscape. Almost as a footnote, he designed a gatehouse in what he called "the Rustic Cottage style." Of this significant design, more later.

In 1838 he began work on what is looked on as his masterpiece, a Gothic Revival home for General William Paulding, a former congressman and mayor of New York City. The site at Tarrytown, a few miles up the Hudson from New York, was as picturesque as any Gothic designer would want: a knoll looking across the river to the magnificent escarpment of the Palisades, with a ravine dropping sharply to one side and the land sloping grandly to the water.

It was named Knoll. On the eastern side a deep porte-cochère opened beneath the pointed roof of a transept. A wide veranda ran around the building and a huge stained glass window faced the west. The roof lines rose and fell in a logical but unexpected pattern. Inside, the rooms were set in useful sequence along a carefully planned axis.

Everywhere the details gave the air of rich assurance—vaulted ceilings, high leaded windows, mantels in different marbles. Davis himself designed the furniture. Armchairs repeated the window motifs, and no two side chairs were alike.

The Pauldings were fussy but freehanded

clients. "The big window must be nonpareil," Davis was instructed. "Here expense may be excused. But don't spend more than $250 on the library window. [Inspect] the marble mantels before they are sent up. If you see anything offensive to your Gothick eye (you don't squint, so no offense) put your veto on it."

Knoll was the talk of New York but not all the talk was favorable. Philip Hone, the famous diarist of the period, called it "an immense edifice . . . with towers, turrets, and trellises; minarets, mosaics, and mouse holes; archways, armories, and air holes; peaked windows and pinnacled roofs, and many other fantastics too tedious to enumerate, . . . which will one of these days be designated as 'Paulding's Folly.'" Hone, who seemed more interested in alliteration than accuracy, was letting out his bile at Paulding, who had beaten Hone when the diarist had run for re-election as mayor.

The Pauldings were people of culture and influence, and Davis was not only their architect but their friend. He had made his way into the city's lively intellectual and artistic circles. When he called a meeting at his office to propose forming a society whose purpose, as he put it, was "architectural conversazione," the "literati and virtuosi" of the city came—the poet-editor William Cullen Bryant, the painter-inventor Samuel F. B. Morse, the aesthete-politician Gulian Verplanck, the botanist John Torrey, the actor-poet John Howard

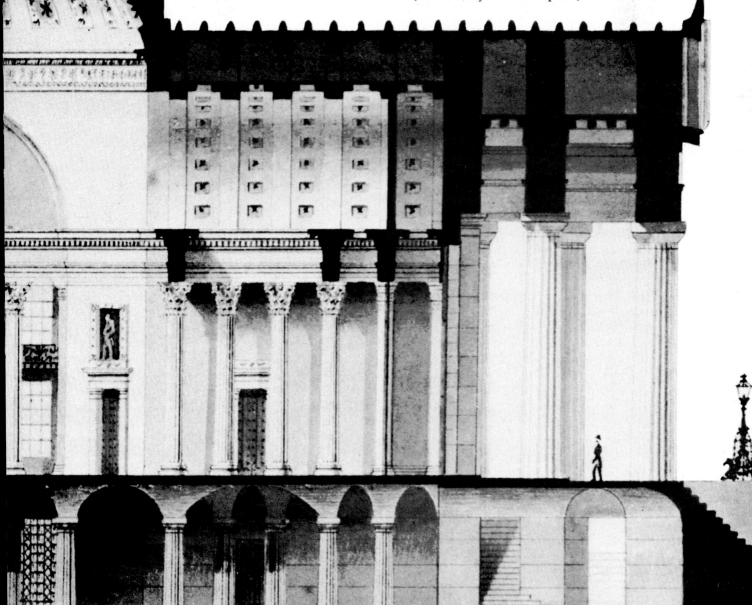

In partnership with Ithiel Town, Davis designed the New York Custom House (later the Subtreasury) in Greek Revival style. This longitudinal section shows the interior of the building from dome to basement, with porticoes at each end.

Payne. Davis went walking with the founders of the Hudson River school to the scenes they painted—with Thomas Cole to Kaaterskill Falls, with Asher Durand to the "Clove," where he did his famous *Kindred Spirits*.

He called himself an "architectural composer" as if he were as much painter as builder—in fact, his drawings and water-color sketches are small gems of art. "Exquisite landscapes, lovely veiled images," William H. Pierson, Jr., calls them in his definitive work on the Gothic Revival, "the finest architectural renderings of his generation . . . richly luminous and vibrant."

Davis was also a methodical, businesslike man, who kept strict records of work and expenses and hounded clients for payment. "Disgraceful!" he wrote next to delinquents' names in his daybook. His fee for designing a house was as much as 7 per cent of the cost, and he gave clients their money's worth, paying as much attention to the curve of a newel post as to the stretch of a façade. For designs "without superintendence or working drawings" he charged (in 1850) from $50 for a $1,000 cottage to $150 for a $20,000 villa. A simple farmhouse was $30, a church of moderate size, $100, and any design already done in his portfolio, $25.

As his reputation spread, so did his work load. F. K. Hunt of Lexington, Kentucky, who had asked Davis to design a mountain villa, was "highly pleased" when he received the plans and told Davis he did not "doubt that you can fulfill my highest expectations." However, there were a few changes he would like—a fireplace in the living room, a storeroom communicating with the pantry. Having paid $150 for ten drawings and specifications, Hunt paid another $153 for revisions. Plan Two included a backstairs and clothes closet, and Hunt kept thinking up changes—perhaps the appearance would be improved if there were a gable over the drawing room. Shouldn't the window sash be of the same black walnut as the doors? What should be done about the shutters, which "folded awkwardly." The letters went on for two years. Finally Hunt sighed, "My house is almost finished." Then, brightening up, he told Davis that "it commands universal admiration as certainly the handsomest building in Kentucky." Today, preserved as a community center, Mr. Hunt's villa, called Loudoun, still commands admiration in Lexington.

Even the poor "labouring mechanic," Mr. Jones, who had asked Davis to charge no more than fifteen or twenty dollars for his plans, made Davis work for his fee. The drawings were "thankfully received," he wrote, but the house had to be made seven feet shorter and two feet wider to fit the lot. And the shutters and verge board could be spruced up. "I shall spare no pains," he had told Davis, "in making this one of the neatest little homes in our village." Davis's clients may have been picky, but they certainly took pride in his work.

The work never ended for Davis and his draftsman. Joseph B. Williams of Augusta, Maine, thanked Davis for "the very kind manner in which you encourage me to offer the suggestions that occur to me," and, thus encouraged, proceeded to offer several pages of suggestions. William J. Rotch of New Bedford, Massachusetts, said Davis's plans "have taken captive the hearts of the builders" (he did not mention that his father, attached to the Federal style, thought them "disgusting"), but the cost was too high and things had to be scaled down. Charles Sedgwick of Syracuse, New York, having spent $2,500 on his house, anxiously asked, "Would agate doorknobs be as good as silverplated for the double doors?"

Clients were not easily put off nor were all of them easily satisfied. Davis worked for decades and for two generations of Livingstons on their great manor, Montgomery Place, up the Hudson, putting up porches, pavilions, hermitages, gazebos, ha-has. "The columns are up," wrote Livingston's daughter about a portico.

The whole thing per se is beautiful. But alas! It squashes down the whole house. Pray pray my dear Mr. Davis think of what can be done. I wish Montgomery Place had the power to make you come up on the *Jefferson* Thursday morning. Mr. Renwick, the architect, was here today and admired the whole thing exceedingly but he was *too polite* to say anything about its crushing the good old house by its magnificence. Your reputation is at stake.

Mr. Renwick was a competitor of Davis's, and the following Thursday dear Mr. Davis debarked from the riverboat *Jefferson* and set to work. "The portico is extremely handsome," his wily client wrote. "The effect surpasses my expectations."

But Davis was never able to please Charles Francis Adams, son of one president and grandson of another. In 1844 he submitted a design for a Tuscan villa for the Adams homestead at Quincy, Massachusetts. "Exceedingly pretty," Adams responded, "and would have fascinated anyone but me. It was wanting in the first element to my mind of architecture: convenience." Davis persisted, Adams rejected. "I do not want you to give me," he wrote some months later, "any of the prevailing fashions of architecture. I dislike them all." The matter went on, actually, until 1873 when, replying to yet another Davis inquiry about the project, Adams wrote that he was now "an old man averse to any new enterprise. So there is no chance for your plan unless"—and Davis could probably hear the Boston Brahmin's sniff—"you can get some of your New York gentlemen to adopt it."

Text continues on page 79

74

May 20. Gothic Cottage Dwelling for Wm. J. Rotch. New bedford. Mass.

1. Basement
2. Prin. floor
3. 2° floor.
4. Attic.
5. Front elevation.
6. Rear. west
7. South end
8. Section. east and west
9. Section. north and south.

100.00

Working Drawings:
A. Cottage window. inch to ft. scale . A² Basement window
B. Plan. elevation and section. oriel window
C. Bay window. plan and inside section. elevation. C² Section
D. Front door D² folding and other door
E. Cornice of Umbrage. F Tudor flower
G. Sash full size. bottom guard. G² ditto.

50.00 150.00ᵗ btt.

Davis sketched the Rotch house in
New Bedford, Massachusetts, in his
daybook (noting fees) and made
a study of it in water color.
It stands today, a masterpiece
of the rural Gothic.

The Architect's Dream, *an allegory painted by Thomas Cole, was commissioned in 1840 by Ithiel Town, Davis's wealthy partner. On one side are the sunlit temples of the ancient world, on the other, the shaded shapes of the Gothic. On a pillar in between, the architect—no doubt Town—meditates. Cole's work did not please Town; he apparently wanted a more personal tribute. What Cole had given him was a summary of the inspirations for American architecture.*

Davis offered a variety of styles in his book Rural Residences. *His Gatehouse (right) makes use of the gables, bay windows, and board-and-batten siding that were basic to many Davis and Downing houses. His Farmhouse offered a Gothic tower as an option. The American Cottage (bottom) made whimsical use of logs as Greek pillars.*

In a sense, none of the splendid work Davis did in designing edifices and mansions made as much of a mark on American architecture as a series of portfolios entitled *Rural Residences*, which he first published in 1837. In them he presented Gothic designs for houses for all classes of Americans— workingmen's cottages, farmhouses, villas. There were already widely used books of designs, but they were concerned largely with details, not with overall design and plan. *Rural Residences* showed the house as a whole with full views, elevations, floor plans. Nothing like it had been done by an American before. Now the man who wanted to build a house could really see what he would be getting. If he liked what he saw, he could buy more detailed plans from Davis.

His designs were persuasive and specific. There was a mansion with octagonal tower, oriels, and spires that could be built for $12,000 in stone or for $7,500 in wood. A three-bedroom Farmer's House with a wide veranda—"simple, economical, and adapted to the American climate"—could be built for $1,500. Several versions were given, including one with a bell tower whose adaptation to the farm was not explained. Just for variety there was an elaborate villa "in Oriental style" and a $500 Greek style log cabin with pillars of rough-cut tree trunks.

But the most interesting design was the Rustic Cottage, patterned after his gatehouse at Barry-town. It had a steep roof, "picturesque chimney tops," a bay window, and was built in a technique Davis had devised: board-and-batten siding— vertical planks with joints covered by thin strips of wood. The four-bedroom cottage cost only $1,200, but its emphatic vertical lines, the irregularity of outline, the variety of detail, all gave this inexpensive house its own strong character. In one way or another, it affected the whole Gothic Revival.

What Davis began with *Rural Residences* was carried on—and with even wider effect—by an admirer of his, Andrew Jackson Downing. In 1838, at the instance of Robert Donaldson of Barrytown, Downing wrote Davis that he had written a book "on Landscape Gardening and Rural Residences with a view of improving if possible the taste in these matters in the United States." He would like to call on Davis and ask his help. The two met and were firmly attracted to each other.

Between them, Downing and Davis might have made a composite hero of one of the Gothic novels they both liked to read. Downing was tall and dark, like those heroes, with a kind of enigmatic hauteur and a habit of startling friends by coming silently into his library from behind a false bookcase door. But in disposition he was mild and generous, given to putting a guest's favorite flower next to his breakfast plate. Davis was fair and open, but with a Gothic disposition—mercurial, ambitious, fierce in expressing himself, quick both to anger and to please. Both were dedicated to the Gothic and scornful of the Greek Revival. By the time their collaboration came to an end in the early 1850's, Downing could say: "The Greek temple disease has passed its crisis. The people have survived it."

Downing began his career as a landscaper working in the family nursery in New-burgh, New York. He was only twenty-six when, in 1841, he set down his ideas in *A Treatise on the Theory and Practice of Landscape Gardening*, the first American book to deal with landscaping as an art and also to be intelligible to almost everybody. He set up two alternative approaches to landscaping: the beautiful and the picturesque. The beautiful was calm and balanced, expressed in flowing curves. The picturesque was angular and unbalanced, expressed in irregular, spirited forms. The extensive, formal gardens of Europe had embodied the beautiful. In the early eighteenth century, the English had turned away from it when Alexander Pope brought "unadorned nature" into his famous garden at Twickenham. Followers of the poet sought to recreate the "beautiful wildness of nature" in their landscaping, but the results, though lovely, were often pictorial and contrived.

In America, wildness did not have to be recreated. It was all around. When Downing began preaching that the picturesque was inherently American, his countrymen were ready to hear him and his argument that architectural beauty must be considered "conjointly with the beauty of the landscape." He emphasized architecture more and more in two subsequent books, *Cottage Residences, Rural Architecture and Landscape Gardening* and *The Architecture of Country Houses*, both of which went into many best-selling editions.

If Davis was an architectural composer, Downing was an architectural moralist. "The national taste is not a matter of little moment," he declared. "Whether the country homes of a whole people shall embody such ideas of beauty and trust as shall elevate and purify its feelings; these are questions of no mean or trifling importance." They applied to houses of any size and cost, from cottages to villas. Downing's cottage was basically the one Davis had designed in *Rural Residences*—gabled, with board-and-batten siding, steep roof, simply decorated. But a veranda or porch could be added "as an expression of domestic enjoyment." The cottage was Jeffersonian in concept, a home for "the cultivators of the soil," the "bone and sinew" of the land.

The villa was a "country house of larger

accommodations, requiring the care of at least three or more servants." The style, Downing said, should fit the owner's personality. The "man of common sense" would naturally prefer the regular horizontal line of classical architecture with "order and distinctness stamped upon its unbroken lines of cornices and regular rows of windows." Its owner "will do nothing without reason; he will have no caprices and no whims either in his life or his house." But the "men of imagination whose ambition and energy will give them no peace within the mere bounds of rationality" must have a picturesque villa with its "unsymmetrical and capricious forms. It is for such that the architect may safely introduce the tower and the campanile." He had one caution: "There is something wonderfully captivating in the idea of a battlemented castle, even to an apparently modest man who thus shows to the world his unsuspected vein of personal ambition by trying to make a castle of his country house. But unless there is something of the castle in the man it is very likely, if it be like a real castle, to dwarf him to the stature of a mouse."

The villa styles he favored were either the steep-roofed Gothic or a variation generally called the Tuscan villa, with flatter roofs, rounded windows, and more sedate details. Though he showed the work of several architects, notably John Notman of Philadelphia, Downing leaned mostly on Davis's designs and ideas, together with plans of his own that Davis rendered in finished form.

Davis made this sketch to promote the sale of houses in a shore-front development planned for the Astoria section of Long Island, across the East River from Manhattan. It is a virtual catalogue of Davis designs, illustrating dwellings that range in style from Greek to Gothic to Tuscan.

Davis would give shape to Downing's conceptions; Downing would amend and promote Davis's work, referring requests he received for fuller plans to Davis. When Samuel F. B. Morse asked Downing to design a house for his young, deaf second wife, Downing sent him to Davis to build one with a four-story campanile, which is still standing in Poughkeepsie.

The decade of the 1840's was the emerging era of popular tastemakers. In their *Lady's Book*, the publisher, Louis Godey, and his editor, Sarah Hale, were beginning to shape the styles and psyches of generations of American women. Downing the promoter and Davis the executer became the country's architectural arbiters. "Nobody whether he be rich or poor," noted an observer, "builds a house or lays out a garden without consulting Downing's works."

The Rustic Cottage became the prototype of houses as far out as the Indian frontier. At the army outpost at The Dalles, Oregon, an enterprising quartermaster, bored with what he called "the piggery system" of barracks architecture, put up several Gothic officers' quarters based on Downing's books. To get architectural unity on the post, he even put brackets on the existing barracks and guardhouses. "Very pretty and conveniently arranged," wrote an officer's wife, but the army bureaucracy was not pleased. An officer sent to investigate reported that it was "quite showy and handsome and fanciful in external appearance" but entirely unsuited to the frontier. Though the army repulsed this Gothic invasion, the Surgeon's Quarters still stands at the post to show how much at home its timbered walls are in the rugged landscape and tapering forests.

Downing, whose views were generally shared by Davis, cajoled his followers with sentiment and sage precepts: "Every copse we have planted," he wrote, "every winding path through the woods, becomes part of our affections, friendships, joys, and sorrows." A tasteful house, he advised, was "a barrier against vice, immorality, and bad habits." A fine house without a porch is as "incomplete as a well printed book without a title page." The picturesque was practical: a natural landscape, with clumps of shrubs and trees, requires less mowing and trimming than formal grounds; and a steep roof rids itself of snow more quickly than a flat one. The use of board-and-batten is "an expression of strength and truthfulness: for its vertical boarding properly signifies to the eye a wooden house"—a judgment anticipating modern insistence that a building's form should be expressed by its material. A house that looked fine in the city, he insisted, should never be built in the country, where it would look "as if it had strayed out in a fit of insanity and had lost the power of getting back again." White should never be the color of a house because nature so rarely uses it. A brown earthy color or warm gray was recommended.

As was inevitable with anything so popular and so malleable, the Gothic got out of hand. Encouraged to suit residences to their clients' egos, builders went on reckless flights and wound up, one critic complained, with "a perfectly awful farrago of libelous details." Downing himself railed against excesses—"the spurious rural Gothic, flimsy verge boards, and unmeaning gables."

The complaints were directed against what became known as Carpenter Gothic, in which builders combined two or three of the Downing-Davis designs, added fillips of molding to doors, created friezes of cutouts, sent sawed-out leaves and vines climbing up the porch posts. When steam power was applied to the jigsaw, inexpensive ornaments were turned out by the thousands, and builders cluttered simple homes with gingerbread brackets and wild flourishes of carved wood.

In 1850 Downing went to Europe, where he was lionized and given a diamond ring by the queen of Denmark. He came home with a partner, a young architect named Calvert Vaux. Downing and Vaux were busy with commissions when, setting out to see a client in 1852, Downing boarded a Hudson River steamer. He found out too late that it was engaged in a dangerous race with a rival boat. At Yonkers, the overheated boilers set the ship afire. Downing was last seen on deck, throwing chairs overboard to keep people afloat.

Downing's fame had overshadowed Davis. "Downing stole your thunder for a while," Donaldson, who had brought them together, told Davis, "but I always claimed for you the seminal ideas which have been so fruitful." Davis himself never felt upstaged by Downing. He had been busy with his own clients. He did Gothic campus buildings for Yale, a lunatic asylum for the state of North Carolina, and a combined ballroom-library for the University of North Carolina.

By the 1850's Davis was ready to supply plans in almost any style: "American log cabin, farm villa, English cottage, Collegiate Gothic, Manor house, French suburban, Switz chalet, Lombard Italian, Tuscan from Pliny's villa at Ostia, Ancient Etruscan, Suburban Greek, Oriental, round, castellated." By now, certain features of his designs had become

BY PERMISSION OF *THE MAGAZINE ANTIQUES*

Davis used a battery of Gothic Revival devices—towers, oriels, castellations, cotes—in the design for Wildmont, his own home in Llewellyn Park, New Jersey.

part of the vernacular of American architecture—board-and-batten siding, recessed double windows divided by spandrels, store fronts of large glass sheets set in between projecting stone piers. Clients were put out that Davis was imitated so often. Joel Rathbone of Albany regretted that he had given Davis's custom-made plans to his carpenter, "who has copied them in everything he has built since so that my windows, mullions, doors, jambs, cornices are duplicated all over the city."

In church architecture Davis was more important as an influence than as a designer. Two of his board-and-batten churches moved his contemporary, Richard Upjohn, to use that style in a series of simple, impressive country churches. And in a parallel to Davis's *Rural Residences*, he published *Upjohn's Rural Architecture*, containing plans that were followed, with many variations, in scores of frontier churches.

While the rustic Gothic Revival style served well enough for country churches, it was hardly suited to grander religious structures in the cities. When Upjohn received a commission to design a new home for Trinity Church in New York, he turned back for inspiration to the authentic traditional Gothic of the English cathedrals. Upjohn's

design, with its thrilling, tapered spire, its pinnacled side buttresses, and its huge stained glass window, was fine enough to overcome the grumblings of many parishioners about "papistical innovations."

Davis felt he had a very specific influence on another famous church architect, James Renwick. In his daybook he complained that the design Renwick had done for Grace Church in New York was based on drawings he and Town had submitted earlier. Davis made nothing publicly of the complaint, even though he disliked Renwick (whose casual intervention at Montgomery Place must have irked him considerably). In any case, Renwick was very much his own man. He was only twenty-three when he won the commission for Grace Church, which served New York's wealthiest parish. His light, economical, delicately ornamented structure was mostly in the English Gothic style. He turned to the traditional Gothic when he built Saint Patrick's Cathedral, filling an entire block then far uptown on Fifth Avenue at Fiftieth Street. Today, Saint Patrick's shoulders its way proudly into the crowded mid-city, its spires challenging the skyscrapers that surround them. Renwick designed many other churches, as well as the Smithsonian Institution, with its extraordinary series of Norman towers, no two alike.

While Upjohn and Renwick were building churches, Davis was helping to give shape to another aspect of American architecture. A rich wholesale druggist named Llewellyn Haskell brought Davis in on his plan to lay out a community on a mountaintop in West Orange, New Jersey, within sight of New York. Davis's ideas and Downing's went into the landscaping—a picturesque complex of curving roads, clumped trees, and craggy slopes, laced with streams and ravines. Davis designed many of the houses in Gothic style to match the deliberate wildness of the terrain. Romantic in concept, functional in execution, Llewellyn Park was the first architecturally integrated community in the country. It still preserves some of Davis's work, including a gatehouse of unfinished stone.

Davis built a home for himself at Llewellyn Park. He called it Wildmont, and it marked a change in his personal life. He had spent his life as a bachelor, charming ladies but never attaching himself to one. In his diary for this period, mostly concerned with the building and landscaping of Wildmont, the fifty-year-old Davis noted: "April 16, 1853: First visit [to Wildmont] with Margaret

The original stone gatehouse in Llewellyn Park is hardly changed today from the way Davis designed the building, its stone walls nestling protectively into its setting.

CASTLEWOOD. SOUTH EAST. ELEVATION   DAVIS. 1858.

Castlewood in Llewellyn Park was slightly changed in structure from Davis's original design—the right wing cut back, the left wing enlarged. But the picturesque feeling is still there today, enhanced by age and ivy.

Davis filled the dining room in Lyndhurst (opposite) with Gothic detail and furniture he himself designed. His rendering of the west front (above) shows the 1865 addition: the square tower and section at left. Lyndhurst was bought in 1880 by Jay Gould, the railroad financier, who spent his last years there. His daughter Anna, duchess of Talleyrand-Périgord, bequeathed it to the National Trust for Historic Preservation.

Lizzy Beale. May 7, 1853: Clearing land. July 14, 1853: Married to Margaret Beale. June 25, 1854: Flora born. May 25, 1856: Joseph Beale Davis born."

The backs of envelopes and paper scraps which Davis used to fill with sketches for houses and minuscule Gothic edifices now showed children at play. Contented with family life, he was fiercely discontented with what was happening in American architecture and became the angry man of his profession. "Hybrid courtesan" he called the eclectic churches going up in New York. "Broken heap of littleness, costly and deformed," he called the New York Post Office, partly, maybe, because his own forward-looking design, employing new techniques of iron and glass, had been rejected on a technicality. The Lenox Library was "depraved." When he wrote to the *Times* disagreeing with its politics, he added gratuitously that the newspaper's weak-minded stand was "rendered obvious by the debased architecture of your building."

Still, his later years—he lived to be eighty-eight—included some triumphs. One was an anticipation of the future: a never-used design for a tall office building whose vertical sheets of glass held in by narrow bands of stone and metal anticipated the Gothic skyscrapers of the twentieth century.

Another was a heart-warming sequel to his past. "Nov. 5," his 1864 diary noted, "went up to Geo. Merritt, Tarrytown, and visited the Paulding house, with a view to additions." Mr. Merritt, newly rich from a railroad-spring invention, had bought Knoll from the Pauldings and, renaming it Lyndhurst, asked Davis to put a large addition onto it. It was risky to tamper with that Gothic jewel. But, to satisfy his client's opulent demands, Davis built a whole new section and somehow added grandeur to the house without diminishing its grace. The new section enhances the old. The joinings are elegant, the transitions skillfully modulated. The new square tower rises companionably over the gabled transept. Seen from the river that it overlooks, the remodeled masterpiece seems altogether in tune with itself, dignified and assured, one part setting off the other—as Alexander Jackson Davis knew the Gothic should—in an animated harmony, a kind of perfect imbalance.

87

Hunt's design for Marble House at Newport, 1888

MORRIS HUNT

NCE
RBILT ESQ[E]

SCALE ⅛ INCH = 1 FOOT

AMERICAN INSTITUTE OF ARCHITECTS FOUNDATION, PRINTS AND DRAWINGS COLLECTION, WASHINGTON, D.C.—PHOTO, JOHN TENNANT

R M Hunt

1827–1895

BY ORMONDE DE KAY, JR.

When, on the morning of August 30, 1904, the liner in which he had crossed the Atlantic steamed into Upper New York Bay, Henry James observed that the city now bristled with skyscrapers, its silhouette reminding him of a "broken hair-comb turned up." Once ashore, the sixty-year-old novelist headed for Washington Square and Gramercy Park, haunts of his childhood, to call on friends. So began a memorable tour of inspection. Having spent twenty years abroad, James would spend ten months rediscovering his homeland, meeting, among others, people from two strata of the population that had barely existed a generation earlier: the one, aliens from Mediterranean and Eastern Europe, and the other, members of America's first real leisure class, the multimillionaire children and grandchildren of self-made tycoons—"robber barons" they would later be called—who had amassed huge fortunes in the decades following the Civil War. Out of his impressions he would fashion a book, *The American Scene;* it would appear in 1907, by which time, satisfied that his countrymen would never stop chasing dollars long enough to constitute a civilized and livable society, he had sailed back to England. His American readers found his insights both illuminating and disturbing, not the least those that touched on architecture.

While gathering material for his book, James repeatedly ran afoul of (as he would today, if the preservation movement had not finally gained public support) a very American "cult of impermanence." Seeking out his birthplace off Washington Square, he found instead a loft building that housed a shirtwaist factory, and when he looked for the house on Fourteenth Street in which he had lived as a boy, it, too, was gone, replaced by a store, as was the nearby church he had watched being constructed, stone on stone. In Boston, he located

Richard Morris Hunt's long and remarkable training in architecture was well behind him when this photograph was made, but his greatest work was still far in the future.

the house in which he had written some of his early stories, but when he came back a few weeks later for a second look, it had been demolished. He foresaw a similar fate—accurately, as events would show—for the mansions that New York's plutocrats had erected along upper Fifth Avenue: despite their solidity they were, he perceived, "flagrantly tentative residences," which their owners' heirs would pull down and replace.

Of all the buildings that had gone up in his absence, one group, in particular, provoked James to indignation: the stone and marble palaces—"monuments of pecuniary power"—which the mansion owners had erected in Newport, that pleasant and previously unspoiled coastal resort he had known as an adolescent. He decried these "white elephants" and "the distressful inevitable waste" they represented, finding them utterly incongruous in a place "where Nature . . . might have shown a piping shepherd on any hillside or attached a mythic image to any point of rocks. What an idea," he protested,

to have seen this miniature spot of earth, where the sea-nymphs on the curved sands . . . might have chanted back to the shepherds, as a mere breeding-ground for white elephants! They look queer and conscious and lumpish—some of them, as with an air of the brandished proboscis, really grotesque—while their averted owners, roused from a witless dream, wonder what in the world is to be done with them. The answer to which, I think, can only be that there is absolutely nothing to be done; nothing but to let them stand there always, vast and blank, for reminder to those concerned of the prohibited degrees of witlessness. . . .

Here again James was prescient, for the white elephants still stand, unoccupied but maintained by the Preservation Society of Newport County and others. Chances are, however, that to the tourists who troop through them they represent prohibited degrees not of witlessness but lavishness, of an extravagance denied to subsequent generations by, most obviously, the graduated income tax.

As James surely knew, the grandest and costliest of these palaces had been designed for assorted Vanderbilts, Goelets, and Belmonts by Richard Morris Hunt, dead these nine years. Hunt was remembered as the architect, too, of George Washington Vanderbilt's French Renaissance château, Biltmore, in North Carolina, the largest private residence in the country; of William K. Vanderbilt's stylistically similar mansion on Fifth Avenue; and of the domed Administration Building at the Chicago World's Fair of 1893. Newspaper readers with long memories may also have recalled that it was Hunt who had designed the pedestal supporting the Statue of Liberty. With the new century barely under way, however, and with their ebullient young president, Theodore Roosevelt,

Jane Leavitt Hunt posed with her children about 1848 in Paris. Clockwise from her daughter Jane, foreground, the others are Richard Morris, Leavitt, William Morris, and John.

keeping things humming, few Americans were inclined to look back. In architectural matters, moreover, the spotlight was now on the virtuoso Stanford White, his partner Charles McKim, and their leading rivals.

But if the public was forgetting Hunt, architects were not, as was demonstrated by a dramatic incident: when, at a dinner of members of the profession, a speaker pronounced his name, all two hundred guests rose to their feet and shouted in unison, "Hunt! Hunt! Hunt!" This spontaneous tribute expressed the diners' awareness that Hunt had done more than anyone else to raise their vocation from one pursued in competition with engineers, contractors, and carpenters to one accepted as the preserve of professionals, that he had been, in McKim's words, "the pioneer and ice-breaker who paved the way for the recognition of the profession by the public."

Today, students of American cultural history are reappraising the long-neglected artistic achievements of the Gilded Age, including those of the man many dismissed until recently as "the Vanderbilt architect" or the "château builder to Fifth Avenue" or "a mere Beaux-Arts copyist." The study of Hunt's work in particular gained impetus in 1980 with the appearance of the first full-length

critical biography of him, by Paul R. Baker, a professor of history.

Not the most brilliant or original architect of his generation—a distinction that belongs to Henry Hobson Richardson—Hunt was nevertheless the most honored by his fellow practitioners, who from the early 1870's on regarded him as their dean. And as his impact on his profession was immense, so was his impact on its practice. The first American designer of buildings to be trained at France's famed Ecole des Beaux-Arts, he never doubted that the best European architectural traditions could and should be transplanted to his own country, and he earnestly sought, through his work, to refine and elevate his countrymen's taste. Hunt's example continued to influence architecture until the 1930's, when it was eclipsed by the search for a new, "functional" aesthetic—only to re-emerge in our own time as a subject for, if not revival, at least respectful review.

Hunt was born in Brattleboro, Vermont, on October 31, 1827, to Jane Leavitt Hunt and Jonathan Hunt, both members of families long established in New England. He was their fourth child, coming after Jane, William Morris, and John. Hunt senior, a lawyer, banker, and landowner, had just been elected to the House of Representatives, where he would work closely with his friend Senator Daniel Webster of Massachusetts; he was thus away from home during much of Richard's babyhood, but his wife, after bearing him a fourth son, Leavitt, early in 1830, joined the re-elected congressman, with her brood, in Washington. Representative Hunt was again re-elected in 1831; but the following April he fell ill of cholera and a month later died at forty-five, leaving his thirty-one-year-old widow grief-stricken but well provided for.

Mrs. Hunt possessed a marked talent for painting, and was, as Henry Van Brunt, one of her son Richard's first students, was to write, "a woman of high spirit, great force of character, and of accomplishments far in advance of her time." Already it was clear that Jane and William had inherited her artistic gift, and before long Richard, too, would exhibit an aptitude for drawing. Although Webster urged her to move to Boston, she settled, at her mother's suggestion, in New Haven. There Richard, at the age of eight, built his first "house," a little cottage in the back yard, with a cellar, a brick foundation, and wooden crossbeams on which his brother William carved decorations with his penknife.

When Richard was eleven Mrs. Hunt moved the family to Boston to prepare her sons for Harvard, placing Richard in the famous Boston Latin School. Living on Beacon Hill, the Hunts came to know some of the city's leading families,

On his travels Hunt sketched whatever caught his eye—in particular, picturesque buildings. He made these sketches in 1852 after completing his studies at the Beaux-Arts. Note, at right, that he used the French names of Belgian cities (Audenarde and Anvers) rather than the Flemish ones (Oudenaarde and Antwerp) commonly used in English.

and Richard met, among others, Martin Brimmer and Joseph Choate, the first destined to become his client and the second, his lawyer. In 1840 brother William entered Harvard, where he was elected to the best clubs and named chief marshal of his class, but he neglected his studies and in his sophomore year was suspended. But Mrs. Hunt, worried by a persistent cough William had developed, decided to take the family on vacation to Europe. Provided with letters of introduction to United States ministers and consuls in France and Italy from Webster, who had recently been secretary of state, they embarked for France in 1843.

Mrs. Hunt had acted impulsively—"I did not realize what I was doing," she later confessed, "until we were half way across the ocean"—but she planned to have her children back in their schools the following fall. In fact, however, the family would remain abroad almost twelve years. Inevitably, this protracted expatriation greatly affected the young people's destinies: John, for one, would become a doctor in Paris and practice medicine there the rest of his life. And the experience would decisively shape the future careers of William and Richard, who, as painter and architect respectively, would achieve greater distinction than any other

nineteenth-century American brothers except William and Henry James.

In Paris the Hunts plunged into a busy round of sightseeing, shopping, and opera- and ballgoing; Mrs. Hunt and Jane were presented at court to King Louis Philippe, while Richard and Leavitt, enrolled in a French school, began learning the language in a hurry. Early in 1844 the family moved to Italy, where Richard roamed the streets and squares of Rome, sketching statues and fountains, churches and palaces, and remnants of antiquity. In the spring the younger Hunts entered an academy in Geneva, informing their schoolmates that they were "Green Mountain Boys."

In Geneva Richard began, on his own, to study drawing and designing with a local architect, but in January 1845 he wrote his mother that he felt "destined to lead a military career, and for this reason, should enter West Point." Four months later, however, he told her he planned to study architecture "at some *first rate* academy in Europe," and then "return to America, where an architect of the *first* quality would be much sought for." In August he rejoined Mrs. Hunt in Paris and, after a year of preparatory studies combined with regular work in the atelier of the noted architect Hector Martin Lefuel, won admission to the famous old Ecole des Beaux-Arts on the Left Bank.

Education at the Ecole consisted of lectures, which few students bothered to attend, and practical design work in nearby ateliers. The school taught no single style but stressed the solving of problems by applying to them principles and ideas derived from the tradition of Renaissance classicism. Students submitted finished drawings for assigned projects every other month and on alternate months participated in day-long competitions, turning out detailed drawings for a structure in a twelve-hour stretch. They advanced according to how juries rated their work, many, in discouragement, dropping out. Richard was to put in five and a half years at the Ecole, never winning a competition but collecting many honorable mentions.

From the start Richard enjoyed student life, even the frantic, around-the-clock scrambles preceding the submission of finished drawings. These deadlines once met, he relaxed happily and noisily in cafés with his companions from Lefuel's atelier. His social contacts, moreover, gave him access to the glittering world of Parisian society: he was presented at court, and his buoyant charm and good looks (he was called "the handsomest American in Paris") made him much in demand for dinners and balls. He relished nightlife, particularly theatergoing; yet he often passed up the city's costlier pleasures in order to acquire more books on architecture for his growing collection.

At his atelier in the Studio Building, filled with pictures and objects he had brought from Europe, Hunt for several years offered formal instruction in architecture.

Richard followed with interest the construction, in adaptations of medieval or Renaissance styles, of the foreign ministry on the Quai d'Orsay and the chapter house of Notre Dame, as well as the restoration of the Louvre. By contrast, he showed little interest in two new railway stations, the Gare Montparnasse and the Gare de l'Est, whose architects had utilized new and radical engineering techniques in boldly overarching structures of glass and iron, remote precursors of present-day sports stadia and airport buildings. Similarly, on a visit to England's Great Exhibition in 1851, he would note only, anent the stunningly innovative Crystal Palace, that it was "not much for a traveller."

While his brother William was winning recognition as a painter, Richard, having completed work at the Ecole, set out in 1852 on travels that would keep him on the go for almost two years. Considering the predilection he would later show for French Renaissance building motifs, his most meaningful trip was probably a tour of the Loire Valley, with its magnificent châteaux. But then, sailing to Alexandria with a companion, he undertook a journey through country few Americans had visited, one that would vastly enlarge his architectural vocabulary. The two young Americans ascended the Nile in a dahabeah, proceeded north on the backs of donkeys and camels across Palestine and Syria (where they narrowly missed being killed by Bedouins), and west along the coast of Asia Minor to Constantinople and finally Greece, where Richard exultantly sketched the ruins of classic temples and statues. By February 1854 he was in Rome; there Martin Van Buren, the former president of the United States, gave him a letter of introduction to Richard Upjohn, America's foremost architect.

Returning to Paris, Richard found that his longtime patron, Hector Lefuel, had been named architect to the new emperor, Napoleon III, and was supervising the construction of buildings connecting the Louvre with the Tuileries; Lefuel offered him a job, and Richard, mindful of both the honor and the opportunity, accepted. Over several months Richard drew the plans and designed many of the details of the ornate, three-story Pavillon de la Bibliothèque opposite the Palais Royal. Lefuel was well pleased: long afterward he would write Richard's wife that his own "greatest work was done while dear Dick worked with me, and he can justly claim a great share of its success." Van Brunt was to view the episode from another angle: "There is a certain picturesque surprise," he observed, "in the spectacle of a Yankee lad giving form and character to one of the imperial monuments of France."

As work on that Louvre extension neared completion, Richard told Lefuel that he intended to go back to his homeland; the older man urged him to reconsider, assuring him that a splendid career awaited him in France. But Richard, still a Green Mountain Boy at heart even though he was constantly taken for a Parisian, was sure that his future lay in America. "It has been represented to me," he wrote his mother,

that America was not ready for the Fine Arts, but I think they are mistaken. There is no place in the world where they are more needed, or where they should be more encouraged. Why, there are more luxurious houses put up in New York than in Paris! At any rate the desire is evinced and the money spent and if the object is not attained, it is the fault of the architects. . . . There are no greater fools in America than in any other part of the world; the only thing is that the professional man with us has got to make his own standing.

Thus, in September 1855, the twenty-seven-year-old Richard Morris Hunt arrived, mustachioed and goateed, in New York, after a preparation in his calling the likes of which no beginning American architect had received before and precious few have since, "accredited" in Van Brunt's words, "as an ambassador of art from the abounding wealth of the old world to the infinite

Hunt's Studio Building contained living quarters, workrooms, and exhibition space for painters and sculptors. Opened in 1858, it instantly became the nucleus of New York's artistic life.

95

possibilities of the new." Crude, unlovely New York, a fast-growing commercial metropolis with two thirds of a million inhabitants, including numerous Irish and German newcomers, was a far cry from Paris, but Hunt felt stimulated by its electric atmosphere. He soon found lodgings and work space in the University Building on Washington Square, a neo-Gothic edifice that contained, besides classrooms, a library, a chapel, the offices of learned societies, and the studios of such well-known painters as George Inness, Eastman Johnson, Edwin Austin Abbey, Winslow Homer, and the artist-inventor Samuel F. B. Morse. In his own studio Hunt installed various objects acquired abroad—tapestries, antique cabinets, Venetian glass, masterpieces of metalwork, and sculptured and painted panels—and his library, described by Van Brunt as "by far the richest, most comprehensive, and most curious collection of books on architecture and the other fine arts which at that time had been brought together in the new world." Hunt's books would more than repay their cost, not only as teaching aids (he would freely let his students consult them and even borrow them) but also as aids in pursuing his own work, for as Henry Ives Cobb, Jr., a distinguished architect and teacher, has written, "Those were the days when to be original meant having an architectural book that none of the other fellows had."

Hunt had hardly settled in when he was summoned to Washington by the eminent architect Thomas U. Walter to work briefly on the extension of the United States Capitol; since this was the most important project going forward anywhere in the country, the job constituted an auspicious debut to Hunt's American career, bringing him wide professional recognition and—while it lasted—the impressive salary of two hundred dollars a month. Back in New York, he drew plans for and supervised the construction of a town house with a façade that was, he noted, "different from any in the city, in its way," that "way" being straight Second Empire. But although its owner, a dentist named Parmly, was well pleased with it, he refused to pay Hunt the customary 5 per cent of the construction cost, asserting that the three hundred dollars he had previously paid him was enough.

More agreeable clients were the Johnston brothers, wealthy art collectors who, feeling that artists needed a building of their own, with studios

The gateways Hunt planned for the southern entrances to Central Park were a project he especially cherished. His designs, ultimately rejected as too grandiose, show the gateways that were to rise along Fifty-ninth Street at, from top to bottom, Fifth Avenue, Sixth Avenue, Eighth Avenue, and Seventh Avenue.

and exhibition space, engaged Hunt to design one. The result, three blocks north of Washington Square, on West Tenth Street, was, in Professor Baker's words, "an immediate success," becoming the principal center of New York's artistic life almost from the moment it opened its doors early in 1858. The Studio Building's first tenants included John La Farge and Frederick Church, and in a month or so Hunt himself took a studio there.

Meanwhile, in his University Building rooms, Hunt had already begun to provide instruction in architecture to two young Harvard graduates, Henry Van Brunt and Charles D. Gambrill, who had asked him to take them on as students. Not surprisingly, he modeled his teaching methods on those he had known at the Ecole des Beaux-Arts. In 1858 George B. Post, a New York University engineering graduate, came to his atelier, now transferred to the Studio Building, and in 1859 William R. Ware joined the group, as did Frank Furness. All five of Hunt's students were to become prominent architects and remain greatly attached to him; Van Brunt and Ware would, as partners, set up an atelier school of their own, and later Ware would head the country's first professional architectural school—at M.I.T.—and organize a new department of architecture at Columbia. Thanks largely to Ware, the Beaux-Arts tradition transmitted by Hunt would become entrenched in the architectural curricula of American universities. Thus, not only by his own example but also through his five "disciples," most of all Ware, Hunt would exert a strong and even dominant influence on American architecture far into the future. And, following his lead, more young Americans would attend the Ecole des Beaux-Arts: in the 1860's, ten would be enrolled there—including H. H. Richardson; in the 1870's, thirty-three; in the 1880's, twenty-nine; and in the 1890's, one hundred fifty-two.

Early in 1857 Hunt was invited by Upjohn to join him and eleven others in forming a new professional association, the American Institute of Architects. Upjohn became its president and Hunt its secretary, an impressive indication of his fellow members' esteem, considering that he was not yet thirty and had been in New York only a year and a half. Over the coming decades the AIA would lead the fight to win recognition and respect for architects, and in 1887 Hunt would become its third president, after Upjohn and Walter.

Before then, Hunt struck a telling blow in a lawsuit against his nonpaying client, Dr. Parmly. The case came to trial in 1861. Although the jury awarded Hunt only half his claim, or 2.5 per cent, he won the suit on principle. "It was," Van Brunt would recall, "a case of much importance to architects, and has perhaps gone farther than any other towards establishing the commissions of the profession upon a fixed basis."

Hunt spent the summer of 1860 at Newport, where his brother William, by now recognized as a leading painter of the day, had established a studio in a year-round cottage called Hill Top. Richard was convalescing from a siege of dysentery, but his visit had a momentous consequence: he met and fell in love with eighteen-year-old Catharine Clinton Howland, the orphaned daughter of a highly successful merchant. They were married on April 2, 1861.

On April 12, Confederate batteries in Charleston, South Carolina, fired on Fort Sumter, and three days later President Lincoln called for volunteers to put down the rebellion. The Civil War had begun. Hunt tried to raise a regiment from among his fellow members of the Century Club,

In a students' competition at the Ecole des Beaux-Arts in Paris, Hunt submitted this elevation for a conservatory. His entries in the school competitions won him several honorable mentions.

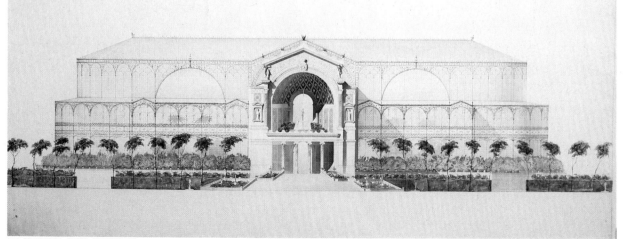

but on being assured by his physician that the effects of the dysentery he had suffered would incapacitate him in action, he put up the money instead for a substitute to serve in his place. And before April was out, he sailed to France with his bride.

Soon after the Hunts returned to New York the next year, bringing an infant son (the first of five children), Catharine came into a large inheritance. As they had arranged with Richard's mother, the couple bought her house on West Thirty-fifth Street; it would remain their city home until 1885, when they would move downtown to Washington Square. In 1864 Richard bought Hill Top cottage from his brother William, and from then on the family spent summers there.

Hunt's most significant project during the war years was a large house in Newport for a couple named Griswold, a commission opening up a new line of work that would lead, via commissions for similar houses, to his vast, palatial Newport "cottages" of the 1890's. In the Griswold house Hunt, according to his biographer, "abandoned the formal, symmetrical exterior composition of his two earlier New York buildings to emphasize the picturesque massing of a seemingly sprawling structure articulated into numerous projecting pavilions, bays, gables, verandas, porches, and dormers." Imposing unity on this riotous assemblage—rendered the more riotous by Hunt's use of contrasting materials and colors—were the multipitched roof, with its repeated pattern of shingles, and an external, all-enveloping "skeleton" of posts, plates, brackets, and braces, the key element of the so-called Stick style that would reach its apogee in the coming decade. The roof, in particular, was typical of Hunt's evolving manner. Playful and romantic, the Griswold house sounded a theme that the architect would sound again often, with variations, in his country houses.

As far back as 1861 Hunt had, at the behest of the commissioners of Central Park, begun work on designs for monumental gateways to the four southern entrances of that exciting new feature of the New York scene; he had submitted plans in 1863, but no action had been taken on them, and in May 1865 the commissioners deferred the matter indefinitely. Hunt may have cared more about this project than any other; he struck back by putting his gateway designs on display and issuing a booklet—

his sole publication—containing the plans and a strong endorsement of them by one "Civis," actually his friend William J. Hoppin. This brought the matter to the attention of the press and public, but did not produce the results he had hoped it would. Calvert Vaux and Frederick Law Olmsted, who had laid out the park, made it known that they considered his grandiose entrances out of keeping with its simple, rustic character. Professional critics agreed; Central Park, wrote Clarence Cook in the New York *Daily Tribune*, was "an American park," based on "the purest and most elevated democratic ideas," while Hunt's gateways were "ugly and unsuitable" copies of contemporary French works, a "barren spawn of French imperialism," and "as un-American as it would be possible to make them." Ordinary citizens who spoke up showed little relish for Hunt's plans, in effect replying to the assertion of "Civis" that the park was "a picture without a frame" by saying that they preferred it that way. And so it has remained.

Now forty, Hunt found himself in a curious position: though a leading, even commanding, figure in his profession, he had designed few notable buildings, and the project closest to his heart, the Central Park gateways, had been resoundingly rejected. But this would soon change: he would take on a succession of major projects, including some of the most important buildings of the Gilded Age, and for the rest of his life would have as many commissions as he could handle.

One of the first was for a building of "French flats." Structures of several stories with accommodations for two or more families on each floor were common in Paris and other French cities, but in America the only multiple dwellings, apart from boarding houses and hotels, were low-rent tenements, crowded, typically, with foreign immigrants. "Respectable" folk consequently associated multifamily housing with low living standards—and also, in view of the scandalous life style widely imputed to the French, low morals. It took courage, then, to propose erecting such a building just south of Gramercy Park, but if you were Rutherfurd Stuyvesant, a descendant of Peter Stuyvesant, with extensive holdings of choice Manhattan land, the attendant risk was less than it might have been otherwise; even so, the project was instantly dubbed Stuyvesant's Folly.

To Hunt, a longtime dweller in Paris apartments, there was, of course, nothing to suggest either poverty or immorality in Stuyvesant's commission and certainly nothing foolish; he undertook the task with gusto, no doubt seeing it as an excellent opportunity to educate his fellow citizens. Early in 1870 the building was ready for

Hunt's eight-story Tribune Building was completed in 1876. Its corbeled clock tower, which recalls that of the Palazzo Vecchio in Florence, rose 260 feet above the street, overtopped on the New York skyline only by the spire of Trinity Church. A vertical extension built in 1905 added nine more stories to the structure but nothing to its appearance.

99

On the night of March 26, 1883, a notable fancy-dress ball marked the opening of the William K. Vanderbilts' new mansion (below). The hostess, Alva Vanderbilt, appeared (right) as a Venetian princess, while her architect, Hunt (right, below), came as Cimabue, perhaps making a wry comment in doing so, since Dante had cited that painter in the **Inferno** to symbolize the transitoriness of fame. Mrs. Vanderbilt's party and house were so majestic that they not only established her social eminence beyond dispute but put her in a position to challenge the reigning queen of New York society, Mrs. William Astor.

occupancy; rising five stories behind a vaguely medieval façade, with a concierge's office off the entrance hall and with twenty-three-foot ceilings in the studios under the mansard roof, it was by then fully rented. The publisher G. P. Putnam moved in, and even Calvert Vaux took an apartment. Until 1959, when it was demolished to make way for a hideous yellow-brick monstrosity, it would almost never lack for tenants and would have one of the lowest turnovers in the city.

The success of the Stuyvesant Apartments naturally inspired other entrepreneurs to put up French flats, and within a generation or so apartment buildings would transform city life. Hunt would design one more such building but would soon turn his hand to private houses, mostly in New York and Newport, and to a variety of specialized structures. Among his larger projects of the next decade were the Tribune Building downtown and the Presbyterian Hospital, covering the city block east of Madison Avenue and north of Seventieth Street. Henry James, who liked very little of what he encountered in the New York of 1904–5, found the latter a haven of tranquillity in the surrounding clamor: "It had . . . in the early evening light, a homely kindness of diffused red brick, and to make out that it was a great exemplary Hospital . . . was to admire the exquisite art with which, in such a medium, it had so managed to invest itself with stillness."

Late in the 1870's Hunt entered into a long and significant association with the Vanderbilt family when William K. Vanderbilt, a grandson of the Commodore, engaged him to create a large country house on Long Island. While it was being built, Vanderbilt had had him design a small church nearby; Hunt fashioned Saint Mark's Church in a style reminiscent of the Scandinavian wooden "stave" style he had come upon in Norway some years before, during his European travels—one example among many of his inveterate eclecticism. The critic Montgomery Schuyler would find it superior "in invention, freedom, and picturesqueness" to any other building of Hunt's. But it was William Vanderbilt's third commission for Hunt that really caused a stir: it was for nothing less than a château—on the corner of Fifth Avenue and Fifty-second Street.

While Vanderbilt ran a vast, inherited railroad empire competently enough, his wife, the tempestuous and relentlessly ambitious Alva Smith Vanderbilt, ran his household, his children, and, often enough, him, so she had at least an equal voice in approving the drawings Hunt submitted. Both Vanderbilts wanted the best they could get, and what they got was, to quote Baker again, "for many years the most remarkable house in New York

Mrs. Astor, pictured above in a magazine illustration, came to Mrs. Vanderbilt's ball and in time ordered her own mansion (below) from Hunt.

City." It was an elegant, complex, richly ornamented structure very like French châteaux of the time of Francis I, when for a few decades medieval Gothic blended with Renaissance motifs in a style countless people—Hunt obviously among them—have since found extraordinarily pleasing to the eye and spirit. Almost everyone agreed that the house was a triumph of elegance and beauty, and its gray Indiana limestone exterior—a refreshing novelty in brownstone New York—was immediately and widely imitated. One critic, to be sure—Hunt's old nemesis, Clarence Cook—called it a "pretentious, fussy building . . . a patchwork made up of bits," and Louis Sullivan, pained by its incongruous appearance in its metropolitan setting, derided it as an anachronism.

The Vanderbilt mansion is long gone, but at least some New Yorkers, living and working in high-rise boxes of perfect austerity, may well, studying it in photographs, feel a twinge of regret and an inclination to endorse, rather than Cook's or Sullivan's, the sentiments of Charles McKim, who regularly strolled past it after leaving his office at the end of the day because, he said, he felt refreshed just looking at it. Of all Hunt's works, it was, in any case, the most widely and lavishly praised.

From the first rough sketches of the house to the furnishing of its interiors, Alva Vanderbilt leaned on Hunt for advice, but she proved "difficult" in the sense that she usually knew what she wanted and insisted on having it, decreeing, for example, that the children's playroom be sufficiently capacious for them to roller-skate and ride their bicycles in. On the other hand, the story that she drove him to distraction is belied by Catharine Hunt's recollection that he "had the greatest admiration for [Alva's] intellect and broad grasp of architecture and he often said: 'She's a wonder!' " But even if she had been far from wonderful, Hunt, a patient, tactful, and hugely amiable man, would still have managed, for he knew very well on which side an architect's bread is buttered. "The first thing you've got to remember," he once told his son Dick, "is that it's your client's money you're spending. Your business is to get the best results you can, following their wishes. If they want you to build a house upside down, standing on its chimney, it's up to you to do it, and still get the best possible results."

While Hunt's fortunes and immediate family grew during the 1870's, the decade brought him much sorrow with the deaths—two by suicide—of three people long dear to him. In 1874 his brother John, in Paris, overwhelmed by a domestic impasse involving his mistress and their lunatic daughter, slit his throat; at the end of 1877, his mother died in New York; and in September 1879, on Appledore Island, off the New Hampshire coast, William Hunt, separated from his wife and exhausted from overwork, drowned himself in a shallow pool. Since Hunt had remained closest to William, the latter's death affected him most.

William was buried in Brattleboro, where all the Hunts of his generation had been born and where Leavitt now lived: a year or so later Hunt had a gravestone of his own design set up at the burial site. Over the years Hunt designed several tombs and mausoleums, most notably one for William H. Vanderbilt, William K.'s father, who rejected his first plan as too "showy" for the "plain, quiet, unostentatious" Vanderbilts, and asked for something "roomy and solid and rich" but without any "unnecessary fancy-work on it."

Along with private memorials, Hunt was increasingly called on to design public monuments. These were all collaborative endeavors, most of them done with the sculptor John Quincy Adams Ward, and the fact that Hunt's contribution in providing the pedestals was, to his chagrin, usually overlooked by the press and public was actually, as William Francklyn Paris explained in an essay on Hunt, a tribute to his skill. "The pedestal," Paris wrote, "poses the problem of perfect proportion, harmony with the sculptural work, and, at the same time, an especial need for inconspicuousness. No attention must be attracted to the pedestal, no one must be conscious of it as having any claim to notice except that it is there, serving its purpose of bearing the sculptor's work."

Frédéric Auguste Bartholdi's Statue of Liberty confronted Hunt with a special challenge. It was, as Paris wrote,

a huge figure and the base must be proportionate. Any pedestal so large . . . could not fail to be conspicuous, but somehow the mass must be contrived in such a fashion that it would not seem mere heavy bulk and, at the same time, not be sufficiently elaborate to turn the eye away from the figure resting upon it. Hunt hit upon the solution of using the fortifications already on the island [Bedloe's Island, now Liberty Island], of molding their solid mass into good proportions and giving them a minimum of ornamentation just sufficient to blend into the general picture. It was a happy choice—and a happy result.

If pedestals were ideally inconspicuous, the same could hardly be said of the mansions going up on and just off Fifth Avenue, buildings plainly intended to impress the viewer—and especially the visitor—with their magnificence. Before long, their owners were to erect similar imposing residences in the country, notably in Newport. And that Hunt would play a leading part in this was inevitable: "By the mid-1880's," Baker relates, "Hunt had become the most fashionable architect

For the country residence Cornelius Vanderbilt II asked him to design, Hunt evidently favored the château style, as in the upper of these presentation drawings, but his client preferred the Genoese Renaissance style shown in the lower drawing. With another story added, this conception became that grandest of Newport "cottages," The Breakers.

103

of his time, and some [people] undoubtedly considered a house designed by him to be a badge of high social position." In the absence of a native American tradition of dwellings grand enough to gratify their appetite for glory, the plutocrats looked to Europe—and there found what they sought in the palaces of Renaissance princes and noblemen, the fortunes of many of whom had been based, like many of theirs, on commerce. These majestic dwellings seemed to the latter-day cisatlantic merchant princes entirely appropriate to their station—with, of course, modern plumbing, lighting, and heating installed. And no architect, surely, was better prepared than Hunt to provide them with such habitations in America.

During the quarter century since Hunt had courted Catharine there, Newport had changed radically: its society, once composed of well-to-do old families from Boston, New York, and the South, with a leavening of artists, writers, editors, teachers, and preachers, was now dominated by the New York superrich, magnates of business and industry. This change had been accompanied locally by a trend toward bigger houses utilizing more stone and less wood, but it was only in the last years of the 1880's that Newport's magnificoes began to think in terms of the immense houses that Henry James would term white elephants. The sums expended on building them was staggering, and the spectacle aroused indignation among citizens aware of the condition of the poor in city slums and immigrant ghettos. But for Hunt the boom in palace building was a wholly welcome development, enabling him to do what he enjoyed most, designing private houses, on a grander scale than ever before, while availing himself, thanks to his clients' enormous wealth, of the finest and rarest materials and the most skilled collaborators. Altogether, it was an opportunity most architects in any era would find irresistible, and for Hunt, now in his sixties, it must sometimes have seemed like the triumphant culmination of his lifework.

Hunt, incidentally, was by no means the only architect designing palaces for the Newport elite: while the fever of construction raged on into the next century, McKim, White, and several others were also at it. Somehow, though, Hunt's four Newport houses outclassed the competition and set the standards for subsequent building.

The first of them, Ochre Court, was commissioned by New York real-estate developer Ogden Goelet and completed in 1891 at a cost, it was said, of four and a half million dollars. French Renaissance in style, with an exterior of Indiana limestone, it faintly echoed the Vanderbilt mansion but was more formal and austere; Montgomery Schuyler called its entrance front "the most artistic composition that its author has produced." Unfortunately, however, the Goelet house, like almost all the other Newport palaces, occupied a parcel of land too small to set it off properly.

In 1892 another mansion, Marble House, was completed not far from Ochre Court on Bellevue Avenue. It was modeled on the White House, with details borrowed from the Petit Trianon in Versailles, and Hunt designed it for his longtime friends and clients William and Alva Vanderbilt. Having gone through it before the gala housewarming, Adèle Sloane, William's niece, told a reporter it was "marvellously beautiful" and "far ahead of any palace I have ever seen abroad, far ahead of any I have ever dreamed of." The structure itself reportedly cost two million dollars, while no less than nine million was said to have been lavished on decorating and furnishing its interior. Hunt, on travels through Europe with the Vanderbilts, had helped Alva select furnishings. He had also personally designed a delicate bronze and steel doorway grille, which a writer in the *New York Times* called "the finest piece of work of this character ever turned out in the United States."

Down Bellevue Avenue from Marble House and finished a year later, the sixty-room, three-million-dollar Belcourt, designed by Hunt for banker August Belmont's son Oliver Hazard Perry Belmont, was a very different sort of place, more hospitable to quadrupeds than bipeds. "A most singular house," Julia Ward Howe called it after lunching there: "The first floor is all stable, with stalls for some thirteen or more horses, all filled and everything elaborate and elegant! . . . The residential part of the house is on the next story, designed by Hunt and palatial in its character." It was, in effect, a magnificent stable and carriage house with living quarters for humans attached— and with a passageway making it possible to drive a carriage straight into the house and up to the front of the grand staircase. Outside, the structure, conceived as a French hunting lodge of the early seventeenth century, presented a curious mixture of French, Italian, and English elements.

Magnificent as they were, Ochre Court, Marble House, and Belcourt would soon be outdone by Hunt's last and biggest Newport "cottage," The Breakers, which Cornelius Vanderbilt II, William K.'s older brother, commissioned late in 1892 to replace a summer house that had burned down.

The ballroom of Marble House in Newport, known not surprisingly as the Gold Room, was decorated in the style of Louis XIV, with the king's emblem on its walls. Alva Vanderbilt's bills for the interiors came to nine million dollars.

Inspired by sixteenth-century palaces in Genoa, it embodied, as Baker notes, the qualities of "harmony, dignity and repose" for which its architect perpetually strove. And it was conceived on a truly heroic scale, occupying two basement levels and a huge attic as well as its three principal stories, and containing more than seventy rooms, almost half of them for the use of servants and staff. The house was about two hundred fifty feet long and a hundred and fifty deep, and its four-chandeliered great hall, surrounded on three sides by galleries on the second-floor level, rose more than forty-five feet from floor to ceiling. The Breakers, vast in scale and sumptuous in decor, was the culmination of Hunt's work in Newport, the largest private house—but one—he would ever design.

In the midst of this activity, Hunt was drawn into the preparations for the World's Columbian Exposition commemorating the quatercentenary of the discovery of the New World. His fellow architects put him in charge of construction, for as Van Brunt, then practicing in Kansas City, would recall, "When . . . in 1893, several of us were summoned to act together again with him on the great national arena at Chicago, the natural domi-

nance of the master again asserted itself without pretension, and we once more became his willing and happy pupils." Hunt's Administration Building was, like all the others, a temporary structure fashioned of plaster of Paris, but as the focal point and ·dominant feature of the fair, it brought him greater notice than had any permanent building he ever designed. Baker's description helps us to visualize it: "Rising at the head of the Court of Honor, reflected in the great basin, its gleaming gold and white dome visible from all over the grounds, this huge, monumental, neoclassical structure set the tone of stately formality for the exposition buildings."

The neoclassical style officially adopted for the fair was to dominate American public architecture for another forty years, to the embitterment of that lonely midwestern prophet of an "American" architecture, Louis Sullivan. In retrospect, however, its persistence would seem to have been dictated by popular taste far more than by, as some historians have claimed, the example set in Chicago by the largely eastern and conservative architectural establishment.

In that year of 1893 Hunt was awarded the gold

medal of the Royal Institute of British Architects, the first American to be so honored, and elected an associate member of the Académie des Beaux-Arts of the Institut de France, Benjamin West having been the only American artist so distinguished before him. He had previously collected awards from the governments of France, Britain, Austria, and Italy, and although he would never be formally honored by his own government, he was pleased to have received, like his brother William before him, an honorary degree from Harvard: a doctorate of laws, awarded in 1892, the first that university ever conferred on an architect.

Although his health was imperceptibly deteriorating, Hunt's last years, covering the early 1890's, were his most productive. In addition to the Administration Building and his four great Newport houses, he designed mansions on Fifth Avenue for William V. Lawrence and Elbridge Gerry and a double residence for Mrs. William Astor and her son John Jacob Astor IV. He drew up plans for U. S. Naval Observatory buildings outside Washington, for an art museum at Harvard, and—at the U. S. Military Academy at West Point he had once hoped to attend—for a gymnasium, a classroom building, and a guardhouse. And for the Metropolitan Museum he designed a monumental extension fronting on Fifth Avenue that is now one of New York's most familiar landmarks.

But even as he worked on these and other tasks, Hunt's thoughts were never absent for long from that grandest of all his undertakings, Biltmore, near Asheville, North Carolina.

When the William H. Vanderbilt who had commissioned a "roomy and solid and rich" tomb from Hunt died in 1885, he left his three sons unequal bequests: Cornelius and William K., the future builders of The Breakers and Marble House, received sixty-seven and sixty-five million dollars respectively, but George got "only" ten million. This discrepancy may have reflected the father's awareness that his shy, bookish youngest son cared little about business, his interests being chiefly artistic and philanthropic. And this, in turn, may explain why Hunt, with his deep affinity for art, came to feel particularly close to George Vanderbilt, sharing what he termed a "perfect harmony"

Completed after Hunt's death from his design, the façade of the Metropolitan Museum of Art is the sole remaining work of his along the thoroughfare, Fifth Avenue, that he so transformed.

with him and regarding him almost as another son.

Having decided, while riding through hilly farm country near Asheville, to build a house on a certain rise commanding a spectacular view of mountains to the west, young Vanderbilt bought the land and asked Frederick Law Olmsted, the cocreator of Central Park, to look it over for him. Olmsted recommended laying out gardens and a small park around the house, leaving the nearby river bottoms under cultivation and pasture, and turning everything else into forest; Vanderbilt accepted the advice. And he asked Hunt to design his house.

Initially, Vanderbilt wanted a modest, conventional residence, but Hunt, excited by the prospect of building out in the open instead of in the cramped conditions of New York or Newport, soon persuaded him to think big, on a scale to match the property and nearby natural features. (As the house took shape, Hunt would exultantly write Catharine that "the mountains are just the right size and scale for the château!") Olmsted backed him enthusiastically. Throughout seven long years, indeed, these two aging masters, who had clashed decades earlier over Hunt's proposed Central Park gateways, worked together in near total harmony toward the realization of their extraordinary collaborative vision. As for Vanderbilt, Biltmore—house, grounds, and forest—became an obsession into which he would willingly pour the greater part of his fortune.

With so many other projects in the works, Hunt had to be away most of the time, but his son Dick—who had graduated from the Ecole des Beaux-Arts before joining his father's firm—was usually there. Little by little, as hundreds of craftsmen and workmen toiled on year after year, the elaborate Hunt-Olmsted plan assumed visible, physical form, until, from grounds organized architecturally into lawns and gardens on several levels, there arose a French Renaissance château awesome in size yet wondrously light in feeling, and strikingly romantic. Vanderbilt was enchanted with his 255-room château and its every feature, including a dining hall seventy-five feet high. In mid-May 1895 he brought the Hunts and the painter John Singer Sargent from New York to Biltmore in his private railway car, so that Sargent might paint the portraits of its architect and landscape architect at the scene of their joint triumph.

After a three-week stay the Hunts returned

For Biltmore, the largest private house in America, Hunt designed this monumental entrance, with an adjoining staircase modeled after that of the château de Blois in the Loire Valley. The full façade of the mansion is shown on page 147.

north, and early in July went to Lenox, Massachusetts, for the wedding of George Vanderbilt's niece Adèle Sloane, the young woman who had rhapsodized over Marble House. Hunt got wet in a sudden downpour leaving Lenox and had to return to New York in damp clothes; the next day, on his way to Newport, he came down with a severe attack of gout. Confined to a sofa in Hill Top cottage, he transacted some business but felt weak and was in constant pain. On July 30 he suddenly began to fail, and around noon on the thirty-first he died. "Upon his deathbed" Van Brunt informs us, "he was seen to raise his hand and, with the fine gesture of the artist, to trace as with a pencil in the air a line of beauty, delicately but firmly fitting the act of grace to the unconscious study of his imagination."

Almost ten years after Hunt's death, in February, 1905, Henry James, heading south in flight from the icy northern winter, stopped at Biltmore for a few days; he arrived in the middle of a snowstorm feeling very much out of sorts, as he was suffering from gout and had just lost a front tooth, and when the incredibly vast house turned out to be cold and drafty, he decided it was no more than "a phenomenon of brute achievement." So he noted at the time; but later, recalling the episode in the comfort of his Sussex study, he remembered the place as a "modern miracle" and tried to puzzle out what made it so:

I had, by a deviation, spent a week in a castle of enchantment; but if this modern miracle, of which the mountains of North Carolina happened to be the scene, would have been almost anywhere miraculous, I could at least take it as testifying, all relevantly, all directly, for the presence, as distinguished from the absence, of feature. One felt how, in this light, the extent and the splendor of such a place was but a detail; these things were accidents, without which the great effect, the element that, in the beautiful empty air, made all the difference, would still have prevailed. What was this element but just the affirmation of resources?—made with great emphasis indeed, but in a clear and exemplary way; so that if large wealth represented some of them, an idea, a fine cluster of ideas, a will, a purpose, a patience, an intelligence, a store of knowledge, immediately workable things, represented the others. What it thus came to, on behalf of this vast parenthetic Carolinian demonstration, was that somebody had *cared* enough— and that happily there had been somebody *to* care; which struck me at once as marking the difference . . . .

What a judgment, coming from that scourge of American shallowness and carelessness, that eloquent denouncer of his countrymen's weakness for the meretricious! It more than made up for his cracks about white elephants. And today, most visitors to Biltmore, architects and laymen alike, agree that they behold in it Hunt's finest memorial, his noblest vision, and even, one might say, his final, triumphant vindication.

109

HENRY HOBSON

RICHARDSON

Sketch for Richardson's Marshall Field Wholesale Store, Chicago, 1885-87
THE HOUGHTON LIBRARY, HARVARD UNIVERSITY

H. H. Richardson —

1838–1886

BY JOHN RUSSELL

It was common ground among everyone who knew him in the late 1870's and early 1880's that Henry Hobson Richardson was one of the great Americans of his day. It was not that he ever talked big—that would have been quite out of character—but that he looked big, thought big, and built big.

Bigness became him, moreover. It stood for things that he had in superabundance: energy, ideas, ambition, assurance. What in another man might have seemed just plain old fat was in the case of Richardson an Olympian amplitude. It was as if he needed to bear down on the American earth with the weight of ten men, knowing full well that the American earth would bounce him back.

In point of fact, his fatness was a pathological condition, his energy was progressively more and more limited, and he knew that he could not count on a long career. But he made the tour, one by one, of the opportunities that could come an architect's way in the 1870's and early 1880's, and to every one of them he brought what seemed to his contemporaries a specifically American vibration.

The opportunities in question were of the kind that the Establishment of the day is always glad to concede to one of its own. By birth, by education, and by conscious choice Henry Hobson Richardson was a member of the Establishment of his day. He went along with it, delightedly; and delightedly it went along with him. By the time he died—at the age of only forty-seven—he had redefined, for the United States, the potential of the public building in one domain after another. To this day, people think of Trinity Church, Boston, when they wish to remind themselves that in this country, as in Europe, a parish church can be as stupendous as many a cathedral. Sever Hall and Austin Hall at Harvard impress the student, even today, by their stately dedication to the cause of learning. Never were legislators more sumptuously housed than in the State Capitol at Albany. If you had to be tried,

found guilty, and sent to jail, Pittsburgh in the last quarter of the nineteenth century was as good a place as any in which to endure it, thanks to Richardson's monumental courthouse-cum-prison. If you were in business, and you felt that business is best carried out in surroundings of the kind that flourished in the ancient mercantile cities of Europe, then once again Richardson was your man, even if his Chamber of Commerce in Cincinnati was not completed until after his death. It was not simply that Richardson was the faithful servant of government, religion, business, education, and the law. It was that he aspired to be—by implication—their leader and their guide. For whether or not it is true that "we are what we eat," it is certainly true that we are formed by what we live in, and by what we look at.

Richardson's was above all things an affirmative art. "No" and "I can't" were noises that he never made when presented with a project that would give the cities and towns of America an ampler, more inventive, and more commanding appearance. It was a part of his general and all-comprehending bigness that within a general commitment to society as a whole he kept a close watch on everything that pertained to his individual buildings, to the status of the architect in society, and to the relations between architect and client (and between architect and contractor). Much as Sir Joshua Reynolds a hundred years earlier had redrafted the relationship between painters and society in England, Henry Hobson Richardson redrafted the working relationship in the United States between architects, on the one hand, and society in general, on the other. A great architect, in his view, came second to no man, and by the time he died in 1886 he had brought a great many people round to his opinion.

There is about Richardson's childhood and first youth an atmosphere of untroubled well-being which makes it pleasant to think about but not easy to describe. All went well for him. He was happy at home, happy in school, and happy in college. He got engaged to be married when he was still in Harvard. (The romance survived an exceptionally long engagement and is reputed to have been without blemish, ending only with his death.) He came of a good family, had enough money to live on, and made friends wherever he went. If he had tantrums, chagrins, reverses, problems of identity, or a run of bad luck, no one has ever brought them to light. Even his ambition evolved slowly and naturally and seems never to have been thwarted. With his combination of northern energy and southern good manners, he was regarded by his contemporaries as the ideal young American.

Henry Hobson Richardson was born on Sep-

In 1884, two years before his early death, Richardson sat for this photograph in his Brookline, Massachusetts, home.

Richardson worked in this parlor-library, amid a clutter of books, drawings, Victorian furnishings, and personal memorabilia. He was photographed there in 1880.

tember 29, 1838, at the Priestley Plantation in the Parish of Saint James, Louisiana. His great-grandfather was Dr. Joseph Priestley, the polymath (author, it was once calculated, of 141 books) who was a nonconformist minister, a master of many languages both ancient and modern, an experimental educationalist, a pioneer chemist who discovered oxygen, an enthusiast for the French Revolution, and an early supporter of the American colonists in their struggle against the British. Joseph Priestley's sons were already well established in America when he himself arrived there in 1794. One of them, Richardson's maternal grandfather, had done very well indeed with sugar cane plantations in Louisiana.

Richardson did not have anything like the intellectual curiosity of Joseph Priestley. Nor did he have anything like Priestley's spontaneous involvement with people who wished to change the nature of society. Neither in his art nor in his life did he look forward to a world transformed. The world as it was was quite good enough for him.

Nor did he have that most engaging of Joseph Priestley's traits: the readiness to follow up a hundred different subjects at one and the same time. From the moment that he settled on his chosen profession he was a man of one subject, one object, and one ambition: to build as well as he could in materials that had been around forever.

Meanwhile, he took his time over that choice of profession. Not only did he not show any precocious vocation, but he showed no particular drive to succeed. He was a very good mathematician in school, but he showed none of that preternatural intellectual activity that is the mark of the mathematician of genius. He was bright enough to be able to play several games of chess at once while blindfolded, but he seems to have regarded chess as no more than an agreeable distraction. He played the flute rather well, and fenced even better. He was more dandified in his dress than was usual at that time. One of his fellow students remembered him as "a slender, companionable Southern lad, full of creole life and animation." He liked talking to girls, and they liked talking to him. He had many friends, and he never lost them. With his "very dark and brilliant hazel eyes," his expressive features, his generosity of disposition, and his delight in amusements of every kind, he could easily have grown into the kind of man of whom his friends say, "What a pity he never stuck to any one thing!"

It is fundamental to his success in later life that, without being either a toady or a snob, he gravitated by instinct toward young men who were likely to become persons of importance. Initially it was they who sought him out—at Harvard he was elected, for instance, to the Porcellian Club, which admitted only fifteen members at a time—but he took care not to lose sight of them. When he moved his architectural practice to Brookline, Massachusetts, in 1874, it was in large part because Brookline was at that time a kind of game park in which prominent people could rub up against one another. Once again, it was not that he was on the make—no one ever accused him of that—but rather that he had got a taste for the company of men and women of a certain kind and saw no reason not to indulge it.

His fellow Porcellians did not spot him from the first as a future architect, let alone as the leader of his profession. It came as a surprise when he decided, at an undisclosed time and for an undisclosed reason, to apply for admission to the Ecole des Beaux-Arts in Paris. To get into the Ecole was in itself an achievement, since the examination was in French, lasted a month, and was conducted in public. At the first time of asking, in the fall of 1859, he failed in descriptive geometry, a subject that he had first looked at only four weeks before. But in November 1860 he came eighteenth in a field of a hundred and twenty and became the second American (after Richard Morris Hunt) to win admission.

He had not intended to stay long in Paris. Louisiana was still his home, and it was taken for granted that he would eventually return there and set up an architectural practice in New Orleans. But before this could come about, the Civil War wrought a total change in his circumstances. His family lost their money. His income dwindled, arrived irregularly at best, and finally stopped altogether. From being one of the richer young Americans in Paris he became a pauper, obliged to work all day for his living and to study by night. Though buoyed and bolstered by his inborn high spirits, he had a difficult time. But, as one of his Parisian roommates said later, "Misfortune gave him maturity of mind." By 1862 this most gregarious and sought-after of men was writing to his fiancée, Julia Gorham Hayden, that "study and society are incompatible. . . . I hardly have time to take my meals. . . . I intend studying my profession in such a manner as to make my success a surety and not a matter of chance. . . . Every day I find new beauties in a profession which I already place at the head of all the Fine Arts."

What were the "new beauties" in question? As to that, surmise is all. Richardson was in Paris at a time of great ebullition for architects and architecture. The Second Empire conceived of architecture as the handmaiden of statecraft. It would have been difficult to be an architectural student in Paris between 1860 and 1865 and not hear talk of the new Opéra, the new Palais de Justice, the new extension of the Louvre, and the new Gare du Nord, the two big new state theaters in the Place du Châtelet, and, not least, the new Ecole des Beaux-Arts. Richardson had taken a job, moreover, in the office of the architect Théodore Labrouste, and must therefore have heard of every major commission that was either going forward or on offer. For Théodore Labrouste, though by no means an architect of genius, was the elder brother of Henri Labrouste, architect of the Bibliothèque Nationale and a key figure in the architectural world of the day.

For the Brookline town hall competition, Richardson designed this richly ornamented structure in the tradition of French civic halls, but with many personal touches. The design was too much for the town fathers, who chose a more workaday building.

Richardson is not known to have regarded any of the new official buildings in Paris in the light of revelation. But the projects listed above set the scale for his American career, insofar as they were, one and all, projects of weight and moment, by which an entire society was to be given a new tone. On this reading, the "new beauties" of which he spoke were a matter of scale, and social responsibility, and enduring moral force.

But the "new beauties" may have resided as much in the practice of architecture itself, and specifically in the Beaux-Arts atelier system. While at the Ecole, Richardson did his studio work at M. André's atelier, a combination of workshop, club, commune, and guild. The members of an atelier were a fraternity, almost a priesthood, rather than a gang of superior day laborers. The atelier was an ideal society in miniature, in which men found fulfillment in an atmosphere of selfless endeavor. This was the atmosphere that Richardson brought back with him from France and later established in his Brookline office.

Where Richardson undoubtedly fell short of the complete Parisian experience in the early 1860's was that, like Hunt before him, he was not interested at all in the new materials that were getting to be more and more important in the evolution of architecture. He was already what he was to be throughout his life: a masonry man, as opposed to an iron-and-glass man. Victor Baltard's Halles Centrales were under way throughout his years in Paris, but there is no indication that he ever thought about them. "Iron, iron, nothing but iron!"—the words used to Baltard by Baron Haussmann, prefect of the Seine—would have seemed to Richardson a meaningless, if not a barbaric, injunction. That buildings should be built as lightly as umbrellas would not have seemed to him desirable. The very openness and candor of iron and glass, their impersonality and virtual anonymity—all these would have been uncongenial to Richardson. Architecture, for him, was a stylish and evocative way of separating outdoors from indoors.

Besides, there was the possibility that radical change in architecture would be the forerunner of radical change in life. Had not Plato said that when the laws of art change, the laws of the state change with them? And Richardson didn't want the laws of the state to change. Where the classic architectures of our own time are metaphors for an open society and a free city of the spirit, Richardson's major buildings have about them something of a fortress or donjon, secure against all comers.

He was, therefore, a convinced and practicing conservative. He liked to work with established institutions, established fortunes, and established individuals. This was a practical preference as well

as a matter of principle. In his concern for "a rich, bold, living architecture," he liked to revise and improve as he went along. ("Architects should not be made the convenience of contractors," he wrote in the margin of a pencil sketch in 1870.) Where possible, he refused to be pinned down to finished preliminary drawings, preferring to work with the growing building as a sculptor works with clay.

This called for steady nerves, a cool head, an understanding builder-engineer, and a client who would not jib at the bills. In Orlando Whitney Norcross (1839–1920) Richardson had an associate who suited his nature ideally. He was, says the critic James F. O'Gorman, "an inventive self-trained engineer" to whom no problem of construction was insoluble. With one or another of the quarries and millworks that he had at his disposal, he could supply a range of materials that satisfied even Richardson, whose first and second thoughts in such matters ranged far and wide.

But before Norcross could be brought into play there had to be both a client and a commission. At the outset of Richardson's career in the United States, both of these were in very short supply. Established in a small way in New York, Richardson found that work was hard to come by. He had to sell the general library that he had bought at Harvard, and before long he was down almost to his last dollar, though still conspicuous for his English suits, his English shoes, his well-chosen cravats, and his strong and still-slender build. Somewhere, somehow, he had to make an impressive beginning as his own master.

As has already been said, Richardson was not the man to spend his time with nonentities. Even when he spent the night in a Paris police station after taking part in a demonstration against the appointment of Violet-le-Duc to the Ecole des Beaux-Arts, it turned out that he shared a cell with Théophile Gautier—poet, novelist, and critic of art—and for that reason was released by the intercession of the minister for fine arts. And when he got his first American commission in November 1866, it was in part because a classmate of his had married well and was in a position to intercede on his behalf. (When told of his success, Richardson burst into tears and said, "That is all I wanted—*a chance.*")

But it is one thing to have a chance and quite another to make full use of it. Richardson never faltered, in a situation of that sort, and in building his Unitarian church at Springfield, Massachusetts, he did as he always did. Deploying the powers of persuasion, which, as one of his friends said, "could charm a bird out of a bush," he invented and reinvented his design several times over. With hindsight we can detect already both the asymmetrical cunning with which he would continue to order his internal spaces, and a delight—never to be lost—in the monumental properties of rough-cut American stone. Some of the detailing was really rather freaky—the narrow slots, for instance, that served as lower windows in the tower—but the general impact of the work seems to have been that of a young man with a future. With his first solo work, and in his thirtieth year, Richardson was on the move.

It was to be quite some time, even so, before his work took on that full-blown look that we call Richardsonian. There is an insufficiency about his work in the 1860's which has nothing to do with his gifts, or his resources, or his ambition. It was in part that the right job in the right place had not come along, and in part that architecture, for Richardson, was like conducting an orchestra: you learned it by doing it. There was no other way to learn it. Nor was there any way not to fall below that ideal of excellence whose fulfillment comes only with time. There might be fine individual features, like the tower of the Brattle Square Church in Boston. There might be demonstrations of ease and fluency in the

adaptation of styles that owed nothing to America, like the Second Empire offices of the Western Railroad in Springfield, Massachusetts. There was the Dorsheimer house in Buffalo, where Richardson adumbrated the kind of baronial living hall that was to give a look of almost feudal splendor to the house that he designed in 1884 for John Hay in Washington, D.C. But none of these had the fulfilled, the almost predestined, look of the work for which Richardson is best known. There was something not quite centered about them, just as there was something not quite centered about Richardson's geographical position, with his home on Staten Island, his office in Manhattan, and most of his major commissions in Massachusetts.

There was a spectacular failure, too: a failure on the grand scale that could not be written off as one can write off a private house that stands behind

Richardson was the chief originator of the Shingle style, which gave grace to many seaside communities in New England. In this early example, the Watts Sherman house of 1874 at Newport, Rhode Island, he used rough stone for the first floor, with shingles above. The house incorporates such distinctive elements of the style as overhanging roofs, plentiful gables, and bulky (or, in this case, high) chimneys.

117

high walls and can be covered in time with creeper. This was the high school in Worcester, Massachusetts. It was an immensely ambitious building: a building almost insanely out of style with the plain and earnest activity that was to go forward within it. The main tower reaches for the sky like a cry for help. The turrets look as if they had been bought on sale and added for no other reason. The external double staircase is absurd. As Henry-Russell Hitchcock says, "The whole educational hive is merely surrounded by four walls and covered with a mansard. Apparently the process of designing the façades was carried out by Richardson in an architectural vacuum, without thought of the interior." It is a building that has no identity either in time or in place. It might be anything, anywhere, any time, where the world was out of joint.

Yet so rich and strong was Richardson's nature, and so speedy its power of assimilation, that when he was asked in 1870 to design the State Hospital in Buffalo, New York, the result was strong precisely where the Worcester High School had been weak.

Sturdy, twinned towers rise naturally from a structure that has precisely the amount of jut and thrust that was needed. Corner turrets look spontaneous and not stuck on. An entrance loggia of three round arches, deep-set between projecting side bays, prevents the eye from moving uninterruptedly upward. Hip-roofed dormers rehearse the forms of the towers and turrets. Lintels and colonnettes between the dormers show a finesse of detailing that is quite new in Richardson's work.

Through no fault of Richardson's, the Buffalo State Hospital took a long time to build. Meanwhile, in June 1872 Richardson won the competition for the new Trinity Church in Boston, with which his name was to be made once and for all. The cornerstone was laid on May 20, 1875, and in November 1876 the work was complete in all essentials. Trinity Church, dedicated in February 1877, was then and is still the most commanding single building in Boston.

Trinity Church as we see it today is not the church that Richardson saw dedicated. Nor is it the

church over whose interior decoration he spent so much time and thought. It has been amended and added to, inside and out, and almost always to its detriment. John La Farge's mural paintings have "sunk" to a point at which we cannot judge them fairly. The "French medieval" stained glass windows are quite out of key with Richardson's intentions, as are the decorations in the chancel by Charles D. Maginnis. The porch dates from the 1890's and is by Richardson's successors, Shepley, Rutan and Coolidge. They are responsible, also, for the tops of the western towers.

It should also be said that Trinity Church as it was designed by Richardson speaks for an aesthetic of *bricolage*, shopping around, that until quite lately was very much out of fashion. To eyes trained by looking at buildings by Adolf Loos, Gerrit Rietveld, the Vesnin brothers, and Mies van der Rohe, it seemed axiomatic that new buildings should be in one style and speak for one man, one time, and one place. But Richardson in Trinity Church was quite prepared to begin with foliage carved in a style

The public library at North Easton was built as a memorial to Oliver Ames II, who made one fortune as a manufacturer of shovels, another as a builder of the Union Pacific Railroad.

Over a period of years beginning in 1877 Richardson designed a series of private and public buildings for the Ames family in North Easton, Massachusetts. The gate lodge of Frederick L. Ames's estate crouches beneath a massive roof of orange tile. Guests who were put up here when the nearby mansion was full could glimpse light through the narrow eyelid dormers.

derived from the High Victorian Gothic churches of England and shift to the round arches of French Romanesque as he went along.

As to the general design, Professor Hitchcock puts it concisely in his *Architecture: Nineteenth and Twentieth Centuries*:

The pyramidal massing of Trinity from the east derived from Auvergnat churches, and there is even Auvergnat polychromy on the apse; the lower portion of the original west front was based on Saint-Gilles-de-Provence; and the executed lantern was an adaptation of that on the Old Cathedral of Salamanca in Spain.

Furthermore, there were echoes of contemporary English practice: "the curious double-curved wooden roof with kingpost trusses derives from published examples of similar roofs built or projected by [William] Burges."

Put like that, Trinity Church sounds like something run up by a dealer in architectural old clothes—all the more so, when we know that the borrowings from Salamanca were made at a late stage and on the basis of photographs sent to Richardson by John La Farge and given by him to Stanford White, who was at that time working in his office. (Richardson had never been to Salamanca.) What kind of a genius is *that*, people would have asked in the 1920's, who relied on cross-continental salmagundi when asked for an original design? Even in the late 1880's Richardson's first biographer, Mariana Griswold Van Rensselaer, felt bound to answer that question. After a point-by-point comparison of the tower at Salamanca

119

Outside Trinity Church in 1893 a great throng gathered for the funeral of Boston's great preacher, and rector of Trinity, Phillips Brooks. The church appears as Richardson designed it, before the addition of a porch by his partners.

with the tower of Trinity Church, she concluded:

We cannot really compare, we can only contrast them. . . . Different ideals were kept in view. Each result has unity and harmony; but the unity of Salamanca is brought about by a general uniformity in features relieved by minor divergencies in treatment, and the unity of Trinity by a strong opposition of features skillfully worked into vital amalgamation. . . . It looks as though the man who built it had been born to build in just this way; it looks like the result of a genuine impulse and not of a lesson learned and then repeated.

Mrs. Van Rensselaer was a friend and contemporary of Richardson's, and she took it for granted not only that his borrowings or adaptations were standard practice among educated architects but that Richardson's creative personality was strong enough to make them his own. She also knew something which cannot be said too often: that Richardson's was an art of color, texture, scale, and pace. Richardson planned Trinity as what he called "a color church" inside and out. Now that more than a hundred years have had their way with the exterior, it is worth remembering what Mrs. Van Rensselaer had to say about its initial appearance:

The yellowish-grey granite employed throughout for the rock-faced ashlar is soft and warm in tone, having much the effect of a sandstone. The trimmings are of that red Longmeadow sandstone which by its admirable texture and beautiful color has done so much for Boston buildings. The lower roofs are of plain slates, the roof and louvre-boards of the tower of semi-glazed red tiles, and the crockets of red terra-cotta. The pronounced yet harmonious effect of color thus produced is one of Trinity's greatest merits . . . .

Even today Trinity Church impresses a visitor with the *moto perpetuo* of its external surfaces. We marvel, in fact, at the unifying energy with which Richardson was able to make of them something more than an anthology of motifs exiled from the southern sun. We also marvel at the way in which he suggests the ineluctable swell of mysterious spaces within. Those spaces were to a certain extent dictated by the commission, which called for a church that would seat a thousand people and have no columns, and by the site, which had a curious trapezoidal shape.

Richardson's idea of a "color church" necessitated an inner space that would be, in his own words, "unembarrassed by conditions." To bring this about, he decided that it would be quite wrong to allow the building materials to dictate the decoration in any way. He embarked, therefore, on a campaign of deception and of dissemblement. Furring and plastering were everywhere, encasing the four great granite piers that bore the weight of the tower and covering the huge barrel vault of trefoil section. Where iron rods were carried across on a level with the cusps of the arches, Richardson disguised them with wooden tie beams. The "material of actual construction," according to

Trinity Church, often regarded as Richardson's masterpiece, faces Copley Square. Of the architect one critic wrote: "To live in a house built by Richardson was a cachet of wealth and taste; to have your nest-egg in one of his banks gave you a feeling of perfect security; to worship in one of his churches made one think one had a pass-key to the Golden Gates."

This meticulous interior design for Trinity Church was executed for Richardson by his gifted assistant Charles McKim, later to be the senior partner of the firm of McKim, Mead and White. Richardson himself did his creative work in the form of quick sketches such as the one at left for another church, leaving to his young colleagues the working up of finished drawings.

Henry Van Brunt, was nowhere visible "to afford a key of color to the decorator."

Color was to be all, in that interior, and it was in that context that Richardson was able to realize what had clearly been a long-standing dream of his: a collaboration between equals in the decoration of a great public building. John La Farge worked on Trinity Church, and to great effect. So did the young Augustus Saint-Gaudens. From England, William Morris and Edward Burne-Jones were called in. What Richardson wanted was nothing less than that the spirit of the age should take up residence in Trinity Church.

He himself had a strong, secure, and well-developed ego. Knowing himself the equal of any man around, he was perfectly at home in Brookline, where he moved his residence and his office in 1874. It was a convenient move, since he needed to be continually on hand in Boston, but it was also a strategic one. Brookline at that time had probably more remarkable residents to the square inch than any other locality in the United States. It was not so much a question of money—though there was plenty of that—as of personal distinction. As O'Gorman has pointed out, Richardson in Brookline had as his neighbors an honor roll of distinguished Americans in the fields of medicine, law, economics, engineering, history, politics, connoisseurship, and the study of trees.

Once again, the spirit of the age was in question. Richardson did not build himself a splendid new mansion in Brookline—in fact he lived and died as the tenant of a house-cum-office that was none too large for his purposes—but he did undoubtedly see himself as the center of an ideal society. There were his wife and children: loving, eager, well-favored, stable. There were his assistants, including Stanford White, who was with him from 1872 to 1878. There was Frederick Law Olmsted, on whose neighborly judgment he relied very much. There were the neighbors, and the distinguished visitors from out of town, who crowded into the house on Sunday afternoons to hear quartets by Haydn and Beethoven and look at the designs that were out on display. There were all the elements, in fact, of a pre-Freudian paradise in which no one was guilty or repressed.

Rash as it is to touch on matters as to which no firm evidence exists, it may strike the Richardson-watcher that what he recreated in Brookline was the atmosphere of the Parisian ateliers that he had known not so many years before. There was the same atmosphere of hard and selfless work powered by high spirits, uninhibited social exchange, and ritual feasting. There was the same enclosed world of collective effort. Richardson was all things in one to his assistants: father, teacher, employer, playmate, and god. Nor was it only architecture that they learned from him. In all his dealings with them he was a model of courtesy, though he was content with nothing short of their best. He gave them the run of his library, the benefit of his experience of the world, and the best of food and wine. They could play tennis on his court (though not for more than thirty minutes during any one working day). And if it was found that three of them could get inside one of his vests, he didn't mind that, either—just once.

He hated to turn young people down. When Charles McKim asked to join his firm in 1870, he said, "My dear fellow, I haven't a thing in my office for my one and only draftsman to do." But somehow he found work for McKim. Even when he was mortally ill with Bright's disease, a professional discussion would bring back color to his cheeks and fire to his eye. He lived for work—but for work done in the company of other men, and warmed by their enthusiasm.

Paris had taught him to love work of that kind. But its origins reached back in time and place beyond the Paris of the 1860's to the Nuremberg of Dürer and Hans Sachs and the Florence of masters too numerous to mention. It may even have brought Richardson consolation of a more secret kind, in that as a very young man he was nominated for West Point, only to be turned down on account of an impediment in his speech. It is never agreeable to be rejected, and to be rejected on that particular ground leaves a lasting mark. Collective acceptance of the kind that Richardson found first in the Parisian ateliers and later in an atelier of his own founding may have been all the more precious to him if it helped to erase the memory of rejection at West Point.

Be that as it may, it is not fanciful to suppose that there was an element as much of thanksgiving as of gluttony in the scale on which Richardson entertained his guests. Something of traditional southern hospitality may have entered into it also, as on the occasion when the Wintersnight Club dined at his house. "The wines came from old cellars in New Orleans," one guest remembered, "the oysters from Baltimore, and the terrapin from Augustin's famous Philadelphia restaurant, with a chef in attendance all the way."

Richardson was only thirty-five when he moved to Brookline, and it was at that time a mere eight years since he had designed his church at Springfield, Massachusetts. His was a prodigious ascension, but it did not leave him winded. (Mrs. Van Rensselaer said of him that "his exuberant frankness and fearless self-trust refreshed one like a breath from some primeval clime.") To get his career in proportion, we must remember that at the time of the dedication of Trinity Church, in 1877, Richardson had but nine years to live. As yet in the future were the libraries, the railroad stations, the two buildings for Harvard, the City Hall for Albany, a house in Washington for Henry Adams, the Chamber of Commerce for Cincinnati, the Wholesale Store for Marshall Field in Chicago, a pyramidal monument in Wyoming Territory, and many other, smaller constructions. We almost believe what he said to one prospective client: "I'll plan anything a man wants, from a cathedral to a chicken coop. That's the way I make my living."

There were of course dangers in that universal readiness. Everyone agrees that Richardson in his last years took on more work that he himself could seriously oversee. But he had something to say, he had not long to live, and he had a very good staff. Besides, he did not wish to fall short of the role that

In his later years Richardson sometimes indulged his taste for medievalism by wearing a monk's robe at work.

house." First making a few marks to get an exact idea of scale, he rapidly drew the first floor plan, almost exactly as it was finally decided upon. The dessert was strawberry shortcake, for which our cook was famous. He asked for a second piece, with the added remark, "Mrs. Glessner, that's the best pie I ever put in my mouth."

But, needless to say, there were commissions that could not be resolved so quickly, just as there were commissions that had wider and deeper social implications. There was the problem, for instance, of the commercial buildings that were getting to be ever more prominent in American cities. Richardson took note of these problems, and when he was asked to build the American Merchants' Union Express Building in September 1872, he went ahead with his habitual elegance and dispatch. He was no less brisk with the commission for the Cheney Building in Hartford, Connecticut, which was

had been thrust upon him: that of Mr. Architecture. From being an obscure beginner on Staten Island, he had risen in hardly more than a decade to being the most talked-of architect in America. And he held that place: in 1885 the *American Architect and Building News* took a poll as to what were the ten finest buildings in the country. Five of them were by Richardson, as it turned out, and Trinity Church, Boston, came top. So there he was: the unchallenged No. 1 in his profession, living within a mile or two of Boston, the architectural metropolis of the United States, and among the cultural elite of the country. Who can blame him if he wanted to redefine the potential of American architecture before he died? What less could be expected of his ardent nature, his inexhaustible ambition, and his sense of societal involvement?

Nor did he find his duties too burdensome. He was a quick study and an even quicker worker. When he was asked in 1885 to do the J. J. Glessner house in Chicago, he took a day or so to think about it. Then, according to Glessner's memoirs, he came to dinner.

When the last course of dinner was being removed before dessert, he called for pencil and paper, saying, "If you won't ask me how I get into it, I will draw the plan of your

124

commissioned in September 1875 and finished in 1876. In 1882–83 he designed the Ames Building in Bedford Street, Boston, for his friend and patron F. L. Ames. If, in every one of these, the forms of long ago were mated with the needs of the late nineteenth century, it was in part because Richardson was determined to uphold what he saw as the canons of great art in the face of architectural practices that were shoddy and mindless to an extreme degree. He upheld those canons for all to see, in exterior elevations that were rarely without strength of mass and distinction of detail; but he also upheld them where almost nobody would see the result—in the central light-well of the Cheney Building, for instance, where the decorative ironwork was like Victorian lace.

There was something paradoxical, even so, in the repeated use of eleventh- and twelfth-century forms in a newly industrialized society. Furthermore, ornamental masonry of the kind that Richardson favored was very expensive. And it served no commercial purpose whatever: who needs balconies, castellations, crocketing, and asymmetrical towers in a department store? There is a point at which practical unfitness overlaps upon aesthetic unfitness and, by way of that, upon moral unfitness. Richardson would never have expressed himself in those terms, but for whatever reason, we

undeniably detect a certain flight from ornament in his last years—above all in what many people now see as his masterpiece, the Wholesale Store for Marshall Field in Chicago.

The Field store represented a particular challenge to Richardson. "There is no public building in Chicago worth seeing," he wrote to his son late in 1885, thereby omitting his own American Merchant's Union Express Building—whether from modesty or from a specific distaste it is now impossible to say. Chicago was, therefore, the place of all places in which a blow could be struck for a new architecture. Richardson was still, and would remain to the end of his too-few days, a masonry man: someone who thought of architecture initially in terms of masonry bearing walls. The Field building had an iron skeleton internally, but in all that could be seen from the street, it was a stone building, with the full thickness of the red Missouri granite walls revealed at second-floor-window height.

We today see the long-vanished Field building with eyes that have over and over again seen plainness in architecture raised to the point of sublimity. But Richardson's contemporaries had never before seen a comparable plainness in a commercial building that filled a whole city block. "The Field Building," said Mrs. Van Rensselaer, "is

This bleak fortress of nineteenth-century justice was designed by Richardson in 1884 as the center for law enforcement in Allegheny County, Pennsylvania. From the courthouse prisoners passed over a "bridge of sighs" to the jail at right. In its stern message to criminals, no less than in its architectural mass, the jail yields nothing to a medieval donjon.

the vast rectangular box in its most uncompromising estate." But with her habitual fine discernment she also noted that "its prime virtues of a solidity commensurate with its elevation and a dignity equal to its bulk are secured in such a way that even a high degree of beauty is not wanting."

Though stark by comparison with some of Richardson's more flamboyant buildings, the Field store is not without its delicacies of detail. Nor in those delicacies did Richardson forbear his ancient loyalty to southern European models. ("Zargossa [sic] cornice," he noted on one particularly handsome sketch now in the Houghton Library in Harvard.) But the overtones of chivalric splendor had been dropped, and in their place there was a new preoccupation. As in other buildings of the mid-1880's, Richardson in the Field building aimed at what he called "a careful study of the piers and a perfectly quiet and massive treatment of the wall surfaces." "Quiet and massive" are not the first words that come to mind when we think of Richardson. "Busty and vivacious" might be more apt, indeed, for the swelling masses and the chatterboxy detail with which he liked to keep the eye consistently alert and amazed. But in his last years there was a marked falling-off in his tendency to "throw the book" at us. (For once that phrase can be used literally, in that Richardson relied for many of his antiquarian motifs on the superb architectural library that he had formed in Paris and elsewhere, as well as—for more recent exemplars—on issues of English architectural magazines.)

He himself thought particularly well of the "quiet and massive" qualities of the Allegheny County Buildings in Pittsburgh, which occupied his firm from 1884 until two years after his own death. The buildings in question are a combination of courthouse and jail. Charm would no doubt be out of place in a complex of this kind, and Richardson ruled out one aspect of charm by choosing a grayish Milford granite instead of the warmer and more varied kinds of stone that he used with such dexterity elsewhere. His jail is one of the more sinister constructions of its kind. One would have to be very sure of the infallibility of justice not to shiver at the evident relish with which Richardson, that kindest of men, made quite sure that the men and women who were sentenced in his courthouse would be committed forthwith to a living tomb. His mastery of mass and his sense of the spectacular are here mustered in the interests of

This baronial entrance hall graced the house that Richardson built for Secretary of State John Hay in Washington, D.C. The Hay house and Henry Adams's house, also by Richardson, shared a façade on Lafayette Square; built together in 1884, they were razed in 1927 to make room for the Hay-Adams Hotel.

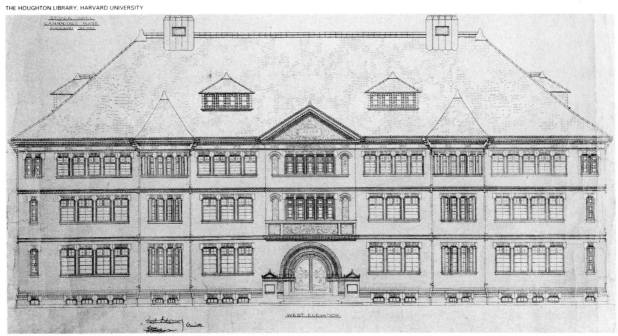

Sever Hall was executed entirely in red brick, supposedly to blend with the colonial buildings of Harvard Yard. The ornamental structures flanking the low, heavy Syrian entrance arch were eliminated before construction.

one thing only: the punishment by men of other men, and their banishment from the sight of all other human beings.

No doubt these matters looked different a hundred years ago, when a watchtower was a necessary element in prison life, rather than a reminder of Belsen and Auschwitz. Even Mrs. Van Rensselaer went along with the general tenor of the design, and thought, for instance, that "the vast voussoirs which Richardson brought home in his mind from Spain are as appropriate in a modern prison door as in ancient portals of defense." Once we think of punishment in terms of panoply, the Allegheny County Buildings, as they were euphemistically called, are indeed a masterpiece in their category; and they have just the kind of Dickensian overstatement that society asked of its prisons in late Victorian times.

Among the later buildings in which Richardson sought for an ordered simplicity, Sever Hall at Harvard stands out. In contrast to the robust and outgoing character of so many of his eclectic constructions, Sever Hall has an aristocratic reticence and a perfection of detail that are all the more noticeable for being executed in one unvarying color—red—and one unvarying material—brick. Red mortar and orange-tiled roofs carry through the same chromatic motif, which was doubtless adopted out of deference to Harvard's older buildings. As Richardson was also guided by current Harvard practice in his management of the interior spaces, it follows that in this subdued and unrhetorical building he put aside the tumult of the senses to which his admirers had grown accustomed. In Sever Hall (and, to a lesser extent, in its successor at Harvard, Austin Hall) Richardson associated the act of learning both with momentous entrances and exits and with a calm, ordered, flowing continuity of external forms. In Austin Hall he thought hard about polychrome decoration, but in general these two buildings were designed *suaviter in modo, fortiter in re.* Richardson was one of nature's educators and—whether in his Harvard buildings or in designing small public libraries—his touch was never happier than when he was making it easier and more agreeable for people to learn.

It would be difficult, and perhaps pointless, to define any one style as "late Richardson." Richardson in the 1880's spread himself very thin, and, like every other architect with a large office, he sometimes took work to keep the office busy. But there is here and there a sovereign plainness that could have come from no other hand but his. The arklike Emmanuel Church of 1885–6 in Pittsburgh is a particularly cogent example. So is the use, in the Stoughton house in Cambridge, and elsewhere, of unornamented shingle as an exterior covering. The severe but hospitable spaces of the Boston and Albany Railroad station at Chestnut Hill could also be adduced as an example of a purified and slimmed-down "late Richardson" idiom.

But no sooner would that be said than other and contradictory evidence would come to mind. Richardson in his last years was a master of the custom-built one-family house. As if still in reaction against the angelic but predictable rectangular living spaces that had been put about by Davis and others in the 1840's and 1850's, Richardson in the Paine house in Waltham, the Hay house in Washington, and others, devised huge baronial halls with staircases wide enough for swordplay and decoration that shamed the oriental rugs on the floor. Forgotten was the slablike form of the Field store, banished, the holy stillness of the Emmanuel Church. Here, as elsewhere, Richardson defies definition. "Like a legendary hero"—I quote from Hitchcock—"he lived for new problems, dreaming of ice-houses and river boats to conquer while the smooth machine of his office turned out the late buildings to which his name was signed."

He was, of course, mortally ill. Had he not died, and had he retained the radiant good health on which people remarked in his youth, he could have lived through World War I. What we fail to define as "late Richardson" might by then have seemed like a transitional phase in a more-than-fifty-years' activity. As it is, the career of Henry Hobson Richardson is one of the great unfinished poems of American cultural history, and Richardson himself is one of America's lost leaders: a man who almost singlehandedly brought architecture from its position as hardly more than a subdepartment of contracting to the very front rank of the professions. Let us hope that somewhere in the Elysian fields Richardson is dining today, as he so often dined in life, off a magnum of champagne and an untold quantity of very good cheese.

Accepting the architectural challenge of an increasingly industrial society, Richardson in his last year of life designed the Marshall Field Wholesale Store in Chicago. In this simple masonry block, almost stripped of the ornamental and historical elements that had been his trademark, the eastern establishment architect gave new direction to midwestern design. Architects such as Jenney and Sullivan found inspiration in the Field store for the development of the Chicago skyscraper style.

FREDERICK LAW OLMSTED

Olmsted's plan for Jackson Park on the Chicago lake front, 1895

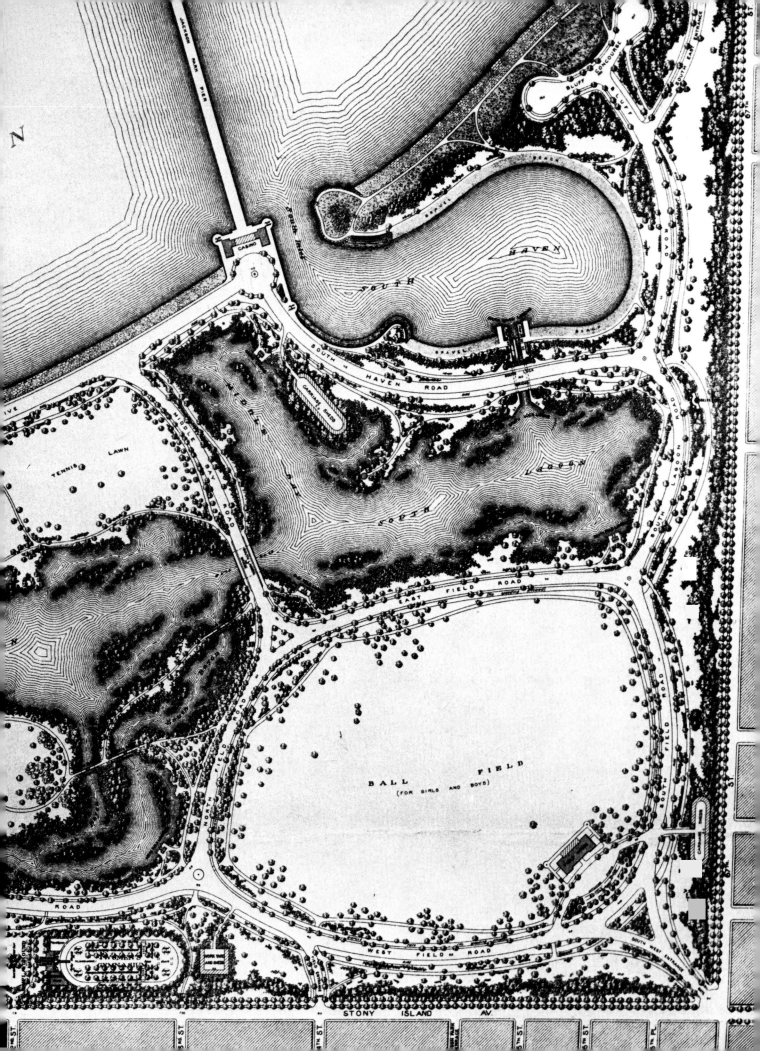

1822–1903

BY JOSEPH KASTNER

On the face of it, there seemed no reason why anyone should offer Frederick Law Olmsted the job of constructing a park in what would become the middle of New York City—the first such park in the city or, for that matter, in the whole country. Or why Olmsted should go on from this to design a park that marvelously suited New York in his time and has saved the city in ours. Or why he should go on from there, while creating the profession of landscape architecture in the United States, to leave his inerasable mark on the cities, towns, and even the wildernesses of America.

When that New York job was casually proposed to him in the summer of 1857, Olmsted was thirty-five and had worked as an apprentice surveyor, a bookkeeper, a seaman, a farmer, a publisher, and a writer of books of travel and social reporting. He was, in fact, finishing his latest book at a Connecticut seaside resort when he met a friend who was serving on the New York park commission. Over tea, the commissioner described the project to Olmsted and worried that they had not been able to find a satisfactory superintendent. Listening to Olmsted's questions and suggestions, he remarked: "I wish we had you on the commission, but, as we do not, why not take the superintendency yourself?"

"Till he asked the question," Olmsted later recalled, "the possibility of my doing so had never occurred to me. I at once answered, however, smiling: 'I take it? I'm not sure that I wouldn't if it were offered me.'"

"Well, it will not be offered you," the friend replied. "That's not the way we do business; but if you'll go to work, I believe you may get it."

The salary was $1,500 a year, and Olmsted, needing a job and money, went to work, which meant getting the support of important friends. He

When this photograph was taken in the early 1860's, Olmsted was doing double duty as the designer of Central Park and the superintendent of its construction.

wound up with the endorsements of Washington Irving, Peter Cooper, William Cullen Bryant, Whitelaw Reid, Horace Greeley, August Belmont, and a few dozen others. They knew him largely as a literary man—and some members of the commission held this against him. They finally voted him the position, but they must have left the meeting wondering just what it was that Olmsted had done to earn this huge job of urban landscaping.

Olmsted himself wondered over the matter, and many years later—when his contemporaries were acknowledging that "no American had been more useful in his time than Frederick Olmsted or has made a more valuable and lasting contribution to civilization in his country"—he suggested an answer. "My pleasure in landscape," he declared, "began to be affected by conditions at an early age, even before I began to connect the cause and effect of enjoyment in it."

It started with his father, a well-off merchant of Hartford, Connecticut, who shared his feeling for nature with his son—"a bothering little chap," Olmsted remembered himself. He took Fred along on long excursions through the countryside, by carriage, horse, and canal boat. From these trips and from visits to his uncle in Geneseo, New York, Frederick's mind was filled with an enormous index of images—of "being sometimes driven rapidly and silently over the turf of the bottom lands among great trees," of stopping at "a house in the dooryard of which there was a fawn and at which a beautiful woman gave me sweetmeats."

Though he dearly loved his son, Mr. Olmsted was an emotionally removed man and sent Fred away for schooling to half a dozen clergymen whose rote learning and pious discipline did little for Fred's formal education. The boy was a wanderer, rambling through the countryside, getting to know, as he put it, "interesting rivers, brooks, meadows, rocks, woods, mountains . . . pleasant old gardens" and making friends with a rural scholar "of musing, contemplative habits," who loved "Virgil and took pleasure in reading and translating him to me."

A self-taught reader, he was taken with two books he came upon in a library—by Uvedale Price and by William Gilpin—on the subject of picturesque landscapes. Another, *Solitude*—"one of the best books ever written," he said enthusiastically— was by a crotchety Swiss named Johann Georg von Zimmermann, who, though longing for the seclusion of country life, admitted that "the world is the only theater upon which great and noble actions can be performed."

A bad case of sumac poisoning blinded Fred for a while and kept him from entering Yale. Apprenticed at fifteen (in 1837) to an engineer, he learned

133

something of surveying and dealing with land. Sent to a New York silk merchant, he worked diligently as a bookkeeper for a year and a half. Then, signing on as a seaman, he sailed to China, enduring seasickness, scurvy, typhoid, and the brutal shipboard discipline.

Back from the sea, lagging behind his friends in schooling, and dependent on his father for upkeep, Fred studied at Yale in a desultory way, getting a smattering of chemistry, geology, and botany, but then decided to be a farmer. He learned what was called "scientific farming" and then took over a farm in Guilford, Connecticut, whose house, as Olmsted described it, was "nasty" and whose land was "juicy." Setting out to retrieve the property, Fred brought a drawing of a proposed house to Alexander Jackson Davis, who thought the design lacked character and sketched him a Gothic Revival farmhouse. But before he could get much done, Fred bought (with his father's money) a larger farm on Staten Island, across the harbor from New York.

"The whole place was as dirty and disorderly as the most bucolic person could desire," a friend wrote. "Fred moved the barns behind a knoll. He brought the road in so that it approached the house by a gentle curve. He turfed the borders of the pond and planted water plants on its edge and shielded it from contamination. Thus, with a few strokes and at small expense he transformed the place from a very dirty, disagreeable farmyard to a gentleman's house."

He also showed ability as a manager. "He introduced system and order to his men," wrote the young lady who would marry Fred's brother and, when widowed, would marry Fred. His men were taught that "at knocking-off time every tool used should be returned to its appointed place and that every chore should be done at the hour fixed."

He was a good farmer and a helpful neighbor. His wheat and turnips won prizes, but his land benefited more than his pocketbook. Even a fine crop did not justify the thirty-four dollars an acre he spent to improve his wheat fields. Still, his neighbors, impressed by his landscaping, asked him how to improve the looks and convenience of their farms. He lived half on the farm, half in the nearby city. His college friends were there and led him into their cultivated circles. One of them, Charles Loring Brace, who founded the Children's Aid Society, showed him the darker side—the hopeless poor, the homeless children. The city was, to Olmsted, "an immense vat of misery."

With money coaxed from his father, he went with his brother and Brace on a tour of the British Isles. His easy ways with people made him quick

friends. One of them, a baker in Birkenhead, a suburb of Liverpool, who had gotten into a discussion of the relative merits of French and American flour, begged him not to leave Birkenhead without seeing its New Park. Olmsted was astonished to find, in this unprepossessing community, a park with "winding paths, constantly varying surfaces, every variety of shrubs and flowers with more than natural grace, large valleys made verdant." And "this magnificent pleasure ground is entirely, unreservedly, and forever the people's own. The poorest British peasant is as free to enjoy it all as the British queen." In the book he later wrote about his trip, he was moved to compose a paean to the art of landscaping:

What artist so noble as he who, with far reaching conception of beauty and designing power, sketches the outline, writes the colors, and directs the shadows of a picture so great that nature shall be employed on it for generations before the works he has arranged for her shall realize his intentions.

Having written this unmistakable signal to himself, he ignored it and went back to farming. He did take time to write *Walks and Talks of an American Farmer in England*, which was well received. Andrew Jackson Downing, the apostle of landscape design and the Gothic Revival, published some of it in his magazine, the *Horticulturist*. Olmsted paid a long visit to him and met his partner, Calvert Vaux.

Feeling that a farmer should have a wife, Olmsted became engaged to a young lady of Hartford but chose not to announce the engagement because he was faced with a bumper crop of cabbages—60,000 heads—and wanted to concentrate on selling them. Before the engagement could be announced or the cabbages sold, his fiancée broke it off and not long after married a young preacher named Hale, who was to write *The Man Without a Country*.

Impressed by Olmsted's book, in which Olmsted had paid almost as much attention to social as agricultural conditions, the *New York Times* assigned him to travel through the South and report on the effects of slavery on the region's agriculture and economics. Olmsted went off with an open mind: he was opposed both to slavery and to outright abolition, favoring a gradual emancipation. During 1853 and 1854 he made two southern trips, from Virginia through Texas, and wrote about them, under the signature "Yeoman," for the *Times* and later for the New York *Herald*. No writer had given a fresher, more acute or unprejudiced picture of the prewar South. "He talked to everybody," said the critic Edmund Wilson, "and he sized up everything, and he wrote it all down."

His readers saw the shacks and mansions of the South, heard the courtly talk of plantation owners and the coarse conversation of the poor whites. They learned of the slaveholder's easy affection for his slaves, but learned, too, of his impersonal cruelty, in Olmsted's coolly controlled description of the beating of a malingering slave girl:

The manager struck her thirty or forty blows across the shoulders with his tough flexible, "raw-hide" whip. . . . "You have not got enough yet?" said he. "Pull up your clothes—lie down." The girl without a word or look of remonstrance or entreaty lay down. The overseer continued to flog her across her naked loins and thighs. She cried, "Oh, God, master, do stop!" . . . The overseer said: "She meant to cheat me out of a day's work."

Olmsted concluded that slavery was not a blessing for the South's economy but a burden—inefficient and oppressive, as frustrating for owner as for slave. He published the reports of his trips in three books, later bringing them together in his classic *The Cotton Kingdom.* They had a significant impact in their time in both the United States and England—Charles Darwin, for one, was very impressed by them. Forgotten for almost a century, the books have become by now an invaluable and trusted source for historians.

While his writing established Olmsted as a social observer of first importance, it left him impatient with the chores of farming, which, in fact, he had been foisting off on his brother and foremen. In 1855 he turned the farm over to his brother and was taken in, more for his money than his skills, to a book publishing firm which also put out *Putnam's Monthly Magazine,* for a brief while the brightest literary magazine in the country. Olmsted proved useful in dealing with contributors such as Longfellow and Melville and in finding new authors, but the firm failed, leaving Olmsted jobless and in debt. At that point he went off to Morris Cove, Connecticut, to work on one of his own books and there met his friend the park commissioner.

The concept of a large public park deliberately set down in a big city was novel and daring in America in the 1850's. London's famous public parks, like Saint James's Park and Hyde Park, had been royal preserves, which, over the centuries, were opened to the public. But public parks were now being designed from scratch. Regent's Park in London was put together by adjacent landholders who realized it would enhance the value of their property. Birkenhead, which Olmsted had visited, had a less selfish motive. Several German cities, too, had for some years been setting aside land for parks.

The nearest thing to them in America were the new cemeteries—Mount Auburn near Boston, Laurel Hill in Philadelphia, Greenwood in Brooklyn—which had become places where people could stroll on Sundays, taking pleasure in green and open spaces. New York, Andrew Downing pointed out, "had contented itself with little dooryards of space, mere grassplots of verdure which form the squares of the city in the mistaken idea that they are parks." Downing led the movement for a proper park and was joined by William Cullen Bryant, poet of nature and editor of the New York *Evening Post.* In 1853, after considerable maneuvering and changes of plan, the city began purchasing (for an eventual seven million dollars) a rectangle of land stretching some two and a half miles north from Fifty-ninth Street and a half mile from Fifth to Eighth Avenues—open land still.

The motives for what was called "the central park" were, to say the least, mixed. High-minded citizens wanted permanent open space to relieve the city and provide a playground for its people. Politicians wanted the patronage it would bring. Businessmen wanted to provide jobs for thousands of unemployed, volatile Irish immigrants given to strikes and riots. Bryant wanted to preserve some of the places where he loved to walk, and less ambulatory citizens wanted a place to drive their carriages. Adjoining property owners wanted to clean out the squatters and slaughterhouses that had moved in. As for the plain people, for whom the park was so nobly and democratically intended, they complained that the rich were fixing things so as to keep them out. The well-off worried that the poor would take over the park for their unkempt pleasures.

Preliminary work was already under way on the park when Olmsted, as the new superintendent, paid a courtesy call on the chief engineer. Looking at his new aide dressed in gentleman's clothes, the engineer said bluntly that "he would rather have a practical man" and sent him right out to be hazed by an assistant—"Mr. Hawkin, a cautious close-mouthed gentleman," as Olmsted described him, "with trousers tucked in the legs of a heavy and dirty pair of boots. My conductor exhibited his practical ability by leading me through the midst of a number of vile sloughs. I had not been aware that the park was such a very nasty place. The low grounds were steeped in the overflow and mush of pig sties, slaughterhouses and bone-boiling works, and the stench was sickening."

When they came to groups of workmen, Hawkin would say, "This is Mr. Olmsted, you'll be taking orders from him after this."

"Oh, that's the man, is it?" one workman responded. "Expect we shall be pushed up now."

And pushed up they were—but not in ways they were used to. Olmsted, who had worked with

Irish laborers on his farm, knew how to handle them. Since park jobs were assigned by ward politicians, Olmsted had no power to discharge them. He found it better to assume that an offender was guilty only of "ignorance and forgetfulness and urge him to give more attendance to his duties." Reacting to this unheard-of treatment, the workmen began to take an interest and even a pride in their work. Olmsted chose foremen shrewdly, laid out work so that it showed quick results, and infected subordinates with his enthusiasm. His scattered experiences began to come into focus—the rudiments of surveying, the detailed discipline of bookkeeping, the toughness he had found on shipboard, the techniques of earthmoving and drainage he had acquired on the farm, his easy ability to approach many kinds of people, the images of nature he had stored up in America and Europe. Within six months, he wrote his father, "I have got the system working like a machine. The confidence of the commission in me has constantly increased and my salary raised to $2,000."

And in an offhand sentence, which held the future both of Frederick Olmsted and American landscape architecture, he added: "I am greatly interested in planning the park."

The park work had been going on without a

In laying out a park Olmsted liked to provide a meadow where people and sheep could mingle in pastoral contentment. This photograph was taken in Prospect Park, Brooklyn, in 1914.

satisfactory plan, and the commission announced a competition for a design with a prize of $2,500. Olmsted's interest in entering a design was aroused by Calvert Vaux, whom Olmsted had first met at Downing's home. After Downing died, Vaux had carried on his partner's work, gaining a considerable reputation as architect and landscaper. Now he proposed that he and the new superintendent collaborate on a plan for the park.

There were stringent problems to be solved. The long, narrow shape of the area was a straitjacket. Much of the land was swampy and treeless, so unattractive that nobody but squatters had built on it. The soil was poor, thin, and broken everywhere by rocky outcroppings. The two-and-a-half mile stretch presented an unacceptable barrier to crosstown traffic. And the demands on the park were rigid and contradictory. It had to be a driving place for the well-off, an airing place for the poor. It had to be handsomely landscaped yet sturdily built to withstand constant and thoughtless usage. There had to be places where people could get away from each other and places where they could congregate, open meadows and paved ceremonial grounds, lakes for rowing and skating, playing fields for the active, and lawns for the idlers. It had to keep out the feeling of the city but invite the people in.

With a full-time job as superintendent and with an unfriendly boss, Olmsted had to squeeze in time for design on nights and Sundays. Vaux took

care of much of the drudgery, and friends who dropped in to see how things were going were given his pens and put to work stippling grass in the endless stretches of lawn and meadow. Olmsted and Vaux worked beautifully together, and neither claimed more credit than the other. The impression remains, however, that the philosophy, the bold approaches, and the over-all concept came more from Olmsted, the details of execution and the architectural niceties, from Vaux. The expression of the philosophy behind the park was Olmsted's: "The park would be a single work of art framed upon a single noble motive to which the design of all its parts in some more or less subtle way shall be confluent and helpful."

The Olmsted and Vaux plan gave the southern section, whose terrain had no consistent character in itself, gentle natural treatment, with open walks winding around small groves, ponds for birds and boaters, secluded glades, and an enormous formal space for promenading. The nothern section, hilly and rough, was left as much as possible in its semiwild state. A low screen of trees and shrubs was planted around the perimeter to define the park but still not close it off. Roadways were gently curved to please carriage drivers but frustrate sporting bloods who kept demanding straightaways for their trotting races. The cross-park traffic was handled brilliantly by sinking four transverse roads below the park level. There was opposition to this. Commissioner August Belmont, known for his financial foresight, insisted there would never be enough traffic to justify the expense, but Olmsted convinced the commission otherwise.

Olmsted and Vaux were shrewd in promoting their plan. To show off its beauty and ingenuity, they brought in a thirty-foot-long rendering with attractive before-and-after sketches. To emphasize its practicality, they showed that they could offset the heavy expenses of blasting by using the rock for park roadbeds, and dispose of the smelly muck from sties and abattoirs by using it to enrich newly filled-in sections. And they gave their proposal the irresistible title of "Greensward."

They won the $2,500 award and Olmsted was appointed chief architect of Central Park. Continuing as superintendent as well as architect, Olmsted made day-to-day changes as much on the spot with his gangs as at the drawing board with Vaux. A careless hole made by blasters would become an unplanned glade, a troublesome pile of dirt would turn into a grassy mound, a surplus of saplings into a noble grove. He worked on two levels. As designer, he said, he carried "a gallery of mental pictures and I constantly have before me, more or less distinctly, more or less vaguely, a picture which, as superintendent, I am constantly laboring

to realize." He could see in himself now the figure he had conjured up after visiting England, that "noble artist-designer who would put nature to work for generations to "realize his intentions." In taking over the post as architect he declared: "I shall venture to assume to myself the title of artist."

More and more, as the park took shape, the title fitted him. Oliver Wendell Holmes recognized this and admired the way Olmsted had preserved the park's inherent beauties. It was the "hips and elbows and other bones of nature," he said, that gave the park its character, and except for Olmsted's practical visions, the park would have "been flattened by art and money out of all its native features."

The physical problems of the park were easier to deal with, in many ways, than the political. Olmsted had to fight off ward leaders who demanded more and more patronage, well-meaning civic leaders who wanted to fill the park with good works like world's fairs and museums, honest penny pinchers who begrudged the money spent, righteous Sabbatarians who wanted the park closed on Sundays. Olmsted grew tactful in dealing with do-gooders and wily in giving politicans no more than he had to. Friendly with the editors and writers of the city, he got a good press and the strong support of the city's elite, who kept coming up to watch proudly as the park took shape.

George Templeton Strong, a cultivated lawyer who kept an invaluable diary of the period, noted in his entry for June 11, 1859:

Footpaths and plantations are finished, more or less, . . . though now in most ragged condition: 'lakes' without water, mounds of compost, piles of blasted stone, acres of what may be greensward hereafter but is now mere brown earth; groves of slender young transplanted maples and locusts undecided between life and death. . . . caravans of dirt carts, derricks, steam engines. . . . Rounds and paths twist about in curves of artistic tortuosity.

A few months later he wrote: "Great progress. The ragged desert of out-blasted rock, cat briars, and stone heaps begins to blossom like a rose. Many beautiful oases of path and garden. . . . Some three thousand men are employed and there are no idlers."

The pressures of keeping the work going bore down on Olmsted. Overworked, beset by politicians, lamed by a carriage accident, he was able to go on largely because he had, at the age of thirty-seven, finally married—the widow of his younger brother. Mary Olmsted was a woman of warm but independent mind, able to support her husband and to stand up to him, and to withstand the loneliness his work would impose. She already had three children whom Olmsted took on as his own. They added another son and daughter.

Text continues on page 140

137

The Greensward Plan

The site of Central Park was a wasteland when Olmsted and Calvert Vaux entered the competition for its design. In their presentation they juxtaposed these "before" and "after" pictures: on this page, photographs of two sections of the area; and on the opposite page, oil paintings of the landscapes they would create in those same places.

Periodically, Olmsted felt he had to quit the park job but was persuaded to stay. In 1861 he took a leave to assume a Civil War job which, if that were all he had ever done, would still give him a significant place in American history.

He was made director of a fledgling organization called the United States Sanitary Commission, which later became the American Red Cross. Its assignment was to "aid the sick and wounded" of the Union army and to insure the "comfort and security" of the troops, who were wretchedly housed, poorly fed, and shockingly undisciplined. It grew into an indispensable medical corps. As director, Olmsted had to fight off the hindrances of the army's own doddering medical corps, which could not do the job itself and wanted no help from outside. He got only halfhearted support at first from Lincoln. But the first battle of Bull Run brought the president and his generals to their senses. Olmsted's report, so scathing that the commission would not distribute it lest it hinder recruiting, described how the army broke down into a "disintegrated herd of sick monomaniacs."

Accepted less grudgingly as he proved the commission's worth, Olmsted was everywhere— supervising the work on the battlefield, in his office soliciting money and volunteers. Going along on the futile Peninsular Campaign, Olmsted turned rat-ridden ships into hospitals, steeled genteel lady nurses to brave the bloody horrors, took in the

140

wounded by the freight car load and sailed them off to central hospitals. He dealt firmly and angrily with generals and bureaucrats, affectionately with wounded soldiers. When beef broth ran low, orderlies went out to shoot local cows and bring their carcasses in. "He is small and lame," wrote an aide to Olmsted. "His face is generally placid and would be beautiful if not perhaps a little too severe. He is a very wise man, born an autocrat."

He "works like a dog all day," wrote George Templeton Strong, who was treasurer of the Sanitary Commission, "sits up nearly all night . . . for five days and nights altogether, . . . sleeps on a sofa in his clothes, and breakfasts on strong coffee and pickles!" He had, Strong said, "talent and

By the winter of 1865 skaters were thronging to the lake in Central Park, and sleigh riders were using the snowy slopes above it. The square-shaped storage tanks that held the city's water supply were later replaced by the Great Lawn and the present reservoir.

energy most rare; absolute purity and disinterestedness, . . . a monomania for system."

His autocratic ways finally led to a break with the commission, and in 1863, having turned his unwieldy volunteer commission into a force that the very life of the Union army depended on, he left his post. The acrimony of the parting was softened when the commission wrote Olmsted that it was "inexpressibly grieved at the thought of parting with you."

Olmsted went to a new project and place—to California, to manage for a group of New York investors a large and lawless tract of mining land called the Mariposa Estate, whose gold and silver lodes never produced the bonanzas they promised. Originally owned by John Charles Frémont, the fabled Pathfinder of the West, it had been neglected and mismanaged. It took Olmsted a year and a half to realize that the mines would never pay and that the investors were not interested in his far-seeing proposal to develop the land's other assets. But the job enriched his own visions. Put off at first by the scale of the wilderness, he came finally to appreciate it. The ancient groves of sequoias exhilarated him—"you feel that they are distinguished strangers, have come down to us from another world." Heading a state commission set up to determine the future of two great tracts of public land, Yosemite Valley and Mariposa Big Tree Grove, he wrote a report that proposed that the lands be kept as parks in their pristine state while being made reasonably accessible to the people. The establishment by government of great public grounds for the free enjoyment of the people "is justified and enforced as a public duty," he wrote, drawing up what became, in effect, the charter for the country's national park system.

While still at Mariposa, Olmsted was notified that he had been named to head the new Freedmen's Bureau, set up to handle the complex task of dealing with the freed slaves. Had he accepted, he might have affected the course of Reconstruction as he had changed the course of army medical practice. But he turned the post down. He also turned down a full-time job as an editor of the *Nation*, which he had helped found.

He went instead back to Central Park. In the fall of 1865 the firm of "Olmsted, Vaux & Co., Landscape Architects, No. 110 Broadway" was set up. In doing this, the two put a firm base under a new American profession and raised their calling, as Olmsted put it, "from the rank of a trade, even of a handicraft, to that of a liberal profession—an art, an art of design."

There had been no true American landscape architects before Downing—there were horticulturists who laid out gardens, but their scope and

To meet the needs of cross-town traffic, Olmsted and Vaux sank transverse roads below ground level; Seventy-ninth Street (above) runs under a bridge of natural rock. The designers fought to preserve "natural, in preference to artificial, beauty." When they had to provide such formal features as the Terrace (right), they blended the stonework into the landscape.

purpose were limited. Downing, concerned with "scenery making," was given more to precepts than practice. The need, however, had been established, and a few architects had set up as landscapers. During his stay at Mariposa Olmsted himself had done several landscaping designs, including a cemetery for Oakland. While Olmsted was away, Vaux had kept a part-time eye on Central Park and had been approached not only to resume as full-time architect there but to develop another large site, Prospect Park in Brooklyn.

Prospect Park became, in its way, as much of a landmark as Central Park. More varied and interesting in terrain to begin with, it needed different treatment—"the maintenance as exactly as possible of the natural scenery," Olmsted decreed. Where Central Park was a marvel of created urban

landscape, Prospect Park was a paradigm of the preserved, setting a pattern for the quasi-picturesque treatment of city parks everywhere in the country.

Central Park was already recognized as a major event in urban history, and cities everywhere stirred themselves to follow New York's example. Institutions and colleges began to understand that the design of the grounds needed as much expert attention as that of the buildings. Even hardheaded land speculators were recognizing this.

Clients coming into Olmsted and Vaux expecting a quick layout for lawns, flower beds, and groves were startled and impatient when the two insisted on going out to study the terrain, the soil, the climate, the surroundings, probing to find out what uses were expected and what could be added.

Olmsted took into account not just the looks of the land but the ways it could enhance the well-being, moral as well as physical, of the whole community. He spoke of creating places "for rational enjoyment," of designing parks that would show a "sympathy with human gaiety and playfulness," of making "improvements by design which nature might by chance." To some clients he seemed to be planning not a park in a city but a city around a park—which, indeed, to his enduring credit, he more and more did.

Olmsted always insisted that Vaux was the artist of the team while he concentrated on the social aspects of their work. He was, perhaps, trying to build up Vaux's importance, because although the two generally got on well together, most of the public credit went to the more articulate and widely known Olmsted. From time to time Vaux broke out with his resentment, only partly appeased when Olmsted declared that "I should have been nowhere" without Vaux. After the two ended their partnership in 1872, they remained friends and occasional collaborators until, on a foggy day in 1895, Vaux fell or walked off a pier in Brooklyn and drowned.

Accustomed to dealing with generals and high officials, Olmsted found no trouble negotiating with the new generation of American wealth and industry. His clients, he made plain, had to look on him as an equal, not a hired hand. He could afford to be independent. He was always being offered jobs as business executive, college president, editor. He was even nominated, without his knowledge or permission, to be vice president on a splinter ticket—and was so embarrassed that he hid from reporters who came to ask him about it. For the first time in his life he was out of debt and financially comfortable. His firm charged as much as $5,000 for a first plan. Sometimes, in developing tracts for builders, it took lots instead of cash.

His first big land-developing job, in 1868, was planning a whole community, Riverside, along the edge of the Des Plaines River near Chicago. Looking back at the design Alexander Davis had helped make for Llewellyn Park in West Orange, New Jersey, Olmsted and Vaux used the shallow river as a focus, laid out long curving drives, clumps of trees, safe walks, houses comfortably but not distantly separated—in all, a place which did not pretend to be rural but still did not smack of suburb. He foresightedly proposed a parkway to connect Riverside to Chicago. The Riverside plan was a little too idealized for the promoters and the Chicago fire stopped work. When resumed, it kept to Olmsted's idea, and today, engulfed by the city, it still accomplishes what he set out to do—and has inspired many twentieth-century garden-city communities.

When Olmsted was born, nine of ten Americans lived a rural life, and Olmsted grew up a Jeffersonian, writing that "rural pursuits tend to elevate and enlarge the ideas." In the 1870's one of three Americans lived in cities, and Olmsted would write that the country's welfare would now depend "on the convenience, safety, order, and economy of life in its great cities." He was forced to become a city planner, the first in America. He fought with small success against the gridiron system, which forced straight streets and square blocks on any terrain, imposing narrow building plots and cutting clumsily across slopes and hills. The dreadful sanitation, choking traffic, increasing crime—all were his concern. And he argued endlessly that cities should acquire not just one site for a park but several for a unified park system.

Buffalo, New York, listened to him, building a series of parks, large and small, which were joined by tree-lined avenues. Boston went along with him as he turned a local complaint into a regional park system. Called in to do something about the marshy area of the Back Bay known as the Fens, which periodically flooded with sewage-poisoned waters, he first took care of the flooding. Digging and filling to create both solid land and an adequate flood plain, he turned a pestilential place into a marshy park. Then by means of boulevards he linked existing and potential park space, giving the city a string of parks clear out into the suburbs— "the emerald necklace," he called it.

Olmsted saved the World's Columbian Exposition of 1893 from becoming on overbearing display of masonry. On the site near the Chicago lake front, he designed this graceful lagoon and, in its center, a wooded island with gardens and small buildings.

In Washington he was asked to finish a job that Downing had barely started a quarter century before: to make sense out of the grounds around the Capitol. Olmsted faced a complicated and tedious problem. Some two dozen streets came into the grounds. Their traffic had to be taken care of. So did the thousands of Americans who, coming proudly to see the seat of their government, were usually oppressed by the summer heat and let down by the graceless backside of the Capitol. To give them the comfort they needed, Olmsted provided pleasant walkways and trees thick enough to offer shade but not so tall as to cut off views. To give them the grandeur they expected, he dreamed up a marble terrace to run around three sides of the Capitol, culminating on the west side in a majestic flight of marble steps.

When Downing had run into trouble with a balky bureaucracy, he had simply had President Millard Fillmore call in the Cabinet to listen to what Downing wanted—and meekly give approval. Olmsted had a stronger-willed Congress to deal with. To show them the final effect he built a wooden mockup of the proposed terrace and slyly pointed out that the addition would provide more and bigger offices for members.

Approval came, but actual appropriations lagged. Bit by bit, Olmsted managed to get at the massive grading, draining, pulling out and replanting, trying to give some coherence to the mall's piebald architecture. Eventually it got done.

By necessity, Olmsted became a lobbyist. When his plan to save Niagara Falls from erosion and industrial encroachment ran into trouble, he helped organize the first coherent conservation campaign to rouse an apathetic and hostile legislature. "Save Niagara" committees suddenly appeared all over New York State. Speakers went out to exhort Americans to rescue their natural wonder. Pamphlets were mailed by the ton, editors were besieged with articles and letters, preachers were offered appropriate texts for sermons. After a while it seemed both unpatriotic and sacrilegious to let the falls go. They were saved, and, said one of the campaigners, "the indispensable factor was Olmsted's thought."

He was still not content, now in his sixties, to sit in the office and draw plans on paper. His commissions would take him to Maine for a campus; Baltimore for a housing development; Montreal for a mountain park; Syracuse for a cemetery; Philadelphia for an army arsenal; Waverly, Massachusetts, for the McLean Asylum; Louisville for a woodland park; Staten Island for an ambitious regional plan; Albany for the capitol and grounds; Boston for the Arnold Arboretum; Brooklyn for a racetrack; North Easton, Massachusetts, for

a memorial; Lenox and Stockbridge, Massachusetts, for private estates; Garfield, Utah, for a Union Pacific hotel development. He argued endlessly with Leland Stanford, who wanted to put up an elm-shaded New England campus on the dry California hills at Palo Alto, and winning as much as he lost, Olmsted did persuade the headstrong Californian that the ambiance required a Mediterranean treatment—arcades, quadrangles, paved areas, native plants.

In the late 1870's Olmsted seemed to sag for a while, losing not only his energy but the heartfelt enthusiasm that always kept him going. He finally gave up Central Park, a constant drain on him. With Vaux gone, he took in young partners, among them his stepson John and then his own son, Frederick, Jr. In 1881 he moved his home and office to Brookline, a suburb of Boston. This revived him as he went on to his two last, grandiose jobs, one for millions of Americans, the other for a single visionary millionaire.

He was called in, with the firm of Burnham and Root, to design the Chicago World's Fair of 1893 and became, said Burnham, "in the highest sense, the planner of the exposition." Years earlier he had presented Chicago with a plan for making something of Jackson Park, a nondescript, boggy area bordering Lake Michigan. Settling now on this site—the fair's commissioners thought it made no sense at all—he made marshes into lagoons and islands; he gave the fairgoers vantage places to take in the great White City and shaded seats to give their feet respite from trudging. It was a consummate bit of specialized landscaping, and when it was all over, and the buildings torn down, Olmsted had presented the city with a ready-made lakeside park.

His historic private commission was for George Vanderbilt, who had ideas to match his inherited wealth. Near Asheville, North Carolina, he had bought some 125,000 acres of worn-out woodland. He had commissioned a 255-room French Renaissance château from Richard Morris Hunt but didn't know how to deal with the land. Had he done something foolish? he asked Olmsted. Well, Olmsted replied, the woods "are miserable," the topography not fitted for a park. The only thing that might be done is to make it into a forest preserve—"a suitable and dignified business" for a young man of wealth, and "of great value" as an example to the country.

And thus, surely not without the idea already in his head, Olmsted set two forces in motion: the use of private wealth to promote public conservation, and the introduction of a concept of wise forest use. The man Olmsted took on to run the

Vanderbilt forest was young Gifford Pinchot, who after restoring Vanderbilt's woods, the first sizable forest management project in the United States, went on, as the first head of the U.S. Bureau of Forestry, to create and implement a national forestry policy and become an apostle of conservation.

By now Olmsted had honor and accomplishment few other men of his time could enjoy. Harvard and Yale gave him honorary degrees on the same day (Harvard stiffly required his presence, Yale obligingly did not). Though his young colleagues did most of the work (Frederick, Jr., carried on the firm with distinction until the 1950's), he kept traveling and getting into everything. His frail body stood up better than his wonderful mind, which finally broke down in 1898. He spent his last five years in the McLean Asylum, still able to recognize its landscape as one he had designed a quarter century before and to complain, "They didn't carry out my plan, confound them!"

He had been, a contemporary wrote, "first in the production of great works which answer the needs and give expression to the life of our great and miscellaneous democracy." That summed up what his century could see of Olmsted's works and barely hints at what the next century would make of his visions—for planned cities and regions, for

At Biltmore, the George Vanderbilt estate in North Carolina, Olmsted framed Richard Morris Hunt's Renaissance château with formal greens and gardens. But most of the 125,000-acre tract became the country's first scientifically managed forest.

communities within cities and outside them, for park systems and parkways, for a balance between use and preservation, for an understanding of ecology (before that term was known), for an art of landscaping that serves beauty and convenience and compassionate social purposes.

But for decades he was shrugged into near obscurity—"a feature of footnotes," someone remarked. By mid-century his fame and philosophy were revived, and finally, in the 1970's, two fine, comprehensive biographies, by Laura Wood Roper and Elizabeth Stevenson, were published.

Olmsted was quietly aware that his own generation could not evaluate him. "The result of what I have done," he wrote in late years to a friend, "is to be of much more consequence than anyone else but myself supposes." Still, he was pleased and grateful at what he had made out of the scattered, seemingly haphazard pieces of his life. "If a fairy had shaped it for me," he wrote of his work, "it could not have fitted me better. It was normal, ordinary and naturally outgrowing from my previous life." And, he said, getting to the nub of the matter, "it occupied my whole heart."

147

STANFORD WHITE

1853–1906

BY RICHARD F. SNOW

One day shortly before the turn of the century a young draftsman named William Kendall, recently hired by the New York architectural firm of McKim, Mead and White, stood on the corner of Fifth Avenue and Twenty-second Street chatting with a Mrs. Garnett. "What sort of a person," she wanted to know, "is this Stanford White of yours?" It was not an easy question. Kendall thought for a moment, then said, "I'll tell you." He pointed to a powerful-looking man who was making his way toward them. "You see that tall, red-haired man hurrying up the street. Well, that's Stanford White. He's ubiquitous."

He still is.

At one time or another, every reasonably florid building put up between the Civil War and the Great Depression—be it a house or an office or a church, whether built in Manhattan or Manhattan's suburbs or in any city with significant cultural leanings—has probably been ascribed to him. "And of course," people will say of anything grander than a glass brick waiting room in a dentist's office, "that was done by Stanford White." With the exception of Frank Lloyd Wright, he is America's best-known architect.

His death had a good deal to do with this, of course, but his life had more. Stanford White was in that rare and happy position of being absolutely in tune with his age. In his energy, his enthusiasm, his appetites and, above all, his architectural vision, he managed to personify a whole era.

His father was not so fortunate. Richard Grant White spent a good deal of time telling about his great-grandfather John, who arrived in Boston aboard the *Lyon* in 1632, and yet, being a lifelong Anglophile, Richard was never entirely happy that his ancestor had made the voyage in the first place. He studied music and dabbled in journalism until the collapse of the family's fortune forced him to

At the peak of his career, the tall, powerful, confident Stanford White seemed to one of his friends to resemble the ancient Gallic chieftain, Vercingetorix.

turn to criticism for a living. While the raw new fortunes his son would help spend grew up around him, he lived under the constant threat of poverty. It made him haughty, arrogant, brittle, and foppish. Nevertheless, he was a fine Shakespearean scholar and, in the London *Spectator*'s generous appraisal, "not at all our idea of a Yankee."

His wife, Alexina, was a gentle, affectionate woman, so modest that when her hair failed to gray with age, she adopted a silvery wig lest people suspect her of dying it. She gave birth to Richard Jr., in 1851 and to Stanford two years later.

A cheerful and lively child, Stannie was the favorite of the family. During summers spent at his aunt's house on the Hudson, he began sketching and painting, and early showed considerable promise. He wanted to become an artist, but this was too much of a luxury in a family that had to survive on a critic's earnings. When Stanford sought John La Farge's advice, the painter told him to forget it: the chances of gaining recognition were faint, those of making money, fainter still. So at nineteen White reluctantly embarked on a career devoid of any social cachet whatever—he apprenticed himself as a draftsman at a time when architects were still widely regarded as pretentious carpenters.

Given the opprobrium of being an architect in the early 1870's, he could scarcely have found a better berth, for he was in the office of Henry Hobson Richardson. Already well on his way to shifting architecture from trade to art, the extravagant, energetic Richardson proved a fine teacher. White worked hard in Richardson's office—as apprentices would later work hard in his—and not long after he joined the firm he was writing his mother about it in gusty letters, half-ebullient, half-whining. "I begin to think that it is my fate to have neither peace of mind nor quiet of body; & both are, I believe, quite necessary to man's happiness. . . . Of course, this may be the pessimism of a fevered imagination—probably is; for (thanks to Richardson and his committees) I feel as if I had been standing on my head all week." While helping supervise the construction of the New York State Capitol, he wrote, "Misery, wretchedness, ennui and the devil—I've got to spend another evening in Albany. Of all miserable, wretched, second-class, one-horse towns, this is the most miserable—not even a church fair, a dance or a saloon to go to."

But for all his picturesque griping, he liked the life and he liked Richardson. While he learned the nuts and bolts of his calling—how brick is laid, how to handle contractors, how to flatter one member of a building committee without getting the others mad, what he called the "small hell" of talking with

a client about closet space—he learned from his boss the larger things: that architecture was truly one of the fine arts, that color could mean as much to a building as to a painting, and that one could borrow from the past.

Also working for the "Great Mogul"—as White impertinently christened his employer—was a young Harvard graduate named Charles Follen McKim, who for his salary of eight dollars a week had charge of the drawings. The two men became friends, and in 1877 they set off on a walking tour of New England, in search of the native American architecture which, in the wake of the Centennial, was just beginning to be studied and restored. Also in the party was a quiet young architect named William Rutherford Mead, who helped with McKim's free-lance commissions. Rambling and sketching their way through Portsmouth, Marblehead, Newburyport, and Salem, the three became increasingly struck by Bulfinch's work and by the idea of a form of architecture based on classical precedents.

Back in New York, White put in a restless year with Richardson and then, having suppressed his

152

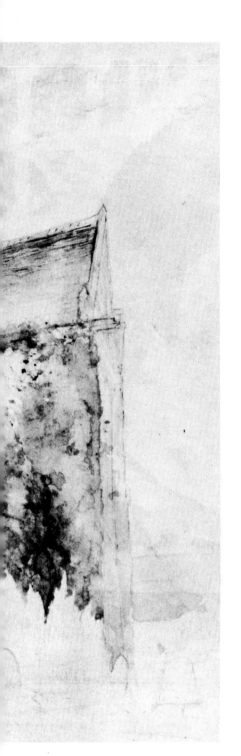

The riotous distractions of his trip through France with McKim and Saint-Gaudens did not prevent White from making careful sketches of the buildings they visited; the one at left shows the Church of Saint Nicholas in Caen. In mock-epic commemoration of the jaunt, Saint-Gaudens struck off the bronze medal above: Saint-Gaudens and McKim—with the immense forehead—stare at each other across a T-square; White is on top, incorporeal save for beady eyes and bristling hair.

extravagant impulses enough to set aside some money, headed for Europe. "The passengers," he told his mother in a typically grandiloquent letter, "are, briefly, McKim and myself. The rest don't matter . . . McKim, by the way, is a low brute. He engages in conversation and leaves me to starve because I dare not ask for anything in bad French—and not a damn waiter understands English. *Tiens*—the laugh will come on him as soon as we strike rough weather." Sure enough, they steamed into a storm, McKim got ill, and White looked after him, full of the mirthful concern that seasickness inspires in those not prone to it.

McKim recovered as soon as they landed at Le Havre, and by the time they got to Paris both were ready to consume the city. White eventually came to rest with his friend Augustus Saint-Gaudens, whom he had met in New York three years earlier. "White lived with us," wrote the sculptor, "our home serving as his headquarters, whence he darted off in extraordinarily vigorous excursions to the towns surrounding Paris that contain those marvels of Gothic architecture of which he was an adorer."

White was still in his twenties when he designed the Newport Casino, whose famous clock tower is here seen through some of the wooden grillework of the interior piazza.

A month after arriving in Paris, McKim and White burst into Saint-Gaudens's studio demanding that he accompany them on a trip to the south of France. The sculptor, having minutes before heard a committee express its displeasure about his monument to Admiral Farragut, was receptive: "Come on," he said, smashing all but the head of his sculpture, "I'll go to Hades with you fellows now."

Their trip launched in such a fine go-to-hell manner, the young artists had a splendid time. White recorded it all as they made their way south through Fontainebleau ("too well known to describe"); Sens ("dirty and decayed without being lovely"); Pont-Saint-Esprit ("a grand old stone bridge of twenty arches, 2,000 feet long, built in the thirteenth century by a company of monks"); Saint Gilles ("a little out-of-the-way town—and in it the

best piece of architecture in France, the triple arch of the church"). White would not forget the journey; years later he would graft that porch whole onto the front of Saint Bartholomew's Church in New York.

Back in Paris with the summer over, McKim said good-bye and headed home, but White could not bring himself to leave the Continent. He settled in with Saint-Gaudens and his patient wife and then struck out for Bruges, Reims, and finally the great cities of northern Italy. Omnivorous and inclusive in his enthusiasms, he liked virtually everything he saw.

Finally, with a solid year of traveling behind him, he wrote his mother, "Turn down my bed spread, dust out my room . . . and above all lay in a vast stack of buttons." Stanford White vowed never again to be "the prey of hotelkeepers, porters, beggars, pretty girls."

White had set out on his trip intending to return to Richardson's office. But when he came

154

home, full of ambition—not an astonishing effect for the Continent to have on a young architect—he found that the infant firm of McKim, Mead and Bigelow had been ruptured. William Bigelow's sister had walked out on her husband, Charles McKim, and the dismayed Bigelow had quit the firm. McKim suggested White as a replacement. Mead was dubious, thought White too showy and inexperienced. "White has not had much training in architecture," McKim conceded, "but he can draw like a house afire." Finally, under McKim's repeated urgings, Mead agreed to offer him a partnership. In September 1879 White put his name to an agreement hastily scrawled on yellow scratch paper: McKim would get 42 per cent of the net profits, Mead 33, and White 25. "It really, after all, was quite as liberal as I could expect for the first year," wrote White, and he flung himself into a year that would leave the partners with total commissions of less than five thousand dollars to share.

Despite this meager beginning, the three young men were uncommonly fortunate: theirs was a perfect partnership. The steady, scholarly McKim was one of only three graduates of the Ecole des Beaux-Arts then practicing in America (the other two were Richard Morris Hunt and the Great Mogul himself). He reined in on White's occasional excesses even as White helped keep McKim's pedantry in check. Mead, a Vermont Yankee so taciturn he bore the nickname Dummy, took less of a part in designing, explaining that his chief job was to keep his partners from "making damn fools of themselves." He was, according to White's son, Lawrence Grant White, much more than the office policeman: "If McKim was the hull and White the sails of the ship, Mead was both rudder and anchor; for it was his sound judgment . . . which steered them safely through the shoals. . . ."

If White's enthusiasms seemed, from time to time, too untrammeled, they nevertheless breathed life into the firm—life, and a ferocious devotion to color. Still regretting not having become a painter, White had written his mother from Bruges:

Here Hans Memling and his school plied their handicraft; and . . . there is a whole room crammed with pictures by him and them. Full of lovely faces . . . all modelled up in beautiful flesh tints without a shadow . . . and green embroidered gowns that make the nails grow out of the ends of your fingers with pleasure . . . To think that such a lovely thing could be done, and that I could not do it! . . . Architecture seems but poor stuff compared with things like these.

Once, riding the Staten Island ferry with William Dean Howells, he saw a stoker fall overboard from a tug and get chewed up by its screw. "The poor devil!" he cried, and then, as blood mixed with the iridescent sheen of oil on the water, "My God! What color!"

Happily for White, the Shingle style he had practiced under Richardson, with its emphasis on the surface of the building, offered him a broad choice of textures, and the play of shadow that he loved. Interiors allowed more latitude still: when he redecorated the Watts Sherman house in Newport, for instance, White put green panels picked out in gold in the library, light blue Dutch tiles in the hall fireplace, and, outside, a dash of inspiriting red in the stucco and mortar. Throughout his career, the man who had wanted to be a painter would, according to the art critic Royal Cortissoz, use building materials "with the same intensely personal feeling that a great technician of the brush brings to the manipulation of his colors."

Nor would White's commitment to the fine arts end with his painterly use of tile, stucco, and marble. In fact, he spent his first weeks of partnership collaborating with Saint-Gaudens on the monument to Admiral Farragut that the sculptor had smashed on the eve of their trip to southern France; Saint-Gaudens would design a statue of the sailor, White would work up a harmonious pedestal. He decided on a tall, elliptical stone seat, and he took it very seriously indeed. One of the many letters he sent that fall to Saint-Gaudens in Paris included this typically agitated passage:

The curved rising line of the back of the seat has lain on my conscience like pancakes in summer. I am sure it will not look well, and I am almost equally sure a straight back or one slightly and subtly rising will. . . . Also, you clay-daubing wretch, why didn't you tell me which site you wished? . . . I myself strongly like the Madison Square site and "so do we all of us."

As it turned out, Madison Square was chosen, and the lovely, brooding monument the two men put up there serves as a clear augury of the unusual rapport White would enjoy with artists all his life.

In the beginning, though, White was far more in demand for private houses than for civic monuments. Before leaving Richardson's office he had, in the opinion of Lewis Mumford, become every bit as adept as his teacher in the Shingle style, and for the first few years of the new firm, his chief job would be designing houses.

One happy early exception seems to have stemmed from the newspaper publisher James Gordon Bennett, Jr.'s truly electrifying social gaffe of relieving himself in the fireplace of his fiancée's home during her family's New Year's Day reception. The lesser results included Bennett's being barred from most of his clubs, among them one in Newport. In retaliation, Bennett proposed to build there a casino where those of his acquaintances who were still speaking to him could go to shop, dine, and play the newly imported game of lawn tennis. McKim got the job but, still rattled by his divorce, bolted to Europe to recuperate, leaving the work in White's lap.

"I cannot tell you how driven I am with business on account of McKim's absence from the office," White wrote Saint-Gaudens. "Damn all strong-minded women! say I." But despite being "nearly frantic," he managed to turn out a spirited shingle building lacy with latticework in its recreational areas and calm and respectful where its shops fronted on the public street. The Newport Casino foreshadowed the particular genius that the mature firm would show in suiting the exterior of a building to its environment while admirably fulfilling the client's needs with the interior. More important for the young partners, the casino's immediate success brought the name of their fledgling firm before a wealthy clientele.

One of these was the railroad magnate Henry Villard, who commissioned a building on a large lot he owned on Madison Avenue. Specific in his wants, Villard demanded six houses around a central courtyard. McKim had started to work up the plans when Villard, evidently liking what he saw, sent the senior partner to the West Coast to design some buildings for the Northern Pacific. Once again White took over, but then he too had to leave New York. Before he left, he turned over the job to Joseph Morrill Wells, a shy, brilliant man who had joined the firm about the same time as White. Wells had a full-blown love of the Italian Renaissance and used it to bring a noble coherence to the half-finished work of McKim and White. It would be hard to overestimate the influence of the Villard Houses. Their Neo-Italian Renaissance façade triggered a vogue that lasted for years, with the hundreds of subsequent imitations finally serving to make the great prototype less startling, if no less handsome.

Wells, who deserved so much of the credit for the project's success, remains a somewhat ghostly figure. He did not live long—disease claimed him in 1890—but for a decade he was indispensable to the firm. "So far as I know," wrote William Kendall, "his work was confined to the detailings of a building. In that he was supreme. Nobody before or since has equalled him in the appropriateness and scale of his ornamentation." A quiet, cynical man possessed of a mordant wit, Wells once said that "a Humanitarian reminds me of the man who does not smoke himself but keeps bad cigars for those who do." But there was nothing of the cynic about his approach to architecture; he regarded it as the highest expression of idealism, and he is said to have refused a partnership in the firm because he could not bear to "put his name to so much damned bad work."

This slight, trenchant figure was a perfect foil to White, who once burst into Wells's room brandishing a drawing he had just finished. "There—look at that! In its way, it's as good as the Parthenon."

"Yes?" said Wells. "And so too, in its way, is a boiled egg."

If the tart reply was typical of Wells, White's self-assessment was equally typical. The hyperbole, however, sprang more from enthusiasm than from egomania; White would have been just as likely to make the same claim for one of McKim's drawings. If he liked a thing, he made noise about it. He was noisy, too, in his dislike. Once, Saint-Gaudens's son recalled, White burst into his father's studio "with his usual effect of being shot from a landslide," demanding to see a relief of a wreath the sculptor was carving for a monument on which the two men were collaborating. "Awful!" he declared when he saw it, "Huh! You might as well paint it green!"

White would probably have been astonished to hear of anyone's taking offense at such an outburst. It was simply jovial bluster, and as much a part of him as his blazing hair and his busy, short-striding walk. To his friend the painter Edward Simmons, White was "that very simple person, child and artist, though he looked like Vercingetorix, bright red hair and the whitest skin, strong as a prize fighter, but gentle . . . and unlike most big men, always in a hurry, dashing about here and there."

It wasn't simply surplus energy that kept White on the move; work was piling up now, the firm's as well as his independent commissions, and he constantly bustled from job to job, checking, re-evaluating, making notes on scraps of paper. Often, after dinner, he would return to the empty office and turn out dozens of sketches for his draftsmen to work up. In the morning they would find torrents of tracing paper covered with White's deft notations, the ones he wanted them to develop circled.

For all this hectic pace, White was never slapdash. He fretted over every detail of a client's job (artistic detail, that is—matters of plumbing and engineering he was happy to leave to Mead) and took endless pains to achieve exactly the effects he wanted. During the construction of the Charles L. Tiffany house on Madison Avenue in 1884, White, unhappy with the variety of commercial brick available, is said to have overseen personally the making of a special recipe. If White loved such subtleties of color and texture, he also loved the monumental, the intricate, the exuberant. Colossal columns, elaborate cornices, and heroic embellishments enchanted him, and he was fortunate enough to live in an era when a new breed of

Medicis, sprung from America's great age of finance capitalism, were happy to furnish the wherewithal to fulfill his most vaunting visions.

Worldly and at ease in society, White was the natural choice for the master designer who would give concrete expression to the inchoate longings of the newly rich. An artist who liked salmon fishing, horse shows, and club life, he never intimidated or confused his clients as he set about building for them what has again and again been called the stage-set of an era.

He did this by borrowing from the architectural vocabulary of the past, but never in too hidebound or stodgy a manner. When, for instance, he designed a baroque tribute to our first president in Manhattan's Washington Square, he was particularly tickled that his memorial arch's thirty-foot single span beat that of any triumphal arch of antiquity. And there were other improvements: "The Washington Arch," wrote White, "differs from its classical predecessors in being generally lighter, in the prominence of the frieze, in the reduced height of the attic."

What White omitted from his description of the arch was the sense of exuberance with which he worked his poetic exaggerations on ancient architectural forms, and the underlying aesthetic that charged these transformations. Once, in a letter to Saint-Gaudens, he spoke obliquely about his art:

By the way, did you ever read the descriptions of the horse in the Book of Job? "Hast thou given the horse strength? Hast thou clothed his neck with thunder? . . . The glory of his nostrils is terrible. He paweth in the valley, and rejoiceth in his strength." Of course, a horse's

neck is not clothed with thunder. It's all damned nonsense. But would a realistic description have gone to your guts so?

McKim was not given to such flights, was more serene and literal in his borrowings from the past, and leaned toward the austerity of Palladian façades and the cool classicism of the high Renaissance. He was, said Lawrence Grant White, "a calm, deliberate scholar—shy, cautious, with a quiet way of speaking which, however, masked a strong will, so that he usually carried his point in an argument." He carried his points on the Boston Public Library, the young firm's first monumental commission. This was a huge and appallingly complex job: it would be the biggest library in America and, in the words of its trustees, "a palace of the people."

McKim, Mead and White knew their palaces, and despite wounded local pride and a good deal of grousing in the Boston papers, the New York firm was awarded the job in 1887. McKim's drawings had done the trick, but apparently his confidence faltered once the task was truly in hand. In December he announced he was going to Europe. Mead wrote him a tough letter:

I found that White held the same opinion I do about the advisability of your leaving the library drawings at this time. . . . You have got a design accepted . . . and if you leave it and get under the influence of Doumet or anybody, you will simply come back and knock into fits the accepted design and all the work done in your absence. . . . You stand in a good position now, and we are

The resounding success of their casino brought the young partners other commissions in Newport; this house, built for Robert Goelet in 1883, was probably designed by White.

157

Happy and at ease amid the gaudy society diversions of the era, White is often said to have designed the fete given by James Hazen Hyde in 1905. In any event, he did design Sherry's restaurant, where it took place—the dining room, above, is ready for the ball—and he attended; he stands in the center of the picture at right, glowering out from behind other guests. Rumors that the extravaganza cost $200,000 provoked such an outcry that Hyde had to surrender control of the Equitable Life Assurance Society and go into opulent exile in France.

all ready to back you, but nobody but yourself can take care of the Library for the next three months.

McKim stayed home.

In fact, he had every reason to be frightened of the project. To the east of the site, Copley Square opened out, ringed with mutually incompatible buildings: the Italian Gothic tower of the Old South Church, the Museum of Fine Arts with its yellow terra cotta and red brick, and the muscular Romanesque masses of Richardson's Trinity Church. "Truly," Walter Muir Whitehill wrote in his history of the library, "it was no easy matter to fill the vacant lot . . . with a structure that would have architectural quality of its own and still not swear at its motley and aggressive neighbors."

Drawing in part on the Colosseum in Rome, McKim had designed a horizontal structure, powerful and austere, featuring, above a high basement, an arcade whose windows lit a reading room that ran across the whole front of the building. Always, as the library rose, McKim badgered the city government for more and more funds, so that the interior would not betray the monumental conception. He ordered the finest European marbles and commissioned John Singer Sargent to

158

159

White could design almost anything, from magazine covers to parades. He did this frame for a picture of his children.

paint murals, Daniel Chester French to do the entrance doors, and Saint-Gaudens to create the panels above them. When the great work was finally completed in 1895, its superb exterior and the gleaming immensities of marble within made it an instant success. Today considered the finest surviving example of the firm's work, the library brought national fame to its designers.

By then White already had more than his share of local fame. In 1892, when he developed the decorations for the parade celebrating the four-hundredth anniversary of Columbus's landing (he chose a color scheme with yellow and white predominating), *Harper's Weekly* said his efforts were "a triumph—Mr. White should have a municipal Commissionership of Public Beauty created for him." Designing a parade seems a curious task for an architect, but White had a hand in everything: magazine covers, yacht and private railroad car interiors, furniture, gravestones, book jackets, jewelry, costume parties.

He was as happy to furnish his clients' homes as he was to build them. At first, he had arranged furniture in the age-old French and Italian tradition: chairs and tables, lining the edges of a room, served as little more than austere wall decorations. But by the turn of the century White had broken up those stiff old patterns. He covered the walls of a room with tooled leather or red velvet or huge oil paintings, and he clustered the furniture in the center or scattered it in casual groupings. This new informality invited people to move around, and imparted an air of liveliness and humanity to what might otherwise have seemed too daunting.

White's interest in furnishings extended to the smallest fixtures. He would come back from European visits with shiploads of vases, inkwells, lamps, clocks, and mantelpieces. He didn't care if these objects had all been born in the same era, or even if they were authentic; he felt that anything truly beautiful would fit in with anything else truly beautiful. Paintings, too, he used as part of the over-all scheme. Despite a personal predilection for the bright canvases of William Merritt Chase and Childe Hassam, White chose for his clients gloomy old masters whose dark surfaces would not compete too stridently with the elaborate gilt frames he liked to design for them.

Such nonarchitectural commissions added yet more distractions to a life of incessant distractions. Once, the story goes, he told an associate, "I'm sorry I can't keep that appointment with you tomorrow, but William C. Whitney dropped in to see me this afternoon and said: 'White, I want you to do me a favor. My new house on Fifth Avenue is ready. I want you to start for Europe tomorrow and select the furniture for it. I want to spend $250,000 for it. It will only take you thirty days because you know just where to go and what to buy. I will pay you $75,000 for your work.'"

White said he didn't want to go to Europe just then. Whitney would have none of it: "You must go. I'll give you $100,000 for your thirty days' work."

Speaking of just such an excursion, McKim once remarked ruefully, "White, in order to maintain his reputation, is planning to return as soon as he arrives."

White did slow down long enough to get married, in 1884, to Bessie Smith, the daughter of an old Long Island family and a lifelong friend of McKim's. A cheerful, steady woman, she adored her husband, but was always happiest in their Long Island home, which White remodeled and filled with his eclectic European plunder. She never cared for the fervid metropolitan social round that delighted the man she had married, and she did not have the temperament to go with him down all the paths of his headlong life.

Certainly his partners were occasionally irritated by White's constant state of motion, but he never wore himself too thin to take an equal part in the firm. How well the equilibrium he struck with McKim worked for the office—and for its city—can be seen in three clubs. All are Italianate, yet they are about as different in spirit as buildings can be.

When J. P. Morgan and men of similar financial clout decided they wanted a new place to

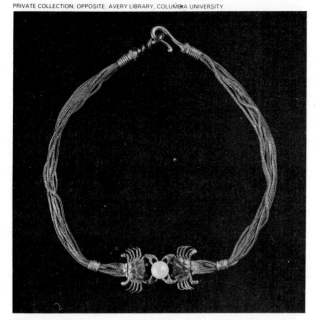

Tiffany and Company executed the crab-and-pearl necklace White designed for his bride, Bessie Smith, who is shown below in a relief by Saint-Gaudens—again, in a White frame.

gather, they approached McKim, Mead and White and got a splendid *palazzo* with a handsome little English carriage entrance thrown in for good measure. Inside the Metropolitan Club a double staircase ascends through a two-story marble hall where everything is dazzling enough to suggest why the firm was sometimes referred to as McKim, White and Gold. The rooms are redolent of wealth: tall, with ornate ceilings and relatively simple walls (White liked to keep walls spare, using them to counterbalance elaborately worked architectural features; often, he bought entire carved rooms just for their ceilings). But their very richness somehow saves these rooms from being overwhelming; there is a sense of buoyancy here, a feeling that the designer of all this splendor was one who greatly enjoyed club life. The Metropolitan Club is, according to the architecture critic Paul Goldberger, "one of the few buildings of its decade which suggest that perhaps there really was such a period as the gay nineties," and it is indisputably White's.

But this building would not have served at all for the more stolid membership of the University Club; they too got a *palazzo*, but theirs is cold, formal, carefully respectful of its architectural wellsprings. White was around while it was being designed—its entrance includes a carving of Athena taken from a statuette he owned—but it clearly reflects McKim.

And then there is the Century Association, a club which White and McKim both joined. Again the building is a Renaissance palace, but smaller, more delicate, and warmer in its ornamentation, as befits an organization founded on artistic and

intellectual interests. The rooms inside are large, but their dark wood and fabric wall coverings render them more intimate and less sententious than those of the University and Metropolitan clubs; like the membership, they suggest the brownstone New York that flourished a generation before the vast infusions of money that gave birth to the other two clubs. The fluency with which McKim and White collaborated is indicated by the fact that the Century's authorship is still disputed.

There is no question, however, about whose vision informed the most monumental of the firm's commissions: it was McKim's, and the building was the Pennsylvania Station.

Perhaps the ultimate melding of the grand classical style and the technology that generated the wealth that made it possible, the station was the Pennsylvania Railroad's effort to challenge the New York Central on its own ground, Manhattan Island. Previously, Pennsylvania passengers going west from New York had to start their journey with a ferry trip across the Hudson to New Jersey; now, however, newly developed electric locomotives could pull them through tunnels under the river.

161

The famous double staircase in the Metropolitan Club is a typical White creation—as is the rest of the lavish building.

But the very solution to this old problem gave rise to a new one: how could the building celebrate the power of the railroad when there would be no trains visible?

To girdle the twenty-eight-acre site, McKim borrowed the simple, powerful colonnade that surrounds the piazza of Saint Peter's. The relentless horizontal formed by its two-block run along the station's front was punctuated with a tall clerestory. Inside, the immense waiting room—modeled on the Baths of Caracalla—gave onto the train concourse, whose ramps and tracks were covered by acres of glass vaulting, supported by intricate traceries of steel.

McKim started designing the station in 1902, and construction began three years later. It took years—it was the largest structure of modern times to be built in one stretch—and both McKim and White would be in their graves by the time it was finished in 1911.

Despite its magnificent scale, the austere, scantly-ornamented building reflected McKim's essential restraint. There was a certain chill to it, hinted at by the fact that amid all the reverent archaeology of that vast main waiting room there was not a single bench on which to wait. Nevertheless, it *was* grand, and when in 1966 the railroad demolished it and reduced the station to the repellent warren it is today, the nation lost something precious. It was a splendid gateway; through it, said Vincent Scully, "one entered the city like a god . . . One scuttles in now like a rat."

Oddly enough, rising above the wreckage of Penn Station is the most recent replacement of still another vanished McKim, Mead and White landmark—one which was equally famous, and which also bore the unmistakable imprint of the partner chiefly responsible for it.

When McKim was complimented on Madison Square Garden, he shook his head and said one word: "White." This quintessential Stanford White structure was born in the desire of some of the New York gentry to revivify what one newspaperman termed "the patched-up, grimy, drafty, combustible old shell" where entertainments had been staged for years. They raised $400,000, bought the land, and commissioned a new Garden from White. He designed a boisterous façade of yellow brick and white terra cotta (a building material he almost single-handedly introduced to the American northeast) enclosing the pale red walls of the largest auditorium on earth. There was also a theater, a concert hall, a roof garden, and a tower, based on the Giralda in Seville, which at three hundred feet stood an insolent five feet taller than its prototype.

The tower caused trouble. As it became clear that the main part of the Garden had eaten up one and a half million of the backers' dollars, the building committee decided to omit the tower. White did not take the decision calmly. A New York

With columns six stories high supporting its coffered, vaulted ceiling, the waiting room of Pennsylvania Station was roughly the same size as the nave of Saint Peter's in Rome.

Sun reporter said, "He . . . kicked furiously to each member of the committee in turn, and afterwards to everyone in any way connected with the building, down to the bricklayers." He made such a nuisance of himself that finally the contractor, complaining that White "is simply hounding me into my grave," at last bought himself some peace by offering to put up half of the $450,000 needed, if the committee would match it. "Mr. White," the *Sun* account concluded, "immediately became reasonable again." Part of White's particular fervor may have

spun off enough income to pay dividends on the common stock.

Still, White probably did not resent his connection with it, for it represented a link with a world that was becoming more and more appealing to him. Although he moved easily and cheerfully in Fifth Avenue society, he found its rituals a bit staid and dull, and sought the flashier diversions of Broadway. He kept a suite in his hard-won tower, where he occasionally entertained his family and often played host to more raffish company. He

White threw even more than his usual compulsive energy into Madison Square Garden. The happy result was a palace that—as the poster above indicates—was at least as much an attraction as the acts of the Forepaugh and Sells circus. Though it never made a profit, the structure stood for many years; on the opposite page, it blooms with bunting for the 1924 Democratic convention.

stemmed from the fact that he had more than an aesthetic interest in his new building; he came to own eleven hundred shares of its stock, and held three hundred and fifty more through the firm.

Despite a gala opening and great enthusiasm in the papers (the *Herald* stated flatly that "there is probably not in the whole world a handsomer building, nor any more exquisitely proportioned"), the huge, costly enterprise failed to make money. Though he worked with all his formidable energy to turn a profit from what the *World* took to calling "Mr. White's yellow-and-white-elephant house"— among other extravaganzas he mounted a toy fair, an industrial fair, a Venetian fantasy complete with canals and gondolas, and a miniature ocean on which miniature American battleships knocked the Spanish fleet into scrap—the Garden never once

loved the sparkle and lilt of the theater, and he adored actresses. But, Aline Saarinen has written, "his pleasure in the ladies of the theater was, in fact, more visual than sexual. . . . He knew dozens of girls. He loved none." Physical beauty enchanted him. In seeking it, he was willing to go to considerable lengths, including paying dentist bills for various chorus girls, so that bad teeth would not compromise their perfection. When, in 1901, he met a startlingly lovely teen-aged actress named Evelyn Nesbit, he exclaimed, "Don't ever grow old! Don't ever grow fat!"

In 1895 he attended a dinner at which a six-foot pie was set on the table, and while the band played "Sing a Song of Sixpence," dozens of terrified canaries volleyed from the crust as a young woman wearing a stuffed blackbird on her head rose from

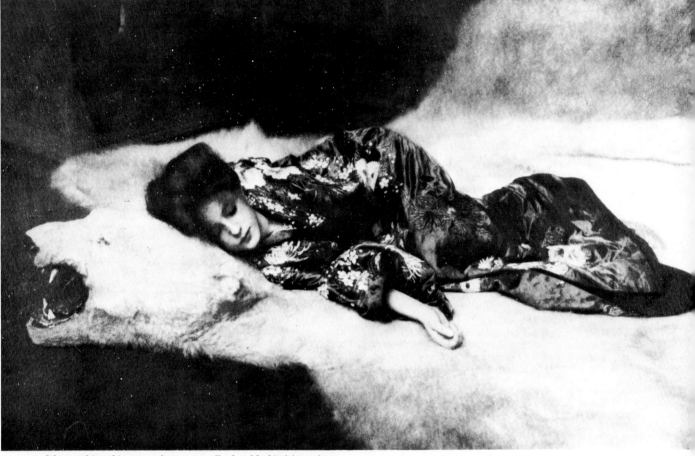

Wrapped in a kimono, a languorous Evelyn Nesbit feigns sleep for the photographer Rudolph Eickemeyer, Jr., who took this portrait in 1901, the year White met her.

the dish. This excruciating bit of dim nineties titillation, which in a decade's time would be raked up by the papers as the nadir of human debauchery, was probably pretty typical of the sort of orgy enjoyed by White and his companions.

However lively White's social life, it did not make a dent in his productivity. Often, ambushed by an idea, he would leap from his seat at the theater, run over to the office for an hour's work, and return in time for the final curtain. The office boys learned to keep on hand a supply of pencils hard enough not to smudge a formal white waistcoat. He was delighted by the coming of the automobile—here was a machine perfectly suited to his way of doing things—and he was probably one of the first men in the country to see it as a business necessity rather than a sporting luxury. In it, said a contemporary, outlining a typical White day, "he would hurry to some country home the building of which he was superintending, then return to the city and look over structures in which his firm was interested. His automobile would take him to three or four clubs, and then he would return home for dinner or go to one of the fashionable restaurants, where he was well known."

During the years following the opening of the Garden, White designed one hundred and thirteen buildings, among them the Interborough Power House, whose four tall stacks White is said to have made "seem almost elegant, with the grace of Lombardy poplars"; the Knickerbocker Trust Company, a daring glass-walled structure whose colossal Corinthian columns were the only masonry to be seen on its façade; the Herald Building, which despite James Gordon Bennett, Jr.'s sulking that "our Italian Renaissance palace will look like a fish market," was hailed by the *New York Times* as "a show, an exhibition, a palace, which drew strangers and sojourners for many years." (When someone pointed out that Bennett had leased the land on which it stood for only three decades, the publisher said not to worry: "Thirty years from now the *Herald* will be in Harlem and I'll be in hell.")

As the year 1906 began, White was just finishing the Madison Square Presbyterian Church, which, John Jay Chapman wrote, was "like a Byzantine jewel, so concentrated, well-built and polished, so correct, ornate and lavish. . . . It brought you to a full stop of admiration." Many considered the church the finest thing White ever did.

On Monday, June 25, White had dinner with his son and a college friend, dropped them off at the theater, then went by himself to Madison Square Garden, where a new show called *Mamzelle Champagne* was opening. He sat at a table near the stage. All his life White had been a highly visible figure, but nobody was watching at the moment three shots killed him.

As White's body fell to the floor and the audience started to scream, a man beside White's table held a pistol over his head, evidently as a signal that the shooting was over. Then the murderer, a neurotic Pittsburgh millionaire named Harry K. Thaw, walked through the seething crowd and rejoined his wife, Evelyn Nesbit Thaw. He had, he claimed, slain White because the architect had despoiled his wife.

The news, of course, received stupendous coverage—and sentiment ran against White. His old friend Bennett saw which way the wind was blowing and cabled the *Herald* from Paris: GIVE HIM HELL. The papers did.

Why did Stanford White [ran a typical report] need the finest studio in New York in the Madison Square Tower? He did not paint or make sculpture. He was an architect, whose work consisted principally in getting orders from rich men and in copying European buildings. . . . He needed that studio for the purposes that have been so abundantly revealed in the disclosures following his tragic end.

In the rich stew of scandal and innuendo, White was transformed from a gregarious aesthetic and social arbiter into a depraved debaucher. Fifth Avenue, its residents fearful lest they be tarred with the same brush, was silent. The man for whom, as John Jay Chapman said, "friendship was a religion" had few friends to defend his memory.

One, however, came forward angry and eloquent. "One who is permitted to write a few true words about a man who never spoke an unkind one," declared Richard Harding Davis, "resents the fact that before he can try to tell what Stanford White was, he must first tell what Stanford White was not. . . . Since his death White has been described as a satyr. To answer this by saying that he was a great architect is not to answer it at all. He was an architect. But what is more important is that he was a most kindhearted, most considerate, gentle and manly man, who could no more have done the things attributed to him than he could have roasted a baby on the spit." Saint-Gaudens, too, stuck by his friend of thirty years.

It did no good. The Thaws had plenty of money to slander the dead man, and when that winter Evelyn Thaw took the stand, the twenty-two-year-old actress proved a brilliant defense witness. Demurely dressed in a schoolgirl's navy blue suit,

she presented her testimony in what Samuel Hopkins Adams of the *World* saw as "a memorable, a magnificent, and a profoundly wicked triumph of dramatic art." The beautiful young woman told, in gaudy detail, of White's drugging and then raping her. The prosecution was not permitted to introduce evidence in White's favor. Harry Thaw was on trial, but Stanford White was convicted. Thaw beat the rap on an insanity plea.

The firm survived White's death, but the festive grandeur of his ornamentation disappeared immediately; it could never be approximated by the other two partners, nor by their successors.

White's reputation did not fare well. By the straitened 1930's the caprice and palpable richness of his buildings made them seem to many nothing more than monuments to an age of witless self-indulgence. Since the 1960's, however, critics, increasingly wary of the barren extensions of pure functionalism, have begun to take a less doctrinaire view. The long-time trend of knocking down columned façades to make way for sheer glass walls has slowed nearly to a halt. There is often a hiatus following the death of an artist during which his work is held in scant regard. The works of McKim, Mead and White are now emerging from just such a hiatus, and we begin to see in them what a British critic named C. I. Reilly perceived as early as 1924: at their best, they are a summation of "the finest aspirations of a great people at a great epoch."

Many considered the short-lived Madison Square Presbyterian Church—shown here in a sketch by Frederick J. Adams—to be White's most successful building.

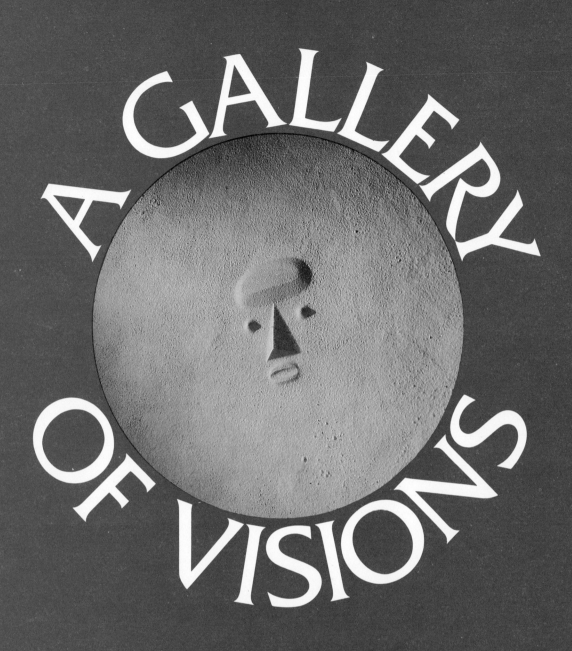

A GALLERY OF VISIONS

Painters and sculptors can, within limits, bring their artistic creations to finished form without outside help. But architects require the money of clients and the labor of workmen to translate their visions into steel or stone. It is not surprising, therefore, that their filing cabinets are filled with designs for buildings that never got beyond the sketching pad.

On these pages we present a portfolio of unfulfilled designs by American architects, some of whom appear elsewhere in this book. The grandiose cone on the opposite page was proposed as a Youth Temple for the Golden Gate Exposition of 1939 at San Francisco. It is the inspiration of Bernard Maybeck, whose earlier, quite different work appears on pages 232–47.

The model on this page is the conception of Isamu Noguchi, a sculptor who has always tried to integrate his work with both land forms and architectural design. In 1947 he proposed this enormous earth sculpture to be shaped by bulldozers on some convenient desert. With a nose one mile long, it would be visible from airplanes and space ships, if not from nearby planets.

OPPOSITE GRAY BRECHIN. ABOVE ISAMU NOGUCHI

MICHAEL GRAVES

MICHAEL GRAVES: A BRIDGE

This exercise in elegant geometry was
proposed in 1978 as a bridge across the
Red River, connecting Fargo, North Dakota,
with Moorhead, Minnesota. The structure
above the roadway would house an art
museum. A windmill on one bank would lift
water for cascades from the bridge.

BRUCE GOFF: A HOUSE AND A HOTEL

The house above was planned in 1956 for a semidesert site near Amarillo, Texas. Beyond the entrance ramp in the foreground a tentlike roof, suspended from a tower, covers the living quarters. One of the tubular wings at top contains a sanctum for the prospective owner, a writer, and the other, a studio for his wife, a painter. At left is Goff's 1961 plan for a Las Vegas hotel. The structure, with its leaning and seemingly melting walls, was to be built of white concrete sparkling with quartz aggregate, and the balconies were to be outlined in white neon.

171

BALTHAZAR KORAB

STUART WEINER

FRANKLIN W. SMITH: NATIONAL CULTURAL CENTER

Mr. Smith, a well-to-do Boston hardware merchant and gentleman architect, believed that the United States badly needed a cultural center to match its industrial greatness. This is the plan for the National Galleries of History and Art that he presented to Congress in 1900. A complex of eight huge buildings, to be erected beside the Potomac in Washington, D.C., would represent the great civilizations of history: Egyptian, Assyrian, Greek, Roman, Byzantine, Medieval, Saracenic, and East Indian. Between them a Sacra Via would lead to the Temple of the Presidents. Within the buildings would be paintings and models illustrating the history and life of ancient times, as well as reproductions of classical sculptures (cheaper than originals and superior, Smith thought, because undamaged). Though it won the support of numerous politicians, scholars, and architects, the plan never got through Congress.

FRANKLIN WEBSTER

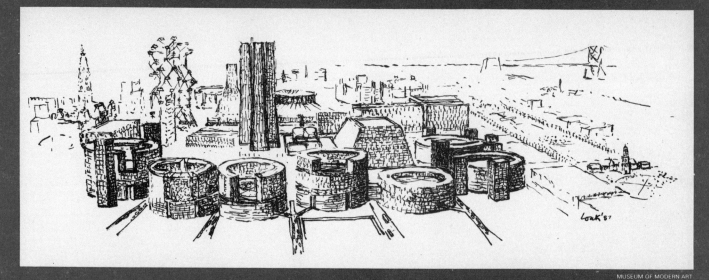

LOUIS KAHN: PHILADELPHIA

ABOVE: This 1957 design for a whole new center city features circular structures that include apartments, offices, shops, and garages. The Tinkertoy construction at top left is a new city hall to replace the old one, still standing in the background at far left. RIGHT: Kahn's model for the new city hall.

STANLEY TIGERMAN: INSTANT CITY

OPPOSITE PAGE: In order not to waste the air space above highways in metropolitan centers, Tigerman conceived in 1966 a series of triangular arches filled with apartments.

PAOLO SOLERI: CENTER OF HIGHER LEARNING

BELOW: This is part of Soleri's 1961 design for Mesa City, an "arcology" meant to house thousands of people. The structures are held up by steel cables beneath a transparent skin.

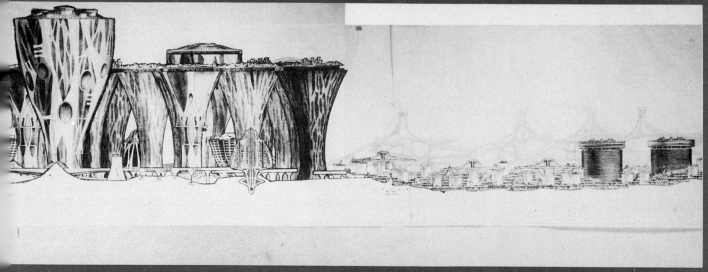

HOW THE WASHINGTON MONUMENT MIGHT HAVE LOOKED

These designs were submitted in 1836 in a competition sponsored by the Washington National Monument Society. Calvin Pollard's Gothic temple (above, left) and William Ross Wallace's colon-naded tower (above, right) had their champions, but Robert Mills's design (center) won out. The marble shaft was to rise from a circular pantheon, with Washington, clad in a Roman toga, driving a chariot above the entrance. For lack of funds the pantheon was eliminated before the shaft was finished in 1884.

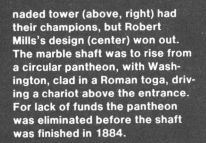

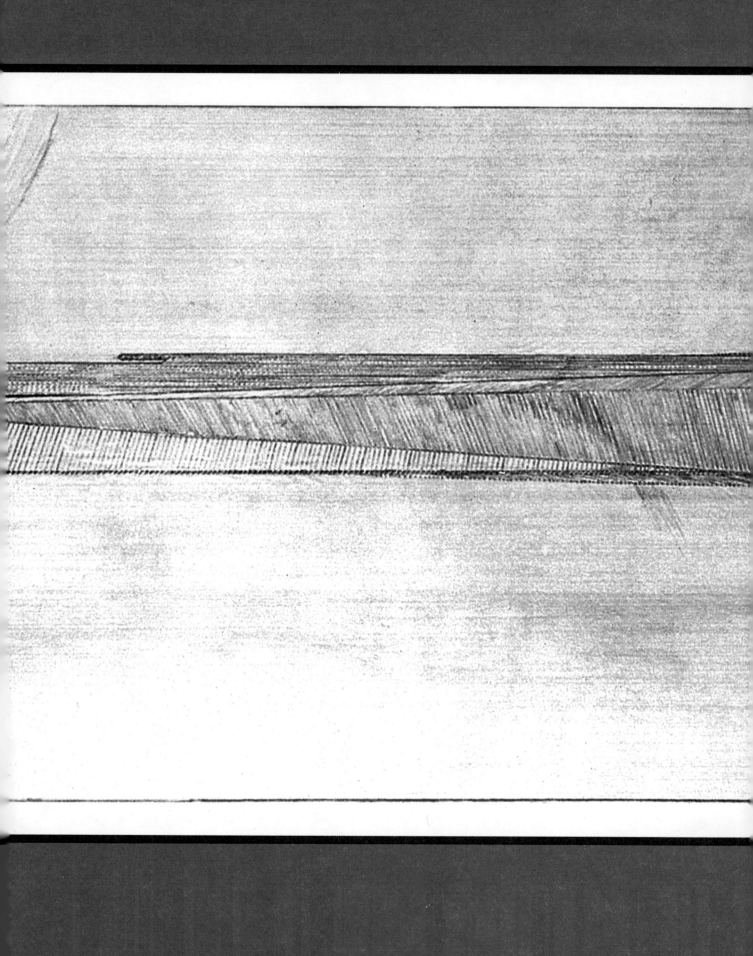

FRANK LLOYD WRIGHT: MILE–HIGH SKYSCRAPER

CENTERFOLD: At Chicago in 1956 Wright unveiled this drawing of the mile-high Illinois. Though he may have meant it as a satirical jibe at the mania for tall buildings, he insisted that the design was completely practical. The 528-story tower would be anchored deep in the ground by a taproot foundation and held up by a steel tripod core with cantilevered floors (a framework like that of a tree, Wright said). The facilities for 130,000 tenants would include atomic-powered elevators and two helicopter pads. Wright predicted that the skyscraper would last longer than the Pyramids.

©THE FRANK LLOYD WRIGHT MEMORIAL FOUNDATION 1957

BUCKMINSTER FULLER: A SKY CITY

To help solve the problem of living space on earth, the inventor of the geodesic dome proposed this floating sphere, half a mile or more in diameter. Under the sun's rays the air inside the aluminum sphere would expand and be partly expelled, thus lightening the structure enough to float it. Fuller conceded in 1967 that construction of such "clouds" might be "several decades" off.

BUCKMINSTER FULLER ARCHIVES

Sullivan's sketch for the Farmers' and Merchants' Union Bank, Columbus, Wisconsin, 1919

HENRI SULLIVAN

Study for New Bank Building
Farmers and Merchants Union Bank
Columbus, Wis.
Louis H. Sullivan Architect   Chicago
Scale ⅛" = 1 Foot   Feb 15th 1919

1856–1924

BY WAYNE ANDREWS

A brilliant success at thirty-three and a miserable failure by the time he died at sixty-seven, Louis Henri Sullivan was one of the great modern architects, no matter if his autobiography betrays a muddled mind. "The lifting of the eyelids of the world is what Democracy means," claimed this naïve genius, whose idea of democracy had nothing whatever to do with the practical political system advocated by our founding fathers. His vision was that of a world from which all selfishness was miraculously removed. No wonder he failed to reckon with the ruthless city of Chicago, where he was to build his career.

Chicago is the city of the first genuine skyscrapers, that is, the first tall buildings expressing their steel frames. Sullivan's achievement was to design skyscrapers that were individual works of art. These are not to be confused with the impersonal glass towers infesting the cities of our time.

Born in Boston on September 3, 1856, Sullivan was the second of two sons of Patrick Sullivan and his wife Andrienne-Françoise List. Patrick, an Irish fiddler turned dancing master in London, came to America by steerage in 1847, and five years later married Andrienne, a musician from Geneva, Switzerland. Andrienne's father, as Louis remembered, "looked upon religion as a curious and amusing human weakness—as conclusive evidence of human stupidity." Louis was never baptized, even though Grandmother List saw fit to join the Baptist Church. In any event, the isolation of the Sullivans from the Roman Catholic community of Boston anticipates the lonely years in Chicago of their gifted son.

Patrick Sullivan apparently did not make much more than a living as a dancing master in Boston. Nor did the summer school he started in Newburyport flourish. He tried Halifax, Nova

Scotia, for a time and then in 1868 moved to Chicago, supposedly in search—although this is hard to believe—of a milder climate for his wife's health. While they were moving about, the Sullivans often left Louis and his older brother, Albert, with Andrienne's parents on their farm at South Reading (now Wakefield), north of Boston. One of the real joys of Louis's childhood was the long walks he took at night to study the constellations at the side of Grandfather List. He came to regard the farm as home and was not unhappy when his parents, upon moving to Chicago, left him behind in South Reading. He lived with the Lists until his grandmother died and his grandfather sold the farm. Then for two years he was sent to board in the household of a neighbor while he finished his schooling.

At Boston English High School, which he entered at fourteen, he found a taskmaster he idolized in Moses Woolson, who insisted on silence, strict attention, and accurate listening. This was not the last time this naturally disobedient romantic was overwhelmed by the voice of authority.

In the meantime, and this was even more important, he had come across on Boston's Commonwealth Avenue a large man of dignified bearing, with beard, top hat, and frock coat, who was obviously accustomed to command. He was an architect, a workman told Louis. "He lays out the rooms on paper, then makes a picture of the front, and we do the work under our own boss, but the archeetec's the boss of everybody."

Determined to be an architect, Sullivan enrolled at sixteen in the architectural school of the Massachusetts Institute of Technology, then headed by William R. Ware of the Boston firm of Ware and Van Brunt. A passionate admirer of John Ruskin, then leading the crusade in England to prove that salvation lay in following the precedent of the Gothic architects of Venice, Ware was more than just a student of the Doges' Palace, even though Louis believed that "he was not imaginative enough to be ardent." With his partner, Henry Van Brunt, he would shortly design Harvard's Memorial Hall, whose polychromy fiercely proclaimed his loyalty to Ruskin.

Aggressive and impatient, Sullivan decided that a year of M.I.T. was sufficient and that he might better advance himself in the office of an architect of standing. In New York he called on Richard Morris Hunt, the first American to be trained at the Ecole des Beaux-Arts. Hunt seems to have been kind to the precocious youngster from Boston, patting him on the back to encourage him. But it was in Philadelphia that Sullivan found his first job, with the firm of Furness and Hewitt. "Frank Furness was a curious character," he remembered in his autobiography, a work in which he cast himself in the third person. "He affected the English in fashion. He wore loud plaids, and a scowl, and from his face depended fan-like a marvelous red beard, beautiful in tone, with each separate hair delicately crinkled from beginning to end.... Louis's eyes were riveted, in infatuation, to this beard, as he listened to a string of oaths yards long." The son of a strenuous abolitionist who was the uncompromising pastor of Philadelphia's First Congregational Unitarian Church, Furness was equally uncompromising, a crosspatch who argued his clients into erecting angry banks and townhouses.

When Furness learned that Sullivan had been to M.I.T., there came "a detonation that set off the mine which blew up in fragments all the schools of the land and scattered the professors headless and limbless to the four quarters of the earth and hell. Louis, he said, was a fool. He said Louis was an idiot to have wasted his time in a place where one was filled with sawdust, like a doll, and became a prig, a snob and an ass."

Finally, Furness burst out: "Of course you don't know anything and are full of damnable conceit." Sullivan agreed with all this but then broke into a hymn of praise to a house by Furness he had spotted on Broad Street. This made some impression. "Of course you don't want any pay," suggested Furness. Upon which Sullivan asked for ten dollars a week. "All right," came the answer. "Come tomorrow morning for a trial, but I prophesy you won't outlast a week." At the end of the week he was told he could stay another, and then: "You may stay as long as you like."

The firm was busy with the plans for the Pennsylvania Academy of Fine Arts, an outrageous thing in Ruskinian Gothic which has only in recent years begun to be appreciated. Sullivan was happy in this environment, tracing the plans for a savings bank on Chestnut Street and admiring Furness more and more for "making buildings out of his head." He also learned to appreciate John Hewitt, who "made of Louis a draftsman of the upper crust." But the Panic of 1873 put an end to all this. "I'm sorry, Sullivan," said Furness, "the jig is up. There'll be no more building.... As you were the

186   *This spirited pencil drawing of Sullivan at the piano was done by his mother when he was twenty-eight.*

last to come, it is only just you should be the first to go." And he slipped a bill into his hand.

The day before Thanksgiving, 1873, Sullivan found himself in Chicago. "THIS IS THE PLACE FOR ME!" he cried in his autobiography. He was mistaken. Chicago was a tough town, dominated by tough men like P. D. Armour, Gustavus Swift, George M. Pullman, Cyrus Hall McCormick, and Marshall Field. Typical was Armour, who bragged that his culture was mostly in his wife's name, and who never failed to put in an appearance at the office "before the boys with the polished nails show up." Typical, too, was his fellow packer Swift, who when he sniffed whiskey on the breath of an employee announced: "I'm glad you liked your job, for you ain't got it now!" Typical, too, was the inventor of the Pullman car, ruling his model town on the far South Side in so pitiless a manner that the Republican boss Mark Hanna was disgusted. Typical, too, was McCormick. The inventor of the reaper was a solid Presbyterian not above calling a loan extended to a pastor who dared mention freeing the slaves. Then there was the immaculate and merciless Field. The builder of the greatest department store in the nation, he claimed that "people do not know how to save." He did, and left Chicago's greatest fortune, $120,000,000.

Forgetting that these big businessmen were setting the pace of the city, Sullivan responded only to the vitality about him. "In spite of the Panic, there was a stir," he recalled, "an energy that made him tingle to be in the game."

Chicago's explosive growth was concentrated mainly in the downtown area, known as the Loop. Land selling at $130,000 the quarter acre in 1880 brought $900,000, or nearly seven times as much, before the decade was over. There was a need for taller buildings, no doubt about that. At the same time, the technology to build them had been created by two engineering innovations: the steel frame, which took the weight of a building off its walls; and the elevator, which gave access to more stories. Thus the market for skyscrapers and the needed technology came together in Chicago in the 1880's.

Conceptually, the skyscraper owed something also to the Gothic Revival of the preceding decades. That popular style, though used mostly for churches and cozy homes, had led architects to study the medieval system of designing buildings from the inside out. In the cathedrals of the Middle Ages, as the French architect Viollet-le-duc pointed out, "walls vanished and became screens, not supports."

The first step *toward* a skyscraper was taken in New York in 1857 when the Haughwout Building was erected on Broadway. Designed by J. P. Gaynor, it made use of the cast-iron frame patented by James Bogardus and was the first structure to boast the practical passenger elevator of Elisha Graves Otis. However, the five-story Haughwout Building was hardly high enough to be called a skyscraper, and in the following decade the lead in tall buildings was taken by Chicago. In 1883 William Le Baron Jenney, who had been an engineer on the staff of General W. T. Sherman, planned the Home Insurance Building on the southwest corner of LaSalle and Adams streets. This nine-story structure, now demolished, is generally considered to have been the first example of a genuine skyscraper. Wrought iron was used up to the sixth story and Bessemer steel beams above that level. This was not a work of art but an amazing achievement in engineering.

Another and more sophisticated engineering wonder was the Tacoma Building of 1887-89 on the northwest corner of LaSalle and Madison. Because it used the riveted skeleton it is a rival claimant for recognition as the first full-fledged skyscraper. The Tacoma, also now demolished, was the work of William Holabird and Martin Roche, both graduates of the Jenney office.

Sullivan was so fortunate as to get a job with Jenney, whose undeniable importance in the history of the skyscraper he was inclined to disparage. But he did not stick with Jenney for long. In the summer of 1874, when not yet eighteen, he managed to scrape up the money to study at the Ecole des Beaux-Arts, then the most respected architectural school in the world. He seems to have spent only a year in Paris, and not too much harm was done. "There came the hovering conviction," he stated, "that this great school, in its perfect flower of technique, lacked the profound animus of primal inspiration."

Moses Woolson's pupil at English High was searching for simple answers, and he found a simplifier in a certain Monsieur Clopet, who had been hired to tutor him in mathematics. There came the day when Clopet announced: "Now observe: Here is a problem with five exceptions or special cases; here a theorem, three special cases; another, nine, and so on and on. . . . I suggest you place the book in the waste basket; we shall not [have] need of it here; *for here our demonstrations shall be so broad as to admit of NO EXCEPTION!"*

To Sullivan this was a great moment. He "stood as one whose body had been turned to hot stone, while his brain was raging. Instantly the words had flashed, there arose a vision and a fixed resolve: an instantaneous inquiry and an instant answer. The inquiry: If this can be done in mathematics, why not in architecture? The answer: It can and shall be! *No one has,—I will!"*

Although he was never to sink to the level of turning out buildings according to a formula, he was obsessed by formulas, and they preyed upon his mind until he eventually evolved the slogan: Form follows function. This phrase has been repeated *ad infinitum* by historians who would be hard put to apply it to any of his creations.

Before returning to Chicago he spent a few days in Rome, two of them in Michelangelo's Sistine Chapel. Here, he tells us, he "communed in the silence with a Super-Man." He also visited Florence for six weeks and found it hard "to break the golden chains that bound him there." These comments are worth remembering, for he was later to develop an all but pathological hatred of the Renaissance.

In Chicago he had the good fortune to meet Dankmar Adler. Twelve years older than Sullivan, Adler was not his equal as an artist but was a masterful engineer and an expert on acoustics, as well as an architect with a sure talent for attracting clients in the Chicago world. The son of a rabbi from the German state of Thuringia, he had gone from one architect's office to another in Detroit and Chicago, besides gaining invaluable engineering experience in the Civil War. Sullivan seems to have immediately recognized that Adler would be a congenial co-worker, open-minded and warm in his enthusiasms. On May 1, 1880, he joined D. Adler and Company, which was transformed into the firm of Adler and Sullivan exactly one year later.

The senior partner was "a solid block of manhood, a terror to any recalcitrant or shifty contractor," declared Frank Lloyd Wright, who at twenty joined the firm in 1887. "What was particularly fine, as we consider human nature," said Sullivan, "was Adler's frank way of pushing his partner to the front." Unfortunately this was not all the junior partner had to say about the senior partner. "Adler's witticisms were elephantine," he emphasized in his autobiography.

Adler's role in the success of the firm should not be underestimated. In 1885 he was asked by the local entrepreneur Ferdinand W. Peck to remodel an exposition building on the lake front to serve as the temporary home of an opera festival. In two weeks' time he contrived a fan-shaped hall whose sight line was ideal—everyone could see and hear—and the sloping ceiling formed an immense sounding board, so that the acoustics were unimpeachable. It was not for nothing that Adler was later requested to be the acoustical adviser for Carnegie Hall in New York.

The triumph of the temporary opera house on the lake front led Peck to decide that Adler and Sullivan should design for Chicago a new Auditori-

um Building, combining in one building a hotel, offices, and a large theater. Sullivan's first sketches for the great granite block on the south corner of Michigan Avenue and Congress Street were hesitant and even confused. However, the final elevation of the ten-story block with tower was commanding. Sullivan had the good sense to take a good long look at the ever so simple granite façade of Richardson's wholesale store for Marshall Field, completed in 1887. There was no idea of using skyscraper or metal frame construction in the Auditorium, and the settling of the seventeen-story-high tower on floating foundations would have presented a formidable problem to anyone with less engineering experience than Adler. "He practically had to dig out his information for himself, and it was a tremendous proposition," Sullivan admitted.

As for the theater itself (the largest permanent indoor theater erected up to that time), it was planned to accommodate not only opera audiences but smaller groups, and by lowering one or a second steel curtain, the seating capacity could be reduced from 4,237 to 2,574. Whether the auditorium was expanded or contracted, its acoustics went unchallenged, and Chicagoans were not the only ones to boast that here was the greatest opera house in the world, surpassing even the masterpiece of Charles Garnier in Paris.

On the opening night, December 9, 1889, when Adelina Patti trilled "Home, Sweet Home" to a choice public including the George M. Pullmans, the Potter Palmers, and the Marshall Fields, the success of Adler and Sullivan was obvious. President Benjamin Harrison, whose interest in music was incidental, leaned over and nudged the elbow of Vice President Levi P. Morton. "New York surrenders, eh?"

It was in the auditorium that Sullivan revealed his gift for decoration. The great golden ceiling arches (which incidentally served as ventilating ducts) became the perfect excuse for the display of his eloquent imagination.

Here was a building that could never be erased from the consciousness of Chicagoans, even though the belligerent Samuel Insull forced the removal of the opera in 1929 to the new Chicago Civic Opera House. The old theater was then abandoned for many years, but after Marshall Field III and the Julius Rosenwald Fund presented the Auditorium Building to Roosevelt University, the restoration of the theater was all but inevitable. In 1967 an immaculate reincarnation was completed, the work of Harry Weese and Associates.

As for Sullivan, he was a lonely figure at the height of his success. "We did not love him, but we had a great respect for him," said one of the

Sullivan's talent as an artist found
frequent expression in personal sketches.
The nude may have been copied from a book,
but the portraits are probably from life.
Below is a sketch of Mephistopheles, from a
notebook Sullivan kept in his twenties.

The evolution of Sullivan's design for the Chicago Auditorium may be followed in these three pictures. The first design (above) with its mansard roof, turrets, and pyramidal cupola, shows a mixture of European architectural influences.

In the second design (above) the cornice has been stripped of decoration and the cupola turned into a tower. In the ten-story Auditorium as built (below) the tower was heightened and squared off. The ground-floor arches were unchanged.

draftsmen on his staff, which at one time ran to fifty. Sullivan's most faithful friend, George Elmslie, who worked at his side for twenty-two years, confessed that "he could be arrogant and unnecessarily decisive at times, and a bit prone to give advice where not needed, to good clients. Of course he lost many jobs because he would not compromise his ideals, nor play fast and loose with vital conceptions of what was fitting for the purpose intended."

Elmslie found that "Sullivan was a bit of a recluse. He liked to be alone, to think and write. He was a solitary man in most ways and constitutionally averse to social display of any kind. He lived alone most of his life and when he drank, he drank alone. Yet," added Elmslie, "he was the most interesting, fascinating, inspiriting and encouraging companion anyone could have. He believed in himself and had reason to do so. He had a true message to deliver and delivered it with eloquence, virility, and great power."

Frank Lloyd Wright, who rose to be chief draftsman of Adler and Sullivan and who supervised the design of the bar of the Auditorium Hotel, gave us a less cordial portrait. "At this time the master's very walk bore dangerous resemblance to a strut," he recollected. He also remembered that the master told him, "I have no respect at all for a draftsman." In spite of this, Sullivan gave Wright a five-year contract and the loan of enough money to build himself in Oak Park in 1889 a home for his growing family. This was delightful. Less delightful was the opportunity to hear the master read from his own writings. Bored, Wright let him know that his prose was "a kind of baying at the moon."

To meet his growing expenses Wright began spending his evenings designing houses on his own. Sullivan found out and was furious. "Your interest is here while your contract lasts," he was informed. "I won't tolerate division under any circumstances." So Wright was fired in 1893.

Wright never left off revering Sullivan's genius but could be impatient with Sullivan the man. Said Wright, "I despised smoking then, drinking and whoring, and do now. I despised the habitual in any form." And he pointed out that his boss came back from Paris with "the standard vices that eventually cut him down before his time."

Sullivan saw no point in being lenient with his rivals, the most significant of whom were Daniel Hudson Burnham and John Wellborn Root, justly famous in those days for such Richardsonian buildings as the Masonic Temple, the Women's Temperance Temple, and the Rookery, the last still standing on LaSalle Street. Even more authoritative was the Monadnock Building of 1889, still visible off Jackson Boulevard. Sixteen stories high, its masonry bearing walls are so dignified that they remain a reproach to anything trivial erected since that time in Chicago.

Sullivan seems to have taken an instant dislike to Burnham, perhaps because here was a man who got Chicago's number and could talk to businessmen in their own language. "I'm not going to stay satisfied with houses; my idea is to work up a big business to handle big things, deal with big businessmen, and to build up a big organization, for you can't handle big things unless you have an organization." So Sullivan recalled their first conversation.

With the glory of the Auditorium Building behind them, Adler and Sullivan began their first skyscraper in 1890. This was the Wainwright Building of Saint Louis, a monument to the ambition of the local brewer Ellis Wainwright and a prime example of Sullivan's disloyalty to the slogan Form follows function. Here was no obvious revelation of the steel frame, the riveted columns, or the spandrel beams that carried the exterior wall on shelves for each of the ten stories. A mere functionalist would have frowned at the elaborate adornment of the tenth story, which served only utilitarian purposes. And a mere functionalist would have been embarrassed by the fact that the alternate piers, enclosing no steel columns, were the same size as the steel-bearing piers. Sullivan gave no thought to this sort of criticism, which was fortunate, since this building was a proud, individualist answer—sheathed in Missouri granite, red brick, and terra cotta—to the problem at hand. Sullivan's own description of what a skyscraper should be is hardly illuminating. "What is the chief characteristic of the tall office building?" he asked. "At once we answer: it is lofty. This loftiness is to the artist-nature its thrilling aspect." The Wainwright Building was more than lofty. It was noble.

To people more familiar with the stark skyscrapers of the International school, one aspect of Sullivan's work is often surprising. The typical Sullivan skyscraper is aflame with a marvelous sheath of decoration. Exactly how he hit upon this inspiration may never be known. Although friends claimed it came from studying the plates of Asa Gray's *School and Field Book of Botany*, this may be too simple an answer. There are parallels to be observed with the work of Hector Guimard, a pioneer of the Art Nouveau movement in France.

Sullivan found another outlet for his decorative gift in a tomb that he designed in Bellefontaine Cemetery, Saint Louis, for Mrs. Wainwright, who died while he was at work on her husband's skyscraper. But this domed sepulcher is surpassed

by that of Carrie Eliza Getty, who had been the wife of Henry Harrison Getty, an associate in Chicago of the Michigan lumberman Martin Ryerson. Her limestone monument in Chicago's Graceland Cemetery is an incredibly inventive design with octagonal panels featuring eight-pointed stars. Sullivan could also refrain from all decoration, as in the august tomb, also in Graceland, that he had composed in 1889 for Martin Ryerson himself.

Sullivan was soon caught up in the exhilaration that swept Chicago with the coming of the World's Columbian Exposition of 1893. This may have been the most successful world's fair in history. Four hundred thousand people poured through the gates on the opening day, and all told, twenty million enjoyed the spectacle. One of the visitors was Ward McAllister, the social arbiter of

Mrs. Astor's Four Hundred, who sighed when Mayor Carter Harrison promised hospitality to all. "Hospitality which includes the whole human race," said McAllister, "is not desirable."

Sullivan would not have smiled at this comment. The fair was serious business, especially since Burnham was dictating the architectural layout. "Burnham performed in a masterful way," Sullivan conceded, "displaying remarkable executive capacity. He became open-minded, just, magnanimous. He did his great share." He also appointed Sullivan secretary of the board of architects.

With or without Sullivan's approval, Burnham went ahead and decided that Richard Morris Hunt and McKim, Mead and White and other firms from the East should be given the opportunity of

Sullivan's flair for decoration is exemplified in the top of Saint Louis's Wainwright Building, his first skyscraper. Whereas other architects had designed tall buildings by piling one story on another, more or less like a cake, Sullivan emphasized the verticality of the building by piers that stretched boldly up the façade. Between them are recessed spandrels of ornately decorated red terra cotta. Under the cornice, completely covering the top, or service, floor, runs a frieze of similar leafy decoration, broken only by small circular windows.

improving the taste of the Middle West, displaying what the recent Renaissance Revival had been accomplishing in New York. Hunt was not exactly a stranger to Chicago, for in 1873 he had planned a dull if imposing mansard-roofed house for Marshall Field on Prairie Avenue. Sixteen years later he revealed his real ambition with the French Renaissance residence on Lake Shore Drive of William Borden. This was very like the W. K. Vanderbilt château on Fifth Avenue. Overcome by this solution to the problem of creating a millionaire's palace, McKim, Mead and White, until that time famous for their "modern" Richardsonian works in the Shingle style, had suddenly transferred their allegiance to the Renaissance and set about turning Manhattan into a Renaissance city.

Burnham was impressed, perhaps too much

impressed, by the presence of these Easterners. "We have been in an inventive period, and have had rather a contempt for the classics," he apologized, proving that he was the latest victim of the well-known Chicago inferiority complex.

No one was more ecstatic during the deliberations than the sculptor Augustus Saint-Gaudens. "Look here, old fellow," he called out at the end of one conference, "do you realize that this is the

greatest meeting of artists since the fifteenth century?" This very thought was to occur to his friend Henry Adams, who fancied that authors, architects, and artists should all belong to the very best clubs. "If," he wrote in his autobiography, "the people of the Northwest actually knew what was good when they saw it, they would some day talk about Hunt and Richardson, LaFarge and Saint-Gaudens, Burnham and McKim and Stanford White, when their politicians and millionaires were otherwise forgotten. . . . Chicago," he concluded, "was the first expression of American thought as a unity."

This was not the opinion of the acute architecture critic Montgomery Schuyler. "Arcadian architecture is one thing and American architecture another," he noted on surveying the classical piles.

The most exciting building at the fair was the work of Sullivan, who had been given complete freedom to do what he liked with the Transportation Building. Its main feature was the Golden Door, a fine frenzy that recalled the twelfth-century Auguenaou Gate at Marrakech in Morocco. That it was not completely original was unimportant. It stunned French visitors, and Sullivan was awarded three medals from the Union Centrale des Arts Décoratifs.

What Sullivan thought of the fair at the time it opened may never be known. In his old age, in his autobiography published the year of his death, he proved a bitter commentator. "The crowds," he wrote, "departed joyously, carriers of contagion, unaware that what they had beheld and believed to be truth was to prove, in historic fact, an appalling calamity. For what they saw was not what they believed they saw, but an imposition of the spurious upon their eyesight, a naked exhibitionism of charlatanry, in the higher feudal and dominating culture, conjoined with expert salesmanship in the materials of decay." So he rambled on, declaring that "the damage wrought by the World's Fair will last for half a century from its date, if not longer. It has penetrated deep into the constitution of the American mind, effecting there lesions significant of dementia."

Thus Sullivan pretended in his last years that the fair had laid a curse on American architecture. This was not exactly the case in Chicago. For in the next quarter century Frank Lloyd Wright had great success, capturing if not every commission he would have enjoyed, at least enough work to win an international reputation. Nor was Wright the only up-and-coming man to win friends and clients. The so-called Chicago school, composed of Sullivan admirers such as Walter Burley Griffin, winner of the competition for the plan of Canberra in

The lightness and elegance of Sullivan's touch in the handling of office buildings is displayed by the Gage Building (below), a small Chicago "skyscraper" of 1899. The arches on the opposite page were green and gold and belonged to the theater of the Schiller Building, built in Chicago in 1892 and razed in 1961.

Australia, and George Elmslie and his partner William Gray Purcell, was flourishing.

The Chicago school, and this will hardly be held against it in our time, was a boon to the middle class: you could have gone to the wrong college, or no college at all, and still live in a remarkable house. Things were otherwise in New York, where McKim, Mead and White were busy designing stage sets for the millionaires, such as Louis Sherry's restaurant or the Venetian palace on Fifth Avenue of Tiffany and Company. Today we see nothing reprehensible in the pageant of Manhattan in those days, but for Sullivan the return to the Renaissance was positively sinful.

Sullivan, who was singularly unsophisticated, also had no interest whatever in city planning, and it is sad that he had nothing to say in his autobiography about Burnham's great achievement, the Chicago Plan. Fascinated by the lagoons and waterways that Frederick Law Olmsted had laid out for the fair, Burnham determined that the lake front should be preserved at all costs and the city given the proudest plan of the western hemisphere. "Beauty has always paid better than any other commodity and always will," he argued coarsely but persuasively to the businessmen of the Merchants' Club. "Make no little plans," he also emphasized. "They have no magic to stir men's blood. . . . Remember that your sons and grandsons are going to do things that would stagger us. Let your watchword be order and your beacon beauty." Here was forceful, direct prose, of which Sullivan was never capable.

Sullivan was, however, capable of setting standards in skyscrapers that no one could equal. He proved that in 1894, when Hascal C. Taylor, a carriage maker speculating in the oil business, commissioned the Guaranty Building in Buffalo, later renamed the Prudential. This could be considered a second version of the Wainwright, although its cornice was thinner and its exterior wall entirely of terra cotta. It was no duplicate, for it was far richer in detail.

The Prudential was completed in 1895, when America had not yet recovered from the Panic of 1893, and it was fortunate that Adler and Sullivan could count on the profits from the Chicago Stock Exchange Building at 30 North LaSalle, opened in 1894. Here Adler used the first caisson foundations in Chicago. The entrance, with a single arch, was emphatic. Singularly successful, too, was the trading room, whose beauty may be appreciated today

The Prudential Building in Buffalo, New York (originally known as the Guaranty Building), was built four years after the Wainwright Building. The style is the same, but its entire steel frame is covered with a terra-cotta surface.

in the Art Institute of Chicago, where it was carefully installed by John Vinci after the senseless demolition of this Adler and Sullivan landmark.

The darkest day in Sullivan's life came in 1895, when Adler, worried sick by the economic depression and the care of his family, retired from the firm to become consulting architect and sales manager for Richard T. Crane's elevator company. Although Adler had brought in the clients on which the two men thrived, Sullivan could neither forgive nor forget what he considered a disloyal act. He first erased Adler's name from the Prudential plans as published and then, early in 1896, when Adler offered to return, snubbed him.

There is no doubt that Sullivan was a genius. But a genius without a wise woman at his side may easily make one mistake after another, indulging in egotism at unfortunate moments. This was to be the fate of Sullivan.

After forty-three years of single life he married Margaret Davies Hattabough, a would-be novelist of twenty-seven. The marriage came at a time when Sullivan had few commissions and was drinking heavily. Often the young wife had to have assistance in getting her alcoholic husband to bed at night. They had no children, and in 1917, after many years of living apart, they were divorced.

With this short, sad marital life, added to the insecurities of his own childhood, it is no wonder that Sullivan took no interest whatever in domestic architecture. His houses are few, and relatively unimportant. In 1892 he designed for his mother a small house, now destroyed, on the South Side. This was to be occupied for some time by his older brother Albert, who rose to be general superintendent of the Illinois Central Railroad and general manager of the Missouri Pacific. Sullivan quarreled with Albert and Albert's wife; there was no family tie to support him in the difficult days ahead. Another, more successful dwelling was planned in 1907 for Henry Babson in the suburb of Riverside. This, too, has vanished, and the only Sullivan house remaining is that of Josephine Crane Bradley, daughter of Richard Crane, erected in Madison, Wisconsin, in 1909. This has been converted into a fraternity house for the University of Wisconsin.

For a while, but only for a while, Sullivan was able to survive on the momentum created by Adler. In the late 1890's he designed the charming Gage Building on South Michigan Avenue, on which he collaborated with Holabird and Roche, and the Bayard Building, New York City's only example of a Sullivan skyscraper. Since renamed the Condict, this apparition on Bleecker Street is wreathed in the most fanciful terra cotta. Here his partner was New Yorker Lyndon P. Smith.

In 1899 Sullivan was at work on the depart-

The rose garden of his cottage at Ocean Springs, Mississippi, was Sullivan's favorite place on earth. Louis and Margaret were photographed there at some time between their marriage in 1899 and their separation six years later.

ment store of Schlesinger and Mayer on the southeast corner of State and Madison streets. Now occupied by Carson, Pirie, Scott and Company, this is one of his revolutionary designs, a horizontally accented skyscraper encased in the richest cast-iron fantasy. The decoration was the work of his assistant Elmslie, who had already proved he could make good use of the master's vocabulary by providing the decorative theme of the Prudential façade. This store was the last dominating structure on which Sullivan was to work his will.

With fewer and fewer clients to inspire him, Sullivan began to imagine a new career as a writer. In 1901 the *Interstate Architect and Builder* published a number of his articles, ultimately reprinted in 1934 under the title *Kindergarten Chats.* Here he voiced his opinions on any number of subjects including American literature, which he found did not amount to much. "Exquisite, but not virile, our latter-day literature illustrates quite emphatically the duality of our tentative and provisional culture," he decided. He was not a well-read man, although he had digested Walt Whitman.

Humor was banished from the world of *Kindergarten Chats.* True, only a sycophantic follower of McKim, Mead and White could object to his saying that "the worm is at the foot of the rose tree" when discussing McKim's library for Colum-

bia University. But he quite failed to comprehend the ravages of social ambition when writing of the W. K. Vanderbilt mansion. "Have you no sense of pathos?" he angrily inquired. "Must I then explain to you that while the man may live in the house physically, he cannot live in it morally, mentally, or spiritually, that he and his house are a paradox? That he himself is an illusion when he believes his château to be real?"

Sullivan was not only a lonely but a pompous man when he applied in December 1905 for the position of chairman of the school of architecture at the University of Michigan.

In view of the incontestable philosophic and practical truth that the schools of architecture now existing in this country are not only worthless to a democratic people but suppressive of their best interests, and of that natural art of expression which should be theirs, but which cannot find form under the present feudal regime now swaying those schools, I feel compelled to address you.

So be began his letter to President James Angell. It continued:

I am taking the liberty to bring myself to your notice, because I assume that it is perhaps the only means by which you are likely to learn of my existence (notwithstanding my international reputation as an architect) or be put on the track of my life-thought that I have given to the development of a democratic architecture in a democratic land.

He did not get the job, and with such an attitude it is nothing less than a miracle that he managed to grasp thirteen minor commissions from 1907 to 1922. The first of these, the National Farmers' Bank of 1907–8 in Owatonna, Minnesota, must be accounted a major monument in the history of American architecture, even though it is a small bank in a small town. He was fortunate in finding that the bank's vice-president, Carl K. Bennett, a Harvard graduate with a taste for music, was heartily tired of the uninspired classical buildings preferred by Sullivan's competitors. He was also fortunate in having at his side Elmslie, who conceived of the two giant arched windows that give this stone and brick structure its undeniable dignity. Elmslie must also have been of help with the enameled terra-cotta reliefs in bronze-green

OPPOSITE: At the Columbian Exposition of 1893 Sullivan's Transportation Building stood in striking contrast to the fair's prevailing Renaissance style. In this painting by Frank Russell Green visitors are drawn to the flamboyant Golden Door.

OVERLEAF (pages 200–201): In the small town of Owatonna, Minnesota, Sullivan designed this strongbox of a bank. Rising from a sandstone base, the red brick cube is broken by great arched windows. The walls are adorned with bands of bronze-green terra cotta and multicolored glass mosaic, and with foliated cast-iron plaques at each upper corner.

accented with bronze. This masterpiece has recently been restored and enlarged with remarkable sympathy by Harwell Hamilton Harris.

Sullivan might well have designed a high school for Owatonna if he had not had an unholy argument with the school board. As for a house for the Bennetts, which was planned but not built, it may never be missed. According to William Gray Purcell, an all but unqualified admirer of Sullivan, "it seemed to be wholly lacking in any feeling for the Bennetts as a living family. It was more in the nature of a club house."

Not every commission of Sullivan's last years needs to be studied in detail, but the Merchants' National Bank of Grinnell, Iowa, dating from 1914, demands attention. Of wire-cut shale brick, with a cornice in brown terra cotta, its glory is the sunburst of ornament above the entrance door. Other small-town banks in Sidney, Ohio, and Columbus, Wisconsin, display the master's touch. So does his last work, the façade of the William P. Krause music store on Chicago's far North Side, since made over into a funeral home.

For Sullivan the last years were dismal. In 1909 he was obliged to move to a smaller office in the Auditorium Tower, to auction off his library and art collection, and finally to let Elmslie resign from his staff. "Emotional expression is almost impossible to me these days," he confessed to Carl Bennett. "It is impossible to discuss my troubles: they seem to be too deep-seated."

After Elmslie was dismissed, he did, however, consult Dr. George D. Arndt of Newark, Ohio. Only after several weeks in Dr. Arndt's care did he begin to recover his hopes. "I have all along," he wrote, "intuitively felt that the cause lay in a flaw in my own character which I could not discover. . . .

An elaborate rose window, in Sullivan's most explosive style, adorns the front of the Merchants' National Bank in Grinnell, Iowa (opposite). The chandelier above hangs in the Owatonna bank pictured on pages 200–201.

Now comes Arndt and puts his finger deftly on the spot. He says that the simple fundamental trouble that has caused all my unhappiness, bitterness, misery and final breakdown is none other than my persistent lack of kindly feeling toward my fellow men. He is right—and I intend to change! . . . I should have twenty to thirty years of hard work in me yet."

This was in 1910, when Sullivan was nearing fifty-four, and it would be encouraging to think that some real relief was in store for this tormented man. No such relief came, although he was able to spend many pleasant hours at the Cliff Dwellers Club atop Burnham's Orchestra Hall. Here he wrote his autobiography and superintended preparation of the plates for his *System of Architectural Ornament*.

He was not altogether friendless, for Elmslie kept in touch and Wright would come by now and then. One friend who has not been identified was the henna-haired milliner who did her best to look after him in his lodgings at the mediocre Warner Hotel on Cottage Grove Avenue on the South Side. She would put up with his forever pounding the table for the coffee that never arrived on time, and may have rescued him now and then from the stupor that overcame him after one drink too many.

On April 13, 1924, after glancing at the plates of *A System of Architectural Ornament*, placed on his lap by his friend Max Dunning, he fell into a sleep from which he never awakened. He was suffering from neuritis and his heart was weakened by an overindulgence in stimulants. He died the next morning and was buried in Graceland Cemetery by the side of his father and mother.

Although he tried to pass for a philosopher-historian and occasionally for a theologian, he was an architect. And as an architect he is there to challenge mediocrity committed by no matter what member of the profession in whatever time. In our own age, when most skyscrapers are anonymous glass boxes, he is an exasperating reminder of what an individualist can accomplish.

203

Frank Lloyd Wright's sketch for Unity Temple, Oak Park, Illinois, 1905

LLOYD WRIGHT

1867–1959

BY WILLIAM MARLIN

In Wales, that primal, emotive place that was the wellspring of Frank Lloyd Wright's heritage, there is a craggy granite mountain called Cader Idris that conceals a mythic excavation. Celtic legend says it was shaped like a smooth stone couch. Whatever explorer happened by it and was tempted to snuggle within its shelter for the night would be found later—either dead, in a frenzy, or having attained the highest imaginable poetic inspiration.

The life of Frank Lloyd Wright, who once said that he had chosen his ancestors "with the greatest of care," is a long, winding, scenic trail that passed by Cader Idris several times.

He was the greatest architect of the twentieth century, though some thought he was the greatest of the nineteenth century, while he himself asked, "What about the twenty-first?" He seemed to have come from a place far in the past, or far in the future—even from both: his mettle an alloy of antiquity and modernity.

He talked to stones, as the druids did. Like the sorcerers, he turned himself into trees. He climbed into the kiln with his bricks and mixed himself into the sand of his plaster. He spun strands of steel into spans of space, the lines of his buildings moving out—like vectors, with direction and velocity—to hover above the landscape and hug it.

The most resonant chord that he struck was his perception of space—before structural, material, and technical elements—as the reality of architectural expression. Space was the loom upon which all other elements were woven together in what he called an "organic" unfolding of form. His buildings made room for human emotion as well as activities, imagination as well as movement, feelings as well as basic functional requirements. A rapport between space, structure, and site was set in

In the studio of his desert compound, Taliesin West, Frank Lloyd Wright sharpens a pencil in preparation for work. Well into his eighties when this photograph was taken, he was turning out an undiminished flow of designs.

motion as "the inside flowed out, and the outside flowed in."

The divining rods used by this first space man to explore for the sources of form were the forked twigs of a profound historical sense, a reverence for the natural landscape and natural light, a responsive attitude toward the nuances of regional climate and culture, and a determination to appropriate the means of advancing technology so that daily life might be accommodated in an atmosphere of convenience as well as enchantment.

Although he has long been hailed as the founder of modern architecture, he had no truck with the finite, uptight, icily aloof forms that would come to be associated with orthodox modernism in the middle third of the century. To him this "woeful trash" was just a stripped-down version of the "pretty boxes" he had challenged at the turn of the century. Nor did he share modernism's disdain for the past, of which he was a serious student. Wright wanted "to continue what was *noble* in tradition, not old forms, not old rules, but the search for *principle*." He was indeed the Great Emancipator of architecture, but this is largely because he was one of its greatest assimilators—constantly taking new bearings on ancient inspirations and, for that matter, traditional bearings on social, cultural, and technological change. Such spliced inspirations explain why his buildings have a primal, emotive appeal, a composure and reasonableness characteristic of the finest classical architecture, and at the same time an engaging futuristic mien. He lived outside time, combining the imagery of the primitive raft, the prairie schooner, and the square-rigger with the streamlines of steamships, trains, cars, and planes. His work left no symbolism unturned.

As American as huckleberry pie and Huckleberry Finn, Frank Lloyd Wright lived almost ninety-two years, designed over a thousand buildings, and saw over six hundred of them to completion during seventy-two years at the drafting board. He was born in Wisconsin in 1867, only forty-one years after the death of Thomas Jefferson, whom he admired, and fifteen years before the death of Ralph Waldo Emerson, whom he worshiped. On the day he died in 1959, the original group of astronauts was announced, satellites were already orbiting, and he had lived exactly half as long as America had then been an independent republic.

Most of us remember Wright as a white-maned patriarch and as something of an imp, given to wisecracks. He had the demeanor of a pastoral squire and the strut of a tribal potentate; the unpretentious, plain-spoken eloquence of a farmer and the dignity of a statesman; the gentle, delightful curiosity of a child and the ebullient, decisive swagger of a Broadway impressario; the patience of Saint Francis preaching to the birds and the impatience of Pope Julius preaching at Michelangelo, to whom the Italians compared him. He could (and did) get up on the witness stand in a court of law and, asked what he did, say, "I am the world's greatest living architect"—because, after all, "I *was* under oath."

Wright was born of a close-knit Welsh clan in the Wisconsin town of Richland Center, not far from *"the* Valley—the valley that taught me everything"—that had been settled by his maternal grandparents, Richard and Mary Lloyd-Jones, in the 1850's. A lot like the hills and hollows of South Wales, from which they had come, it lay just south of the wide, sandbarred Wisconsin River and near the town of Spring Green. A bedrock-solid feeling for their heritage was implanted in the soil of the valley and in the psyche of their offspring, including Wright's mother, Anna.

To understand Frank's character, one has to deal with the uneasy union of Anna Lloyd-Jones, whose "abiding passions were knowledge and

nature," and her husband, William Russell Cary Wright. A lawyer, preacher, a teacher of music, Wright's father had a wanderlust that no one person, opportunity, or place ever resolved. The newly married couple moved from Richland Center to McGregor, Iowa, and then to Pawtucket, Rhode Island, and then again, in 1874, to Weymouth, Massachusetts, where William Wright took over the pulpit of the First Baptist Church, and where the pull on young Frank from each of his parents became strong.

He was imbued with the compositional, even architectural, geometry of Bach and Beethoven as he pumped the bellows of the church organ that his moody father played for hours. ("My God, Bach required a lot of air.") Even before he was born, his mother had made up her mind that her son would be an architect. At the Philadelphia Centennial Exposition of 1876 she discovered the kindergarten "gifts" of the German educator Friedrich Froebel— blocks, spheres, and cylinders of maple, and paper in various shapes, colors, and textures. Though by this time Frank was nine, she sat him down to play and build with these "gifts." Between Bach and the

blocks, he acquired a tactile as well as a visual sense of spatial and structural organization.

Anna longed for Wisconsin, for the comparative prosperity and stability of her clan, and she wanted her children to know them. In the spring of 1878, assured of work as an itinerant preacher by Anna's prominent brother, the Reverend Jenkin Lloyd-Jones, William Wright moved his family to Madison and into a small house near Lake Mendota. Its porch posts were wrapped with vines, and inside its floors were of gleaming maple. Anna left the floors bare, but for a few Persian rugs, and hung the windows with white sheer curtains: lessons in simplicity for her son, perhaps.

Frank, now eleven, was off to the farm of his Uncle James in the Valley for a hard summer's work. This was the beginning of his "tired to tired" period—the predawn rapping on the stovepipe to awaken him, the never-ending toil (along with several attempts to hide or run away)—and of his gradual harvesting of a bumper crop of clues about nature's patterns, cycles of growth, textures, and colors. During his early teens his formal studies did not interest him much, but up in the attic of the

In 1904 Wright sat on a wall by his home in Oak Park with members of his first family: his six children; his wife, Catherine (second from right, behind Lloyd); his sister Maginal (next to Catherine); and his mother-in-law, Mrs. Samuel Tobin (holding the baby). Wright had enlarged the house as the family grew, and had built an adjoining studio (below) in 1895.

The Robie house, with its sweeping horizontal lines and cantilevered roofs, was built in Chicago in 1909. The most famous of Wright's Prairie houses, it is now a national landmark.

Madison house he surrounded himself with books, materials for drawing and painting and handicraft, and a printing press. This was his "Sanctum," as he spelled it out on the door.

He was not oblivious to the gradual break-up of his parents, especially after the fall of 1883, when he was sixteen. The reason usually given for this crucial turn is that his restless father was hardly ever around, what with his preaching all over southern Wisconsin and his assorted musical activities. Clearly, however, Anna's devotion to her son took on a domineering tone. This may well be why his father retreated, as much out of anguish over a "lost" son as anything else, and he divorced Anna in 1885.

There is something mysterious about Wright's life that may be buried in this mighty woodpile of psychological and familial disruption. Wright maintained that he was born in 1869, not 1867. He also maintained that he had come within three months of getting a degree in civil engineering at the University of Wisconsin (he came within three years of getting it). Historians Thomas C. Hines and Robert C. Twombly have documented the falsehood of both contentions, shedding new light on

Wright's youth and thus on his psychological motivations and personal conduct in later years.

Though we do not know why, we know that Wright expunged two years from his chronology, probably for some very personal (and painful) reason. It has been speculated that he tracked down his father and tried to rekindle a relationship with him—only to be rebuffed. But, as we shall see, the expunction of two years may have been caused by a later, harrowing upheaval. Certainly it behooves us, in dealing with a man who wrote so rich a script for the cultural development and destiny of us all, to keep an eye out for the lost passages in his own persona. Besides which, the Wisconsin lad expected us to.

Not long after his parents' divorce and his dropping out of high school (his attendance had been spotty), Wright went to work for Allen D. Conover, a professor of civil engineering at the University of Wisconsin, doing office chores, some drafting, and a little field work. He entered the university as a "special student" in January 1886. That summer he supervised the construction of the Lloyd-Jones clan's chapel, out in the Valley. It was designed by Joseph Lyman Silsbee, a Chicago proponent of the picturesque Shingle style and a close friend of Wright's Uncle Jenkin. The following winter, at the age of nineteen, Wright dropped out of the university and took the train to Chicago.

Chicago—big, crude, crowded, ambitious—had all the subtlety of a Bessemer furnace compared to his bucolic roots. But the city was experiencing some bracing architectural breezes. A progressive, structurally forthright idiom of design was emerging from men such as Major William Le Baron Jenney, and from firms such as Burnham and Root, Holabird and Roche, and Adler and Sullivan. They were raising the first steel-framed towers, making Chicago the birthplace of the skyscraper, and spouting the first functionalist rhetoric.

Wright knocked about the streets and assorted architectural firms for several days. Starved and scared, he finally showed up at Silsbee's and, without mentioning the Lloyd-Jones connection, was hired. By the time his relationship to Jenkin became known, he had shown such skill that he was given time to design and supervise the construction of his first building, the Hillside Home School for his aunts Ellen and Jane, located back home in the Valley. Opened in 1887, it was one of the first progressive coeducational institutions in the country.

Early in 1888 Wright went to see Louis Henri Sullivan of Adler and Sullivan, then planning the mammoth Auditorium Building. Wright's fine hand and quick, incisive mind greatly impressed the usually imperious, impenetrable Sullivan. Hired, Wright became "a good pencil in the master's hand" and, according to the benign "big chief," Dankmar Adler, the highest-paid chief draftsman in town.

The completion of the Auditorium coincided with Wright's marriage in 1889 to Catherine Tobin, whom he had run into (and literally knocked down) at a dance at his uncle's church. He bought a lot in the village of Oak Park and, with an advance on a five-year contract with Adler and Sullivan, began building a modest gabled house for himself and Catherine.

Wright's brambly prairie lot was a conservator's delight, with a tulip tree, a ginkgo, a number of willows, a honey locust, black and white walnuts, and some butternuts. Beyond lay the tall grass and native flowers of the ancient, unspoiled prairie, few patches of which are still to be found today. The shingled gable nestled on a base of brick that, in turn, extended to form terrace walls. Inside, there was an extraordinary warmth of tone and openness of space. As his family grew, finally numbering six children, Wright added more rooms. On the second floor he created a high barrel-vaulted, skylit playroom. Family concerts and cotillions, puppet shows and magic shows, poetry readings and glittering parties—all were held in the playroom. A fireplace was at the far end,

with a fanciful mural above the mantel. Rising above and behind the low entrance were stairs leading to balconied galleries. A few years later, Wright installed a grand piano beneath these stairs in an ingenious way. Only its keyboard protruded out of the wall, into the room. The rest of the piano was concealed, suspended by chains, deep within the structure. The risers of the stairs leading to the galleries could be opened when the piano was played, thus transforming the galleries into an acoustically effective sound chamber—making the room an aural as well as visual entity. Toward the end of the 1890's he added an architectural studio, entrance loggia, private office, and library. The home-and-studio complex is one of Wright's most inventive and magical creations.

It was all so wonderful—this low-flying labyrinth of a house, sending out calls of courtship to the prairie, enclasping peaceful gardens and terraces between the intricately dovetailed buildings. A tall willow grew up between the house and studio, giving the effect of growing through the roof. Angular roof peaks leaped up from low angular wall planes to fraternize with the branches of the trees. Skylights and clerestories ensnared the light, and beneath them a whole new epoch in architecture was configured.

During his first three years in Oak Park, Wright designed several houses for clients of Adler and Sullivan. He also started to do work of his own on the side—"bootlegged" jobs, as he called them. Ingenuously he did not believe that this would constitute a betrayal of Sullivan's trust or of the terms of his contract with the firm. Sullivan, happening by one of the "bootlegged" houses and recognizing the style of his chief draftsman, thought otherwise. The contract, it turned out, read otherwise, too. After a stormy scene between the two, Wright stalked out of the office.

Moving into the Schiller Building, on which he had worked for Sullivan, Wright struck out on his own. His first independent job was the Winslow house in River Forest, west of Oak Park. Even today, almost ninety years after its conception, this building, with a simple, symmetrical street façade of brick and terra cotta beneath a generous overhanging roof, looks astonishingly modern.

For the next seven years leading up to the turn of the century—from his twenty-sixth to his thirty-third year—Wright would struggle to gather together the strands of his own identity and idiom. This crucial period has been glossed over by many observers as a stylistically unkempt time during which Wright tried on everything at least once—Dutch Colonial, Georgian, Tudor, even something he called Hans Christian Andersen. Indeed it was almost as though Wright didn't quite trust himself with the delicate counterbalancing of forms and effects that he had packed into the Winslow house. He was feeling his way, testing this and testing that, gradually gaining confidence.

In 1896, with the Hillside Home School prospering, his aunts needed a windmill above a newly dug reservoir, uphill from the building he had designed for them while working for Silsbee. They asked Frank, but when the unusual scheme for "Romeo and Juliet" arrived, his pragmatic uncles protested. They said it would fall down in the first storm to hit the valley. Wright wrote, "Build it!" They did, and it is still there: a sixty-foot-tall octagonal barrel, braced by a diamond-shaped "storm prow."

To take another example of Wright's confidence, in the late 1890's his Uncle Jenkin, fast becoming a world-famous humanitarian through his All Souls' Church in Chicago, decided he needed a larger building, combining a church and community center. Inspired by his close friend Jane Addams, he wanted it to "do for the rich what Hull House was doing for the poor." He asked Frank to design it, but from the start the two couldn't agree on a scheme. His uncle said, "I've been all over the world; have seen more great buildings than you've ever seen. Can't you trust me?" The spunky nephew shot back: "No . . . not with 'my' building. Besides, you couldn't possibly have seen more great buildings than I've ever *imagined*."

By the turn of the century Wright was imagining some of the most inventive and beautiful residential buildings in the history of architecture. These so-called Prairie houses had a chimney-anchored, evanescent horizontality, a flowing spatial affinity between rooms, an honest, unadorned handling of materials, and an underlying structural pattern out of which every visual element emanated.

Starting with the publication of his earliest work in the *Architectural Review of Boston* in 1900, and with the airy, interlocking pavilions of the wood-and-stucco Willits house in Highland Park the following year, Wright's architectural shots would be heard around the world. The prominent English architect and critic C. R. Ashbee, having gotten to know Wright and his work during a visit to Chicago, started spreading the word throughout Europe. Wrote Ashbee,

This new spirit has for us in Europe a peculiar charm and piquancy, just because we do not see in it that reflection of European forms to which we have been so long accustomed. Its characteristics are a departure from tradition, a distinctiveness of surrounding, and a consequent character of its own, a delight in new materials, and an honest use of machinery.

Through to the close of the Oak Park years in 1909, and of what Grant Manson called Wright's first golden age, this new spirit, tethered closely to the native ground, natural elements, and new technological and social conditions, shaped the snug, low-slung Heurtley, Cheney, and Thomas houses in Oak Park; the brick-enfolded fantasia of wide eaves and earthy hues for Susan Lawrence Dana in Springfield, Illinois; the sprawling, richly articulated estates for Darwin D. Martin in Buffalo and Avery Coonley in Riverside, near Oak Park; and, finally, the most famous Prairie house of all—that for Frederick C. Robie, which rode upon its site down by the University of Chicago like a long brick ship, and, through the use of long steel beams, flung its cantilevered roofs into space.

Since Wright's objective was a total integration of elements, it was impossible to see, at the Martin house, the brick piers, the heating elements, and the lighting fixtures as separate pieces of the environmental fabric. Free-standing quartets of these piers composed the plan, the radiators were tucked in the center, and light came from fixtures on the piers themselves—all one unit in visual and functional performance.

It was similarly impossible to see, at the Coonley house, structure as one thing, windows as yet another thing, and ornamentation as something else again. In almost all of the Prairie houses, Wright would select one or two or three motifs, each inspired by a native plant or flower, and reduce what he called its "pattern of growth" to a basic, severe, geometrical abstraction, variations of which would appear in the windows and doors throughout the house. In the Dana house, the thriving motif was derived from sumac; in the Martin house, from wisteria.

Wright tended to design everything—rugs, curtains, napkins, tableware, furniture (which he preferred to build in)—so that every element of the environmental experience could flow together. He even designed the dresses of some of his clients' wives (as indeed he did for his own). Usually these dresses had natural, soft colors and graceful lines so that Mrs. Avery Coonley, for example, could feel herself blending into his scheme, or so that Mrs. Frederick Robie, whom he didn't like, could feel herself disappearing completely.

Wright's concept of total design carried furniture a long way from the days when, as he said, "tables and chairs were still at large." Yet his furniture could be infuriating. Certainly it was refreshing to see clean, crisp lines and natural, plain wood, but his chairs were almost as hard to move as his built-in benches. Many of them were uncomfortable to sit in, because a chair whose geometry is meant to evoke the geometry of a house plan or its related leaded-glass abstraction of flowers may not be easy on the human frame. At dinner, for instance, some people had to wonder whether they were sitting there to enjoy the food and company or to participate in and reaffirm the otherwise joyous geometry of the architecture. At least Wright was honest about this: "All my life my legs have been banged up somewhere by the chairs I have designed."

These often entertaining quibbles aside, the Prairie house was a triumphal integration not only of space and structure and site, but also of new materials and technologies, such as plate glass, central heating, and electricity. These enabled Wright to fulfill his sense of space and simplicity, to replace the old heavy walls with bracing vistas, and to cease "reproducing with murderous ubiquity forms born of other times and other conditions."

Wright's buildings for the public realm, with the spatial zest and technical inventiveness of his houses, had the air of ensconcing families of spirited, creative, productive individuals. In 1904 he designed the Larkin Company Administration Building in Buffalo. Its milieu, held within "simple cliffs of brick," was molded around a fetching skylit well running through the center and flanked by several gallerylike floors. On the top level, at either end of the light well, conservatories were placed so that the visual experience culminated in a luxuriant, inspiring display of foliage as well as in a bath of diffused light. A restaurant overlooked the offices below and gave onto a rooftop recreation area.

Wright's other notable public building of the Prairie period was Unity Temple in Oak Park, designed in 1905 as "a frank revival of the old temple form." Eschewing the customary steeple pointing at the heavens, Wright envisioned "a modern meeting house and good time place . . . in which to study man for his God's sake."

Turning inward from a noisy street and nearby train track, the temple is a strongbox of poured-in-place concrete which contains a square, skylit sanctuary. Few rooms in the history of architecture match its intricately reasoned spatial relationships and glowing serenity. People are guided into it, as if by some invisible force, across an entrance terrace and through a low vestibule to cloisters, from which the main room is glimpsed. Then, up a few steps, they fully experience its interconnected

The exterior of Unity Temple, built in 1906 for the Unitarian church in Oak Park, is a massive box of poured concrete. Within the sanctuary the walls, columns, stairs, and balconies make an intricate composition of squares and rectangles.

AARON SISKIND

213

The Imperial Hotel, built in Tokyo between 1917 and 1922, was a palatial fantasy of brick and concrete with sculptured lava trim. Set upon a flexible foundation, it rode out the earthquake of 1923 that destroyed much of Tokyo, but was torn down in 1968.

columns, stairs, and balconies, which rise to the light-flooded pattern of intersecting concrete ceiling beams and to curtains of glass sweeping along the upper edges of the exterior walls.

The creation of Unity Temple was pure genius. Working in his studio three blocks to the north, wolfing down his favorite baked Bermuda onions beside a roaring fire while his wife played the piano in the background, Wright here first consciously codified his perception of space as the reality of architectural form—the same year that Albert Einstein codified his perception of the speed of light as the reality of measurement in physics. Unity Temple was Wright's $E=mc^2$.

On the surface of things, Wright by this time seemed destined for universal acclaim. His son John later recalled, "He was an epic of wit and merriment that gave our home the feeling of a jolly carnival." But something was starting to go wrong with his marriage and family life. In fact, Wright, despite his success, and with such masterworks as the Robie house just ahead, was coming to his first encounter with Cader Idris.

The house he designed for Edwin and Mamah Borthwick Cheney, completed in 1904 and a short walk from his own place, is to this day haunted by wraiths that will come, with a little coaxing research, out of the deep fireplace to help explain what happened. The Wrights and the Cheneys had spent a lot of time together since the late 1890's, the two women collaborated on various civic and cultural projects, and Frank and Mamah became

very fond of each other. Furthermore, as Wright rationalized it later, Catherine's vocation had become motherhood; besides which, the shenanigans of his children were getting on his nerves. He began to draw away from Catherine and fell deeply in love with Mamah, a progressive, free-spirited graduate of the University of Michigan. Although she had three children, she was anything but a doting mother.

At the same time, Wright was becoming disenchanted with the way his work was being interpreted. Its outward stylistic effects—not the social and cultural significance that he saw in it—were being widely discussed. He found himself being lumped in with a new "Prairie school," and a school of style was not what he had set out to mold. Although he would later contend that he had battled against overwhelming odds for acceptance,

and although some traditionalists did find his houses "crazy-looking," what really irked Wright were comments like those in *National Builder* magazine, which could report in 1905 that his ideas, especially his fluid, uncluttered interior spaces, were happily becoming "typical." In other words, Wright, the torchbearer of a new architectural order, was finding it difficult to reconcile his self-image as a revolutionary with the fact that his work, precisely because of its freshness of form and fecundity of invention, *was* being accepted.

As Wright tells us in that long fireside chat of a book, *An Autobiography:* "Weary, I was losing grip on my work and even my interest in it. . . . Everything, personal or otherwise, bore heavily down upon me. Domesticity most of all. What I wanted I did not know. I loved my children. I loved my home. A true home is the finest ideal of man,

215

and yet.... Because I did not know what I wanted, I wanted to go away."

By 1909 Wright was behaving in an increasingly eccentric, distracted manner. He took wild rides on his horse, raced around the area in his car, disappeared for days at a time, asked Catherine for a divorce—and was asked to take a year to think it over. He also began planning a house "for his mother" up in the Valley on a hilly piece of land that had come to her. This was the beginning of Taliesin—literally "shining brow"—named for the ancient Welsh bard. It was not built for his mother at all, but as a home for himself and his new love.

Then, during the construction of the Robie house, he abruptly announced to his admiring client that he had an opportunity to go to Japan to do a little hotel. He left Oak Park in September of 1909, not for Japan but for Europe—and with Mrs. Cheney. They went to Berlin, where the prestigious Wasmuth publishing house had invited him to prepare a portfolio of his work. The result, *Ausgeführte Bauten und Entwürfe von Frank Lloyd Wright* of 1910, hit all of Europe, as Ludwig Mies van der Rohe was to say, "like lightning."

As the noted historian and critic Edgar J. Kaufmann, Jr., has written, Wright, having triumphed over the "cold-storage classicism" of the Beaux-Arts influence, appealed to the Europeans because he "could be inventive without losing a sense of the living past." Wright agreed: "Radical though it be, the work . . . is dedicated to a cause conservative in the best sense of the word. At no point does it involve denial of the elemental law and order inherent in all great architecture; rather, it is a declaration of love for the spirit of that law and order, and a reverential recognition of the elements that made its ancient letter in its time vital and beautiful."

There are indications that Wright felt guilty about leaving his family. In any event, Mamah returned to Oak Park in July of 1910, and having told Edwin the year before that she was leaving for good, she went off somewhere with her children until Wright's return in October. But for him, "getting home" meant building a brick wall between the original house, which he moved into, and the studio, which he remodeled for his family. Until the Cheneys' divorce in August of 1911 he lived and worked, off and on, in the house, while Mamah lived nearby in the one he had built for her and Edwin. He was also working furiously to complete Taliesin, and the following Christmas it became public knowledge that Mamah Borthwick Cheney had moved into the new house.

The year 1912 started out stormily. Preachers, assorted social groups, and "right-minded" citizens generally denounced the couple. Taliesin was

hooted at as a haven of pleasure, crazy house, love-cote, and as a palace of folly. Early in 1913 the two took a five-month trip to Japan, where Wright had a commission to design a hotel in Tokyo.

Back home, while refining plans for what would be the renowned Imperial Hotel, Wright went to work on the design of the Midway Gardens, a spectacular, block-square entertainment center in Chicago. Wright was hopeful and happy in his work and in the home he had made at Taliesin. Its genesis was best described in his own words:

I scanned the hills of the region where the rock came cropping out in strata to suggest buildings. . . . And so began a "shining brow" for the hill, the hill rising unbroken about it to crown the exuberance of life in all these rural riches. . . . Finally it was not so easy to tell where pavements and walls left off and ground began. . . .

The strata of fundamental stone-work kept reaching around and on into the four courts, and made them. Then stone, stratified, went into the lower house walls and up from the ground itself into the broad chimneys. This native stone prepared the way for the lighter plastered construction of the upper wood-walls. Taliesin was to be an abstract combination of stone and wood as they naturally met in the aspect of the hills around about. The lines of the hills were the lines of the roofs, the slopes of the hills their slopes, the plastered surfaces of the light wood-walls, set back into shade beneath broad eaves, were like the flat stretches of sand in the river below and the same in color. . . .

And when the snow piled deep on the roofs and lay drifted in the courts, icicles came to hang staccato from the eaves. Prismatic crystal pendants, sometimes six feet long, glittered between the landscape and the eyes inside. Taliesin in winter was a frosted palace roofed and walled with snow, hung with iridescent fringes, the plate-glass of the windows shone bright and warm through it all as the light of the huge fire-places lit them . . . and streams of wood-smoke from a dozen such places went straight up toward the stars.

On August 14, 1914, while Wright and his son John were taking lunch at the Midway Gardens site, he received a telephone call from the Valley. Taliesin was in flames. When Wright got there he found a charred, smoking ruin. Mamah Borthwick lay dead, along with two of her children (who had been visiting), and four other victims. The ghastly scene was the work of a deranged butler, who had set the house afire while the occupants were at lunch and then hacked them down with an axe as they tried to escape.

"Men from Taliesin dug the grave, deep," Wright later wrote. "I cut her garden down and with the flowers filled the strong, plain box of fresh, white pine to overflowing.... My boy, John, coming to my side now, helped lift the body and we let it down to rest among the flowers that had grown and bloomed for her." He filled the grave alone, standing by past sunset and into the night.

Only a part of his architectural studio escaped the blaze—this and a little bedroom and sitting room tucked behind it, with a fireplace. When Wright wasn't taking long, directionless walks at night, he spent days darker than night inside, venturing outside of himself only to eulogize in the Spring Green paper "a brave and lovely woman" and to express his gratitude for the compassion of a community that had once kept a discreet (when not condescending) distance from "the freedom in which we joined." Only the thought of rebuilding Taliesin sustained him as "the equivalent of years passed within my consciousness in the course of days."

Wherever Mamah was buried—her marker, placed there after Wright's death, does not mark the exact spot—may also be buried the reason why he expunged those two years from his life—why he began saying that he had been born in 1869 rather than 1867.

In pursuing this mystery to at least one of several possible conclusions, one must keep in mind that Wright had in him that deep, Celtic, indeed congenital, bent for symbolic signs and gestures. Mamah was forty-five in 1914, when Wright was forty-seven. Instead of having "flat

The Millard house in Pasadena, California, was a product of Wright's interest in ancient Mayan temples during the early 1920's. It was built of patterned concrete "textile blocks," so called because they were "knit" together with steel rods.

217

forgot" when he was born (Wright never "flat forgot" a thing), it can now be surmised that either before or after her death he decided to "twin" the year of his birth with hers as a symbolic gesture of affection. It would have been completely in Wright's nature to make this gesture—and not think of it as a lie. When he lowered Mamah Borthwick down amongst the flowers and into the earth, he did not lose two years to seem younger; he lost them to be with her.

By November of 1914 Wright had pulled himself together enough to go down to Chicago, where since 1912 he had maintained an office at Orchestra Hall and an apartment on Cedar Street, on the Near North Side of town. Preparing to rebuild Taliesin, he also resumed work on the design of the Imperial Hotel.

This immense complex of brick and hand-worked lava trim, meant to be earthquake-proof, was carried on a flexible foundation of concrete pads, each supported in turn by slender pinlike piers sunk down through the topsoil to the sea of mud beneath Tokyo. The building—H-shaped in plan and interspersed with courtyards, gardens,

and pools—was in effect "floated" on this underground sea to ride out tremors. In construction from early 1917 until late 1922, the Imperial looked like a sprawling, primordial eruption of ornament whose cavernous interiors seemed to have been carved out by the flow of subsurface streams.

In December 1916 Wright departed for Tokyo, where he would live most of the time until the Imperial's completion, taking with him a well-off Kentucky-born divorcee named Miriam Noel. A flamboyantly attired sculptress who was living in Paris at the time of the tragedy in 1914, she had written to Wright, offering her sympathy, help, and presumably her companionship. In fact, her money helped substantially in the rebuilding of Taliesin—underscoring Wright's psychological vulnerability at this point.

From the start, their relationship was weird. She was mercurial and sparkling, imperious and intellectual, possessive and open to advanced ideas. She flew into rages at the very mention of Mamah, turning the rooms upside down; she crawled to Wright on her hands and knees, begging forgiveness. She left in a huff, flooded him with love

In 1932 Wright and his third wife, Olgivanna (opposite page), founded the Taliesin Fellowship to train young architects. Learning by doing was the basic tenet of the program, and students were immersed in all aspects of everyday life from carpentry (left) to kitchen duty; the weaver on the opposite page finds one of the many bronze arms of an ancient Indian god a useful yarn holder. In return for their labor the apprentices and even their children received instruction by the master (above), as well as an exhilarating round of parties, concerts, and picnics (left, above).

hock House for Aline Barnsdall, an oil heiress. It surrounded a lushly landscaped courtyard with low and heavy concrete shapes, trimmed with long rows of abstract hollyhocks (Miss Barnsdall's favorite flower). Taking the theme all the way, the stiff backs of the dining room chairs also carried this abstraction. And to underscore the material continuity of the house, there was even a concrete *door*. Miss Barnsdall used to say that it took several men to help her in and out.

In the early 1920's Wright developed a system of concrete-block construction, opening the way for yet another building medium. These "textile blocks," threaded onto steel rods, were the warp and woof of the mysterious Millard, Storer, Freeman, and Ennis houses—intriguingly mute creations, as silent in their isolate imagery as anything then on the silver screen.

By 1923—the year of the Tokyo earthquake that the Imperial rode out to international acclaim—Wright had entered an uncertain period in his life which would score high on any seismograph of human discord and upheaval. The mentally unstable Miriam was driving him crazy.

letters that were made public by a disgruntled housekeeper, and then returned to escape the sordid repercussions of the published letters.

When Wright was not in Japan he spent most of his time in southern California working on a series of exotic houses that reflected a new enthusiasm for Mayan temples. Among these was Holly-

The spacious living room of Taliesin North, the home that Wright built in Spring Green, Wisconsin, was the gathering place for his family and the whole community of young architects and students who came to learn from him.

Having finally returned to Taliesin late in 1922, he got a divorce from Catherine, suffered the death of his mother the next February, and then inexplicably married Miriam in November. Things only got worse. She left in April 1924.

Around Christmas of that year another figure appeared at Taliesin. Olgivanna Milanof Lazovich, twenty-six, whom Wright had met at the ballet in Chicago, had been born of an influential family in the mountainous principality of Montenegro, now part of Yugoslavia. Schooled in Russia, she had become a student of Georgi Gurdjieff at his Institute for the Harmonious Development of Man, near Paris. She was (still is) aristocratic, mystical, beautiful, and tough.

Wright had not heard the last of Miriam, whom he tried to divorce after her departure. During the next two years he was embroiled in a tangle of lawsuits and public attacks instigated by her. As if that were not enough, Taliesin, struck by lightning, burned down again. At last, in 1928,

Wright got his divorce, wed Olgivanna, and returned to the long-besieged, but rebuilt, Taliesin.

Although the storms of his private life had interfered with his work, and the crash of 1929 cost him commissions, Wright was undismayed. He had encountered Cader Idris, had survived its death and its frenzy, and had emerged with the highest imaginable poetic inspiration intact.

In May of 1930, hardly looking the part of the harassed outcast genius, Wright swept onto the campus of Princeton University in his white Cord convertible and, cutting quite a figure at the age of sixty-three, delivered six lectures that were published the following year in book form as *Modern Architecture.* In 1932 Wright published his *Autobiography* as well as *The Disappearing City,* his first epistle about the decentralization of our urban centers. Also that year Wright and his wife founded the Taliesin Fellowship as a training ground for architects. Its essential idea was to produce well-rounded, hard-working men and women who could deal with (and design for) every aspect of human life. Others have likened it to King Arthur's Round Table, a druidic priesthood, a monastic order, an offshoot of the American utopian communes of the nineteenth century, and a Byzantine court.

Life for those who joined the fellowship was a constant round of rotated duties, interspersed with stretches at the drafting board: tilling, sowing, reaping; splitting wood; stoking the furnaces, looking after the electrical generator down by the dam; cutting wood and doing carpentry; quarrying limestone and laying it up; feeding the lime kiln and doing plasterwork.

A most absorbing account of fellowship life has been given by architect Edgar Tafel in *Apprentice to Genius*. Running into Wright on his first day at Taliesin, he was asked to help the master move a piano. Soon Wright learned that Tafel could play it, so he was frequently told to climb up on the little balcony above the architectural studio and knock out a fugue or sonata.

Another apprentice, the photographer Pedro E. Guerrero, arrived in 1939. His talent appealed to Wright's long-standing interest in photography and, besides doing all the work that the other apprentices did, he became the court cameraman. But as he recalls,

I wasted little time in becoming an architect and carpenter. And the first week I was also assigned to the kitchen, an elaborate K.P. In the summer our kitchen abounded with fresh vegetables, and at times it was the Wrights' happy boast to a visitor that the meal we had just put away was entirely Taliesin-grown. Harvest time was splendid. Great mountains of pumpkins and squashes were piled high at the entrances of the remodeled Hillside Home School buildings, and basket after basket of apples were stored in the cool root cellar. The need for the crop was important, but the way in which it was used to enhance the beauty of our surroundings was equally important. Mr. Wright felt the same way about music, feeling that the apprentices working out in the fields should have as much access to Bach and Beethoven as those in the drafting room. His solution was to install a speaker atop "Romeo and Juliet" connected to the Scott record player at Hillside. The whole countryside came alive with music.

There have been less rhapsodic accounts of life at Taliesin. Many of the apprentices—most came from fairly comfortable circumstances—did not like being farm hands, household servants, construction laborers, and chauffeurs. But the Wrights' insistence that their apprentices be immersed in every aspect of cultivating and maintaining a complete living environment was quite valid in principle. Moreover, the Wrights themselves joined in most of the work. Olgivanna recalls,

Oh, how he loved moving furniture. I believe I have moved more of it, helping him, than any woman alive.

A desert sunrise enlivens this metal, geometricized standard, keeping sentinel at the entrance to Taliesin West. The sculpture incorporates Wright's insignia, the red square.

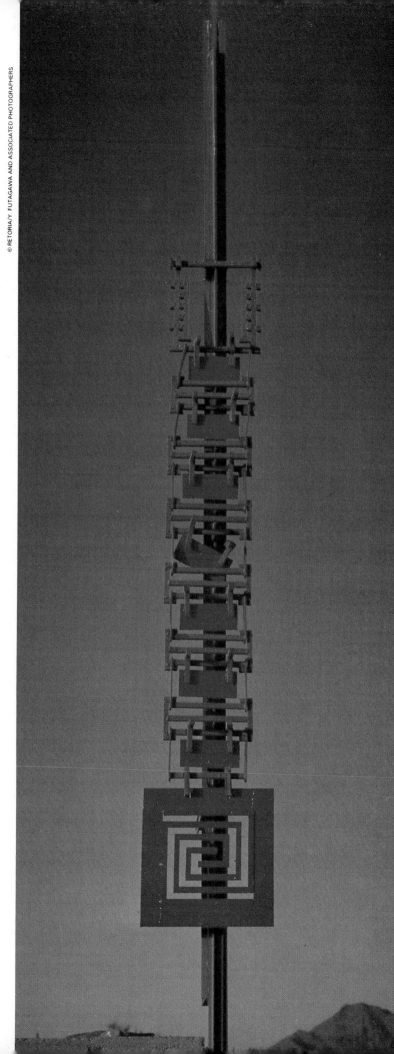

You see, there was no differentiation for him between physical, spiritual, and creative energy, and none between scrubbing floors, working out in the fields, concentrating on a design, coming up with a wonderful dinner, or sitting at the desk to write. It is this sense of the integration of life that Frank wanted to instill in those who came to study. . . .

Life at Taliesin was leavened by a flow of prominent people from the intellectual, scientific, theatrical, business, and political worlds. The list of guests who came for a day or weekend, or for a week or two, is endless. Sinclair Lewis, Lawrence Tibbett, Charles Laughton, Sessue Hayakawa, Alexander Woollcott, Carl Sandburg, Paul Robeson, only hint at the richness of the discourse, the diversity of the fun. "Where else but at Taliesin," said the builder Morton Cohen, "could I have dinner seated between Adlai Stevenson and Clare Boothe Luce?" On weekends especially, with lavish dinners, the latest movies, lots of conversation, and a chorus or

Taliesin West, a testament to man's primordial ties to nature, proffers a great prow-shaped terrace to the terrain that inspired its form and supplied the stone for its walls. The parallel beams to the left mark the roof of the drafting room; to the right rise the living room and the Wrights' personal quarters—all interspersed with cool pools and gardens.

chamber concert, the place was sparkling in its urbanity—a kind of dream community that expressed Wright's belief that American society should *plan* communities "with all of the advantages of the city and the country and without the disadvantages of either."

Wright's most caustically criticized and (until recently) least understood project embodied his thinking about cities, the impact of suburbanization, and environmental planning. It has long been said that Wright hated cities, which he called "great mouths." This is patent nonsense: He hated the chaotic, coercive characteristics that so many cities had taken on. In 1934 he conceived Broadacre City as a framework for giving order to the social, economic, and technological forces that were contributing to the decentralization of our urban centers. Hooted down by the "experts" as hopelessly romantic, it was based on the allocation of one acre per person. Houses were built to the contours of the land, all interlaced with roadways and punctuated here and there by towers.

Actually Broadacre City was a serious socioeconomic diagram and, as things have turned out, extraordinarily prescient. For Wright understood

both the allure and the potential evils of the automobile. While he felt it to be an emancipating machine, he also cautioned that America, amidst the massive exodus from the city that he saw as inevitable, might well end up strip-mining its natural landscape with unkempt sprawl. Thus Broadacre City addressed the physical, functional, and visual relationship between farms and adjacent built-up sections containing homes, schools, stores, professional offices, business and public buildings, and parking. In this he understood what we, in the 1970's, were to hear a lot about—the impact of suburbanization on agricultural lands or other open space, and the risks of not handling the "urban fringe" carefully. He proposed combining high-speed public transit lines with the run of his highways, based on his belief that the government, if it wanted to subsidize something really practical, should subsidize this. Thus, while Wright saw clearly that the coming of the car was encouraging decentralization, he also saw that America—for environmental and ecological as well as aesthetic reasons—should not be turned into one endless Autoland. By putting public transit and financial assistance for it at parity with the construction and

improvement of highways and roads, he was fifty years ahead of his time.

Broadacre City, whether we know it or like it or not, has come to pass—but without the order, harmony, and sense of community that Wright envisioned. Robert A. M. Stern, among the most talented of the younger generation of architects, points out: "Though Broadacre City can be dismissed as an extreme vision of the Arcadian ideal such as Detroit might dream of but never have the genius to propose, it did articulate principles for a new kind of land planning based on the automobile which have come to govern suburban development since 1945."

In 1936 Wright designed his best-known building, Fallingwater, a country retreat for Edgar J. Kaufmann, Sr., at Bear Run, Pennsylvania. Hovering above a waterfall in a lovely ravine, its dynamic, even rambunctious demeanor is held in check, anchored into the ancient rock ledges by tall piers of native stone. Ledgelike floors and terraces of concrete are cantilevered out over the waterfall, overlapping one other. The largest of these cantilevers carries a lairlike living room where a big boulder emerges out of the flagstone floor beside

the fireplace. And through a glass-encased "hatch" a hanging staircase flutters down to the stream, which is sensed throughout the house, even when it cannot be seen. Fallingwater, Wright's most brilliant essay about the relationship between nature and architecture, is the first space ship.

Also in 1936 Wright got the job of designing the administrative headquarters for the Johnson Wax Company in Racine, Wisconsin. Its president, Herbert F. Johnson, had a genuine interest in enriching the daily lives of the employees. And so, in the depth of the Depression, Wright produced a building that was clearly meant to leaven the outlook as well as the efficiency of workers.

The main element of Johnson Wax is the enormous, luminous workroom—a brick receptacle with rounded corners and streamlined surfaces. The whole structure is covered with skylights, which are actually the interstices between the round lily-pad tops of the tendril-like concrete columns supporting the roof. The feeling inside can be likened to being immersed in a vast clear pool of water permeated by the play of light. The fluid spaces, alternately compressed, interlaced with long bridges and balconies, and soaring to the lily pads configuring the roof, are conducive to camaraderie. Stories are legion about how people would come in early and stay late, as drawn into the experience of work as to the warmth of their own hearths at home. The spirit of the place encouraged rituals, such as singing by the company choir on the bridges overlooking the main floor, and the serving of tea at appointed hours. At a time when "free enterprise" was widely thought of as a euphemism for organized avarice, this building was a deliberate message to the business community that, for the most practical reasons of productivity, its buildings must make room for the needs of its employees in the broadest sense.

Not all his corporate clients were as amenable to Wright's ideas as Johnson Wax. While he was dealing with one of his rich clients he once remarked: "There is nothing so timid as a million dollars." Ironically, at about the same time as Fallingwater and Johnson Wax, he was to find out that there is also nothing so courageous as $5,500, which is what a Madison newspaperman named Herbert Jacobs had to spend on a house. Wright had long been concerned with the challenge of designing average-size, affordable dwellings, and

Fallingwater at Bear Run, Pennsylvania, is the most famous and most spectacular of all Wright's houses. In a creative marriage of nature and modern technology, floors and terraces of concrete, anchored in the native stone ledges, are cantilevered out over a waterfall. Built in 1936 for Edgar J. Kaufmann, Sr., the house is now open to the public.

the one for Jacobs was the first of many "Usonian" houses. *Usonia* was Wright's name for America.

Showing the same sensitivity to site and climate as the Prairie houses, the Usonians were logical, economical, and unostentatious. Shop-fabricated "sandwich walls" of plywood, with horizontal boards (usually of cypress) screwed on either side, replaced the conventional two-by-four stud construction. The floors were simply mats of concrete, scored with delicate lines depicting the planning grid; these were laid over a layer of gravel in which was embedded a filigree of heating pipes—the first radiant, or gravity, system. The low roof lines and deep eaves not only underscored the affinity between structure and terrain, but they were extended out as a shelter for the family car—the first "carport," which Wright named as well as devised. Inside, the Usonians typically combined living and dining areas into a single space looking out upon and drawing in the garden. Back to back were the fireplace, kitchen, and utilities. The bedrooms were ranged along what Wright likened to a polliwog's tail, usually at a right angle to the living area, and the corridors in this wing were lined with built-in closets, storage space, or bookshelves. Lighting was usually recessed or indirect, so one had the feeling that the house itself was the light source. In its uncramped, uncluttered ambiance, in its frank and consistent expression of materials and of the underlying structural grid, the Usonian house was one of Wright's most noble and disarmingly beautiful creations.

The late 1930's saw Wright's reputation soar. During this period he designed the campus plan and a number of buildings for Florida Southern College at Lakeland, with a lattice of covered walkways interconnecting the villalike complex; a never-built thicket of towers called Crystal City in Washington, D.C., combining hotel facilities, apartments, offices, and commercial and cultural space—pioneering the so-called mixed-use principle of urban development; a studio for Gutzon Borglum near Mount Rushmore; a palatial spa for Elizabeth Arden in the Arizona desert; one hundred all-steel, factory-fabricated houses in Los Angeles; and another hundred four-family houses, each clustered together like a cloverleaf, for defense workers in Massachusetts. The latter housing project was killed because Representative John McCormack agreed with protesting Massachusetts architects that such a plum shouldn't be given to somebody from Wisconsin when they themselves were out of work.

It probably wasn't helped along either by Wright's own pronouncements about the design standards of the government. Speaking to the

Association of Federal Architects in 1938, he said, "The cultural influences in our country are like the floo-floo bird. I am referring to the peculiar bird who always flew backwards. To keep the wind out of its eye? No. Just because it didn't give a darn where it was going, but just had to see where it had been." Perhaps Wright was thinking of one particular federal floo-floo who had written asking him to send his "brochure and a few examples of your work" so that the government might consider Wright for a commission.

Each winter, beginning in the early 1930's, the Wrights led the fellowship on a trek from Wisconsin to Arizona. These annual caravans—over 2,200 miles of driving, plus any number of miles of walking, depending on which natural wonders Wright wanted to absorb—included one car that served as a chuck wagon; the others would make a circle around it and several campfires at night. A couple of apprentices would find themselves driving the Wrights' dog; another couple, looking after a car full of canned goods and big tanks of the homemade sauerkraut that were frequently dragged to the desert from the root cellars of Taliesin; still another couple, guarding the rolled-up architectural drawings.

In the winter of 1937–38, having got hold of several hundred acres in the foothills of the McDowell Mountains near Scottsdale, Wright began building his "ship of the desert," his "look over the rim of the world," Taliesin West. Day after day Wright wandered amidst the vastness, communing with cliffs and cacti to get the sense of what his wintertime oasis would be.

As he described the scene, "For an architect, what a marvel of construction that *sahuaro!* Or the latticed stalk of the *cholla!* Nature, driven to economize in materials by hard conditions, develops, in the *sahuaro,* a system of economy of materials in a reinforcement of vertical rods, a plaiting of tendons that holds the structure upright for six centuries or more."

Taliesin West—its plan, structural elements, and procession of spaces—was a symphony of triangles abstracted from the desert's colors, patterns, terrains, textures, and plant life. Wright had his apprentices scour the slopes for rocks, which were placed into wood forms that were then filled with cement. This method was used to build long canted walls, both enclosing the interconnected buildings and extending out to define terraces. Springing up over the large drafting room, the spectacular living (or "garden") room, and Wright's private studio were angular redwood beams, between which were stretches of canvas diffusing the strong sunlight. From a distance, Taliesin West looked like a collection of tents, but as

you were drawn into its composition, there was a never-ending, constantly changing quality of discovery and sense of direction. To one side of the living room fireplace, canvas flaps could be pushed aside to reveal, across a small, beautiful green lawn, the Wrights' private quarters, encased in an ensemble of stone shapes. Pushing out into the desert

In the Johnson Wax Building at Racine, Wisconsin, slender concrete columns rise and flare out like lily pads. Between them the luminous ceiling admits daylight during working hours.

from this area was the prow-shaped main terrace, with steps rippling down to a triangular pool. From this vantage point ninety miles of desert sweep up to the house with an environmental majesty that no other work of architecture in our time has so successfully embraced.

    After the end of the war it seemed that

The Usonian house was Wright's answer to the need for simple, low-cost dwellings. In this one, built for journalist Loren Pope in 1940, he used cypress and brick, inside and out, to complement the site in a grove at Falls Church, Virginia. In the mid-1960's the house was relocated to a site near Mount Vernon.

everyone wanted access to Taliesin's master. The flood of honors had begun with the English, who gave him the Royal Gold Medal for Architecture in 1941. In addition to many honorary degrees, the high school and college dropout was to receive the Medici Medal at the Palazzo Vecchio in Florence (the first time it was given to a non-Italian), and the rarely conferred Star of Solidarity at the Doges' Palace in Venice. Even the American Institute of Architects, which he had often called the Arbitrary Institute of Appearances, gave him its Gold Medal. He alternately tickled and jabbed the audience in the ribs for forty minutes; after all, the profession's official body had kept him waiting for forty years.

The demand for and diversity of his work was running at high tide as the 1950's unfolded. He designed a laundry in Milwaukee shaped like an ore boat; a country club in Hollywood for Huntington Hartford; a synagogue near Philadelphia, its towering translucency an abstraction of Mount Sinai; a hexagonal theater that looked like a cubistic outcropping of concrete, next to Turtle Creek in Dallas; a suspended tentlike sports pavilion for Belmont, New York, obviously decreed by some visionary in Xanadu; a state capitol for Arizona, which would have housed state functions beneath a golden hexagonal canopy sheltering cool gardens and pools; and an opera house for Baghdad, where the soon-to-be-deposed king of Iraq made a point of bowing to *him*; a gas station in Minnesota where the pumps hung down from a cantilevered roof; bridges for San Francisco Bay and for the Wisconsin River; a train depot for San Antonio; a birdhouse for a former client; a doghouse for another former client; and the beautiful Meeting House of the First Unitarian Society in Madison—its crisp copper roof planes, folded like hands in prayer, soaring above walls of native stone.

He also built the Price Tower in Bartlesville, Oklahoma—employing a treelike system of steel floor slabs (or branches) cantilevered out from a concrete core (or trunk). There is a munificent richness to the Price design, which included both offices and apartments. No four-square box rising up to proclaim its mechanized independence of nature, it is a multifaceted totem with variations of color, material, shape, and rhythm. The juxtaposition of vertical and horizontal window bands fitted with sun-controlling metal fins on the exterior make for not only visual delight but also climatic common sense.

There was considerable fantasy in his work by this time. In 1956, as part of Mayor Richard J. Daley's official Frank Lloyd Wright celebration, Wright unveiled a breathtaking twenty-two-foot drawing of his 528-story "Mile-High Illinois" (see page 179), which he offered as either a solution to or, more probably, a satire on the frenzied bunching up of banal, anonymous high-rises that was coming to characterize so many downtowns. Rising from a series of stepped-back decks with parking, parks, terraces, and helicopter pads, and containing offices and apartments, the tower was a variation on his old love affair with the cantilever, its floors branching out from a concrete-covered steel tripod core. Transit was by atomic-powered elevators. To be sheathed in gold-colored metal, the Illinois had a soaring rapier shape, which was apt enough in symbolic terms, for with this design Wright was engaging in a fencing match with the architects, developers, builders, and city planning officials across the country who had reduced the high-rise to a dispassionate formula for center-city renewal.

Soon construction started in New York on Wright's last major public building undertaken in his lifetime, the controversial, spiraling Guggenheim Museum on upper Fifth Avenue, its ramped galleries coiled up and around an immense skylit chamber. Wright had begun work on the scheme for Solomon R. Guggenheim in 1943. Not dedicated until the fall of 1959, six months after Wright's death, the interior made one imagine what it might be like to crawl up into and conduct reconnaissance amidst the contours of a huge seashell. The debate continues as to whether Wright's concept produced a place conducive to the contemplation of art. Peggy Guggenheim called the building "my uncle's garage," while others have more recently observed that, with all its ramps, it would make a great skateboard park.

When Wright wasn't at the Taliesins, or traveling for business or speaking engagements, he received people at his magnificent suite at New York's Plaza Hotel, built by architect Henry Hardenbergh—a rare example of "the founder of modern architecture" admiring a premodernistic masterpiece. While there he explored "the greatest mouth of all," and since he was known for having a pretty big one of his own, his pronouncements about architecture, society, and the degradation of the environment were frequent and were fully covered by the media. People found him approachable and gentle in person. He would strike up conversations with strangers who recognized him in department stores, auto showrooms, art galleries, museums, theaters, or during his walks to and from the Guggenheim site.

Wright could be sarcastic and yet endearingly gracious. Six months before his death he was invited by the floo-floo birds in Washington to give his advice on what a national cultural center should consist of and look like. Asked if he would consider designing it himself, he said, "Of course I would . . . and I would never be paid for it in this world . . . I would have to give it." This was a moment after he had wondered out loud why, with so many "half-baked" classical buildings all over the nation's capital, he didn't see any of the bureaucrats wearing togas.

As he freely admitted, Wright chose "honest arrogance" over "hypocritical humility." But his dramatic public persona was a natural extension of an innate dignity and unshatterable spiritual strength—not at all an act for the press. Pedro Guerrero recalls,

I was once asked to assist in the repair of a cantilevered table in Mr. Wright's study that had come unmoored from the wall out from which it was built. It became my job to hold the table in place, against the wall, from underneath, while the other fellow attempted to screw it to its supporting stud. The screws turned out to be the wrong size, and I was instructed to stay put, not to move a muscle, until he returned with the longer screws. While hidden from view, I was able to observe Mr. Wright enter the room. He walked briskly, dressed for the day in starched collar, flowing tie, and tweed suit. His keen and critical eyes, ever alert to the slightest imperfection, fell on some *objets d'art* on a shelf. He glided toward them and shifted them, one forward, one to the right. He walked backwards, looking at them with his head slightly tilted, hesitated, scooted toward them again, decided he was satisfied, glided to the piano and ran through a few bars

of Bach. . . . He cleared his throat, picked up his hat and cane, and disappeared out the door. He had played the classic role of Frank Lloyd Wright as if he had been before an audience.

As he entered his nineties Wright was as busy as he had ever been. Designs came "shaking out of my sleeve"—from the Marin County Civic Center, which was built north of San Francisco, to a house of native stone that was to interconnect three little mountaintops not far from Taliesin West. After the winter of 1958–59 the *bianana*, the beautiful desert spring, came quickly—and outside on the prow of Taliesin West, Easter was celebrated with a sumptuous feast and bright conversation, in an atmosphere of pageantry, with music filling the air. Then early in April Wright was struck by severe abdominal cramps, and taken to the hospital down in Phoenix, he was operated on to remove an obstruction. In the ensuing days he bounced back with marvelous strength. His progress was followed by the profession and the public in the press, and out in Los Angeles his granddaughter, the actress Anne Baxter, who had been at the Easter festival, was reassured by her mother, Catherine, that things were going fine.

In the early morning hours of April 9, 1959, Miss Baxter was awakened by a dreadful nightmare—the vision of an immense bird bearing down on her against a vast twilighted horizon. At the same moment her grandfather had died with a simple sigh in Phoenix.

Frank Lloyd Wright was brought home to the Valley and laid in the great living room of Taliesin, beside his piano and surrounded with hundreds of petunias in red clay pots. At sunset his coffin, covered with a single pine bough and a rose-colored cloth, was placed on a horse-drawn dray and taken down the hill to the little family chapel he had helped build in 1886. Its bell tolled. He was carried inside. An old pot-bellied stove gave off warmth, and the aroma of candles blended with the smell of pine. The minister from the Unitarian Meeting House he had built in Madison ten years before read from the Bible. Then he was taken outside to the burial ground. His own spot was surrounded by pine boughs, yellow chrysanthemums, and birds-of-paradise. Migrant memories converged. His mother, Anna, and all her people were here—and nearby, in an unknown spot, Mamah Borthwick.

Three years before, he and his wife had

The Guggenheim Museum in New York City, first conceived in 1943, opened in late 1959, six months after Wright's death. The soaring central chamber and the spiraling galleries create a theater in which the movement of people becomes an integral part of the architectural experience.

Frank Lloyd Wright, whose father taught him that a symphony is "an edifice in sound," invariably had a piano around—even here, on the Guggenheim site. He "let the piano play itself," as, he sometimes said, he let nature shape his buildings.

traveled to the ancient land of the Lloyd-Joneses and Cader Idris to receive an honorary doctor of philosophy degree from the University of Wales at Bangor. "He was as gay and happy as a young boy to be there in that wildly picturesque country," she was to write later.

We walked on many roads and through the fine gardens and once, when we came across an old cemetery, we looked for some of his ancestors' graves. We tried to read those complex Welsh names which were almost impossible to pronounce, even for him, though he did not want to admit it: Evrawac, Manawyddan, Wledig, Llevelys, Fflwch. At last we found one tombstone with the name Wriaeth inscribed on it. He was overjoyed. He walked all around it, then "A vague sense of belonging here comes over me," he said. "Let's go on."

They went on. Back in town, there was another architect named Wright, and a meeting had been arranged—just for the fun of it—for this other architect worked in a traditional style. The two talked amicably. Afterward, coming out, he was asked by an eager entourage what he thought of the other one's buildings. His eyes twinkled. "Well . . . we are both doing God's work," said Frank Lloyd Wright. "He has been doing it his way in there . . . and I have been doing it God's way."

231

Maybeck's drawing for the Palace of Fine Arts, San Francisco, 1913

MAYBECK

233

Bernard R Maybeck

1862–1957

BY RICHARD REINHARDT

In the winter of 1953, a few days after his ninety-first birthday, Bernard Ralph Maybeck granted a tape-recorded interview of several hours to a public-service radio station in Berkeley, California, the city in which he had lived and worked for six decades. In some respects the interview evidenced little more than the casual curiosity that people feel about someone who has been around for a long, long time. But, to a greater extent, it denoted a sudden, belated realization in his home town that Maybeck, whose work was almost entirely concentrated in a small area of northern California, whose best-known buildings were unclassifiable hybrids of contemporary materials and traditional forms, and whose career had flowered and faded so long ago that almost everyone thought he was long dead, was an architectural genius of major international importance.

The claim was in dispute, of course. In Maybeck's ninetieth year, the American Institute of Architects had at last awarded him its gold medal, largely in recognition of buildings he had completed thirty or forty years earlier. Still, the words most often used to describe Maybeck and his work—such words as eclectic, poetic, anachronistic, improvisational, romantic, neobaroque, mystical, and idiosyncratic—were certainly not the words that describe the dominant qualities of twentieth-century architecture. To the contrary, most of the words applied to Maybeck describe precisely what modern architecture is *not*. Maybeck's view of himself, he told the interviewer from Station KPFA, was that he had "never been an architect." He had been merely a discriminating participant in the human search for beauty, "a man who appreciates the ideas of other men, that's all."

Maybeck had never established a "school" or a

Like a gnome in his forest workshop, Bernard Maybeck at the age of eighty-six was still at work on designs for structures of eccentric, haunting beauty.

style that bore his name. He had never propounded a coherent philosophy, a theory of architecture, save that architecture must aspire to "beauty," a slippery attribute at best. He seemed to have few imitators. (Perhaps he was inimitable.) He had never fathered a skyscraper, the characteristic monument of his age. He had not scattered the spores of his inspiration in Europe, Asia, or South America. Much of his work, by cruel chance, had been destroyed by fires or other natural disasters. And yet, there was that church, those homes, that huge and haunting palace by the bay . . .

Inevitably, Maybeck's late-blooming fame became entwined with his longevity, his eccentricities: his odd, gnomelike little figure, scarcely more than five feet tall, dressed in bib overalls of his own design, sporting a Seven Dwarfs beard and a crocheted tam-o'-shanter; his grandiose proposals for unbuildable cities and campuses conceived on the scale of imperial Rome; his weird social circle of Berkeley aesthetes, domiciled in wind-swept redwood sleeping porches, pseudo-Grecian temples, and gunny-sack cloisters up in the misty, dripping eucalyptus forests above the University of California; his exaggerated horror of milk, dairy products, tobacco smoke, and honey ("It gets into your elbows"); his faddish flirtations with vegetarianism, antivivisectionism, Japanese diet regimes. It was all too easy during Maybeck's last years to attribute his renown to his peculiarities, to think of him always as he was at the end, sitting barefoot, bright-eyed, sunburned, in a canvas camp chair by his radio, or standing at his drafting board in the patio of a breezy house with a great redwood-timbered ceiling and a view of the bay through restless branches—an enormous fireplace, pine cones, pastel chalks, large dogs, fresh air; an old man whose life, like his creations, linked the present to the past.

As for Maybeck, his thoughts had a way of running back a century or two, with the selective hindsight of the aged. When the interviewer from the station asked him on that February afternoon to recount the high points of his career, Maybeck remembered his days as a student at the Ecole des Beaux-Arts in Paris in the 1880's, the days that he now believed had shaped the pattern of his life. It was at the Beaux-Arts, Maybeck recalled, in the atelier of Monsieur Jules-Louis André, that he had learned the significance of the line and had encountered the Romanesque. It was there that he had developed the ambition and the passion to become an architect.

Born in New York City in 1862, Maybeck had gone to Paris at nineteen to study furniture design. His father, an immigrant from Germany, was a master woodcarver in a furniture manufactory in lower Manhattan; his mother, who died when Maybeck was three, had hoped her son would become an artist. Respectful of his wife's wishes—and impressed by the attainments of Eugene Carrière, whose portraiture was in vogue—Maybeck's father imposed artistic tutelage. ("Other boys played ball. I had to draw and draw.") Maybeck was an indifferent student in reading and writing, but he was apt in handicrafts. After a brief try at college, he joined his father's firm as an apprentice at three dollars a month, working on interior decorations for Pullman Palace cars. In spare moments he devised and patented a reversible passenger seat. (Maybeck never profited from his invention; he sold the rights to it in 1886.) By the time he boarded the ship for France, reeling from the fumes of his first cigar, he had already developed a taste for rich colors, deep textures, and the sheen of well-tooled wood.

In Paris his attention wandered. From the windows of the furniture shop he could see young men in shiny black "pot hats" pushing cartloads of drawings through the entrance of the nearby institute of fine arts. He felt a twinge of envy on learning that they were architects. The mystery of artistic inspiration, the challenge of creating shapes and spaces, began to stimulate and disturb him, drawing his thoughts away from the drafting table. Stopping once at midday in the Church of Saint-Germain-des-Prés, he experienced for the first time a complex and marvelous emotion, a sort of spiritual awe, animated by an almost personal affection for the anonymous, twelfth-century builders who, in their "sincerity," had created the masterpieces of Romanesque religious architecture.

Maybeck wrote home and asked his father's permission to enroll as a student of architecture at the Beaux-Arts. He passed the rigorous entrance examinations a few weeks after his twentieth birthday and was admitted to the atelier of Monsieur André, who ran a relatively independent studio within the rigidly traditional school.

The Beaux-Arts, with its emphasis on academic "laws" of composition, its formalized aesthetics, its reverence for the great works of the past, had infuriated Louis Sullivan, who blamed the pervasive influence of Beaux-Arts training for much that was inappropriate, imitative, and pretentious in American architecture. To Maybeck, however, the school was neither stifling nor totally consuming. He mastered its classical principles of grand-scale planning and of carefully balancing masses and spaces to achieve the required "composition"; yet, at the same time, his soul yearned back to the earthy, hand-hewn craftsmanship, the humane medievalism, that was momentarily out of favor at

the Beaux-Arts. He sought the Gothic spirit as a tonic for the classical. He absorbed the lectures of Henry Lemmonier on the Romanesque and Gothic structures of the Middle Ages; he wandered with a sketchbook through the churches of Le Puy and Vézelay; he devoured the essays of John Ruskin and the *Dictionnaire* of Viollet-le-Duc. With his singular gusto he admired and retained both of the opposing principles that had often divided the school. As William H. Jordy, the art historian, has observed: "He accepted both worlds—the elite world of the academician and the humble world of the craftsman, the realm of splendor and that of nature, a sentimental viewpoint toward building and one of common sense."

Throughout his life Maybeck gave full credit to the Ecole des Beaux-Arts for teaching him to infuse a composition with "beauty"—"the essence of architecture," he called it. He often told a little story about the time when Monsieur André, having examined one of Maybeck's first drawings, took a soft pencil and worked over the carefully placed lines "until the beautiful paper was just black." Comparing the master's smudgy inspiration with his own sterile outline, Maybeck understood one of the first processes of creation. Thereafter, he put aside his T-square, rulers, and calipers and began his compositions with "a dirty drawing" in charcoal or chalk—rubbing, erasing, changing shapes and masses, until (as Monsieur André put it) he had "studied it." Looking back seventy years later from his hillside in Berkeley, Maybeck fondly remembered even his master's sarcastic comment about a blank sheet that Maybeck had tidily mounted on a board: "You will never do better."

Back in New York after five years of study in Europe, Maybeck went to work for a new architectural firm that had been formed by one of his classmates, Thomas Hastings, and another young adept of the Beaux-Arts, John Merven Carrère. Carrère and Hastings rejoiced in the sort of upward social connections that so often have advanced the fortunes of American architects. They had just landed a commission to design a resort in Florida for the indefatigable land developer Henry M. Flagler. Soon after Maybeck joined the firm, Flagler added a second luxury hotel, two churches, and a residence to the project. Maybeck helped plan the Hotel Ponce de Leon and its six-acre site in Saint Augustine. When construction began, the firm sent him to Florida to supervise the work, and his father went along to install several hundred yards of wood carvings from the New York shop. Historians in search of the earliest evidences of Maybeck's uninhibited style have found them in the lavish, neo-Spanish Ponce de Leon, which flaunts a playfulness never again shown by Carrère and Hastings; a parasol-like central dome and roof garden (echoed several years later in the California pavilion at the World's Columbian Exposition, a building that was also designed by a firm employing Maybeck); and some raffish graffiti in the dining room. ("Perhaps the muralist selected the texts," Kenneth H. Cardwell says in his definitive biography of Maybeck, "but suspicion falls on a young architect whose sense of humor included the art of gentle ridicule.")

Predictably, Maybeck fell out with Carrère and Hastings—or, perhaps, merely fell away from them. He never worked long in harness with other architects. In search of a job, he took the railroad west to the aggressively growing town of Kansas City; but his only success there was meeting Annie White, whom he married the following year, after he had found work as a draftsman in San Francisco. Maybeck's wedding present to his beloved "Doddy" was a one-half interest in the patent rights to a lady's fan he had invented. Later, as a more substantial token of affection, he worked Annie's initials into the pattern of a cornice on an office building. The Maybecks were married sixty-five years. Annie was with him, supplying an occasional forgotten word, laughing indulgently at his lapses of memory, scolding a barking dog, on that winter day when the interviewer from the station came up to tape-record the recollections of an old man who was suddenly famous.

Maybeck completed his apprenticeship during the next few years with an established architectural office in San Francisco. (He was associated in designing the much-admired Swedenborgian Church of the New Jerusalem, a wildly syncretistic project in which the pastor, several prominent artists, gardeners, lumberjacks, and members of the congregation worked in collaboration with the firm of A. Page Brown to produce a tiny but enduring masterpiece.) But it was only after he and Annie moved to Berkeley in 1892 that Maybeck began to develop the distinctive style, outlook, and clientele that made him for several decades the most important residential architect in western America.

Berkeley, as now, was the seat of the University of California, which had established its campus there only twenty years earlier. A lively young faculty, some woodsy utopians, and a few hundred families of commuters had settled around the campus. Maybeck found the company, the climate, and the daily ferryboat trip to San Francisco entirely to his liking. On the boat one evening he got acquainted with an engineering professor who suggested he apply for a position teaching descriptive geometry in the university's newly formed

department of instrumental drawing. Maybeck's class, the closest thing the university offered to architectural training, attracted a group of students interested in design. Maybeck invited them home for discussions of art and architecture, put them to work building additions to his cottage, and urged the most promising of them to continue their studies at the Ecole des Beaux-Arts. (Among those who did so were John Bakewell and Arthur Brown, Jr., the designers of San Francisco's City Hall, perhaps the ultimate expression of Beaux-Arts baroque in the United States, and Julia Morgan, another brilliant eclectic, who was the first woman to be admitted to the Beaux-Arts. A prodigious and versatile designer, Miss Morgan is best known as the supervising architect of William Randolph Hearst's Casa Grande at San Simeon.)

Birthdays and holidays in the Maybeck family were made festive with homemade costumes and colored paper decorations. In this photograph Bernard, Annie, and their two children, Wallen and Kerna, are dressed for a family pageant.

Maybeck's closest friend in Berkeley was Charles Keeler, an incipient poet, who observed with passionate attention the growth of the Maybeck house at Grove and Berryman streets. It was "something like a Swiss chalet," Keeler recalled, many years later, in an unpublished memoir. There were interior walls of unfinished knotty pine boards, a furnace of molded sheet iron, and a lot of rough-hewn wooden furniture that Maybeck had planned and built. "It was a distinctly handmade house," Keeler wrote, with obvious relish. (He, too, was deeply imbued with the principles of Ruskin and Morris, and he had founded a local Ruskin Club to stimulate Berkeley's appetite for medieval sincerity.)

Maybeck and Keeler had met on the jolly five o'clock boat from the city. Keeler, out from Wisconsin with a year or so of college behind him and a job at the California Academy of Sciences, was barely twenty, but he affected a long black cape and a gold-headed cane. Maybeck, the European-educated intellectual, was nearly thirty. By comparison, he was a muddy peasant.

"He was of solid build with a round face and chin," Keeler remembered. "His complexion was ruddy, like an outdoor man's. His eyes were dark and his expression benign. He seemed to me like a European rather than an American. . . . Instead of a vest he wore a sash, and his suit seemed like a homespun of dark brown color."

Maybeck and Keeler shared an intense commitment to architecture as art. When Maybeck learned that his friend owned a vacant lot on a hillside north of the university, he immediately volunteered to design free of charge a house that would be an example to the community—perhaps to the world. Keeler became Maybeck's first client, and the little studio house on Highland Place was like the first enunciation of a prophetic religion. To see it today, altered in many details but fundamentally as Maybeck laid it out almost ninety years ago, is to be startled by its "modernity." The interlocking beams of unpainted redwood, the windows reaching to the roof line, the hill-hugging configuration, tucked into the landscape "as if it were a part of it"—all these have become the familiar characteristics of hillside homes in northern California.

To understand how novel, not to say peculiar,

Maybeck designed more than 150 houses in California, using a wide variety of styles to achieve his goal of "making the home fit the family." The shingled Goslinsky house in San Francisco (top) was distinguished by carved window overhangs and a drainpipe with a Byzantine onion dome. The stucco Kennedy house in Berkeley (middle) sports Gothic details in the windows and balconies. The Chick House in Berkeley (bottom) makes use of the trellises that are characteristic of Maybeck's later work.

the Keeler house was in 1895, one need only think of the thousands of mass-produced row houses, conspicuously decorated with carved wood gingerbread, that were then under construction along the residential streets of San Francisco; or the Italianate mansions around the shores of Lake Merritt in Oakland; or the white, Neo-Gothic farmhouses of California's rural valleys: crowded parlors, widow's walks, wrought-iron fences, hedges of clipped yew. Maybeck's domestic architecture, a personal but logical application of the cloister-and-hearth medievalism of Viollet-le-Duc, was revolutionary both in concept and in purpose.

Maybeck saw the Keeler house as a demonstration model, a statement of principle. He often read it aloud to Keeler (and others) as a priest might read the scriptural stories from a stained glass window to an illiterate parishioner. He pointed out the "sincerity" of the unpainted, shingle exterior and the unfinished indoor paneling. He discoursed upon the *meaning* of the beams: a house must show what it is made of—that was an absolute dictum. Just look at the structure of the Romanesque, the early Gothic churches! Those rafters, those pillars, those flying buttresses, were elements of structure, not decoration. Their repetition was like the beat in music, the meter in poetry, beautiful because it was justified, because it was *essential* to the composition.

The lesson caught on, at least around Keeler's cul-de-sac. In the next few years Maybeck designed half a dozen homes—"Gothic houses," he called them—among the oaks and boulders. And in 1898 Maybeck and Keeler and their neighbors formed the Hillside Club, whose goal was nothing less than to turn the entire community into a woodland garden—a gentle, parklike encampment of "simple homes" and winding lanes, pedestrian walks and flowering stairways.

At a later date the Hillside Club would have been called an "environmental" organization; but its ideology, unlike that of many contemporary environmental groups, did not involve a commitment to wilderness or a hostility to the effects of technology. Its underlying cause was evangelism, and its overt mission was to apply Bernard Maybeck's ideals to all the homes and landscapes of California. Keeler, as the club's chief propagandist, became Maybeck's public voice. The views of an architect were seldom expressed more dogmatically than in the various pamphlets and yearbooks Keeler wrote for the Hillside Club. Every pronouncement was infused with Maybeck's powerful bias against late Victorian taste: let there be no more of these marbleized wood panels, wooden arches, rounded wooden towers, and curving wood-framed bay windows; no more of these oil-base paints (especially paints used to simulate masonry); no formal gardens; no useless balconies. Year by year the advice grew more specific. It turned into a set of specifications for a typical "Berkeley Brown Shingle," as occupied by a typical member of the Hillside Club.

The exterior, of course, must be unstained, unpainted wood shingles, weathering in time to a soft brown or gray. ("The colors bestowed by nature always improve with time, and therefore are the safest.") Let there be no white trim, no rainbow-tinted window frames. In the garden, if one were longing for a splash of color, it was permissible to plant wisteria, clematis, passion vine, ivy geranium, masses of banksia roses. On the east side of the house there must be a wide, roofless porch. (The porch might go on the south, provided there was a wall of wood or glass to the west, to divert the prevailing wind.) The windows: grouped together to avoid cross-lighting. ("Three or four windows side by side give a far better light than the same number scattered about the room, and the wall space can be used to better advantage.") The eaves: wide. ("A house without eaves always seems to me like a hat without a brim.") The fireplace: huge. ("As the life of the house centers about the fireplace, this may appropriately be the most beautiful feature of a room.") The walls: unpainted wood or stucco, if one's taste ran to that. ("The wooden house may be varied by the use of plaster, either on the exterior or the interior. The point to be emphasized is never to use plaster with wood as if the construction were of masonry.") The rooms: spacious. ("A generous living room of ample dimensions is preferable to several small rooms without distinctive character. . . . The dining room may open off from this assembly room as an annex or alcove.") The interior: cozy. ("A high ceiling, with its wide expanse of unused wall space, commonly gives a room a dreary effect which is almost impossible to remove, although an extremely high ceiling, relieved by exposed rafters, is sometimes very charming.") The occupants: comfortable. ("No home is truly beautiful which is not fitted to the needs of those who dwell within its walls.")

That the "simple house" was destined to influence the lives of its occupants as well as to affect the appearance of the Berkeley hills was evident in every communication from the club. The mission was moral as much as aesthetic: "Let those who would see a higher culture in California, a deeper life, a nobler humanity, work for the adoption of the simple home among all classes of people, trusting that the inspiration of its mute walls will be a ceaseless challenge to all those who dwell within their shadow. . . ."

Hearst Hall on the Berkeley campus of the University of California was commissioned by Mrs. Phoebe Apperson Hearst in 1898. A great hall supported by twelve arches of laminated wood, it served as an art gallery and reception pavilion and later as the women's gymnasium, before it burned down in 1922.

Perhaps it is unfair to attribute these recipes for perfection directly to Maybeck. They show his influence, but his own desiderata extended beyond the garden gate of his new aerie on Buena Vista Way. His work at the university led him inevitably toward the other world, the realm of splendor.

The university's most generous patron, Mrs. Phoebe Apperson Hearst, proposed to endow the campus with a mining building in memory of her late husband, George Hearst, who had made a fortune in the Comstock Lode. Maybeck saw an opportunity to guide the institution toward a rational future. He convinced Mrs. Hearst that it would be rash to site the building without the guidance of a master plan. Next, he persuaded her to sponsor an international competition to design "a City of Learning in which there is to be no sordid or inharmonious feature . . . [a] plan for centuries to come."

For more than three years Maybeck was immersed in the Hearst competition, designing announcements, supervising the preparation of an architectural program, recruiting a jury of eminent

For Wyntoon, the Hearst family retreat on the McCloud River, Maybeck in 1903 dreamed up this romantic Black Forest castle, constructed of gray lava stone with dark green roof tiles. It too was destroyed by fire, in 1929.

architects, traveling to Europe and Great Britain to distribute information. Out of 105 entrants, eleven were brought to California at Mrs. Hearst's expense to complete on-site drawings for the final stage. The winner, Emile Bénard, was a Parisian, trained at the Beaux-Arts. His grand scheme, to no one's surprise, bore a certain resemblance to the Place de la Concorde superimposed upon the bumps and creases of the Berkeley highlands. As required by the competition, Bénard's plan envisioned a campus for 8,000 students, although there were then only 2,000 in the university. Critics called it absurdly visionary. (The number of students is now close to 30,000.)

Bénard declined an invitation to serve as supervising architect at California. No one, apparently, thought of putting the wild young Maybeck in command. The university brought in John Galen Howard, a New Yorker, whose entry had won fourth place. Howard became the university's first professor of architecture, founder of its architecture school, designer of the Hearst Memorial Mining Building (and numerous others), and supervising architect for a quarter of a century. Maybeck's tenure as an instructor ended with Howard's arrival. (The real Beaux-Arts traditionalists in Howard's firm thought Maybeck's notions were hilarious.) Except for two buildings that he designed—the Faculty Club (1902) and the Women's Gymnasium (1925, with Julia Morgan)—Maybeck exerted little influence thereafter on the appearance of the campus. Fifteen years later, Howard replaced Bénard's composition with a new plan, based on his own entry in the international competition. The university today bears little resemblance to Bénard's classical dream city (or, for that matter, to Howard's dream city, either).

Mrs. Hearst, however, continued to be enchanted by Maybeck's work. For her he designed two elaborate structures: a reception pavilion

In the First Church of Christ, Scientist in Berkeley, Maybeck brought together a dizzying variety of architectural traditions to create an unlikely masterpiece. In the construction he used such miscellaneous materials as rough-cut wood, concrete, metal windows, and asbestos sheeting.

(Hearst Hall) adjoining her home in Berkeley, and a country house (Wyntoon) on the McCloud River in northeastern California. Both were imaginative extensions of Maybeck's Gothic mood; and both, had they survived, would probably be landmarks in the history of American architecture. Hearst Hall, which eventually was moved (as planned) onto the university campus, was a 140-foot-long gallery supported by twelve towering arches of laminated timber. Inside and out it was clothed in redwood barn shakes. After serving Mrs. Hearst as an art gallery and party center, and a generation of students as a women's gymnasium, it was consumed by fire in 1922. Wyntoon was a Teutonic castle of gray lava stone and dark green roof tile, glowering on the edge of a torrent. Maybeck thought of it always as it looked in a misty dawn, bathed in pearl-gray light, with fragrant fir logs smoldering in the massive stone fireplaces, and the cold blue river foaming ceaselessly below the

leaded window panes. Wyntoon also was destroyed by fire, in 1929.

Maybeck never was more popular, more professionally "successful" than during the decade that followed his large projects for Mrs. Hearst. He designed houses, churches, schools, and clubhouses, elaborating and refining the principles that emanated yearly from the Hillside Club. A distressing number of his "simple houses" were swept away by a fire that devastated the Berkeley hills in 1923, and other of his buildings succumbed to the changing pressures of taste, utility, and real-estate development; but those that remain are precious possessions that knowledgeable Californians identify with the magic phrase, "It's a Maybeck." For the cognoscenti, that is a signal to look for the touches that typified Maybeck's mature style: the exposed ceiling beams with Swiss carvings at the ends; the patented, two-hole Venturi chimneys; the built-in window seats, fireside benches, inglenooks; the carved wooden traceries in hinged, wood-framed windows; the carvings on gables and balconies; the austere interior panels, like Japanese screens; the sleeping porches; and, of course, the banksia rosebushes, tumbling over the garden gate.

It is not always easy to know whether one is in the presence of the master or a disciple. The Berkeley Brown Shingle, unlike Maybeck's larger works, was easily imitable, as it was meant to be. Thousands of homes aspiring to Keeler's ideals (and nowadays commanding far from simple prices) are scattered through the hills of Berkeley and Oakland, the pine forests of Bolinas and Inverness, the older parts of Palo Alto, and even a few sequestered neighborhoods of San Francisco. The Bay Region's "natural" style, or something like it, was promulgated not only by Maybeck but by other eclectic Californians, including Maybeck's friend and occasional associate, Julia Morgan; Maybeck's partner, Henry H. Gutterson; his sometime employers Willis Polk, Ernest Coxhead, and Albert C. Schweinfurth; and even by John Galen Howard, who was sternly Beaux-Arts/classical in his architecture for the university but mellowed to Brown Shingle Gothic in the home territory of the Hillside Club.

In southern California at about the same time, the brothers Charles Sumner Greene and Henry Mather Greene fathered a similar breed of heavy-browed, brown-shingled houses along the tranquil boulevards of Pasadena. Greene and Greene's innovative style, drawn from the same assortment of domestic and foreign influences that affected the northern Californians, spread into middle-class residential neighborhoods in many parts of the United States, where it quickly lost almost every attribute except its name, "California bungalow."

In a sense, Maybeck *was* the founder, or one of the founders, of a regional style, a unique approach to housing, adapted to the climate, building materials, and terrain of the cool coastal slopes of the Pacific. While others strayed from the principles of the "simple house"—or, like Keeler, bogged down in repetitious orthodoxy—Maybeck continually reinvigorated his own concepts with new ideas: fireproof hill houses of stucco or masonry; lightweight walls of "Bubblestone" concrete; sheet-metal roofing, prefabricated sash. If someone had found a way to make Sheetrock "beautiful," Maybeck surely would have used it.

Still, on the basis of his residential architecture before 1910, Maybeck's reputation probably would be equivalent today to that of his forgotten colleagues who also worked with shingles and raw redwood. It was in 1910, when he was forty-eight, that Maybeck began to work on the First Church of Christ, Scientist, in Berkeley, which some critics have called the most significant ecclesiastical building in the United States.

The commission came to him on the strength of his houses in Berkeley—or, possibly, in recognition of the constructive spiritual outlook expressed by the Hillside Club. As Maybeck remembered it, five women came to his office in San Francisco one day and told him they had been authorized by the Christian Science congregation to hire him to design a simple church of natural materials that would exemplify the basic tenets of their faith. Maybeck, whose religious sentiments were pantheistic, not to say pagan, warned them that he would prefer to work in coarse materials—rough-sawn wood, factory glass, concrete poured in crude forms. The congregation, perhaps sensing more clearly than Maybeck himself did that his desire to use primitive materials was motivated by a search for ideal form, sent back word that they would like him to start work.

The outcome of this commission was a building of intense originality, shaped out of a diversity of symbolic elements that only a historian of architecture could identify. "The mere mixture of his borrowings boggles the imagination," Jordy has written. "Byzantine, Romanesque, Gothic, Renaissance, Japanese (or possibly Chinese), Swiss chalet, and domestic wooden vernacular commingle in this unique building; with metal factory windows and asbestos sheeting thrown in for good measure!" Although Jordy implies there is something reprehensible about all this "borrowing" (not to mention *mixing!*), he rates the church a brilliant success: "Splendor is opposed by the commonplace; levitation by weight; expansion by concentration; the romantic by common sense."

To builders, the church is the most interesting of Maybeck's designs because it uses so many ordinary materials to such sympathetic effect. To architects, it is the realization of a tantalizing goal: to create a structure that does not resemble a conventional religious edifice yet is obviously a church. And to laymen, entering in curiosity or devotion, it is a mysteriously compelling building, human in scale but exhilarating in spiritual grandeur. This rare combination of attributes has sometimes been attributed to the Romanesque style that Maybeck so much admired; and there are echoes here of the Romanesque, as in the Church of the New Jerusalem. Maybeck, when asked to name the style, always said: "Modern."

Considering the almost universal acclaim that now surrounds the First Church of Christ, Scientist, it is difficult to account for the slump in Maybeck's career that followed the completion of the contract. But construction was sluggish in northern California, and Maybeck was an indifferent salesman. The

The interior of the Christian Science church displays Maybeck's genius for mingling architectural elements: Romanesque columns, Gothic tracery, Byzantine inlay, Japanese timberwork.

244

critic Winthrop Sargeant, who once described him as "my favorite San Francisco genius," pointed out that Maybeck never, at any time, was what is commonly regarded as a successful architect.

"His Diogenes-like view of life was against it. He hated contracts, estimates, and all the rest of the business side of architecture. Businessmen seldom understood him, with the result that he never built a bank, and was a mere collaborator in most of his office-building ventures."

Sargeant drew a charming word-picture of Maybeck, the wayward genius, in the huge living room of his home on Buena Vista Way, surrounded by his whole family—Annie and Wallen, their son, and Kerna, their daughter, "who looked like a princess out of an old German fairy tale."

Apart from this living room, there wasn't much to the house. Maybeck used to remark jokingly that a human being can't occupy more than one room at a time, so why bother with more? . . . It was kept in a continuous state of Bohemian disarray. An old-fashioned player piano with a huge collection of rolls thumped out piano arrangements of Wagnerian opera, the "William Tell Overture," and Lieder by Schubert. In the midst of this joyful din,

Maybeck would stand, stroking his gnomelike beard, pondering the mysterious relations of lines, masses, nature, and human beings—the factors that, put together in the proper proportion, constituted the art of architecture as he saw it.

When the directors of the forthcoming Panama-Pacific International Exposition in San Francisco selected a board of advisory architects, Maybeck was not included. He understood the reasons: "I hadn't even done a warehouse."

But it was a harsh snub to a man who regarded himself as a planner of dream cities, one who had looked upon the Beaux-Arts grandeur of the World's Columbian Exposition in Chicago in 1893 as the finest example of urban planning in America. San Francisco's 1915 fair, which would mark the completion of the Panama Canal and celebrate the reconstruction of a city devastated only nine years earlier by earthquake and fire, was to be a repetition and extension of the White City, an even more exquisite sample of Beaux-Arts composition.

Left out of the planning of the exposition, Maybeck busied himself entering (unsuccessfully) competitions for the privilege of designing various public buildings and monuments. Finally, with what must have been considerable agony of spirit, he took a job as a draftsman in the office of his old friend Willis Polk, the chairman of the exposition's architectural commission. Talented, mischievous Polk, the self-appointed gadfly of Bay Area architecture, had charge not only of over-all planning but also of designing the most important single building at the fair, a steel-framed gallery to house the exhibits of painting and sculpture. Polk had done some preliminary sketches of a conventional museum with a massive central lobby and long wings on either side; then, dissatisfied and overworked, he called in his office staff and challenged them to an in-house competition for alternative designs.

Maybeck, sketching as usual with charcoal on tracing paper, produced an impressionist vision of a lonely, vaguely classical building that looked like one of Piranesi's drawings of the ruins of Rome. His plan was to set this Palace of Fine Arts at the edge of a small lagoon that Polk had planned to fill and cover. (It lay between the site of the building and the central pedestrian concourse of the exposition.) In Maybeck's scheme, crowds pouring down the concourse would be deflected by the lagoon and would follow the shore and enter the picture gallery through a splendid, semicircular colonnade, open to the sky. On a peninsula in the center of the lagoon, embraced by the arms of the colonnade, would stand an immense dome, forming the center of the complex and serving as an enormous loggia for the display of statuary. The gallery itself would be a simple, barnlike building, curved like the colonnade and forming a sort of buffer around the western end of the fairgrounds.

Polk's staff was dazzled. They voted it the best submission. Polk looked at Maybeck's much-erased charcoal and said with easy grace: "The job is yours."

Maybeck's Palace of Fine Arts was (or appeared to be) a Greco-Roman temple in a state of decay. But if it was in that respect a classical building, it was one that had been stripped of its imperial pretensions. Softened by time, humbled by neglect, it seemed to tremble and melt like its own reflection in the pool, an ironic commentary on the futility of power and vanity. Maybeck wanted the building to induce a mood of gentle sadness in visitors as they wandered through the colonnade. This, he thought, was an appropriate state of mind for persons who were about to enter a treasury of art. On every side were reminders that empires wither, buildings crumble, idols fall, and the carefully drawn lines of architects are rubbed away by ineluctable hands. Beauty alone endures. Art is the consolation of the soul.

The Palace was the singular artistic triumph of the exposition, the most popular structure ever built in San Francisco. Although the rotunda and colonnade had been constructed of staff and plaster of Paris on a framework of wood and laths, the city allowed them to stand for four decades, deteriorating in reality as they had done in illusion. No one attempted to duplicate the Palace: it was *sui generis*, the capstone of Beaux-Arts romanticism (although there were academic architects who pointed out that Maybeck had taken outrageous liberties with proportions.) Strictly speaking, the part of the Palace that everyone loved was not a building at all, but a monument, a colossal outdoor sculpture, whose function was purely decorative. It was a plaything, like a Victorian gazebo or a kiosk in a pasha's garden. The real building—the curved, flat-roofed gallery where they showed the pictures—was as nondescript and practical as a railroad roundhouse. The army used it as a warehouse during World War II. Later, the Recreation and Parks Department laid out tennis courts inside.

In 1957 the California legislature, spurred by an offer of two million dollars from a wealthy lumberman named Walter Johnson, agreed to put up two million dollars to match a similar contribution from the city to reconstruct the Palace from Maybeck's original plans. It took a decade to tear the structures down, recast the statues, and reconstruct the colonnade and rotunda out of tinted, steel-reinforced concrete. In the process, the build-

ing lost its faded, parchment-colored melancholy; but it was "saved." The city rededicated the Palace with several days of concerts, folk dances, organ recitals, films, lectures, and sound-and-light shows in October 1967, exactly ten years after Bernard Maybeck died.

Maybeck had never rested on the glory of the Palace, although the public regarded it as his masterpiece. His architectural office was busy through the late 1920's designing houses, studios, college campuses, hotels, town plans. He completed (with his associate Henry Gutterson) a Sunday school wing for the Church of Christ, Scientist; a pretentious villa in Los Angeles and two fanciful sales buildings in Oakland and San Francisco for Earle C. Anthony, an automobile dealer; a mountain resort; a studio for himself with walls of gunny sacks dipped in lightweight concrete.

For almost eighteen years he worked, as well, at a master plan for The Principia, a small, Christian Science college in the Midwest. Maybeck approached the assignment with his usual glee and his usual blend of assiduous research and unfettered fantasy. With a small team of associates he toured campuses from Illinois to Delaware, sketching dormitory floor plans, cafeteria serving lines, laboratory spaces. Much of what he saw he dismissed as "Early Peorian." His first scheme for the new Principia was Imperial Beaux-Arts, like the Bénard design for the University of California: a series of symmetrical, interconnecting courtyards, surrounded by cloisterlike buildings and with a sort of domed pantheon lording it over the central axis. Then, as years passed and the site of the planned campus was moved from the outskirts of Saint Louis to the bluffs of the Mississippi near Elsah, Illinois, Maybeck shifted into his "humble" mode. He decided that a college in the softly rolling hills of mid-America should seek its spiritual kinship not with the Areopagus but with an English village—intimate, tranquil, sequestered in a dimple of the Cotswolds. He designed a scheme of winding roads, buff stone cottages, and Tudor half-timbers. Even though Maybeck withdrew from the assignment before the college was built, the English imprint on The Principia remained.

Despite Charles Keeler's efforts to enunciate Maybeck's views, the genius of the architect remains in some respects elusive, enigmatic. How can one reconcile the operatic flamboyance of the Anthony showrooms with the finely textured cottage craft of the Keeler house? Or Phoebe Hearst's fun-Gothic castle at Wyntoon with the First Church of Christ, Scientist? From one point of view, Maybeck appears to be old-fashioned, a borrower and manipulator of traditional forms. From another, he seems bizarre: a bearded pixie

The Palace of Fine Arts at San Francisco's Panama-Pacific Exposition of 1915 owed its inspiration to classical forms, softened and mellowed through Maybeck's romantic vision. The domed rotunda and the curved colonnade, originally built in plaster and lath for the fair, were faithfully reconstructed in the 1960's of tinted, reinforced concrete.

building funny houses out of burlap soaked in concrete, a man who once designed a vast, useless, ochre-colored temple in San Francisco that looked in passing like a melted-down set for the last act of *Samson et Dalila.*

In truth, there was a constant element, running like a tightly braided thread through all of Maybeck's work. It was the element of spirituality. For Maybeck was at heart a Platonist, a believer in abstract virtues—goodness, beauty, truth—which he found as readily in the textures of a piece of wood as in the soul of a human being. Like all the best of the Beaux-Arts architects, he always saw architecture as an art. Only secondarily, if at all, did he look upon it as a servant of technology, an expression of ideology, a pragmatic response to instant problems. The value of architecture had to be judged by the mood it evoked. A "simple house" should bespeak an atmosphere of domestic felicity. A museum should produce nostalgic sadness. A church might preach the unity of the natural world. A college campus might suggest the awesome majesty of knowledge—or the modest comfort of a country village.

Maybeck never appeared to be troubled by the dichotomy others saw in him. While tape-recording his last opinions, drawing on a memory spotted by age, he recalled with admiration the Bénard plan for the university, which would have created an overbearing, terraced city of palaces and triumphal boulevards. He seemed to sense no incongruity between this pompous layout and his adjoining neighborhood of simple houses, rustic steps, and little roads that dodged among the trees. Both ways of doing things were beautiful. Both were appropriate to their use.

Maybeck remembered that Bénard had started his grand design for the university with the sewer line. Laughing, he said he thought it was as good a place as any to begin. The point was not where you started but where you ended, with a beautiful composition. *That* was the essence of architecture.

247

RAYMOND
HOOD

1881–1934

BY CARTER WISEMAN

During the design stages of what eventually became known as Rockefeller Center, Raymond Hood, one of the architects, was discussing with John R. Todd—the contractor John D. Rockefeller, Jr., had picked to direct the job—what sort of material should be used to clad the great buildings. Hood was set on stone, but Todd, in the interests of economy, was pushing for brick. When Hood had a moment alone with Todd, he said he didn't think brick was such a bad idea after all. The buildings' purpose, Hood conceded, was "to make money." And if the purpose was to make money, "then brick is good enough, even common brick. In fact, when you come right down to it, if corrugated iron—painted, of course—is good enough for the purpose, then that is what should be used." Todd was a tightwad, but he had one of the most important pieces of urban architecture ever conceived on his hands, and the prospect of corrugated iron was too much even for him. He promptly decreed that Rockefeller Center be sheathed in limestone.

This scene, which is recorded in a biography of Hood by Walter Kilham, Jr., one of the architect's former associates, provides a key insight to the man. Hood hadn't for a moment thought that corrugated iron was the stuff of a Rockefeller monument, and the good-naturedly duplicitous manner in which he got his way was typical of someone described by a contemporary writer as the "brilliant bad boy" of architecture. Despite conventional training, Hood was never a conventional designer. Not much taller than a jockey, with a quizzical smile and dark hair that he wore brushed straight up from his scalp, he was fond of ruffling the feathers of colleagues and public alike. "This beauty stuff is all bunk," he used to say. But he clearly didn't believe it. Neither did his close friends and associates, including Wallace K. Harrison, a collaborator on the Rockefeller Center

Rumpled and down-to-earth as usual, Hood posed at his home in Stamford, Connecticut, at the height of his career.

project, who said after Hood's death in 1934 that "everybody knew he was the best designer in town." Since then, the praise has grown stronger. Vincent Scully, the architectural historian, has called Hood "the greatest skyscraper architect of all time."

There is ample reason for such an accolade. In the course of a professional career that spanned only slightly more than a decade, Raymond Hood proved to be a major force in carrying the quintessentially American form of the skyscraper out of provincial eclecticism and into the modern era. Unexpectedly tapped by a friend to help out on the pivotal Tribune Tower competition in Chicago, Hood won with a design that at once acknowledged the decorative pull of the recent past and looked forward to the massing and formal simplicity of the future. His American Radiator Building in New York City was an unorthodox step into the use of color in architecture and showed a new appreciation of design as a corporate symbol. Hood's building for the *Daily News*, also in New York, all but abandoned decoration and became a model for many later buildings. In his headquarters for the McGraw-Hill Publishing Company, Hood carried the use of color even further and began to flirt with the emerging International style. And in Rockefeller Center he made a key contribution to what is generally accepted as the best piece of modern urbanism in the world. "While New York lagged behind Chicago in the development of the skyscraper," Lewis Mumford wrote in 1953, "it had the ironic task in the Thirties of bringing that task to its logical end." Raymond Hood was present all the way.

There was little in Hood's early life to suggest the prominence he would eventually achieve. He was born in 1881 in Pawtucket, Rhode Island, the son of a prosperous box manufacturer and the great-grandson of the town's first Baptist Sunday-school teacher. Upon finishing public school he went to Brown University, which he left after two years for M.I.T. and a bachelor of science degree in architecture. Hood's first job was as a draftsman in the New York office of the Boston firm of Cram, Goodhue and Ferguson, who were then working on the design of Saint Thomas's Church on Fifth Avenue. It was a choice spot for a young architect, but Hood decided after only six months to move on to Paris and the Ecole des Beaux-Arts.

Hood arrived in Paris only to flunk the Beaux-Arts drawing examinations. A year later, in 1905, he did better and embarked on the Ecole's rigorous course of study. Life in Paris took some getting used to for the new arrival: at first Hood refused to enter Notre Dame on the grounds that it was improper for a good Baptist to be caught in such a Catholic sanctuary. But his landlady (who had trouble pronouncing "Monsieur Ood" and dubbed him simply Le Jeune Homme) helped smooth the way. Having heard that her young lodger was pained by the early morning cold of the communal toilet, she thoughtfully scheduled her own visits just before his, in order to warm up the seat.

After a year at the Beaux-Arts, the peripatetic Hood was back in New York for another stint in Goodhue's office, but the city had temporarily lost its allure. In a letter to a friend written at the time, Hood complained, "Here, you get out of bed, eat a breakfast—and then submerge yourself in a foul smelling subway—and hanging on to a strap, you are carried three miles downtown to the musical accompaniment of all the dins and crashes which are peculiar to subway travel. Downtown, where you pass the day, is a place in which the sun never penetrates." His irritation must have got to his work, for he was evidently sacked by Goodhue. His next stop was Pittsburgh and the offices of Henry Hornbostel. But not long afterward, Hood was in Paris again, and he finally got his degree from the Beaux-Arts in 1911. Then it was back again to Pittsburgh, but after three more years with Hornbostel, Hood felt he was ready to head east once more and try architecture on his own. He intended, he announced grandly to his Pittsburgh friends, to become "the greatest architect in New York."

The year 1914 was an exciting time for a young architect in the big city. Following the introduction of the passenger elevator and the structural steel frame, office buildings had been reaching unprecedented heights. D. H. Burnham's Flatiron Building was finished in 1902; Ernest Flagg's Singer Building went up six years later, followed in 1913 by Cass Gilbert's 800-foot Woolworth Building with its lavish Gothic detailing. Two years later the enormous Equitable Building was completed, casting giant shadows down an unsuspecting Broadway (and leading to the passage of New York's first zoning law).

For all the architectural excitement bubbling around him, Hood's office on the top floor of a brownstone on West Forty-second Street remained a depressingly quiet place. (He papered part of the premises in gold in an attempt to cheer things up.) He produced a grand Beaux-Arts scheme for a courthouse in Providence, Rhode Island, but his income depended on piecework for other designers' competition entries. Hood did get one commission during this period, from the wealthy Mrs. Whitelaw Reid, who asked him to redo a bathroom in her Westchester estate. The problem was a cracked wall, and the architect's solution was: "Hang a picture over it."

At the time, Hood was taking most of his meals at Mori's, a restaurant on Bleecker Street, and the proprietor, Placido Mori, took a shine to the impecunious architect. Mori asked Hood to remodel the place, and in exchange provided him with a small apartment and a long cuff. Hood was already forty years old, but Mori had confidence in the man. "He must be a genius," Mori told a doubting friend. "He eats so much."

Even though Hood was deeply in debt, he managed to hire a secretary, Elsie Schmidt, and not long afterward they were married. By scraping together bits and pieces of work—including a project designing "Directoire," "Jacobean," and "Empire" radiator covers—he raised enough money to set himself and his new wife up in an apartment on Washington Square. And then the break came. An architect friend of Hood's, John Mead Howells, had been invited to enter the competition for the design of the Chicago Tribune Tower and asked Hood to join him in the project. A total of 263 architects from the United States and abroad, including Eliel Saarinen of Finland and Walter Gropius and Adolf Meyer of Germany, submitted designs. But when the decision was announced on December 23, 1922, the $50,000 first prize went to design No. 69, by John Mead Howells and Raymond Hood.

When Hood heard the news, he touched Mori for enough extra cash to buy a new coat and went out to Chicago to receive the award. When he got back, he and his wife settled up with Mori, splurged on a cab, and toured the town, paying off all the other creditors who had thought Raymond Hood might—or might not—have a future as an architect.

Hood's design for the Tribune Tower was hardly revolutionary. But then, the rules of the competition required only that the building be beautiful, and that it serve the practical needs of a major newspaper. As Howells and Hood put it in the statement accompanying their design: "Our desire has been not so much an archeological expression of any particular style as to express in the exterior the essentially American problem of skyscraper construction, with its continued vertical lines and inserted horizontals. . . . We have wished to make this landmark the study of a beautiful and vigorous form, not of an extraordinary form."

By the lights of the times, they succeeded admirably. The drawings show a tower soaring into space from a solid base punctuated by a large, arched entryway. The "vertical lines" the designers spoke of were etched emphatically in stone, giving the building an almost palpable feeling of upward thrust. The Gothic detailing reached its climax in a complicated openwork top of buttresses and pinnacles, which, the architects pointed out, was designed "not only for its own outline and composition, but for the possibilities of illumination and reflected lighting at night."

Many architectural critics have scoffed at Hood's design since it went up on Michigan Avenue, arguing that its fussy references to the Gothic ignored the pioneering work of Louis Sullivan in developing a spare skyscraper idiom appropriate to the technology of the day. "Woolworth Gothic" is the way Sigfried Giedion described the winner, referring to the style of Cass Gilbert's famous New York skyscraper, which was already nine years old at the time of the Tribune competition. Henry-Russell Hitchcock termed the building "medievalizing."

Looking back, those criticisms seem excessively harsh. In fact, Hood's design was not all that far removed in spirit from Saarinen's slimmer, more austere entry, which won second prize (and had a far greater immediate impact on American design). Hood's early sketches for the building make clear that his primary concern was the fundamental form of the building, and that the Gothic detailing was frosting meant, no doubt, to reassure the *Tribune's* owner, Colonel Robert R. McCormick, that he was getting something with firm cultural—which was to say, old and European—roots. Ely Jacques Kahn, an architect who was to become a close personal friend of Hood's, explained Hood's attitude in an appreciation written shortly after he died. "It is easy to see why Hood's scheme won out," Kahn wrote. "There was clarity and logic in plan and mass. The fact that his detail was Gothic amused him some years later, for, as he put it quite tersely himself, the building was erected when embroidery was in vogue, and he was more concerned with the actual structure than its shell."

That concern became increasingly evident in Hood's subsequent work starting with the American Radiator (now American-Standard) Building on New York's West Fortieth Street, done in association with J. André Fouilhoux, a French engineer. In this side-street skyscraper Hood showed an appreciation of the simplicity of Saarinen's Tribune entry, and produced a much cleaner, setback form marked by thin piers. It was suggested at the time that the elaborate top, which again was designed to be lit at night, was intended to represent a glowing coal in symbolic reference to the owner's heating business, but Hood evidently saw it merely as after-hours advertising of the company's presence. ("It stimulates public interest," he observed.) The building's real distinction, apart from its spare shape, was its color. To avoid the inevitable dilution of a light-colored building's visual unity by the dark "holes" created by

Before Hood won the Tribune Tower competition, he and his wife lived briefly in a small apartment over Mori's restaurant on New York's Bleecker Street. He made this drawing of the establishment in 1919 while remodeling it for the owner, who credited the work against Hood's substantial tab.

windows, Hood sheathed the tower in black brick. Of course, the effect was reversed at night, when the windows were lit, but during the day, with its sleek black mass topped by gilded finials, the Radiator Building created an entirely new awareness of what height in architecture could mean.

Raymond Hood had covered a lot of ground—professionally and personally—from the time of the Tribune competition to the completion of the Radiator Building in 1924, and he was enjoying the fruits of his efforts. He and his wife had a comfortable house on Long Island Sound in Stamford, Connecticut, which Hood had designed (in the English manner), complete with tennis court and a dock for his boat. But his domestic life was unpretentious, especially for a man who was emerging as one of the most prominent designers of his day. The furniture was a nondescript mixture of antique and modern; Hood liked milk and ginger cookies on weekend afternoons, and fancied applejack late at night. If an idea for a design struck him out of range of a drawing board, he improvised—to his wife's dismay—on whatever was handy. "Nothing is sacred," Mrs. Hood once complained to a friend. "He spares nothing. Look at those columns—disgraceful; and my tablecloths are all

253

covered with pencil marks. It's impossible to keep a laundress."

If the design direction from the Tribune Tower to the Radiator Building suggested an emerging consistency in Hood's style, he showed during this period that he was still an able eclectic, adjusting his work to suit the customer. The Saint Vincent de Paul Asylum in Tarrytown, New York, would have fit comfortably into a French provincial landscape. He did a comfortable and unexceptional house for some friends in Greenwich, as well as the Masonic Temple and Scottish Rite Cathedral in Scranton, Pennsylvania. Working with an English architect, J. Gordon Reeves, Hood designed the National Radiator Building in London, whose smooth dark façade suggested a solid knowledge of contemporary European developments in architecture. Only in an apartment house on Manhattan's East Eighty-fourth Street does a sense of what is to come appear with any authority. Considerable ornament persists in the spandrels beneath the windows, but the treatment of the limestone strips between them is strongly vertical and altogether unembellished. The residual decoration of the Radiator Building is here being shaken loose by the spareness of modernism.

Hood himself would never have put it that way, of course. As far as he was concerned, the look of a building derived from its purpose (which could include a need for voguish "embroidery"), and modernism as a theory had nothing to do with it. He took up the subject directly in an article in the December 7, 1929, issue of *Liberty* magazine entitled "What Is Beauty in Architecture?" Beauty, Hood concluded, "is utility, developed in a manner to which the eye is accustomed by habit, insofar as this development does not detract from its quality of usefulness."

By this time, ornament was evidently beginning to detract from Hood's perception of usefulness in newspaper buildings, for when he (and his Tribune associate, John Howells) set to work on a project for the New York *Daily News*, embellishment virtually disappeared.

Hood had long entertained a fantasy about a city made up of enormous towers standing singly or in clusters, and he got his first chance to experiment with the concept in the Daily News Building. The original scheme called for a structure of only six stories to house the paper's printing plant. Hood

The Chicago Tribune Tower, designed in 1922 and completed two years later, has been criticized for the use of Gothic ornament at a time when the modern American skyscraper was coming into its own as a spare architectural idiom. But Hood's preliminary drawings show that the decoration was far less important to him than the building's fundamental form.

254

argued that a larger building would allow the *News* to accommodate its offices as well, and to rent out any additional space at a profit. Working with plasticine models—which were much better suited to a "mass"-conscious designer like Hood than were the more common perspective renderings—Hood began, literally, to manipulate the rough form of the building to take best advantage of the city's zoning restrictions. Hood's solution was a thirty-seven-story tower stretching through the entire block from Forty-first Street to Forty-second Street. At first, Captain Joseph Patterson, the owner and editor of the *News*, balked at the idea, but the economics of Hood's plan finally convinced him.

Once the decision to go ahead with the tower was made, Hood proceeded with the details in typical fashion, cannily probing and pushing until he got his way, justifying the whole thing on the basis of usefulness, but quietly attending to the look of it as well. Two elements of the final design make the workings of the Hood method clear. Because of the way the site was laid out, three of the building's four sides would be facing streets, while the fourth would, at some point, inevitably face another tall building. The normal solution would have been to leave the fourth wall without windows in anticipation of later construction on the adjoining site. This would have ruined Hood's hopes for a free-standing tower, so he proposed giving up a narrow strip of the News site for a midblock street, guaranteeing air space all around, no matter what kind of structure later went up next to it. The idea struck Captain Patterson as downright wasteful, until the architect gently explained that office space without windows—"loft" space— would rent for about $1.50 a square foot, while offices *with* windows, which they would get in Hood's plan, would rent for twice that. The proposal was accepted, and similar trade-offs subsequently became common in skyscraper design.

After the Daily News Building was finished, a number of contemporary critics, loyal to the modernist dictum that buildings should be "honest" expressions of their structure, attacked Hood for using twice the number of vertical piers on the exterior as there were structural steel columns to "justify" them. Whether Hood chose the number of piers for aesthetic reasons (which is possible) or not, he found a purely functional explanation for his decision. What really determined the spacing,

Hood sheathed his 1924 American Radiator Building in black brick so that the dark openings of the windows would interfere less with the tower's visual unity. The Gothic touches at the top, residuals from the Tribune Tower, were highlighted in gold and illuminated at night "to stimulate public interest."

he insisted, was the size of window that a typical office worker could open and close with ease. To establish that, Hood chose a young woman for a test and concluded that the ideal window width was four feet six inches, leaving a four-foot space between windows. The space between the structural steel columns was, however, much wider and would have meant leaving unsightly gaps between the windows and the "real" piers. Since columns normally carried much of a building's wiring and piping—and in this case a widening of the corresponding piers would have been necessary to handle the unusually heavy load—Hood simply added an intervening pier to handle the utility lines. He thus created an "aesthetically" even rhythm for his exterior, while satisfying the "functional" needs of the building and its prospective users.

One historian has noted approvingly that the Daily News Building "marks the end of the era of eclectic experimentation" in architecture. But at the time not everyone was pleased by the de-emphasis of ornament on such an enormous building (decorative panels over the entrances and patterned brickwork on the spandrels are among the few concessions). The slightly coy attitude with which Hood greeted the complaints is clear in an article he wrote in the November 1930 issue of *Architectural Forum*:

Naturally, the exterior of the News Building is so simple that a great many things could be done to it, but whenever I wanted to do anything, I never knew where to begin or where to stop; and I took comfort from a remark that Laloux [a Beaux-Arts teacher] made occasionally to a student who was at a loss as to what sort of ornament to use in a particular place. Laloux's remark was: "Why not try nothing?"

Even at this stage, though, Hood was perfectly willing to use ornamental devices if the situation called for them. One such was a huge mockup of a refrigerator that he designed as the crowning element on the showroom buildings he did for a General Electric distributor. A country house Hood built for Captain Patterson is another example of how willing he was to accommodate a client's decorative requirements (or to use the client's requirements as a vehicle for his own experimentation). Patterson had decided to build a house in Ossining, New York, and he wanted lots of windows in it, windows placed where *he* liked them, not where an architect thought they looked best. So Hood dutifully sprinkled windows over much of the surface of the building, giving it what now appears to be a radically—if somewhat inadvertently—modern look. The cubistic exterior was almost without ornament, but it was striking for more than its shape: whether out of a desire to have

In his soaringly vertical design for the Daily News Building, completed in 1930, the architect all but abandoned ornament. An exception was the decorative panel above the main entrance. The inscription, "He made so many of them," apparently referred both to God's creatures and the readers of the News.

the house blend into the landscape, or some nostalgia for the military, Captain Patterson insisted that the walls be painted in the irregular patterns of wartime camouflage.

Several other projects were filling the boards of the Hood office during these years, including one for the interiors of a steamship for the United States Lines, as well as a second New York City apartment house, and portions of the 1933 Chicago World's Fair plan. It was a far cry from the days when Hood was doing odds and ends for other architects in order to cover his tab at Mori's, and he was hard pressed to handle all the work. During a particularly hectic period, it became clear that the shop needed another draftsman, but there was no more room to set up an additional drafting board. "Hire another man anyway," declared Hood. "There's always one guy on the can."

With the Tribune, the Radiator, and the Daily News buildings behind him, Hood had established himself as a major force in office building design, and his next project offered him a chance to carry even further his thinking about towers, color, and the building-as-corporate-symbol. In 1929 the

258

McGraw-Hill Publishing Company decided to build a new headquarters and invited Hood to do the job. Like the *News* project, this one required the housing of production as well as clerical functions, but in the case of McGraw-Hill, which turned out a wide range of publications, the demands were more varied. In a day before extensive air conditioning and lighting systems, a prime consideration was making maximum use of natural light and ventilation. To do this, Hood came up with a design for the West Forty-second Street site that marked a significant departure from the strict verticality of earlier American skyscrapers, including his own. He wrapped the building in strongly horizontal bands of windows, stacking one "layer" atop another in a series of setbacks that culminated in a narrow, almost nautical, bridge displaying the McGraw-Hill logo in bold Art Deco lettering.

Striking as the horizontal treatment of the building was at the time, its color was even more so. A number of different colors had been suggested at the outset, including black with orange trim. But James McGraw, who had two sons at Princeton, reportedly declared, "There's too much Princeton around here," and decided on green. There was more to it than that, though. Hood described the color scheme in greater detail as "Dutch blue at the base, with sea green window bands, the blue gradually shading off to a lighter tone the higher the building got, until it finally blends off into the azure of the sky."

The McGraw-Hill Building has had a mixed critical response in the years since it was completed in 1931. (Scully has called it "proto-jukebox.") But there is no question that it was a landmark on American architecture's road toward modernism. And that was clear immediately after it was finished: McGraw-Hill was the only American building Henry-Russell Hitchcock and Philip Johnson included in their highly influential book, *The International Style*, published in 1932.

When the enormously ambitious planning for the future Rockefeller Center got under way, Raymond Hood was an obvious choice for the design team. The beginnings of the project lay in the search for a new home for the Metropolitan Opera, which was to become the focus for a complex of other cultural and commercial buildings. Benjamin Wistar Morris drew up the initial plan, and in 1928 John D. Rockefeller, Jr., at first just another investor, began to assume control of the project. Rockefeller eventually put his developer friend John Todd in charge of carrying out the job. Todd in turn added the architectural firm of Reinhard and Hofmeister. But the undertaking clearly required more manpower, so the firms of Corbett, Harrison and MacMurray, and Hood, Godley (a new partner) and Fouilhoux were invited to join in, creating a group that became known as the Associated Architects.

The financial crash of 1929 forced the opera to withdraw from the project, and Morris went with it. The solution to the crisis, as Rockefeller and Todd saw it, was to go all out for a commercial office venture that would sustain itself through the troubled times. Hood, for one, found the new pressures and restraints a challenge.

Far from being a handicap [he wrote], this discipline, I am convinced, of being obliged to make a project stand on its own financial feet and to submit its details and materials to a constant critical analysis leads to honesty and integrity of design. Under this stimulation, the cobwebs of whimsey, taste, fashion, and vanity are brushed aside, and the architect finds himself face to face with the essentials and elements that make real architecture and real beauty.

This is vintage Hood, and although he was only one of a talented team, he soon became the dominant member in the refinement of the over-all scheme, which now provided for an enormous office tower in place of the opera building and several lesser structures arrayed around it. The layout of Rockefeller Center, with its clear axial relationships and symmetries, was classic Beaux-Arts from the outset. This is hardly surprising in light of the fact that six of the eight architects on the job were graduates of the Ecole (the exceptions were Reinhard and Hofmeister). But the evolution of the details, in which Hood had such an important role, saved it from academic sterility. One of the most significant details was the Prometheus Fountain. The original plans provided for a small plaza at the foot of the main skyscraper, and Hood suggested using it for a fountain to relieve the great expanses of hard surfaces that would be going up around it. Predictably, Todd thought the idea an extravagance and declared that it would involve recirculating some 30,000 gallons of water a day. At that point Hood pulled out his pencil, did some quick arithmetic, and revealed that the cost of recirculating that much water would run to $8.30 a day. Against an estimated cost of $250,000,000 for the entire complex, the water bill struck Todd as acceptable after all, and Hood's fountain went into the plan.

Another detail that shows yet again Hood's dual sensitivity to cash return and human needs is the system of rooftop gardens he proposed for the

One of Hood's many contributions to the vast and complicated design of Rockefeller Center was the idea of using the roof areas for gardens. This 1932 rendering, by John Wenrich, includes one of several planned pedestrian bridges, which ultimately proved impractical and were never built.

center. And the way he went about proposing them is, again, typical. Apparently the flinty Todd was not happy with the prospect of his future tenants having to look down from their elegant offices on a bleak panorama of blank roofs. According to Walter Kilham, Jr., the architect turned to Todd one day and said, "By the way, John, thinking of Radio City and getting the best possible rents for the space, I was wondering if office space that looked out on a garden would be worth any more than, say, space that just looked out on another roof?" Todd said he thought it would be worth about a dollar more per square foot, and Hood, again doing some quick arithmetic, pointed out that there would be roughly seven acres of roof space on the center's lower buildings, offering the prospect of a handsome return. "At a dollar more a square foot extra you could afford to landscape those roofs like the hanging gardens of Babylon," he told Todd. So that plan, too, went ahead, although when the bridges that Hood had proposed to link the various roof gardens proved impractical, it was much reduced.

Rockefeller Center is one of the few pieces of modern urban design about which there seems to be almost no aesthetic debate. The American Institute of Architects' *AIA Guide to New York City* says simply: "An island of architectural excellence, this is the greatest urban complex of the twentieth century: an understated and urbane place that has become a classic lesson in the point and counterpoint of space, form, and circulation." It is always difficult to separate out the influence of any one member of a team in assessing their final product, but there is no doubt that Hood, the man who had declared that beauty was "bunk," was a prime mover behind Rockefeller Center's form as well as its urbanity. In the words of historian William Jordy: "Hood was the key member of the team in the sense that his newly completed Daily News Building haunted the Associated Architects throughout their deliberations."

Even as Rockefeller Center was under construction, Hood was pursuing the next stages of his vision of a city of towers. One far-sighted scheme was for a free-standing apartment tower set in the middle of a country site so that the residents could share the use and view of their common ground while minimizing the maintenance of individual buildings. Far more ambitious was Hood's plan for Manhattan 1950, a great grid of clustered towers housing businesses, residences, and industries, served by a mass-transit net and linked across the rivers by mammoth bridges that themselves contained thousands of apartments. For those of us who have suffered the effects of modern megastructural theories in the various forms of urban renewal, the implications of Hood's grand designs may cause a shudder. But one has to wonder how such plans might have developed in the hands of an architect whose ambitions as a builder were always so well tempered by his sympathy for the user.

Hood never got the chance to see his grandest plans become a reality; he didn't even get to see Rockefeller Center in its final form. In the wake of the Lindbergh kidnaping, Hood received an anonymous note threatening his own children. He sent his family to Bermuda for safety and later joined them there. But he was not well at the time, and not long after their return, on August 14, 1934, he died of heart and circulatory problems complicated by rheumatoid arthritis. He was fifty-three, and it had been a mere twelve years since his winning Tribune Tower entry had plucked him out of obscurity.

Hood occupies a curious limbo in the history of American architecture. In 1932 Hitchcock said, "He is not an idealist and he is not a creative artist." It is true that Hood railed at public displays of aesthetics, and he remained a client's man all the way. ("To Hood," wrote a colleague after the architect's death, "the client was always the boss—his job was to solve the client's problems.") And he didn't have the flamboyance of a Wright or the arrogance of a Le Corbusier. "It may be my building," Hood once told a friend, "but it's their skyline."

Yet what is one to make of Hood's clear-headed manipulation of commercial demands to produce such livable, workable buildings? Or his plans for cities of towers surrounded by gardens? Is there no idealism—or art—there? The Dutch architect and writer Rem Koolhaas has called Hood "a specialist in pragmatic sophistry at the service of pure creation." But the architect himself was not fond of such high rhetoric. Perhaps the truest appreciation of his role lies in something he said once when discussing his main line of work, the design of office buildings. "For the client it is a chance to get a return on his money," he explained, "for the manufacturer a chance to sell his products, for the contractor a chance to make a profit. There remains the architect, the building's only friend."

The greatest testament to the work of Hood and his associates on Rockefeller Center is that the complex has come to be widely regarded as the finest piece of urban design in this century.

LUDWIG MIES

Mies's montage drawing of the interior of a row house, 1931

VAN DER ROHE

1886–1969

BY M. W. NEWMAN

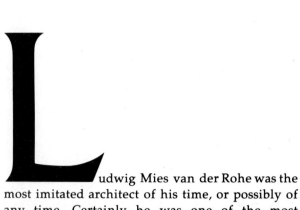

Ludwig Mies van der Rohe was the most imitated architect of his time, or possibly of any time. Certainly he was one of the most influential. This laconic master of "Less is more" set his imprint on a mid-twentieth-century Miesian Age, and he lived long enough to suffer the inevitable rebellion in the ranks, a post-Miesian era stamped with his name. His legacy and his legend in any case are immense, and his buildings are among the most serene, decisive, and beautiful ever crafted.

Nearly everyone in architecture, and many outside the profession, called him simply Mies (pronounced *Meece*). Reticent but vastly sure of himself, he was at once the modern classicist and the classic modernist.

In two decades after World War II he achieved a towering reputation as the master of steel and glass, the uncompromising designer of "skin-and-bones" buildings, the austere prophet of reason, the distiller of absolutes. Dedicated to a credo of structure, clarity, and order arising out of its own time, Mies was the architect against whom other architects measured themselves.

Such comparison never was easy. The man in his Olympian way appeared to dwell on mountaintops. "I don't want to be interesting, I want to be good," he said in his heavy German accent, turning his broad back on mere flights of architectural form for form's sake.

His was a moral quest. In the impeccable grid lines and rhythms of curtain-wall architecture, in the impersonal harmonies and hierarchies of structure, he sought a sacred "significance of facts." "Beauty is the splendor of truth," said Mies van der Rohe, echoing Saint Augustine.

Mies never said very much, although he was given to devising nuggety maxims. "Don't talk, build," was his theme. He made his students squirm

Clouds of cigar smoke and long periods of silence were signs of concentration on architectural problems. This photograph of Mies was taken in his Chicago office in 1957.

by peering coolly over their shoulders until their sketches and design projects turned to jelly before their eyes. "Try again," he finally would say.

Mies chilled and distilled architecture to bare essentials, to "almost nothing," as he put it. In theory and practice, "Less is more" banished flab, excess, and overt ornament in favor of the thing in itself—the building as all-purpose box, as stripped-down object, as monument.

But did Mies, in his zeal for an unattainable purity and order, take the stuffings out of architecture—the messy element of humanity? Was less a bore? It was one of the many arguments made by his critics, and even by some of his friends. "Mies based his art on three things: economy, science, technology," his former celebrator and collaborator, Philip Johnson, said in 1959. "Of course, he was right. It's just that I am bored. We are all bored."

Bored or not, we can never dismiss Mies's buildings. Actually, they are as challenging as they are calming, arising from a high discipline welded to a compressed passion. They are the works of a master, regardless of their implacable consistency of style or the Xerox landscape of lesser, look-alike buildings they spawned. For they are elegant and, for all their seemingly weightless transparency, solid and enduring. Johnson may have stepped down from Mies's shoulders in a search for new paths, but he noted as he left: "Mies is such a genius."

The evidence surely is there in the bronze-coated Seagram tower in New York (designed with Johnson), soaring thirty-eight stories above its stately plaza without a dissenting line. The austere Federal Center (1964–1975) is a superb complex in Chicago's Loop, despite its bleak lobbies. The glass-walled Farnsworth house, a supreme masterpiece completed in 1950, seemingly floats in air beside the Fox River in the Illinois prairie.

Mies and his students remade the Chicago skyline, and there is a recognizable family of unadorned buildings by the master, as well, in Mexico City, Baltimore, Detroit, Newark, Montreal, Des Moines, Washington, Berlin. And a prewar jewel: his legendary German Pavilion for the International Exposition at Barcelona in 1929, which virtually enshrined revolutionary concepts of space and structure—only to be dismantled and vanish forever.

Mies was a stonemason's son and grew up in the ancient Rhineland cathedral city of Aachen, learning the heft of materials firsthand from his father. (The architect later devised the name Mies van der Rohe by combining his father's and mother's last names. It was a name as ordered, balanced, and patrician as the man himself turned out to be.)

267

He never earned a high-school diploma, let alone an architectural degree, but enjoyed an astonishing sixty-five-year career anyway. Two careers, in fact. As form-giver and prophet of the glassy skyscraper long before it was feasible to build one, he was a large eminence in his native Germany—thinking, theorizing, and teaching, for the most part. After Hitler came to power, Mies joined the exodus of German émigrés to the United States. And in 1938 he settled in Chicago, where he spent the second, and most productive, thirty years of his professional life, remaining creative into his eighties.

More than anyone else, this deliberate Bauhaus master defined the image of the office tower that in turn defined corporate America of the mid-twentieth century. He was the right man, at the right time, in the right place, to stylize the glassy, air-conditioned skyscrapers that erupted in the downtowns of the world. Many of them were little more than vertical work machines dedicated to paper shuffling and button pushing, but the stonecutter's son placed a cachet of art and status on these big boxes. The word got around fast in a time of almost instantaneous communication. For as long as he reigned and well beyond, it was fashionable to clad office towers in neutral grid skins made of industrial materials.

Above all, Mies did it, paradoxically, with two brilliant apartment houses—the Chicago Lake Shore Drive "glass houses" of 1951, which were primary art forms of the 1950's. Framed in black-painted steel, they gleamed at night like lanterns lighting up a new world.

Paradox—in this case, apartment houses that set the high style for corporate office skyscrapers—was an essential of Mies's work, whatever his intent may have been. He combined the utmost pragmatism ("reason" was his word for it) with an almost visionary pursuit of absolutes.

The Miesian curtain wall somehow joined a seeming weightlessness to an uncompromising grid of manmade materials—steel, glass, aluminum, concrete. It managed a marriage of tension and serenity. And it was set forth in classic proportions: three bays on the narrow side, five bays on the wider, in the Seagram Building and in the Lake Shore Drive glass houses. The Federal Center courthouse in Chicago (designed in association with three other firms) fills its broad envelope of space to the precise, magical inch.

Mies's buildings look simple, but "simplicity isn't so simple," he pointed out. Do they look alike? So do Greek temples. Mies felt he was on to something classic. Novelty was beneath him. "I don't think every building I put up needs to be different, since I always apply the same principles," he said.

"But, Mies, what about self-expression in architecture?" one of his employees asked him one day, with a worried look. She happened to be the granddaughter of Frank Lloyd Wright, the ultimate romantic of American architecture. So the story goes, anyway.

Mies, a slow starter, told her, "Wait—first let me get a cup of coffee. Come back in two hours."

When she did, the old master politely asked her to write her name on a slip of paper. "There," he said, "so much for self-expression. Now let's design a good building."

That was a Miesian dig, we can be sure, that would have brought a heated retort from Wright. The two men had long admired and influenced each other's work, although they spoke very different languages of architectural expression. In 1938 Wright had even introduced Mies to a VIP Chicago audience as "my Mies van der Rohe," but had then swept out of the hall before Mies could say anything.

Years later Wright, as the high-riding dean of American architects, turned against Mies, deriding his restrained development of form. It was flat-chested, look-alike, unwholesome, imported, and even "totalitarian." Wright had prided himself on destroying the "box," but it had come back stronger than ever under the hand of "my Mies." Mies shrugged and kept on working. He was cool.

"The only time I ever saw Mies lose his temper was after he stayed up all night on a student design project," a Chicago architect recalled. "We ran out of cigars at two in the morning. There weren't any available in the neighborhood. About an hour later, Mies became irritable and blew up at a student. But at 6 A.M. a store opened and Mies finally got some cigars and relaxed."

Cigars and brandy must be considered Miesian. Late at night, he confessed, he sometimes felt an overwhelming desire to work at something he liked. But as high priest of the architecture of reason and impersonal truth, the iron-willed elder wouldn't give in. "I shake it off by smoking a cigar and drinking a glass of brandy and going to bed," he said. "I don't want to do what I like. I want to do what is right."

Mies played variations on this moral code with oft-quoted aphorisms as spare, polished, and tautly profiled as his best designs. "God is in the details" was a Miesian saying. The seventeenth-century French painter Nicolas Poussin, a strict classicist, had said much the same thing.

It was hardly Mies's fault that architects and developers slavishly copied a few of his formulas, while ignoring his painstaking thought, the deeper values of his canon. Almost always, they copied for the worse. Few, or none, had his eye for proportion and detail, for the nuances in the relationship of the parts to the whole, for sheer workmanship. Mies, indeed, could have traveled to almost any large city and seen a pseudo-Miesian world. The glassy acres of Park Avenue or Third Avenue in New York are largely a monument to this kind of hack work and fashions of the hour.

He startled New York (and incidentally broke the formidable architectural wall formed by Park Avenue) by setting a ninety-foot-deep plaza in front of the Seagram Building. But what he did there, so magnificently, soon turned into a deadly cliché—the skyscraper on the plaza—in less skilled hands.

Miesian doctrine, supposedly so teachable, turned out to be elusive. His formulas, and those of his more talented colleagues of the International style, were converted into assembly-line staples, marketplace commodities. When they lost their sales appeal, they were replaced with other instant stylings.

What was his credo? It emerged from his world view in an epoch of science and the machine triumphant, and embraced clarity, order, truth, serenity, balance—while leaving room for asymmetry and dynamism (the Farnsworth house, for example, and the Barcelona Pavilion of 1929). It was the architecture of unadorned structure, but Mies's grid lines and precisely placed metal beams ornamented his curtain walls anyway. He elevated technology but was far from a mere technologist. Mies clung to a certain idealism, an ambiguity, an aesthetic, that on occasion almost seemed to remove his buildings from their immediate setting and time, regardless of his expressed will. It was confusing. Mies did not or could not always abide by his principles.

"Whenever technology reaches its real fulfillment, it transcends into architecture," he assured the world. Or, putting it another way: "The structure is the fundamental of it. We don't think about the form when we start. We think about the right way to use materials. The esthetics . . . come later, much later. This is the refinement of it." These supposedly simple rules were in reality complex, difficult, remote.

There is, for example, a mystical but ultimately impossible oneness with naked technology—with black-painted steel and glass wrapped around space—in the very heart and soul of the Miesian imperative, Crown Hall at Illinois Institute of Technology in Chicago. Here Mies achieved an immense open workroom, 120 feet by 220 feet and 18 feet high, encased in crystal. He did it by suspending the roof from four enormous girders supported by eight columns.

Crown Hall is Miesian "universal space," designed to adapt to varying uses, to changing needs. Form need no longer follow function, he announced: in the new age a universally convenient form (the box, typically) is created and the uses are fitted in. (It was at about this time that the architecture department of the University of Illinois in Chicago was housed in a one-time brassiere factory, and accordingly was dubbed the Brahaus.)

Mies headed the school of architecture at Illinois Tech for twenty years, placing that university on the world map. He planned and designed many of its buildings and fashioned Crown Hall's main space for the study of architecture.

Some see Crown Hall's grand open room as a democratic space, some find it bureaucratic. A better word might be aristocratic. For all of Mies's seeming modesty, for all of his manifestoes demanding an impersonal architecture, for all of his proclamations that architecture emerges from a fulfilled technology, Mies enshrined architecture itself. He sought to remake the world with orderly, clean-lined design, like many other architects who matured in the heady aftermath of World War I. It was an uplifting dream, even if life messed it up. "Architecture wrote the history of epochs and gave them their names," Mies announced, in the pontifical style he sometimes favored.

Crown Hall in consequence was designed as the most striking, epochal building on the campus. It was dedicated on a memorable night in 1956 with a student prom. Colored lights roamed over the tall, precisely divided glass walls, which are the same inside and out. Duke Ellington's orchestra played, and the Duke said with a smile, "The acoustics are crystal."

Mies was fascinated. He puffed on a cigar and beamed. As an architect with no clients in the broken Germany after World War I, he had envisioned the future with a series of awesomely prophetic designs for office buildings and houses. Working with glass models, he had "discovered that the important thing is the play of reflections and not the effect of light and shadow as in ordinary buildings." The dream crystallized in the noble spaces of Crown Hall.

But—always there is a *but*—Crown Hall's immense rectangles of glass had a way of turning the space into a sweatbox in summer. And where in this universal clear-span room could one find a corner of his own, a place to pin up a picture, to control the light, or to escape from noise? And why does the building rather resemble a temple—or, as one critic put it, a president's house? Why did the supposedly adaptable universal space prove so stubborn when later invaded by dry-wall cubicles installed by lesser artists?

Perhaps the most suitable Miesian answer is that "simplicity is not so simple." Mies, more than any of his contemporaries, strove for an anonymous architecture using the grammar of its day. But it demanded a painstaking, individual skill after all. A seeker after universals must expect contradictions, and they are abundant in the master's work.

His split-level School of Social Service Administration at the University of Chicago contains one of Mies's most uplifting open spaces—balanced, symmetrical, calm, ordered. Possibly he thought it was too good for social workers, because he achieved this Renaissancelike luxury by relegating staff members to the lower levels. The building is hard to move around in, besides.

"Mies doesn't like people" was a perennial complaint of his critics. He never did live down one of his sorriest manifestoes, dating from 1924 when he was deeply involved in Berlin's avant-garde polemics. Those were the days when Mies talked, or at least wrote, rather than built—since there was little else to do. He wrote at that time:

We are concerned today with questions of a general nature. The individual is losing significance; his destiny is no longer what interests us. The decisive achievements in all fields are impersonal and their authors are for the most part unknown. They are part of the trend of our time toward anonymity.

If one chose to do so, it was easy to detect a soulless, bureaucratic spirit in this ice-cold rhetoric. Mies might have thought of it as reason or realism. In spite of his iron-Teuton pronouncements, he himself was indubitably human, a tailored gentleman of fixed habits. In later years in Chicago he never even moved out of his high-ceilinged old apartment into one of his own "glass houses." A divorced bachelor, he sometimes bounced children on his painfully arthritic knees, and relaxed over brandy at night with favored colleagues. He would spend hours fussing over the placement of a chair or painting.

Was he, then, rigidly "antipeople?" Or as "impersonal" as he possibly liked to think? Certainly not, if one looks carefully at the famous twenty-six-story towers, 860-880 North Lake Shore Drive, finished in 1951. Mies placed them at right angles to each other. They don't just sit there but command their site and maximal lake views dynamically. And the spaces between them were as important to Mies as any other aspect of the design. With two Miesian towers that later went up just north of them, they form an astonishingly exciting ensemble.

Glassy, charcoal-framed cubes raised on stilts, all four buildings create openness and a serene

formality at ground level. As you move around them, their uniform grid façades actually seem to change. The taut network of lines opens when viewed head-on, and becomes opaque when seen from an angle. It is the art of perspective, among other things, with a complex play of major and minor rhythms.

"You either like Mies or you don't," a Toronto real-estate man once noted, eyeing the master's stalwart if aloof Dominion Centre there. Lewis Mumford, America's distinguished urban philosopher, had severe reservations about Mies. He accused him of creating cold, inhuman monuments to the technocratic ice age—jewels of chaste design.

For many people, however, the Miesian milieu is profoundly satisfying, even lyrical. They are living or working, or perhaps both, in works of art that mirror sky, water, the seasons, the cityscape. True, the apartments in Mies's buildings tend to be routine—or "democratic," according to his defenders, who say that the very simplicity of the spaces permits each occupant to mold them to his own purposes. (Mies's boldly original plans for 860 proposed open-space apartments divided not by rooms but by partitions, and were rejected by the developer.)

In any event, there is nothing routine about the way his buildings manage, in effect, to stand aloof and closed, while reaching to the outdoors. Miesian space goes right through walls.

For some people there is nothing routine, either, in living behind glass. If you have a feeling you are being spied upon, a Miesian shaft is not for you. And what happens to the view if you must pull down the shades in summer to keep from broiling in the sun? That did happen in 860, which at first had no air conditioning.

Mies's old Bauhaus colleague, the city planner Ludwig Hilberseimer, once needled him about the way 860 had been designed without regard to sun orientation. As the architect Reginald Malcolmson recalled the incident, Hilberseimer even dredged up Socratic doctrine: with proper shading, a house should face south so as to get as much winter sun and as little summer sun as possible.

"Socrates never saw a skyscraper," replied Mies.

"I did not know that the truth changed with the number of floors," replied "Hilbs."

There were aesthetic ambiguities in 860, too, and Mies allowed himself to chuckle about them. He sought to express its structure, its framework of

These twin towers, built on Chicago's Lake Shore Drive in 1951, established Mies's pure-as-ice skyscraper style.

steel, as clearly and minimally as possible on its façade. This was Miesian truth. But the Chicago fire code required that he coat the steel skeleton, the true framework, in concrete. At some expense, therefore, in terms of money and of the strictures of Less is more, Mies developed a stunning solution. He added an outer framework of steel over the concrete. It did not hold up anything but stated the position and nature of columns and spans. It was the artifice that tells the truth, the refinement that is art.

Mies's fondness for glass walls posed even more of a problem in domestic architecture. Dr. Edith Farnsworth was a friend until Mies built an exquisitely detailed country house for her in Plano, Illinois, crafted in sheets of glass and bands of white-painted steel. The living space in the Farnsworth house is, in effect, a single room divided into areas, and seems to float through the glass. House and setting look as though they were made for each other. But Dr. Farnsworth was so displeased by the design, as well as by the cost and the five years it took to build the house, that she brought (and lost) a suit against the architect.

Philip Johnson's renowned glass house in Connecticut was inspired by Mies's concept, although the two structures are quite different. Johnson's house is firmly rooted to the ground. Mies's slabs and cantilevers appear to be in flight.

There were other problems in Miesian design. In Baltimore his One Charles Center office block spruced up the downtown, but its connecting marble-paved pedestrian bridges have not weathered very well, according to civic officials. At Lafayette Park, near downtown Detroit, Mies placed skyscraper apartments and town houses on ample lawns. The site, however, first had to be cleared of nearly two thousand families who lived there. Even Crown Hall replaced a remarkable building of an earlier day—the Mecca Flats, a once-elegant atrium apartment house that had been taken over by hundreds of squatters in crowded postwar Chicago. There just was no simple way to tidy up the world with architecture.

The Miesian Age, to be sure, did not begin with Mies. He was but one of the founding figures of modernism, of the so-called International style notable for its unadorned clean lines and resolute banishing of historical quoting from the past.

Besides, it was always hard to typecast Mies. He did not emerge from "almost nothing," and he never really turned his back on history. It was all around him in the ancient, ruggedly honest buildings of Aachen, where he was born March 27, 1886. He knew stone, and later brick, because he worked so closely with them. "How sensible is the small, handy shape [of a brick], so useful for every

purpose!" he once rhapsodized. "What logic in its bonding, pattern and texture! What richness in the simplest wall surface! But what discipline this material imposes!"

In Aachen, undoubtedly, began Mies's extraordinary sense of discipline, of "God in the details." Mies vividly recalled how his father had rebuked another son for arguing that details on the upper levels of a high building were not vital, because no one could see them from the street. The senior Mies angrily suggested a climb to the top of Cologne cathedral, where all details were as carefully done as at ground level.

Mies learned early, too, the economic necessity of precision. One of his earliest tasks was to inscribe graveyard headstones. He could not afford to make a mistake in marble.

It was in those days that Mies developed his fabled skill as a draftsman, doing full-sized sketches for stucco ornamentation. He could draw freehand, his awed students later reported, while he stood with his back to the blackboard.

Mies went to Berlin in 1905, and there his first great career flowered. The decisive three years of his early period, 1908–11, were spent in the office of Peter Behrens, a leading architect and industrial designer with an innovative, ordered, classical style that brought together large areas of glass and precise detailing. Walter Gropius and Le Corbusier also worked in the office at times. All of these modernist giants went to school with Behrens.

There were other influences, too: the Dutch architect Hendrik Petrus Berlage, proponent of structural truth; the nineteenth-century neoclassicist Karl Friedrich Schinkel; Frank Lloyd Wright, the American master of free-flowing space. And Plato, Goethe, Aquinas, Saint Augustine, Nietzsche. Mies's early work was clean, spare, unstartling. By 1912 he had his own practice; in 1914 he began four years as a soldier in the engineer corps of the embattled German army.

If the Mies who returned after the war was different, so was Germany. It was crippled by defeat but freed of the overbearing Kaiser. Berlin seethed with new movements in the arts. Mies was suddenly caught up in it all—in architectural groups, architectural publishing, architectural social reform, architectural aesthetics. This was the period of the "radical" Mies.

Starting in 1919, he executed his then-visionary schemes for prismatic glass-walled skyscrapers, for a concrete office building with bands of ribbon windows, for brick and concrete country villas shaped in overlapping, free-flowing forms and spaces. He was influenced by Cubism and Constructivism, by Dutch de Stijl concepts of interlocking lines and spaces, and certainly he knew the abstract grids of the artist Piet Mondrian.

But it was only after a second world war, when Mies designed the glass-steel-and-brick boxes of Illinois Institute of Technology, that architects saw in their traceries and proportions an eye as subtle as Mondrian's. "Better than Mondrian's!" Mies is said to have blurted, in a rare explosion of self-esteem.

By the mid-1920's Mies clearly was a formidable figure of modern architecture, although known mainly to cognoscenti. In 1927 he organized the celebrated Weissenhof housing exhibition in Stuttgart. Gropius, Le Corbusier, J. J. P. Oud, and other eminences contributed. But if this was to be model housing for the people, most of the buildings turned out to be rather expensive; Mies's own steel-framed design was one of the more modest.

Indeed, he already had a reputation of being a rich man's architect. This was always one of the anomalies of Mies's life. He loved materials— marble, stone, brick, steel—and used them lavishly when he could: in the Barcelona Pavilion; in the Tugendhat house of 1930 in Brno, Czechoslovakia, with its Macassar ebony; in the grandly expensive Seagram Building of 1958. He nonetheless made economy and prefabrication in construction a watchword, and he brought in the Lake Shore Drive glass houses of 1951 for about 10 per cent under conventional costs. His Illinois Tech "boxes" are for the most part exceptionally modest, reflecting budget constraints.

In the Barcelona Pavilion (designed with his partner Lilly Reich), Mies had no need to stint. The pavilion's sole purpose was to celebrate its sponsoring nation, Germany. Mies made free use of marble, glass, onyx, and chromium-plated steel. It was a brilliant demonstration of some fundamentals of modernism, with overlapping walls and a clear separation of space and structure. Cruciform columns stood clear of walls, and, typically, the pavilion itself rested on a platform, a concept probably borrowed from Schinkel and one that was to appear in many of Mies's later buildings.

Behrens predicted that the pavilion would eventually be called "the most beautiful building of our century." It has frequently been called that since then, although it vanished so quickly after the fair that relatively few of Mies's contemporaries ever saw it except in photographs. It has had an enormous design influence, however.

From the pavilion, as well, came the Barcelona chairs (again conceived in association with Lilly Reich) and X-base coffee tables that established themselves as high-style symbols of our time. The chairs are, quite simply, twentieth-century classics, fashioned of elegantly finished leather on a curving steel base. Supposedly, they were built wide and generous, like a throne, to accommodate the Spanish king. Another explanation is that their ample lines provided the kind of seating acceptable to a man of Mies's frame of mind and matter.

Mies, indeed, devised an entire royal family of furniture, and he apparently lived on the proceeds for several years in Germany after the Nazis took

A warm light glows from the glass front of the chapel at Illinois Institute of Technology. In one of Mies's rare concessions to privacy, the other three walls are of brick.

FRANK SCHERSCHEL, *LIFE* MAGAZINE. ® TIME INC.

power and in effect banished his architecture. His cantilevering tubular steel chairs are just one more example of the touch of the master, who said it was harder to design a good chair than a good building.

An even more difficult task was the director-ship of the Bauhaus, the "House of Building" that had become the center of modern architectural theory in Europe. Mies took it on in 1930 at the suggestion of Gropius, its former leader. But the emergent Nazis were already hounding the school in Dessau, and it moved to Berlin. Mies had run-ins, as well, with dissenting left-wing students. He cracked down harshly—he was a better educator than an administrator, according to a colleague—and tried to get the divided school back on track. By late 1933 it was closed, a victim of Nazi culture bosses.

Mies appears to have had as little use for the Nazis as they had for him. Seemingly, however, he was apolitical. In the mid-1920's he had designed a powerful memorial (later razed by the Nazis), in massings of brick, for the slain Communists Karl Liebknecht and Rosa Luxemburg. He surely was no Communist.

There was, in any event, no place in Nazi Germany for the cool, unadorned Bauhaus design. It was *Kulturbolschewismus* by Nazi standards. Mies was the last director of the Bauhaus. He and his colleagues closed it rather than bow to Nazi supervision. "We, not they, will close the Bauhaus," he said. Other Bauhaus figures were already leaving for the United States, or soon would go. But Mies, ever deliberate, lingered on, hoping for commissions that never came, and this provoked critical comment later. Finally, he too arrived in New York, pressed by the urgings of his disciple Philip Johnson, then known primarily as a histori-an of the International style. By 1944 Mies was a United States citizen, and among the many honors bestowed on him over the years was the Presidential Medal of Freedom, conferred in 1963.

Hitler's mad policies had brought America a rich stream of exiled practitioners of the arts and sciences, and Mies was just one of them. At Harvard University Gropius trained a generation of Ameri-can architects, emphasizing the disciplines of teamwork and comprehensive design. In Chicago László Moholy-Nagy launched the New Bauhaus. It

was to become the Institute of Design at Illinois Tech—where Mies eventually consigned it to the lower levels of Crown Hall. The Bauhaus had moved to America.

Harvard, in fact, had sounded out Mies before appointing Gropius to head its architectural school. But Harvard wanted to place Mies's name on a mundane list of candidates. He said no. Didn't Harvard know the difference between him and Gropius?

Mies got to Chicago because Armour Institute, possibly as obscure as Harvard was eminent, wanted to freshen its Beaux-Arts-oriented school of architecture. The year was 1938, that blurry boundary between Depression and World War. Mies was fifty-two, and it was time to settle in somewhere.

But Chicago? The great gray city, after ten years of hard times, had sunk, exhausted, into its own slums. Mies took a quick look and was dismayed. "I felt I ought to turn around and go home," he once recalled. On the other hand, his former students who were living in Chicago assured him the city was open to the new architec-

ture, even if few people there had heard of him.

Actually, Chicago was the city of all cities most likely to embrace the doctrine of Less is more. Here was the cradle of rugged, no-nonsense commercial buildings. The Reliance, the Carson Pirie Scott store, the Marquette, and the other definitive steel-frame masterworks had revolutionized architecture in the late nineteenth century. Hustling Chicago had elevated technology to art, in the name of dollars and common sense. It was a Miesian concept, before Mies.

He began to yield, and looked around a little at the city that had spawned the architecture of Louis Sullivan, Daniel Burnham, John Root, William Le Baron Jenney, Holabird and Roche, and Frank Lloyd Wright. Later Mies was to say he never looked very hard. But he must have seen something, because he said yes to Armour Institute.

In turn, he got the freedom to develop a design

275

curriculum based on practical work methods—drawing, firsthand knowledge of materials, construction and function allied to "the spirit of our times." He also began to build a new campus on the slummy South Side. Armour Institute was growing up into Illinois Institute of Technology.

For the campus Mies evolved a surprisingly romantic proposal of overlapping planes on a cleared site. His Barcelona Pavilion had already prefigured this arrangement. The final plan, although modified, was a subtle procession of seemingly simple boxes, efficient and adaptable, in a landscaped setting of grassy courts and spaces. Everything had been laid out precisely, on a modular grid. It was a campus of ordered rectangles, of boxes within boxes, so to speak. And it was extraordinarily decisive in its use of American technology: steel framing, glass and brick infill. He had caught on to America very fast, but was always refining and refining.

Mies, for instance, turned the corners of his buildings deftly, with subtle in-and-out framings of metal beams. He had a way of setting major works on platforms (Crown Hall, the Seagram) and of leading the eye to "floating" travertine marble stairs or grandly arcaded lobbies. Architecture was not a playland, said the master. His work was formal, processional, and earnest.

Not everyone joined in acclaim. Mies's Illinois Tech chapel particularly baffled many architects. It was a variant on the all-purpose brick-and-glass box, and its exterior offered no clues to its content. Was this recognizable religious architecture? On the other hand, everything inside enhanced its purpose: a place for meditation. There was nothing showy about the travertine altar, the silk curtains, the slender steel cross. In the populist 1970's this effortless restraint bothered some people at the university so much that they attacked the space with pop art hangings and beanbag pillows. If it wasn't blasphemy, it surely proved that more could be less.

There were many contradictions in Mies's life. Not the least was the fact that he made Illinois Tech's reputation, but was waved away by a new administration in 1958, before he could design such key buildings as the student union and the library. He was hurt, but went on to other and bigger things. Illinois Tech sacrificed a rare chance for a unified campus. Some of the buildings put up after Mies are painful parodies of his concepts.

Be that as it may, Chicago gave the architect a home base, a building platform. He and his students responded by molding the skyline into Mies country, with Mies himself designing several dozen buildings, many of them along the lake front. Among the immense achievements of his followers were the Richard J. Daley Civic Center (1965), a massive skyscraper courthouse clad in rusting steel, that culminated seventy-five years of Chicago construction technique (Jacques Brownson, principal architect); the enormous McCormick Place convention center (1970), with its steel-truss roof and Miesian clear-span space (Gene Summers, chief designer); and Lake Point Tower (1968), a sculpturesque, shimmering, seventy-story apartment house recalling Mies's early experiments with glass skyscrapers (Schipporeit and Heinrich, architects, with Graham, Anderson, Probst and White).

Two major Chicago-based architectural firms, C. F. Murphy Associates and Skidmore, Owings and Merrill, borrowed, adapted or extended Mies's ideas freely. The trend, unfortunately, was to giantism, a machinelike technology for technology's sake, reaching a peak with SOM's 110-story Sears Tower. Mies himself had warned that technology could be used for good or evil. Just because one could do something, should one? He felt that his own 860 Lake Shore Drive should have stopped at twelve stories.

The principle of Less is more, applied to residential architecture, produced the Farnsworth house of 1950 in Plano, Illinois (above and opposite page). The unhappy client complained that less also meant more in time (five years) and cost (from an estimate of $40,000 to a final bill of $73,000).

While Chicago built, journalists and historians began to talk about—and argue about—the Mies-inspired "second Chicago school of architecture." Was it an outgrowth of the structural achievements of the Sullivanesque first school? Or was it too spare, refined, austere, to qualify? Cases were made on both sides. Mies by then was so eminent that the distinguished Chicago architectural historian Carl W. Condit described his life as "the most extraordinary in the history of architecture." Mies and his school, Condit wrote, "left a mark on the metropolitan area so profound that one could find a parallel only in imperial Rome, or Florence under the Medici, or Paris in the heyday of the monarchy." That paean was sounded in 1974, five years after the architect's death. Yet by 1980 Condit had concluded that Mies's influence had been all too pervasive, leading to a monastic severity. "It was a prime misfortune that the so-called International style should have swept everything before it," he wrote ruefully.

Chicago, of course, was only part of Mies's world. American industry and corporate wealth had given him the chance to do what he had merely thought about in Germany. He had waited decades for life to catch up with him. And when life rushed past into the new age of revisionism, Mies remained influential even while architects began reshaping the traditional flat-top box. Mies's early-1920's sketches profoundly affected Philip Johnson's crystalline variations in Minneapolis, Houston, and other cities fifty years afterward.

Johnson, like many architects, first found it necessary to put space between Mies and himself in the late 1950's. Miesian doctrine could be dogma if extended *ad infinitum*. Buildings should be interesting as well as good, said the anti-Miesians, and they should be readable. It was more important for them to declare their place and purpose—whether apartment, office, factory, or whatever—than merely to symbolize the way they were constructed. The new

277

credo was forcefully articulated by the architect Robert Venturi in the mid-1960's. Its essentials were complexity and contradiction—pluralism rather than purism—and a revival of historicism.

In other words, relax. Use familiar images from the past. Mix it up. Venturi and his associates sought meaning in the roadside strip and in the neonized spaces of Las Vegas. He announced that Main Street was almost all right. The word for this new trend was pop architecture.

Modernism was declared passé, and architects began talking about designing for context, for the cityscape, for continuity and connection. Just as in 1920's Berlin, there was more talk than reality to it, but the age of the architect as moral hero was presumably over. Architecture, having failed to reform the world, had decided to join it. The new architecture would have to put reins on soulless science and technology and address itself to the human condition.

Mies's critics ran up a long list of complaints. His buildings, with their hard materials and edges, turned people off. Besides, they repeated themselves. And they had sunk behind increasingly neutral skins that sacrificed some of the articulated force of the first Lake Shore Drive apartments. Mies tended to drop his sealed, glassy boxes into the cityscape arbitrarily, whether or not they fitted the surroundings. They were exclusivist monuments, did not always work as well as they should, and seemed to be at their best with no one in them. They were dinosaurs in the new age of high energy costs. Buildings should be designed to suit their circumstance, climate, and use. They should bring back color and joy. The world need not be clad in Miesian black or silver-gray.

So the indictment read, even as glass boxes continued to proliferate in the burgeoning downtowns—the box, after all, being the most inclusive and convenient shape.

The case against Mies was stimulating and even overdue—but also overcooked. His genius as designer, his passion for precision and detail, his zeal for structure, order, and clarity, his sense of his times, kept architecture honest. He was the teacher. And he remained consistent to his own principles, even if they were at times inconsistent with the cityscape.

Always there were ambiguities about his work that make any repudiation of Mies very difficult. In Chicago, his towering One IBM Plaza is a routinized version of the Seagram and the Federal Center courthouse. It is the last building on which Mies

placed his imprint, and that only nominally, for he died at age eighty-three on August 17, 1969, some two years before the IBM was completed.

This fifty-two-story shaft thrusts an immense and somewhat chilling wall along the Chicago river front, and is coated in dark olive ribbing. The plaza is windswept. A taut, precisely gridded box, the building tells us only too clearly what it is: a work machine housing machines and people who tend them. One IBM Plaza, seen in this way, seems to have little to do with its neighborhood, or with the city itself.

But look again. The lobby, a monumental twenty-six feet high, is encased in Miesian crystal and arcaded with imposing columns. This majestic space opens to the downtown panorama—skyline, water, bridges, the city in its stunning diversity—on all sides. Everything is exceptionally clear. There is no mystery involved in finding the elevators, contained in six travertine-walled banks. As always, the materials are hard but superior. Granite floor blocks are laid precisely, to the fraction of an inch, following a module. The building, despite its streams of glass, was engineered and computerized for energy efficiency. Its office spaces are open and generous—in contrast to the understated bust of the architect in the lobby. One IBM Plaza simplifies complexity. If it throws up a skyline wall, it also connects.

The same can be said of Mies's Federal Center, consisting of two high cubes and a pavilion post office. Mies arranged the spaces in such a way that they open up the shadowed Loop. It can be argued, although not easily, that he did not put the buildings where they should have been—but he sweated out the placement through long hours of painstaking study. He took the setting into account.

But was he too candid, too uncompromising, in expressing the cell-like nature of the federal bureaucracy in the vertical tracery of the wall beams? At the end of the 1960's the courthouse served as the unhappy stage setting for the wild trial of the "Chicago Eight" conspiracy, so-called Yippie protesters against the Vietnam War. Miesian order, along with cool modernism, took a beating. Still, the courthouse is an elementally great building.

Mies van der Rohe lies in Chicago's Graceland Cemetery, where are also the tombs of his predecessors in that city's architectural lineage: Root, Burnham, Sullivan. He is part of history now, and history will decide his ultimate role. There is little doubt that it will be a very large one, for Mies was not so much repudiated as absorbed into the ongoing architectural synthesis. He remains a titan in the post-Miesian Age.

The Seagram Building on Park Avenue, expensive and beautiful in its sheath of bronze, stands today, after almost a quarter century, as the purest and finest of modern skyscrapers.

279

Louis Kahn

1901–1974

BY CHARLES L. MEE, JR.

W hen Louis Kahn was three years old, he stood at the open hearth before a coal fire in his home in Estonia, watching the firelight. Ordinarily the coal burned with an intense blue flame, but at the moment, as Kahn later recalled it, some of the coals burned with an unusual, bright green flame. Kahn thought he would save the rare light, and so he reached into the fire and took the coals that burned green and put them in his pocket. His clothes caught fire and went up in flames. He put his hands up to cover his eyes, thus he saved his sight; but his face was dreadfully burned, and healed in grotesque folds of scar tissue.

Soon after this traumatic accident, Kahn's father moved the family to Philadelphia. The father went to work in the construction business, was injured on the job, and never worked again. Kahn's mother barely managed to support the family; in the course of two years, they moved seventeen times. As a young child, Kahn never had a secure or solid place.

He spent his childhood in hand-me-down clothes, and when he was put in school—at the age of seven, in 1908—he would make his way to school each morning by slinking along the sides of the houses, ashamed for his scarred face to be seen. When he got to school, he would wait across the street until, at the last minute, he would make a run for the classroom just before the bell rang.

At school the teacher, noticing that he had a talent for drawing, asked him to take one subject after another and work it up into large-scale drawings to be put on the wall for the instruction of the class. Kahn drew unstintingly, and even at that age, he had an unusually vital line in his drawing. It would always be said that his trees could get up and walk off the page, and he had an uncommon sense of color. He returned from school each day with his arms covered with gold stars in recognition of his drawings: his teacher pasted the stars to his skin.

His scarred face gave him the look of a street tough, but Louis Kahn talked with the voluble grace and passion of a poet.

Kahn's mother played the harp—and claimed she was a descendant of Felix Mendelssohn—and Kahn himself learned to play the piano, well enough that he played for money when he was a teen-ager, at a silent-movie house. (In later years he would entertain friends by sitting down at the piano and improvising. He would take a copy of The *Saturday Evening Post*, open it to one advertisement or another, and, at the guests' bidding, "play it like Bach," or "play it like Beethoven," or Vivaldi or Mozart.)

His father, though invalided by his building accident—and given to tyranny and an occasional child-beating—was a talented man: he spoke five languages fluently and was a skilled craftsman in stained glass. Kahn remembered vividly how he had traveled once with his father aboard a train, and his father called the boy's attention to the patterns of frost on the window pane, and the two of them practiced tracing the crystalline patterns.

Kahn thought he would be a painter until, in the latter half of his senior year at Central High School in Philadelphia, he enrolled in an architecture course that was taught by an inspiring man named William Gray, who set a number of students out on careers in architecture. Within three days, Kahn declared that he wanted to be an architect.

At the University of Pennsylvania, on scholarship, he had the good fortune to have an entirely unfashionable architectural education. He was trained in the tradition of the French Ecole des Beaux-Arts, which was devoted to massive masonry architecture, to clearly defined blocks of space, to an insistence on a solid, emphatic sense of structure. Kahn did not adopt the highly ornamented aspect of Beaux-Arts building, but he did take the sense of solid structure to develop into his own modern, and idiosyncratic, idiom.

Kahn was an intercollegiate wrestler, a muscular young man with powerful arms and hands and broad, strong shoulders, and from the beginning his buildings looked just like him. He had a natural affinity for Beaux-Arts building—a sense, even in his early student drawings, of how to shape and place mass and weight, and he had no affinity at all for the new International school. Aside from his instinctive feeling for solid structure, Kahn had difficulty with the sort of smooth finish that the International school gave their steel and glass buildings—with what is commonly called the skin of the building.

In any case, prepared as a student of the Beaux-Arts, Kahn graduated from architecture school in 1924 and spent two decades completely unfit by training or inclination to design much of anything that a world enamored of the International style would want. He did, however, get a job

283

immediately in a Philadelphia architect's office, because, as usual, he could draw better than anyone; and he worked on plans for the Philadelphia Sesquicentennial Exhibition of 1926.

By 1928 he was able to get together enough money to take a trip to Europe and make a grand tour of architectural masterpieces. Although he could have seen something of the new architecture if he had wanted to—Le Corbusier was at work at the time, and one of Kahn's Philadelphia architect friends was even working for Le Corbusier—Kahn headed straight for a look at the ancient Greek and Roman buildings.

On his way through Italy he stopped off to do some sketches of the turreted town of San Gimignano, south of Florence. Done in bold strokes with the side of a carpenter's pencil, the sketches are alive with a sense of the afternoon Tuscan sunlight, the deep shadows of the narrow streets, the hefty

blocks of stone with their roughly textured surfaces pierced here and there by a small window, the towers built up cube by cube. In Assisi he sketched the cathedral, its doorway set beneath a perfectly semicircular stone arch. Cube, circle, rough surface, sunlight: Kahn took them all for his own.

Of all that he saw, nothing impressed him more than the Baths of Caracalla. "Consider the beauty of the Baths of Caracalla," Kahn later said. "Why a one-hundred-and-fifty-foot ceiling when an eight-foot ceiling would do? What has this evoked? Certainly not only a bath!" Feeling, said Kahn, must come before mere functionalism. An eight-foot ceiling would do if all one wanted was a bath; but to have the feeling of luxuriating in a bath, to be overcome by the sensation of water and stone and sunlight: this required the power of a vast space. Before functionalism, before design, even before an understanding of materials, must come feeling. Kahn never stopped talking about the Baths of Caracalla.

When he came to consider how anything might be built, he wanted, he said, to begin his work not at "volume one" but at "volume zero."

Perfect children amid an idyllic landscape play London Bridge Is Falling Down, *in a sketch Kahn made when he was a child. He gave the drawing to Fannie Seligman; indeed, for a time he left drawings on her desk every morning at school, because she hit the children who teased him about his face.*

I think of a school as an environment of spaces where it is good to learn. Schools began with a man under a tree who did not know he was a teacher, discussing his realizations with a few others who did not know they were students. The students reflected on the exchanges between them and how good it was to be in the presence of this man. Soon the needed spaces were erected and the first schools came into existence. . . . Schools must reflect the spirit of the man under the tree.

The building of a home, said Kahn, must begin not with considerations of so many square feet for a kitchen, so many square feet for a laundry room, but rather with a consideration of the nature of a home, of the nature of the center of the home, of the hearth, of the feeling of sitting in the warmth and security of the center of the home. The feeling is the Form.

After Form, said Kahn, comes Design. Design translates the feeling of home or school into tangible shapes. The best shapes were, for Kahn, the basic ones that he found in Greek and Roman buildings: the square, the triangle, the cube, the arch, the sphere, the column. The best materials were brick, stone, concrete.

When he returned to Philadelphia, he found there was little demand for such ruminations as these. Once again, it was his sheer mastery of drawing that gave him a livelihood: he went to work for a firm that designed the Folger Shakespeare Library in Washington, D.C., doing renderings with his customary vitality. When the Great Depression struck, however, not even Kahn's drawing abilities could sustain him, and he was often out of work and on relief. The Depression, the unfashionableness of his work, and the resulting idleness all combined to force him to spend years buried in thought about what a building was and should be, to read, to think, to firm up his convictions.

In 1932 he organized the Architectural Research Group, bringing together about thirty unemployed architects and engineers to think about city planning for Philadelphia, the design of low-cost housing, slum clearance, new building techniques. They built nothing, but they drew, and thought, and talked. "Money," Kahn said later with characteristically determined optimism, "is not scarce, it just does not know where to go."

In 1930 he had married Esther Israeli, a young woman who was interested in the sciences, particularly in neurology, and the two of them moved in with Esther's mother, and never left. Esther got a job as a neuropathologist and supported the family; Esther's mother cooked and kept house, and Lou, as everyone called him, drew, and talked about architecture, and stayed out late at night—sometimes in the company of women, but more often than that, working at the office.

Half imp and half melancholic, sporting a bow tie, Kahn drew this charcoal self-portrait when he was in his late forties.

He loved to dress well. He always wore a tie and jacket at meals. When he could afford it, he bought his clothes at Brooks Brothers—and always saw to it that they were slightly rumpled, and that his tie was askew. When his daughter, Sue Ann, was born in 1940, he hardly knew how to talk to her, but he would get down on the floor and play with her blocks with her and work on drawings with her. He liked movies and comics. (He never read the comics but only looked at the pictures, and he liked Prince Valiant most of all.) He never missed a Saturday football game at Penn. (He loved winners and couldn't stand losers.) But, in general, he preferred to keep his schedule free so that he could go to his office and work whenever the mood struck him.

He was a great talker. When he wrote, he wrote poetically, and often incoherently, and he worried terribly about his grammar. But when he spoke, the flow of words—however abstract and loosely defined, or merely suggestive, however mystical or simply mysterious—was always spellbinding, full of passion, and almost never about anything but architecture.

By 1941 he was back in practice with the fine and well-established Philadelphia architect George Howe, and in 1942 Kahn and Howe were joined by Oscar Stonorov. Even so, at the age of forty Kahn had not yet built anything of particular distinction;

285

and although his wife said he never became discouraged or depressed, his aspirations invariably surpassed his achievements.

In 1945 Anne Tyng joined Kahn's firm. She was an elegant young woman who had just graduated from Harvard's architecture school, bright, stylish and passionate about architecture. They fell in love at once, and had a daughter together, although they never married, for Kahn could never bring himself to part from his wife. He began, rather, to live in a personal turmoil that characterized his life from then on: he stayed with Esther and their daughter, and also with Anne and their daughter, and later on with another well-born woman of the Northeast, Harriet Pattison, and the son they had together; and he had, too, a great many love affairs. Even while Anne Tyng was off on her

With a few quick strokes of a pencil, Kahn caught the sunlight and the stone in Assisi, looking toward the duomo, *in 1929.*

own in Italy to give birth to their daughter, Kahn was having an affair with a young Chinese woman who worked in his office. He seemed always to fall in love with women who were architects or designers: as much as he enjoyed making love (as Anne Tyng said he did), he enjoyed, perhaps even slightly more, talking architecture.

By the late 1940's Kahn's work and talk had begun to attract the notice, at least, of other architects. In 1947, when one of the faculty members at Yale retired, Kahn was given an appointment as a visiting critic in the architecture school. He was soon made a professor of architecture and chief critic of architectural design, and he began to turn out graduates who were not so much students as disciples. To this younger generation the International style was arid Establishment design. Kahn was fresh, and he spoke with a sense of authority that made him seem a guru. "Consider," he said of the ruins of Paestum, "the great event in architecture when the walls parted and columns *became.*"

"The room," he said, "is the beginning of architecture.

"It is the place of the mind.

"You in the room, with its dimensions, its structure, its light, respond to its character, its spiritual aura, recognizing that whatever the human intends and makes becomes a life.

"Enter your room and know how personal it is, how much you feel its life. In a small room with just another person, what you say you may never have said before.

"The plan is a society of rooms. . . ."

Nevertheless, for all his talk, at the age of fifty Kahn had still not built a major building. His chance came when Yale decided to build a new art gallery, and George Howe persuaded the trustees to give the commission to Kahn.

The spine of the Yale Art Gallery is a massive concrete cylinder—inside of which is a concrete stairway in the shape of ascending triangles. Near the cylinder is a rectangular concrete box that contains the elevator and all of the ducts, pipes, and wires necessary to serve the building. Kahn always made a sharp distinction between the "servant" and the "served" areas of his buildings. He said repeatedly that since servant areas were necessary, they ought to be designed forthrightly into the building by the architect and not left to engineers or others to fit them in and hide them behind smooth, cosmetic walls. In the case of the Yale Art Gallery, the servant cylinder and box also give the structure the core from which the ceilings take off over the open spaces filled with light, air, and art.

Kahn was working on his plans for the gallery when Buckminster Fuller visited Yale and talked,

For the Richards Building Kahn stacked scientists' studios one atop another like translucent building blocks. Some of the scientists, who needed darkness for their biological research, covered their windows with sheets of aluminum foil, as at upper right—marring the skin of the building.

ceaselessly, about his domes supported by triangular or tetrahedral bracing. Whether Kahn got the notion from Fuller, or from Anne Tyng, who was always fascinated by geometry, he finished off his plans for the gallery by supporting the vast expanse of ceiling with a tetrahedral frame, like an egg carton, in poured concrete—which he left open, to show the servant ducts and pipes as they came out from the central core through the whole building.

All of the concrete in the building was left unfinished, its surface marked with the flaws and blemishes left by the rough wooden molds into which the concrete had been poured. Then he gave the building a light glass and metal skin, as precisely geometrical as a Mondrian painting, as smooth as the International style, and somewhat out of character.

The geometry of the Yale Art Gallery, along with its exposed pipes and unfinished concrete, caused a sensation. "It was about this time," as the architecture critic Vincent Scully has written, "that architects were saying that Kahn, whom they now deeply respected, was designing the ugliest buildings in the world. ('But I love them,' one said.)"

Still, commissions did not pour in on Kahn. He did not get his next major job until 1957, back on his

OVERLEAF: Phalanxes of studios face the Pacific Ocean from the open court at the Salk Institute in La Jolla, California.

287

The Street is a Room by agreement A community
Room the walls of which belong to the donors *dedicated to the city for common use*
From The street must have come
The Meeting House also a place by agreement
its ceiling is the sky

Under this elegant didactic sketch Kahn wrote, "The Street is a Room by agreement"—and, in a smaller hand, "From the street must have come the meeting house, also a place by agreement."

home ground at the University of Pennsylvania, where he was asked to design the Richards Medical Research Building. For that project Kahn began by asking not how many square feet a scientist in the biological sciences needed for his laboratory, but what sort of space is appropriate to a man or woman exploring the fundamental mysteries of life. "If I were to define architecture in a word," said Kahn, "I would say that architecture is a thoughtful making of spaces. It is not filling prescriptions as clients want them filled. It is not fitting uses into dimensioned areas. . . . I believe that the architect's first act is to take the program that comes to him and change it . . . to put it into the realm of spaces."

What a laboratory "wants to be," Kahn thought, was a studio, a place that is at once enclosed and open to the world, private and accessible to colleagues, a place to turn in on the work at hand, but open to the sunlight, to the world.

He conceived of crystalline clusters of small studios that seem to be suspended in midair around a core of servant areas of pipes and elevators and other utilities. The stairways, and the ducts for air intake and fume exhaust, are set into roughly textured concrete towers that rise up along the sides of the studios like the towers of San Gimignano. The studios have built-in work counters that face large windows, to let in the light and to give the

Standing in the library court of the Yale Center for British Art, a visitor can look through a rectangular window into one of the intimate galleries on the top floor.

scientists companionable views of one another's laboratories, and of the world outside—to be enclosed but accessible, private but open.

Each studio is suspended on a hollow frame that has been fitted together from rectangular precast concrete pieces. (It is through these hollow frames that the pipes and tubes of the servant areas snake out to the laboratories and back again.) Just how these basic units are made, and how the whole building is made of them, is openly displayed by Kahn at the entrance to the building, where the frame underpinning the first studio is left naked for the visitor to see. Indeed, the entrance to the Richards Building, with this display of the principle of its structure, announces the theme of its structure like the opening bars of a musical composition.

What Kahn forgot was that researchers in the biological sciences need darkness, not light, for much of their work. He provided dark spaces at the center of the building, but not enough of them. He had called for louvers to keep out the brightest sunlight in the studios, but some scientists needed total darkness, and so they covered their windows with plywood or aluminum foil. From the outside, then, the skin of the building has been defaced.

Inside, Kahn's studios, although they offer flexible open spaces, are not flexible enough; they are sometimes larger than they need to be for some sorts of work, sometimes too small. And so the scientists sometimes luxuriate in their laboratories, sometimes crowd in their assistants and equipment, sometimes let their projects spill out into the

In the lower right corner, beneath his sketch of two people by a hearth and a window, Kahn wrote, "Natural light gives the time of day and the mood of the seasons to enter."

Architecture comes from The Making of a Room
A society of rooms is a place good to live work learn
The Plan

The Room

A great American Poet once asked the Architect "What slice of the sun does your building have, what light enters your Room" as if to say the sun never knew how great it is until it struck the side of a building.

s The place of the mind. In a small room one does not say what one would in a large room In a room with only one other person could be generative The vectors of each meet. A room is not a room without natural light *natural light gives the time of day and the mood of the seasons to enter.*

hallways, into the servant areas, jamming up against elevators, until the interior of parts of the building takes on the appearance of a crowded submarine. Some scientists became so enraged at the building that they took to painting Kahn's bare walls, like Huns among the Roman ruins.

Such problems with the Richards Building has not yet become apparent when Jonas Salk, the discoverer of the polio vaccine, commissioned Kahn to design a research center for the Salk Institute for Biological Studies in La Jolla, California. Salk, said Kahn, was the ideal client—"one who knows not what he wants, but what he aspires to." If, Kahn said, "a client knew what he wanted, he would not need an architect."

"The architect," said Kahn, "must know the nature of man's activity enough to reveal to the client what could be; that which could give him the most resourceful method of getting what he wants. It must be good enough so that he wants it, so that he hates the fact that he cannot afford it and tries to get more money.

"The client asks for areas, the architect must give him spaces: the client has in mind corridors,

The Phillips Exeter Library appears from the outside (above) to be a brick cube with small carrel windows to read by. Inside (at right), its center is a concrete frame embracing a huge invisible sphere—large enough to invite the mind to expand.

the architect finds reasons for galleries, the client gives the architect a budget, the architect must think in terms of economy; the client speaks of a lobby, the architect brings it to the dignity of a place of entrance."

The confrontation of an architect with his client, said Kahn, "is a creative thing. The client erodes the initial Design—destroys it and forces the architect to reconsider and find the essentials to come back with a stronger Form. The principles, however, must never be given in to. The fight between that which wants to create and that which wants to destroy produces a resultant which is Form."

The two men spent several years together before they knew what the Salk Institute "wanted to be." (Meanwhile, as the shortcomings of the Richards Building became apparent, Kahn made sure he did not repeat his mistakes in his work with Salk.) Kahn began making drawings in 1959 and continued through 1965, when the construction was finished. Such time-consuming working methods made it impossible for Kahn, even now that commissions had begun to come to him in increasing numbers, ever to make money; in fact, he never got out of debt. Salk told Kahn what was needed for the laboratories, but he had no aesthetic program except to say that he wanted a building "that he could invite Picasso to."

"This consideration," said Kahn, "changed the Salk Institute from a plain building like the one at the University of Pennsylvania to one which demanded a place of meeting which was every bit as big as a laboratory. It was the place . . . of arts and letters. It was a place where one had his meal, because I don't know of any greater seminar than the dining room."

Salk also talked to Kahn of the monastery of Saint Francis of Assisi. "I remembered the cloister there," Salk once said, "and I conveyed to Kahn the idea that this is what I would like—the cloistered garden." In Kahn's drawings, the cloistered garden became a central court that opened out onto a cliff and a view of the Pacific Ocean. The court was lined on either side by rows of studios, and the two rows of studios were backed by long laboratory buildings, containing flexible, loftlike spaces similar to the open space of the Yale Art Gallery.

Once again, Kahn put in the servant areas as integral parts of the design—horizontally this time, instead of vertically. In the Salk Institute the lab floors are interlayered with nine-foot-deep service spaces for the ducts and pipes. Salk characterized the air-conditioning ducts running through these spaces as the respiratory system of the building, the other pipes and wires as serving the circulatory and nervous functions, and the laboratories and studios as serving the cerebral functions.

The Salk Institute has been criticized—not for having the sort of functional flaws that the Richards Building has, or for looking ugly or "unfinished," but for being too beautiful, for seeming altogether too monumental. To some architectural critics, there is something distasteful in the fact that a medical research center is so far removed from the suffering it is meant to address. The institute, set off sybaritically by itself, with its sweeping view of the Pacific, its pristine laboratories and quiet Franciscan studies, strikes them almost as an affront to the purpose it is meant to serve. Architectural critics have been, for the most part, censorious, or apologetic, about this aspect of Kahn's work. Kahn himself seemed unembarrassed about it; he kept the company of the builders of Paestum and the Baths of Caracalla; his eye was always on some more sempiternal notion of the human adventure.

Salk never did receive Picasso at his cloister, but Françoise Gilot, one of Picasso's mistresses, found her way to La Jolla to take a tour of the institute. Salk himself showed her around the laboratories, pointing out their features with his customary enthusiasm. The two fell in love in the course of the tour, and married soon after.

A large reading room in a library, said Kahn, "is really for browsing, for deciding what books you want to read, for boy meets girl." This romanticism of Kahn's—and his warmth and sweetness as well—were given free scope in the library he designed, beginning in 1967, for Phillips Exeter Academy in New Hampshire. "Exeter began with the periphery," he said, "where light is. I felt the reading room would be where a person is alone near a window, and I felt that would be a private carrel, a kind of discovered place in the folds of construction."

Kahn was extraordinarily modest in his design for the exterior of the library: it is a cube, done in brick, which fits in easily with the older brick buildings on the campus. The modesty of the exterior, the proportions, the windows that give natural light to the readers within, all give the building simplicity and grace. Kahn said of the library: "No decorative elements are resorted to because I did not feel in the air the approval for decoration. I felt the striving not for severity but for the purity I sense in a Greek temple."

Bold, completely intellectual geometric shapes give the building its structure. The outer brick wall forms a cube. Inside, the cube is hollowed into an interior court. The walls of this interior cube within the cube are made of massive slabs of concrete. And

"Consider the great event in architecture," Kahn said, "when the walls parted and columns became"—and sunlight was let into the room. On a Mediterranean tour in 1951 Kahn made these sketches of the Temple of Apollo in Corinth (top left), the Acropolis (top right), and an interior space in Egypt (above).

A crescent of sunlight sears the terrace (above) of the Kimbell Art Museum in Fort Worth, Texas. At right, visitors enter the museum and its undulating succession of vaults that Kahn slit in order to let in floods and slashes of sunlight.

the four concrete walls are pierced by enormous circles that suggest an imaginary sphere. To have put a sphere within a cube would have been a nice enough trick; but to have made an invisible sphere within the cube gives the building a feeling of mystery and power that makes it one of Kahn's greatest works.

By the mid-sixties Kahn had more commissions than he could handle. He had always worked uncommonly long hours; his office had always been the center of his life. When he went off traveling to see a building or a client, he would return first, when he arrived back in Philadelphia, to his office, not his home. He sent out his laundry from his office, and on the bit of identification that he carried in his wallet, he put only his office address. When he referred in conversation to a time "when we lived at" such and such a place, he meant his office, not his home.

"He worked best at night," one of his colleagues said.

The office was quiet and most everyone had gone. The phone stopped ringing and there would be no more interruptions. Back in the drafting room, under the warm glow of a drafting lamp, Louis Kahn would sit staring silently at the yellow tracing paper unrolled on a drawing board, a stick of vine charcoal in his hand poised above the paper. Sitting by his side a draftsman, or perhaps the man in charge of the job, would wait patiently for a word or question to break the silence: ". . . what if we did it this way?" and he would lightly touch

At street level the Yale Center for British Art comes to terms with downtown New Haven. Above the first floor the building has a skin of smooth concrete, dull steel, and glass—so beautiful as to look, as Kahn said it would, "on a gray day . . . like a moth; on a sunny day like a butterfly."

the tip of the charcoal to the paper. . . . The marks of the vine charcoal barely adhered to the smooth paper, sitting on the hard surface as black dust ready to be brushed away by his hand the moment a better thought arrived. He had invented this technique for himself: vine charcoal on the smooth yellow paper. Drawing and erasing became immediate and as rapid as his thoughts. He would smudge away one idea and follow it with another, leaving only a faint trace of the original sketch. The layers of charcoal left a translucent, animated image of the new ideas superimposed on the ghosts of the old.

In the Kimbell Art Museum in Fort Worth, Texas, Kahn returned to the column and the vault—to the column and the vault alone—and built the entire building with them. He set out a succession of long vaults, side by side, each vault supported by only a few columns. The whole building, like the Yale Art Gallery, like the laboratories at Salk, is a single vast loft space that can be divided at will into exhibition spaces with no fixed walls. Yet the enormous space is not formless: the vaults give it a sense of "grain," so that a visitor always feels he is moving either with or against the grain, conscious always that he occupies a particular place, with a particular orientation, within the

great open space. The vaults alternate, too, with galleries—low, flat-ceilinged areas, six feet wide, that contain the museum's servant elements.

Each vault is slit open at its apex to let natural light in, to let the light spill down the curving walls. With this extremely simple combination of column, vault, and sunlight, Kahn came as close as he ever did to a kind of elemental architecture that suggests the universals that so captivated him. "Architecture," he said, "like music, must be a part of the composer, but it must also transcend him to give something to music or architecture itself. Mozart is not only Mozart, but music."

Curiously enough, the very last building that Kahn designed is infused with a sense of music, and particularly of Mozart: the Yale Center for British Art, which was built just across the street from the Yale Art Gallery.

Built to house the great collection of art that Paul Mellon gave to Yale, the Center for British Art is a symphony built upon the square. The whole building is composed of two cubes placed side by side, four stories high, both with hollow interior courts. All spaces—cubes, courts, galleries, servant and served areas—are divided into squares twenty by twenty feet. Once again, the theme of the building is announced at its entrance, where four twenty-by-twenty-foot squares have been removed

298

from the corner of the building—making a negative space with the dimensions that will be repeated throughout the building.

Just in case a museumgoer misses the point, the doors repeat the announced theme: the doors themselves are squat rectangles containing glass panes divided into squarish rectangles, and set on either side with four rectangular windows. Through the entrance doors the visitor steps into the first interior court, a cube, whose skylight ceiling is divided into four square panes of glass that are in turn divided into smaller squares. Around the interior court is light oak paneling, inlaid with rectangles of oak with a variant grain, and pierced by rectangular windows that open into the upstairs galleries. The triumph of the building is that the squares and rectangles, far from becoming boring, have the playfulness and lightness of Mozart variations on a theme.

The repetition of cube and square seems not so much geometrical as stable, and is constantly reminiscent of a small, intimate room. Even the elevator, which is placed in the servant area between the two cubes of the building, is smaller than most public elevators; it is a cube of scaled-down, domesticated proportions.

As at Exeter, the building is saved from excessive sweetness by bold geometry at its center: the spine of the building is a massive cylinder in unfinished concrete. Inside the cylinder is the stairway, ascending in flights and landings that describe a series of squares within the cylinder. Throughout the building, oak and concrete alternate in squares and rectangles—their quiet, smooth blond surfaces changing constantly as the natural light coming through the skylights and windows alters.

While he was working on his sketches for the British Art Center, Kahn kept mentioning an English country house, and how he wanted to have each of the galleries in the museum feel like a small room within the country house. The living room of an English country house was the "Form" for Kahn for the art center. The rooms are grouped around the building's two interior courts and are divided by movable partitions—covered in a linen that complements the colors of oak and concrete. And while each room has a sense of being intimate and contained, none is claustrophobic: each has a rectangular window looking out onto the interior court—and into the rooms across the way. From each room it is possible to see into eight other rooms—and in each room Kahn has managed to place an oak door, so that the room does have the feeling of the living room of a country house.

With his last buildings—with the Exeter library and the Kimbell Museum, and especially with the British Art Center—Kahn seemed to have less trouble with the skin. With the British Art Center he used a smoother, almost silky, finish for his concrete; and he sheathed the exterior of the building with dull steel and glass. He wanted the steel to have the quality of lead or pewter—to give even steel a softness that would convey a sense of the bold and of the domestic at the same time. Before the art center was finished, the director of the gallery asked Kahn impatiently what he imagined this pewterlike steel would look like. "On a gray day," said Kahn, "it will look like a moth; on a sunny day like a butterfly."

Even while he worked on the finishing touches for the British Art Center, Kahn traveled ceaselessly to keep up with the commissions that now came his way in profusion. He often went to Dacca, the capital of Bangladesh, to oversee his work there. At Dacca he put together a cluster of buildings for legislation, prayer, and public assembly. "The prevailing idea of the plan," he said, "is the realization that assembly is of a transcendent nature." Cylinders and cubes of concrete and brick—pierced by circles and half circles—are arrayed along a water plain, their massive walls bathed in sunlight in such a way as to recall Kahn's remark that "the sun never knew how great it was until it struck the side of a building."

"The great American poet Wallace Stevens," Kahn wrote, "prodded the architect, 'What slice of the sun does your building have?' To paraphrase: What slice of the sun enters your room? What range of mood does the light offer from morning to night, from day to day, from season to season, and all through the years?"

For Kahn, all architecture was in the service of light. As a child he had been captivated by light; as an adult, he would move brick and concrete for its sake. Architecture, he said, "is the Treasury of Shadows. Whatever is made of Light casts a shadow. Our work is of Shadow. It belongs to Light."

Returning from overseeing one of his projects in the spring of 1974, Kahn died of a heart attack in New York's Penn Station. He was not recognized, and so his body was taken to the city morgue. Because it was the weekend, and because Kahn's wallet contained only his office and not his home address, the police did not inform Esther Kahn of his death. In addition to his wallet, his pockets contained the small sketchbook he always carried with him, in which he had made sketches of trees, lively studies of the play of light and shadow among the leaves. And in his lapel buttonhole, as usual, he wore not a flower but a sprig of bright green leaf.

299

ELIEL AND EERO

SAARINEN

Eero Saarinen's pencil sketch for the Ingalls hockey rink at Yale, 1953

301

1873–1950   1910–1961

BY PAUL GOLDBERGER

Both Eliel Saarinen, the father, and Eero Saarinen, the son, were born in Finland. Yet they were quintessentially American architects in outlook: in each case a somewhat romantic, picturesque impulse fired their designs far more than did any theories. Father and son were very different architects in personal temperament and in stylistic preference, but they showed a reluctance to be bound by ideology, a sense that architecture emerged out of the molding of space and form in a way that was intuitive more than it was theoretical.

Both father and son were architects of great popular acclaim, Eero so much so that *Architectural Forum* could suggest, a year after his death at fifty-one in 1961, that he had been "the most famous young architect in America, perhaps in the world" in his final years. Eliel, too, had achieved early fame; he designed the Finnish Pavilion at the Paris Exposition of 1900 when he was twenty-seven, and by 1904 had received the commission for the monumental Helsinki railway station. And he was not yet fifty when he was awarded second prize in the competition for the Chicago Tribune Tower in 1922, for a graceful design that was to be more influential in the evolution of twentieth-century skyscraper design than the winning scheme that was actually built—and, indeed, was so celebrated that it led to Saarinen's decision to leave Finland and launch a new career in the United States.

There is no easy way to characterize the buildings of either Saarinen. Both father and son felt themselves to be modernists; Eliel rejected the heavy hand of Beaux-Arts classicism as he struggled to evolve a simpler style based more on a picturesque order and on a love for materials than on any of the technocratic underpinnings of the Bauhaus. His work was invariably subtle and restrained, above all an attempt to come gently to

The Saarinens, father and son, stood for this stiff portrait before the doorway of their home in Finland when Eero was nine. Four years later Eliel brought the family to the United States.

terms with the powerful forces of modernism swirling about him. Eliel neither rejected modernism totally nor embraced it but sought, instead, a middle ground. From that middle ground he tried to explore architecture's basics: proportion, light, mass, volume, scale, and decoration. Eliel's buildings had neither the elaborate ornament of most revivalist architecture nor the utterly austere quality of orthodox modernism. They lacked the tension of either extreme. Saarinen had the ability to create a quality of repose, an air of serenity that is present in almost no other architecture of the twentieth century.

Eero embraced the tenets of the modern movement somewhat more directly than did his father, but interpreted them in a way that was very much his own. He reveled in the ability of technology to create unusual structures; the two airports he designed toward the end of his life, the TWA terminal at Kennedy airport in New York and the buildings at Dulles International Airport outside Washington, D.C., are flamboyant exercises in the potential of concrete, buildings full of theatrical swoops which seemed, to a public already showing signs of boredom with the glass boxes of the 1950's, to be signs of a brilliant new age.

It was Eero's inventiveness more than anything else that brought him popularity—he seemed forever able to evolve a new shape, a new form; from the three-pointed dome of his Kresge Auditorium at M.I.T., of 1955, to the nervous concrete grid of the façade of the United States Embassy in London of 1960, his buildings did not look like the buildings of any other architect. Yet they seemed to speak to certain impulses that were very much part of their time. The curves and bulges and swoops of Eero's work were, in their way, as much a part of the 1950's as the Miami Beach hotels of Morris Lapidus or the amoebalike shapes of the hung ceilings in coffee shops. All were attempts to break out of the rigid rationalism of European modernist architecture, to show that modernism did not have to be dull and austere. Eero was responding to an urge in postwar America to be at once modern and amusing, to have no contradiction between the two.

Eliel Saarinen's work, admired as it was, spoke to no such strain of popular desires. His buildings were more thoughtful, and surely more subtle, than were his son's. They do not appear to leap; they sit with a solid, even somber, air to them, and they reveal their special qualities slowly. Yet they seem, for every inch of their being, made to have human functions. In the monumental grandeur of the Helsinki railway station or in the intimate cloisters of Cranbrook at Bloomfield Hills, Michigan—the multibuilding campus that was to be Eliel's greatest American work—there is a sense always of human

303

scale, of a quiet, sure order based upon the human figure and the way it fills and moves through space. Saarinen was never abstract: in this sense, though he disliked the architecture of historical cribbing and felt himself a modernist, he had something in common with the traditions of revivalism.

Eliel Saarinen was born in Rantasalmi, Finland, in 1873 to a rural minister and his wife. He studied first to be a painter; he credited visits to the Hermitage, in Saint Petersburg, with awakening his eye. The museum became far more to Saarinen than it is for most children; he recalled spending hours alone there, and was attracted in particular to the haunting light of Rembrandt. But Saarinen's own painting was not exceptional. "Rather than become a third-rate cobbler, a common craftsman, I was willing to sacrifice my dream to be a painter," he told Albert Christ-Janer, his biographer, in 1948. Whether his drift toward architecture in his mid-twenties emerged out of a recognition of his own limits as a painter or out of a sense that painting was a more limiting pursuit is difficult to say, but Saarinen does seem to have had a conscious desire to take a revolutionary stance, and he may have felt that the potential for having a social impact was greater in architecture. His conservative and fairly conventional upbringing was hardly evident in his statement that at the beginning of his career "architecture was a dead art-form. It had gradually become the business of crowding obsolete and meaningless stylistic decoration on the building's surface. And it was a sacrilege to break with such a procedure, which was held to be as sacred as the dogmas of religion."

Saarinen's words were not so far from those of H. P. Berlage, of Louis Sullivan, of Adolf Loos, of Henry van de Velde, of Frank Lloyd Wright—in each case the revivalism of the 1890's was seen as an evil, as an almost immoral act, and the call to revolution was clear. "Architecture has gone astray; something has to be done about it; now is the time to do things," said Saarinen. And he joined with two of his fellow students at the Polytechnic Institute in Helsinki, Herman Gesellius and Armas Lindgren, to form a firm dedicated to the practice of an architecture which would be new and admired.

The direction that Saarinen's career was to take was shown in his first major commission, the Finnish Pavilion for the Paris Exposition of 1900. The building that he and his partners produced looks like a cross between a Romanesque Revival library and a fanciful Finnish cottage—with hints of Art Nouveau in it—as if Henry Hobson Richardson had designed a gingerbread house with an assist from Henry van de Velde. But for all of the

Eliel's pencil drawing of his pensive young son gives evidence of his talent for fine art, a vocation that he set aside early in life in favor of a career in architecture.

competing decorations, the pavilion seems resolved—it is a serene and simple object, in which the various influences are brought together as part of a firm and disciplined, if romantic, pictorial vision. The pavilion was at once fanciful and stark, and Saarinen's ability to unite such distinct moods was to become a keynote of his work.

Not long after the pavilion's completion, Saarinen and his partners erected an immense villa called Hvitträsk, north of Helsinki, as their shared living and working quarters. This was as romantic, surely, as the pavilion in Paris, and once again the design seemed to emerge out of the Finnish vernacular traditions—here simplified into a picturesque play of masses—with some influence from the developing styles of modernist churches. The house has a red-tile roof, walls of granite and pine timbers, and a round stone entrance tower. Here Finnish folklore is made truly majestic; it was Saarinen's gift to be able to create a storybook house at vast scale without having it appear excessively cute or coy. Though Hvitträsk was built by all three partners, Lindgren resigned from the firm in 1905 and Gesellius in 1907, three years after Saarinen had married the latter's sister, Loja. So by 1907 Hvitträsk had become a house for the Saarinens alone; it was there that Eliel produced his architecture, his wife sculpted, and their two children, Eva-Lisa, called Pipsan, and Eero, were born. He was to live and work in the house until he moved to America in 1923, and in those years the house was a destination for such Saarinen friends as Maxim Gorky, Gustav Mahler, and Jean Sibelius. Sibelius was Eliel's favorite composer as well as a close friend; there was clearly a kinship felt between the two men, each a romantic modernist in his field.

Saarinen's major project of the early years in Finland was surely the Helsinki railway station of 1904-14, a monumental mass that, in terms of design, was far ahead of the stations being built at the same time in the United States—and most of Europe. Saarinen swept away the Beaux-Arts fronts of most of Helsinki's predecessors and substituted a solid, clean structure, a building that feels as if it were carved out of a great, solid mass instead of built up piece by piece. There is a handsome, austere arched entrance that suggests that of the Stuttgart railway station by Bonatz and Scholer; a corner tower with graceful setbacks that calls to mind the tower at Josef Hoffmann's Palais Stoclet, in Brussels, though it is rounder and bigger in every way; and there are vertical piers dividing several floors of windows that suggest the great factories of Peter Behrens in Germany. Saarinen's work was neither so clean nor so forceful as any of these buildings, but its design preceded all of them, and though there is no likelihood of any direct influence, it is only fair to state that Helsinki made it clear that Saarinen's work was paralleling that of many bigger modernists who were his contemporaries. But the railway station is more gentle than the work of the architects who were then evolving what was to be called the International style; it never loses its romantic sense of composition, and in this sense recalls the work of the American master of the picturesque, Bertram Goodhue. Like Goodhue, Saarinen sought to evolve a style that would appear to be modern and would show no signs of literal revivalism, yet would not break away radically from past architecture; and like Goodhue he indulged in the art of composition, blending sculpture into structure with a certainty that he was doing something that had not been done well since the Beaux-Arts.

The distance between Saarinen and the architects of the International style seemed clearer than ever in 1922, in Saarinen's famous scheme for the Chicago Tribune Building. His second-prize-winning design called for a tower that rose gracefully, even sumptuously, with four even setbacks in its upper half. The lines were primarily vertical, and the effect was Gothic in spirit, if not in detail: it looked as if certain middle sections of Cass Gilbert's great Woolworth Building had been recast into a building of altogether different shape. As in so much of Saarinen's work, massing told the story; this tower seemed to carve itself into the sky, to float upward, in a way that almost no other skyscraper had done.

But for all the Tribune design's lilting quality, it was still a fairly conservative building. Nowhere had Saarinen tried to demonstrate structure, say, as Walter Gropius and Hannes Meyer did in their stark entry, or as Knut Londberg-Holm did in his sleeker and more suave tower proposal. Saarinen's romanticism had won out again, and for all the

In the competition for design of the Chicago Tribune tower in 1922, Eliel Saarinen won second prize with this drawing. Although Saarinen's tower was never built, it had greater influence on skyscraper architecture than the winning design by Raymond Hood and John Mead Howells (see page 254).

305

Eliel Saarinen's major work in the United States, and his home for twenty-five years, was the Cranbrook educational complex at Bloomfield Hills, Michigan. His first project there was a school for boys, shown in his 1925 rendering at right. The last was the museum and library (above) of the Cranbrook Academy of Art, completed in 1943.

306

The classic simplicity of line and form that marked Eliel's late work is exemplified in the First Christian Church at Columbus, Indiana. The church and freestanding campanile were designed with his son in 1940.

quality of the design—this was romanticism as opposed to pure sentimentality, far less self-indulgent than pure revivalist skyscrapers were—one nevertheless wonders at Louis Sullivan's famous eulogy of it. Sullivan's praises, written in the *Architectural Record* of February 1923, was doubtless a reason that Saarinen's losing design became so celebrated. It revealed much about the aspirations of the American himself, then old and near death.

"One glance of the trained eye, and instant judgment comes; that judgment which flashes from inner experience, in recognition of a masterpiece," Sullivan wrote. "The Finnish master-edifice is not a lonely cry in the wilderness, it is a voice, resonant and rich, ringing amidst the wealth and joy of life."

And he concluded: "There remain, for some, two surprises: first, that a Finlander who, in his prior experience, had had no occasion to design a soaring office building should, as one to the manner born, have grasped the intricate problem of the lofty steel-framed structure . . . second, that a 'foreigner' should possess the insight required to penetrate to the depths of the sound, strong, kindly and aspiring idealism which lies at the core of the American people."

It did not take long for Saarinen's design to become real, not in the form of buildings by him but in echoes of it in the work of other architects. Raymond Hood and John Mead Howells, the winners in the Tribune competition, themselves let Saarinen influence their later work—Hood in the American Radiator Building in New York, completed in 1924, and Howells in his Panhellenic Tower in New York of 1929. But the most significant child of Saarinen's Tribune scheme was Ralph Walker's Barclay-Vesey Building in lower Manhattan for the New York Telephone Company; its massing and delicate details could not have existed without study of Saarinen's project.

All of the attention that followed his second-prize award—not to mention the honorarium of $20,000, a substantial fee in 1922—led Saarinen to visit the United States in February 1923. Building was slow in Finland, and the exposure he was receiving as an architect in a country that was away from the centers of European cultural activity was far less than he wished. Meanwhile, building activity in the United States was mounting toward the hectic peak of the late 1920's. Saarinen had never visited this country, but he seemed to have

The Jefferson National Expansion Memorial in Saint Louis is a monument to the Louisiana Purchase and a symbolic "gateway to the West." The stainless steel arch places Eero Saarinen in the select company of architects, including Gustave Eiffel and Robert Mills, who have created an emblem for a great city.

"Need a church be rectangular?" Eero asked, and in 1950 he designed this cylindrical chapel for Massachusetts Institute of Technology. Within the brick drum, light streams down from a skylight, glinting from pieces of brass on a hanging screen and flooding the altar (below).

309

In the David S. Ingalls Hockey Rink at Yale (above), designed in 1953, Eero combined new technology with a dynamic spatial feeling reminiscent of the baroque. The spinelike concrete arch and swooping roof made it look to some like a beached whale, but it drew this ultimate tribute from a player: "It makes me feel go, go, go." In the TWA terminal at New York's Kennedy airport (right), designed soon after the hockey rink, Saarinen achieved another striking sculptural effect. Though not so intended by the architect, the structure reminds many people of a bird in flight.

sensed intuitively that it was a better place for him to do his work.

The Saarinens settled first in Chicago, where Eliel worked on a monumental plan for the city's downtown—an updating, in a sense, of Daniel Burnham's classic scheme for the city. The plan was a grandiose and quite formal ordering of streets and plazas, which had as its centerpiece a great underground garage at Grant Park; Saarinen seemed especially concerned with the problems of traffic and general disorder, and he sought more than anything else to clean out the city, to smooth over its rough edges. The plan was too ambitious for its time, though it was surely in tune with the instincts of most of its era's planners, and its suggestions were never carried out. But Saarinen stayed on, moving to the school of architecture at the University of Michigan at Ann Arbor, where he taught for the first time. Despite the quality of much of the architectural output of his American years, he was ultimately to have his greatest influence in the United States as an educator, in a place quite near Ann Arbor. This was Cranbrook, at Bloomfield Hills, a school and an art academy that he was to design, live at, teach at, and serve as elder statesman to, for the rest of his life.

Cranbrook was the philanthropy of George Booth, the publisher of the Detroit *News*. Booth had long envisioned an arts-oriented school on his estate, and the first unit, an elementary school, had already begun under the design of his son, Henry,

who was a student of Saarinen's at Ann Arbor. George Booth's loyalty to his son was put aside when he met Saarinen; they became good friends, and by late 1925 Booth had enticed the Saarinens to move to Cranbrook and Eliel to take on the commission to design Cranbrook's second unit, a boys' school, which was completed in 1926.

Saarinen was ultimately to design an arts academy for Cranbrook, of which he became president in 1932; a home for himself and his wife on the grounds; a science museum; and a school for girls at Cranbrook called Kingswood. The Cranbrook projects, taken together, tell the whole story of Saarinen's gradual but deliberate evolution of an American style. The boys' school is of dark brick, and as an over-all composition it feels not unlike

the romantic Gothic campuses so many American universities built in the 1920's, except for some strikingly original details that allude loosely to Art Deco but are very much Saarinen's own. It is a romantic grouping, and in this sense calls to mind Saarinen's work in Finland; once again he has taken historical forms and reinterpreted and relaxed them. But the finest aspect of all is the skillful way in which Saarinen manipulates our movement through the complex; it is an array of quadrangles and courts and open spaces, brilliantly arranged with changes of level and scale and vista to create a constant sense of surprise. It is a reminder that Saarinen, for all his picturesque tendencies, was far more than a maker of façades: he was as well a maker of space and movement through it.

There are notable spaces in Saarinen's own house of 1929, most particularly an exquisite dining room with a low dome that recalls the great breakfast room of Sir John Soane's house—now the Soane Museum—in London. But the house is most impressive as a collection of details and furniture— a glowing tiled fireplace with a pair of peacock-shaped andirons; a dazzling tiled bathroom; a dining room table and chairs of holly wood with ebony inlays; a set of simple floor lamps with metal bowls shining light up to the ceiling. Stylistically these call to mind Art Deco, but no aspect of this house precisely resembles any well-known object by another designer.

Kingswood, the girls' school, completed in 1931, is another large, multibuilding composition;

By night as by day, the Dulles International Airport terminal stretches upward and forward to welcome air travelers. Here Saarinen used his flair for soaring shapes to create a striking but practical landmark of the age of flight.

EZRA STOLLER

The John Deere company wanted "an iron building" to proclaim its eminence in the manufacture of heavy farm machinery. Shortly before his death in 1961 Saarinen designed this headquarters, at Moline, Illinois, enclosed in a framework of a special steel that rusts to a permanent cinnamon brown.

here Saarinen has clearly been affected by the work of Frank Lloyd Wright. But the buildings are not literally Wrightian; once again a powerful style has been moderated, made lighter and more graceful, by Saarinen. Kingswood is probably Saarinen's masterwork at Cranbrook—the Wrightian and Art Deco influences with which Saarinen had been experimenting were brought together with considerable imagination. The later buildings, the science institute of 1933 and the art museum and library of 1943, are more classicizing; they bear a certain resemblance to the stripped-down classical style that was becoming so popular in the design of government buildings at that time. The only really special element is the open portico of the art museum, before which figures in a sculpted fountain by Saarinen's friend and Cranbrook colleague, Carl Milles, dance in pleasing counterpoint to the hard lines of the architecture.

The modern classicism of the art museum was the style of Saarinen's best final works in the United States, most notably the Kleinhans Music Hall in Buffalo of 1938, and the Tabernacle Church of Christ (now the First Christian Church) of Columbus, Indiana, of 1940. At Columbus Saarinen created the first, and what remains perhaps the finest, of all the buildings by well-known architects that have made that small city so notable. The church is cleaner and starker than the Cranbrook buildings, but once again Saarinen's gifts for picturesque composition of controlled spatial sequences, not to mention for well-crafted details, bring great life to a structure that at first glance appears stark.

Saarinen's home remained Cranbrook, where he died in 1950, as Loja was reading aloud a letter that had just been received from the couple's old friend Jean Sibelius. To Cranbrook he left a double legacy—not merely an architectural setting but an institution to grow and develop within that setting. Cranbrook became particularly noted as a center of furniture design, but it yielded fine architects as well: among those who studied or taught there were Florence Knoll, Harry Bertoia, Warren Platner, Charles Eames, and Harry Weese. There was another architect who, though he graduated from Yale in 1934, spent much time at Cranbrook and became its most celebrated alumnus—Eero Saarinen.

Eero had a tragically short life—though long enough to permit two marriages (the second, in

314

1953, to Aline Louchheim, the well-known art writer who was to become NBC television's on-air art critic), three children, and more than thirty major projects as well as a host of furniture designs. Saarinen's success as a furniture designer was considerable, from his first place with Charles Eames in the Museum of Modern Art furniture design competition in 1940, to his molded plastic furniture and "womb" chair which became classic pieces of the 1950's.

Eero's independent career spanned little more than a decade before he died at fifty-one in 1961. He had worked in partnership with his father at the Cranbrook studio throughout the forties, and during that time had been somewhat in Eliel's shadow, although a number of the sleeker, more stripped-down pieces of the elder Saarinen's work during this decade bear the mark of Eero's influence: Eero took the dominant role in one 1939 design, the winning entry for the Smithsonian Institution Art Gallery in Washington—a project that was never built—though it was still credited officially to Eliel. In 1948, however, Eero produced a truly major project on his own, the 590-foot-high catenary arch that was his entry into the Jefferson National Expansion Memorial competition for Saint Louis. Eliel had entered the competition with a design of his own, and the telegram announcing the winner was at first thought by both father and son to be heralding Eliel's success. But it was Eero's scheme that had won—and from then on, his reputation as an architect was secure.

Eero's design method was at once simple and complex. He thought largely in terms of basic geometric forms, but he worked with great intensity to refine them; in his unadorned office in Bloomfield Hills he would feverishly sketch scheme after scheme long into the night. He became famous for designing with models as much as with paper, though: the Saarinen office was known for its remarkable array of tiny cardboard buildings, teaching and learning tools for the architect as much as they were presentations for the client.

Saarinen's commitment to basics, to certain easily grasped, fundamental design forms, showed itself not only in his finished work but in his process of design. Saarinen used to love to tell the story of the time in 1959 when he and a number of other architects had been invited to Berkeley, California, to take part in a test on the nature of creativity. Each architect was put into a small, private booth, given a set of colored tiles, and asked to make a design. After the test, Saarinen asked Philip Johnson what he had done, and Johnson told Saarinen how much he had disliked all the colors, and therefore had thrown the colored tiles away and used only black and white.

"I told Philip I used only the white, and he was so jealous," Saarinen later recounted.

But Saarinen did not necessarily come to his simple forms instantly. For the great croquet wicket of the Saint Louis arch, for example, he had originally thought he would propose a domed structure, "sort of a lacey Pantheon." It was only much later, after visiting the site, that he reversed himself entirely and felt that the conditions required something altogether different—a great arch of stainless steel, a gate that would reach as high as a skyscraper.

The arch was not to be completed until 1964, and thus it was another project—the General Motors Technical Center in Warren, Michigan—that brought Saarinen's work more directly into the public eye. This was a multibuilding complex of low, Miesian office and research buildings arranged precisely around a reflection pool, with a great stainless steel water tower and a low, earth-hugging dome as visual accents. The buildings had brightly colored brick walls, a theatrical touch Mies van der Rohe himself would, in all likelihood, have shuddered at; the complex as a whole had a quality at once theatrical and technological, as if Saarinen's goal had been to prove that an expression of postwar technology need not be stark and boring.

That was to be a characteristic of numerous other Saarinen projects throughout the 1950's. More than any other architect, he seemed able to respond to a certain need on the part of corporations and institutions for buildings that would create a strong, clear image. A Saarinen building looked lively; it was never bland, and yet it was never superficially decorative, as were the works of such architects as Edward Durell Stone and Philip Johnson, men who shared Saarinen's sense that the Miesian style that was remaking the American landscape was too austere, too stark, to express adequately the needs of postwar culture. To an era of boxes, Saarinen offered symbols instead—buildings that seemed to relate to specific programs and specific situations. They looked different from one another, and they were. Saarinen could create a Miesian building of glass for the Bell Telephone Laboratories in Holmdel, New Jersey, of 1962, a mock-Italian hill village for Ezra Stiles and Samuel F. B. Morse colleges at Yale of 1962, not to mention the flamboyant forms of his two airports. To the architect there was no contradiction at all in these vastly different forms, for each had been created to serve a different need.

"I feel strongly that modern architecture is in danger of falling into a mold too quickly—too rigid

a mold," Saarinen said in 1958. "What once was a great hope for a great new period of architecture has somehow become an automatic application of the same formula over and over again everywhere. I feel, therefore, a certain responsibility to examine problems with the specific enthusiasm of bringing out of the particular problem the particular solution."

Saarinen had given another key to his feelings in an interview in *Time* magazine in 1956, when he said, "Our architecture is too humble. It should be prouder, more aggressive, much richer and larger than we see it today. I would like to do my part in expanding that richness."

Together, these statements sum up Eero Saarinen. To *Time* he revealed what instinct it was that led him to such bold, flamboyant shapes; in his 1958 remarks he offered the beginning of a philosophical justification for this instinct. In retrospect, it was Saarinen's emphasis on the "particular solution"— his avoidance of a consistent style—that was to have the greatest impact on American architecture in the decades to follow. The years since Saarinen's death in 1961 have been a time of collapse of the ideology of modern architecture; buildings that could be called modern are still produced, but without the theoretical underpinnings that were present in the 1950's. There is less of a sense, in other words, that the orthodox modern style is the only proper way to make architecture; what has replaced this certainty is a tendency to rely more heavily on historical forms, and on romantic, somewhat eccentric, invention.

Saarinen's work played a considerable role in establishing the climate that made this attitude possible. By rejecting the notion that a certain kind of stark, austere modernism was the one true way, Saarinen, though he still relied heavily on the Miesian style, nonetheless helped to break down the ideological force of modernism, and to shift the mood of his time toward an acceptance of a more relaxed and more problem-directed approach.

Where Saarinen built Miesian buildings, he varied them considerably, as he had done at the General Motors Technical Center. At the IBM research center at Yorktown Heights, New York, for example, he let a Miesian box sprawl into a great generous curve, and detailed it with rough stone and a flamboyant entrance canopy.

But it was not in his variations of Mies that Saarinen's inventiveness achieved its best results. Saarinen's more original forms, though they some-

times came off as awkward and pretentious—as at the Ingalls hockey rink of 1959 at Yale, which sits on a suburban hill like a great beached whale, or the dormitories at the University of Pennsylvania, which might best be called brutalism decorated— could also succeed admirably. The tower for CBS in New York, completed in 1964, is an imposing shaft of black granite, at once expressive of height and a certain urban sophistication; it feels solid and dignified in a way that few postwar skyscrapers do, and its only failing is that it stands so aloof from its neighbors, as if any inflection toward the rest of the city would destroy its perfection.

At his Yale colleges, completed in 1962, Saarinen tried something more unusual still for the 1950's—a complex that was to depend almost entirely on mood, an impressionistic stage set. The desire was to evolve a style that would fit comfortably in Yale's Gothic context without being directly imitative of that context, and the result, though highly picturesque, succeeds at this. It is at once solid and fanciful, and its romanticism seems, as much as anything Saarinen designed, to suggest the philosophical direction of the next decade.

But Saarinen's finest works, surely, were Dulles airport and the headquarters for Deere and Company, the farm equipment manufacturer, in Moline, Illinois. Dulles is as flamboyant a form as Saarinen ever created, but here the result is not mere exhibitionism—there is controlled drama to this form and to the space within it, and it never appears self-indulgent or excessive. The attempt to evolve a monumental style of architecture appropriate to the ceremony of air travel succeeds here in a way that it has not at any other airport. The system of "mobile lounges" to move passengers from terminal to plane was not as successful as the building, but if nothing else it stands as evidence of Saarinen's deep commitment to programming. He thought through the functional systems of an airport and produced a design that offered not merely a new kind of architectural enclosure, but a new kind of airport operation.

For Deere, Saarinen created a stunning eight-story structure of exposed, rusted steel to span a ravine. The building is not only framed in steel, but feels covered in steel, with beams and girders creating a gentle, subtle grid along the façade. The form is at once graceful and powerful, and in this sense sums up the best of Saarinen. It is a building that uses the most modern technology and the most modern materials, but does not use them in the most direct or expected way. It uses them for ends that are picturesque as much as technological; it was Saarinen's gift, almost alone among architects of his time, to see no contradiction between these goals.

To show his clients how their buildings would look, Eero Saarinen often worked with three-dimensional models. Here he stands behind a model of Ezra Stiles and Samuel F. B. Morse colleges, built at Yale University in 1962.

ARCHITECTS OF TODAY

Robert Venturi's design for a ski house at Vail, Colorado, 1975

BY PAUL GOLDBERGER

In the closing decades of the twentieth century, it is difficult indeed to state with certainty which of the architects now most active are going to assume the roles history has already given to Kahn, to Saarinen, or to Hood. It is simply too soon, either to see the full scope of their work, for much is yet to come, or to measure the full sweep of their influence. There can be no doubt, of course, as to the lasting importance of at least a few figures, architects such as Philip Johnson, I. M. Pei, Kevin Roche, and Paul Rudolph, each of whom has designed buildings that have already become part of the legacy of twentieth-century American architecture. But to cast the net wide, far beyond the work of these architects, it is clear that architecture in the past few years has been a source of immense public interest, perhaps more so than at any other time in this century, and that those architects responsible for this great surge must inevitably find their way into the permanent record of time.

Some of this outpouring of public interest has come from the work of architects such as Johnson and Pei, but a great deal of it can be attributed, directly or indirectly, to architects such as Robert Venturi, whose writings as well as his buildings suggest alternatives to conventional modernist practice; to Charles Moore, whose energetic work, inspired by vernacular architecture, has set off a generation of new houses; to the firm of Hardy Holzman Pfeiffer, whose brash and lively buildings have played a particularly significant role in turning public perceptions to the values of older buildings; to Romaldo Giurgola, the thoughtful heir to Louis Kahn; to Frank Gehry, the apostle of the "unfinished" building; or to Richard Meier, Charles Gwathmey, Michael Graves, John Hejduk, and Peter Eisenman, the New York architects whose work was published in the early 1970's and who rapidly became known as the Five Architects, the title of the book.

The late 1970's have been much discussed as the time in which modern architecture died—when it ceased to be a universal and expected style for our age. Now, modernism was never so rigid or so orthodox as its critics might have suggested (or its advocates might have wished), but it was, for most of the years following World War II, the common way of making large-scale public buildings in the United States. Virtually every city of any size by the end of the 1960's had acquired a glass office tower, usually housing the headquarters of the local bank; suburbs became dotted with low-slung, flat-roofed schools and shopping malls; and places in which the economy permitted them were filled with sleek, tall apartment towers. Very few of these buildings came from the drawing boards of architects of any distinction, and most of them were banal at best, sterile and austere at worst. Most of them were simplistic echoes of the ideas of the twentieth century's great modernist architects, dropped without comprehension into the midst of America's cities.

It would be unreasonably optimistic to suggest that we have seen the last of such buildings, but there has been a dramatically different attitude prevalent in the last few years. Young architects, and old architects influenced by young architects, have been producing a series of large- and small-scale buildings containing both physical forms and social goals that set them apart from conventional modern buildings. The rejection of the glass box sitting in the midst of a concrete wasteland of its own making is perhaps the central theme of the architecture of the moment: there is a vast variety of alternatives to the glass box, from visually active, almost nervous, abstractions to buildings that seem almost literally to imitate styles of the past. A desire to use the materials of modernism, to make crisp, sleek surfaces of glass and aluminum, remains strong, but these materials are combined into forms far different from what modernism's early decades offered. The new breed of towers is more romantic, and more picturesque, than its predecessors, and in this sense has something in common with the other major strain of the time, the romantic desire to echo the forms of the architecture of the past. So while no really coherent style of the time has emerged, the work of these years is surely unified by a certain underlying picturesque impulse—not to mention a desire to stand apart from what came just a few years before.

It is worth beginning, perhaps, with the story of one architect whose career encapsulates the evolution of the past few decades, and who himself has become as well-known to the general public as any architect in America: Philip Johnson. The son of a wealthy Ohio lawyer, Johnson graduated from Harvard with a degree in classics; he had no real grounding in architecture but did have a certain tendency to embrace causes, and in 1929 he joined

Henry-Russell Hitchcock, the young writer who was to become one of America's eminent architectural historians, on a tour of modern architecture in Europe. What resulted was the book *The International Style*, a significant early treatise in support of the steel, glass, and concrete architecture of orthodox modernism. After years as a critic and museum curator, the urbane, elegant, and fiercely articulate Johnson became an architect himself in the mid-1940's; he achieved his greatest early renown, surely, with his Glass House, the structure he built for himself in New Canaan, Connecticut, in 1949. Johnson was Mies van der Rohe's most earnest and creative disciple in those years; although the Glass House has a formal, classicizing air that Mies's similar projects, such as the Farnsworth house, lack—it sits firmly on the ground like a Greek temple, instead of floating above, as Mies's projects do—there can be no doubt that without Mies's example it could not have been built.

Johnson followed the Glass House with a series of similar, if less refined, houses in the Miesian mode, until the late 1950's, when despite his collaboration with Mies himself in the design of the Seagram Building, which was finished in 1958, he began to drift toward something more visually rich and picturesque. Johnson turned toward a rather fussy kind of decorative classicism, and this phase of his work, which came to fruition in the early 1960's, yielded such buildings as the New York State Theater in New York City, of 1964; the Sheldon Memorial Art Gallery in Lincoln, Nebraska, of 1963; and the Amon Carter Museum in Fort Worth, Texas, of 1961.

The lively, energetic mind that led Johnson to anticipate by more than a decade the widespread movement away from the International style that came in the late 1970's did not permit him to rest long in his period of classicism. With John Burgee, who became his partner in 1967, Johnson embarked upon a series of skyscrapers which as a group played a crucial role in shifting taste away from the conventional glass box. First came the Investors Diversified Services Center in Minneapolis, completed in 1972, a fifty-one-story multisided tower of glass joined to a nineteen-story hotel and a retail wing, all arranged around a central, glass-covered court. IDS offered both a lively shape and a new social program: it was the skyscraper joined to the agora, the tower as a part of a town's marketplace and central square. IDS rapidly became a symbol not only of the Minneapolis skyline but of the ability of the postwar skyscraper to be more than a pure abstraction, to play an active role in the cityscape.

Less notable urbanistically, but surely as important from the viewpoint of pure form, was

Johnson and Burgee's next major skyscraper, the twin-towered Pennzoil Place in Houston of 1976. Here, two towers with trapezoidal plans were placed side by side, with their tops sliced off at dramatic angles and their bottoms joined by a shared, greenhouselike lobby. Pennzoil, even more than IDS, rapidly awakened other architects, not to mention the public, to the potential of the skyscraper as an unusual and striking visual form. In the years following its completion it came to represent the movement away from the box that was to be joined by dozens of major American architects.

Pennzoil Place was what might be termed a "late modern" building; it still uses modern materials and has a certain kind of sleek, modernist imagery, but the result is something livelier, more flamboyant, than the puritanical International

CERVIN ROBINSON

In his office at the Seagram Building, a landmark of the International style, Philip Johnson leads the movement away from that style to a "postmodern" architecture. At a desk in the background is his partner, John Burgee.

Three Johnson skyscrapers now under construction promise a new variety in the skylines of American cities: above, left, 33 Maiden Lane, in New York's financial district; above, right, the American Telephone and Telegraph headquarters on Madison Avenue; below, the PPG Industries Building in Pittsburgh.

style would have permitted. Though Johnson and Burgee created other designs in a similar mode—most notably the exquisite Post Oak Central in Houston, a complex of three towers with rounded corners and more than a hint of 1930's streamlining—not long after Pennzoil's completion they were already looking elsewhere. Johnson had complained in the late 1950's, when he made his break with Mies, that architects were too quick to reject history—"One cannot not know history," he stated—and this time he turned, more literally than before, toward the architecture of the past. What resulted was the design for the American Telephone and Telegraph Company headquarters in New York, made public in 1978—a thirty-seven-story granite skyscraper topped by a broken pediment and entered through a six-story arch and a colonnaded base. AT&T, which is expected to be completed in 1982, uses a number of elements from historical styles, some literally and some interpretatively, merged into a whole that is altogether Johnson and Burgee's. No less historicist—and no less startling—are Johnson and Burgee's schemes for a Gothic tower in glass as headquarters for PPG

Industries in Pittsburgh, for a castellated tower of brick for lower Manhattan, and for a soaring glass tower of setbacks, based on the great 1920's skyscrapers of Raymond Hood and John Mead Howells, for Houston.

If Johnson's work can on occasion be criticized as too intellectual, too self-consciously concerned with ideas rather than with the poetry of form, Kevin Roche's architecture might be said to be the opposite. Roche, who with John Dinkeloo inherited Eero Saarinen's office after Saarinen's death in 1961, has built on Saarinen's reputation for picturesque modernist forms. But Roche's work is more thoughtful and consistent than Saarinen's was: he is less likely to appear, as Saarinen did, to be a dozen different architects at once.

Roche is a quiet, private, and shy man, the utter opposite of the flamboyant Johnson. He was born in Ireland, where he took his architectural degree; he did not come to the United States until 1948, by which time he was twenty-six years old. He worked briefly for Mies and then joined Saarinen's office in Bloomfield Hills, Michigan, where he was to play a crucial role in such late Saarinen projects as the CBS headquarters in New York and the Deere and Company headquarters in Moline, Illinois. After Saarinen's death he and John Dinkeloo relocated the practice in Hamden, Connecticut, a move Saarinen had initiated but had not lived to complete; there it still remains, in an old mansion in a strikingly rural setting in the midst of a New Haven suburb.

Much of the early work of Roche and Dinkeloo seems rather overbearing and excessively monumental: the Knights of Columbus headquarters in New Haven and the New Haven Arena, both completed in the late 1960's, seem like immense constructivist fantasies, powerful and inventive but hardly benign. Far pleasanter was Roche's use of the same vocabulary for the Ford Foundation in New York, of 1964, where glass and granite and Cor-ten steel, materials similar to those used at New Haven, were this time combined into an urbane and graceful urban monument, a building that manages to remain welcoming despite its grandiose scale. Roche has generally been most successful in glass: he is a true sculptor of glass, from the delicate shed of the Irwin Union Bank addition in Columbus, Indiana, to the lively form of the United Nations Plaza hotel and office tower in New York. In each case a glass skin covers the building like a blanket, with little articulation of interior function; the building is proudly abstract but visually alive at the same time. Roche's Worcester County National Bank in Worcester, Massachusetts, is similar; a glass skin of great subtlety and elegance uniformly covers a relatively active form.

These buildings, like Johnson and Burgee's Pennzoil Place, seem to occupy a middle ground between the cool formality of the modernism of the 1950's and something more pictorial, even eccentric. A view of Roche's United Nations Plaza tower from the East River shows this. To the left is the stern, austere form of the United Nations Secretariat Building, and to the right is the whimsical Chrysler Building. Roche's tower is in between—it uses the vocabulary of modernism to create a theatrical effect more like that of the Chrysler. (Indeed, the interiors of the United Nations Plaza Hotel are particularly illustrative of this: the dining rooms contain a dazzling array of mirrors and trelliswork.)

But Roche is too inventive, and too conscious of the currents of the time, to be a simple "late modernist." Whereas some of his works, like the huge series of limestone and glass wings for the Metropolitan Museum of Art, are rather heavy

In the Investors Diversified Services Center at Minneapolis, Johnson broke away from the four-sided glass slab of modern skyscrapers by adding vertical setbacks at the corners.

BALTHAZAR KORAB

exercises in late modern monumentality, others, like the series of corporate headquarters buildings Roche has done in the New York suburbs, are at once civilized and inventive. The headquarters of Richardson-Vicks, the pharmaceutical firm, is set discreetly in a Connecticut woods; parking is on the roof, and the low-slung Cor-ten steel and glass structure appears slipped neatly between the trees. But still more indicative of Roche's potential as a designer is the General Foods headquarters in Westchester County, now under construction; it is a vast structure of glass, with a central atrium under a glass vault. The Beaux-Arts derivation is clear—this is a great, classical manor house rendered in the materials of modernism. Roche here united the two impulses of architecture in the 1970's—the desire to express the potential of technology and the desire to express history—in a single structure.

That merging of essentially separate strains has not been accomplished by Philip Johnson, who has tended to design buildings of either one strain or the other, or by I. M. Pei, whose work is much more along the lines of conventional, if visually active, modernism. It has been tried, however, in some promising designs by Helmut Jahn, an articulate and deeply serious architect who in the 1970's took over the design department of C. F. Murphy, a huge commercial architectural firm in Chicago, now renamed Murphy/Jahn. After several years of producing extremely sleek, not to say slick, buildings that glittered as examples of late modernism, Jahn turned at the end of the 1970's to an attempt to incorporate historicism in his work. His addition to the Chicago Board of Trade is cool and refined but echoes in its shape the 1930's

setback forms and pyramidal top of the original Board of Trade building.

Similarly, Cesar Pelli, who like Roche began his career with Saarinen, has created a series of skyscrapers which employ the sleek, smooth imagery of "high-tech" modernism, but which through their shapes attempt to echo older architectural forms. Pelli's condominium tower addition to the Museum of Modern Art in New York is to have setbacks reminiscent of Raymond Hood's McGraw-Hill Building top of 1931, but rendered in glass; his pair of apartment towers in Houston will have something approximating mansard roofs of glass. The gracious, Argentinian-born Pelli, who is also dean of the Yale School of Architecture, is likely to have a major impact on the New York skyline: he is designing a complex of skyscrapers for Battery Park City in Lower Manhattan.

Jahn and Pelli seem likely to make their mark in the coming decade; Ieoh Ming Pei clearly has done so already. Pei, who was born to a wealthy banking family in China in 1917 and came to the United States in 1935, began his active practice in 1948 as the staff architect for William Zeckendorf, one of the most adventurous of American real-estate developers. Although the buildings that Pei designed for Zeckendorf—structures such as the Mile High Center in Denver, Place Ville Marie in Montreal, and Kips Bay Plaza in New York—were radical indeed as the output of a private developer,

The model below is that of the General Foods headquarters, now being built by Kevin Roche, John Dinkeloo and Associates in Rye, New York. At their Ford Foundation building in New York City (opposite), glass-walled offices look out upon an interior court planted with trees and flowers.

the experience of working directly for a real-estate developer nonetheless started Pei's career off with a strongly pragmatic slant. He left Zeckendorf in 1955 to found his own firm, I. M. Pei and Partners, which now has a staff of 160, built around a core of partners who were with Pei from his earliest days at the Zeckendorf office.

The Pei firm, which is based in New York, is among the few architectural firms to have made a mark equally in the design of commercial and institutional work. Its style, like Pei's own, is corporate and sleek, more that of a sophisticated business institution than an artist's atelier. Pei's first major commission on his own was the Earth Sciences tower at Massachusetts Institute of Technology, the gridded concrete façade of which was to become a Pei theme, repeated in a number of noteworthy housing towers. The M.I.T. building started Pei's practice off in an institutional direction, and the acclaim the architect received for such works as the Everson Museum of Art in

For the East Building of the National Gallery of Art, I. M. Pei (right) was given a trapezoidal site between the Mall and Pennsylvania Avenue. He designed a building that abounds with angular spaces and surfaces. In the triangular central court (below) a Calder mobile moves above the heads of visitors.

Paul Rudolph's sculptural use of striated concrete gives a unique roofline to his Endo Laboratories at Garden City, Long Island, completed in 1964. The curved bays are skylights.

Syracuse, of 1965, and the Herbert F. Johnson Museum at Cornell University, of 1973, confirmed the institutional emphasis of his practice. It is a stream of development that culminated, surely, in the call to design the East Building of the National Gallery of Art in Washington, D.C., which was completed in 1978. For the East Building, as for all of his institutional buildings, Pei evolved a solution based on abstract geometries—in this case a set of triangles. The strong, crisp structure makes considerable use of both glass and masonry, but the feeling is altogether different from the glass and stone buildings of, say, Kevin Roche. Pei's reliance on geometric shapes makes itself felt all through his buildings; diagonal lines seem as powerful as the spaces themselves, and yet the sense of structure that is often visible in Roche's work tends to be hidden here. Pei's buildings are abstract shapes within which there is often an active variety of kinds of interior space; we do not feel them as structures per se.

Oddly, there has been a feeling of structure in much, though not all, of Pei's commercial work. The 88 Pine Street tower in lower Manhattan, done with Pei partner James Ingo Freed, is a delicate and refined skyscraper of white-painted aluminum and glass, its windows set in wide bays that seem almost an homage to the early Chicago skyscraper window. On the other hand, in the John Hancock Tower in Boston, done with partner Henry N. Cobb, a neat glass skin tightly covers the sharp geometric form. Here the feeling is more like the work of Kevin Roche—though the Hancock is a bit more rigid, more strait-laced in its sleek, high-tech imagery, than Roche's skyscrapers have been. Pei seems to want every aspect of his building to have a purpose other than pure visual pleasure: the glass skin of the Hancock, for example, reflects floor divisions as Roche's at the United Nations Plaza does not; similarly, the nips and tucks that carry the over-all tower form away from the box are not simple and arbitrary gestures but inflections made with reference to the demands of the building's relationship to its neighbors in historic Copley Square.

Pei's best work, including the Hancock, the

Rudolph's Art and Architecture Building for Yale University at New Haven, Connecticut, is a monumental structure of concrete and glass. Behind the striking façade, however, teachers and students find the interior spaces difficult to work in.

Robert Venturi (below, right) has pointed the way to a postmodern style, both in his buildings and in his influential 1966 book, Complexity and Contradiction in Architecture. *Two of his houses, built in an adaptation of the Shingle style, are on Nantucket Island (above). "These two stand very much alone," writes Vincent Scully, "and their tall vertical stance gives each of them a special quality as a person; we can empathize with them as the embodiment of sentient beings. . . ."*

National Gallery, the Overseas-China Banking Center in Singapore, and the New York City Convention and Exposition Center, which will be completed in 1984, has a luxurious quality that seems to put it at odds with the austere image of the modernist traditions from which it comes. But it is determinedly modernist nonetheless—Pei has kept a conspicuous distance between himself and architects like Johnson who are engaging in the literal use of historical forms.

But Pei's active, precise, geometric late modernism is markedly closer to more recent developments than is the work of Paul Rudolph, an earnest and driven man who burst into prominence with a set of remarkable, light, tensile houses in the early 1950's. Born in 1918 in Kentucky, Rudolph came north to teach at Yale and eventually became chairman of the university's department of architecture, a position he held until he moved his practice to New York in 1965. Rudolph's work in the late 1950's moved from a light picturesque modernism, as shown in the Jewett Art Center at Wellesley College of 1958, to the immense and monumental Art and Architecture Building at Yale, completed in 1963. "A & A," as the building has generally been known, is a beautifully composed structure of striated concrete and glass, its façade an

essay in balance reminiscent of such radically different modern masterworks as Frank Lloyd Wright's Larkin Building and Le Corbusier's monastery of La Tourette. (Indeed, it is no surprise that one critic referred to the building as "a locomotive collision between Wright and Le Corbusier.") But if Rudolph succeeded in uniting two such diverse strands of modernist architecture, he did so at great price to practicality. The building sits sumptuously on a New Haven street corner, most of its interiors unworkable, a monument to formalism and to a certain kind of modernist hubris more than to accommodation to the needs of its users.

At the Haystack School (opposite), a crafts workshop on Deer Isle, the shedlike wooden buildings of Edward Larrabee Barnes seem at home with the rocks and pines of the Maine coast.

331

Venturi's ski house for the Brant family rises among the aspens on a hillside at Vail, Colorado (above). The outsize top floor contains a living room with large dormer windows and vaulted ceiling (left). "I was thinking," Venturi says, "of eighteenth-century Polish synagogues with their wonderful vaulting."

The plainest of Venturi's buildings sometimes borrow from the grandest architecture of the past. By his own account, the split gable of the house he designed for his mother in Chestnut Hill, Pennsylvania (opposite, top), derives from the monumental façade of Blenheim Palace in England.

For the same family that built the ski house in Vail, Venturi designed this home in Greenwich, Connecticut (opposite). The Palladian arrangement of windows in the curving façade of glazed green brick calls to mind the English country house.

CERVIN ROBINSON; ALL OTHERS: VENTURI, RAUCH AND SCOTT BROWN

Since the Art and Architecture Building, Rudolph's work has not changed significantly. The quality that might be called picturesque brutalism that marked the Yale building became more noticeable in other works, such as the Endo Laboratories at Garden City, New York; Tracey Towers housing in the Bronx; or the Boston Government Center. Much of Rudolph's work has a futuristic air to it as well, as evidenced in a number of houses which, like the larger-scale buildings, are exquisite compositions, but which frequently appear unrelated either to the architecture around them or to the functions within them.

The generation of which Rudolph, Roche, and Pei are members—Johnson, who was born in 1906, is older—has produced other architects of note as well. There is Edward Larrabee Barnes, born in 1922, whose practice, like Pei's and Johnson's, has contained a mix of institutional and commercial work, but who is coming increasingly to be known as a shaper of the skyline. Barnes's IBM building, a forty-three-story skyscraper in midtown Manhattan due to be completed in 1982, will be a five-sided tower of dark green granite, with a glass-enclosed, greenhouselike park at its base. In its provision of such a social amenity as a central aspect of the design, it seems to derive from Johnson's IDS Center; Barnes has tried, however, in the use of granite and in the unusual shape, to integrate the tower into the larger urban context as well as to

provide a restrained hint of the sleek imagery that has become so common in the past decade.

Barnes made his mark originally with a series of smaller, institutional structures, such as the Haystack School in Deer Isle, Maine, of 1962, and the Walker Art Center in Minneapolis of 1974, both of which attempt to combine stark geometries with the moods of older, more traditional building forms. The fortresslike Walker is generally acknowledged to be among the most successful new museums in the United States; its interiors are powerful yet flexible, and hospitable to a wide range of types of art. But Barnes's work is not easily categorized, at least not in visual terms; if Roche might be thought of as a picturesque modernist, Barnes might be called a thoughtful one—an architect who attempts to evolve modernist forms into something less abstract and more closely related to the demands of the building's program and the urban situation in which the building is to be placed. His new museum for the Asia Society in New York, for example, is a structure of reddish granite, with a powerful façade intended as a force to define the building's presence on Park Avenue; behind the billboardlike front the building steps back and becomes more modest.

Ulrich Franzen was born in 1921 in Germany; he trained at Harvard, as did Barnes, and for some years his work showed that influence clearly. Franzen, like Philip Johnson, tried through the 1960's and 1970's to find some sort of alternative to orthodox modernism; at first his work was rather heavy and brutalist, mixing, in such buildings as the Agronomy Laboratories at Cornell of 1968, influences as diverse as Le Corbusier, Pei, and Rudolph. But by the late 1970's Franzen was taking

The Occupational Health Center at Columbus, Indiana (below), was designed by the firm of Hardy Holzman Pfeiffer to serve the employees of the Cummins Engine Company and other industrial concerns. Bright colors, used to highlight the structural and service elements of the building, give patients plenty of distraction in the reception area (opposite).

Charles Moore (above) designed this complex of vacation houses for the Sea Ranch community on the northern California coast. Drawing inspiration equally from rural Vermont and Italian hill towns, it is intricately planned to afford ocean views from all the units, together with areas of shelter from the strong winds.

a more direct antimodernist stance and had begun to produce structures such as 800 Fifth Avenue in New York, an apartment house with a limestone "false front" intended to relate it to the smaller-scale buildings around it; and a headquarters tower for Philip Morris, due to be completed in 1982, that will make more overt classical gestures and have different limestone façades to emphasize the different role each of its sides plays in the cityscape.

If Franzen's 800 Fifth Avenue and Philip Morris seem to place urbanistic concerns over purely formal ones, that approach might be said to owe a major debt to the writings and teachings of Romaldo Giurgola, an Italian-born architect who became a disciple of Louis Kahn. Giurgola views the building not as a pure object in itself, as Pei, Roche, and even Johnson tend to do, but as a fragment of a larger urban whole. To him, the building's ability to successfully integrate parts of this larger whole is more important than its unity as a single object.

Giurgola, who was born in 1920, practiced for many years in Philadelphia; in 1967 he came to New York to head Columbia's department of architecture, and since then his firm has been divided between an office he heads in New York and one in Philadelphia directed by his partner,

Ehrman B. Mitchell. Among the major works of Mitchell/Giurgola Architects are two Philadelphia towers, one for Penn Mutual Life Insurance Company and the other for the INA Corporation, both completed in 1976. Penn Mutual, a structure of glass and concrete that has a number of different façade treatments, articulates Giurgola's views with particular clarity. So does his Fairchild Center for the Life Sciences at Columbia University, where a set of panels of reddish quarry tiles comes together to make a façade that fills a difficult and tight site. Giurgola's buildings are not as graceful as those of, say, Roche or Pei, and they are even somewhat harsh—in this sense they recall those of Giurgola's mentor, Kahn. But they are harsh only in visual terms; they emerge out of a deep understanding of the functions they contain and the cities in which they are placed, and they are almost invariably

Richard Meier (above) was called upon to design a visitors' center for the restored community of New Harmony, Indiana. In the early nineteenth century New Harmony was the site of two utopian experiments, the first launched by the Harmonists, a strict German sect, the second by the intellectual followers of Robert Owen. Meier's Atheneum, a "high-tech" structure clad in shiny white porcelain enamel, rises starkly from the green landscape, at odds with the multiperiod architecture of New Harmony but in tune with later visions of Utopia.

civilizing influences. And Giurgola's own deeply philosophical leanings make him seem personally as well as professionally Kahn's heir.

Almost a contemporary of these architects—he was born in 1925—is Robert Venturi, who with his wife and partner, Denise Scott Brown, and his partner John Rauch, has created an architectural firm that has come to have an impact far in excess of the amount of built work it has to its credit. Venturi, too, was deeply influenced by Kahn, but in a less literal sense than Giurgola was. His buildings have never resembled Kahn's, but Kahn, as well as Venturi's Princeton professor Jean Labatut, led him early in his career away from the strictures of orthodox modernism. Venturi became probably the most articulate and influential critic of the orthodox modern movement; his now-classic book, *Complexity and Contradiction in Architecture* (1966), argued strongly that the modernist architecture of the International style was cold, dull, and insufficiently expressive of the complexity and irony of modern times.

Venturi's own work is highly complex and ironic; though he has often argued that the "dumb and ordinary" vernacular architecture of the American landscape is a more appropriate model for imitation than the work of the modern masters, his own buildings are not simple at all. They tend to be highly studied, mannered essays on architectural themes, with references to the architecture of the past. His house for his mother, built in 1964 in Chestnut Hill, Pennsylvania, for example, has an immense split gable, an allusion to the gable of Sir John Vanbrugh's Blenheim Palace, but the over-all form is quite simple, so simple as to recall the drawings of houses done by children. The house is thus at once simple and complex—an image intended to be almost innocent, on the one hand, and studied and knowing, on the other.

Because its work is more sophisticated than that which most corporations tend to commission, the Venturi firm does a greater proportion of houses than do most architects of such substantial reputation. The physical forms of such buildings of the mid-1970's as the Tucker house in Westchester County, New York; the Brant house in Greenwich, Connecticut; the Brant-Johnson house in Vail, Colorado; the Trubek and Wislocki houses in Nantucket; and the Brant house in Bermuda are all quite different; but the themes are essentially those established in the Chestnut Hill house—that of commenting both on the vernacular of the house and on architectural styles of the past, all the while attempting to create something that is inventive and handsome on its own terms.

Although Venturi, Rauch, and Scott Brown's houses and other buildings, such as their checker-

Fifth Avenue facade
Portland

Graves
'80

board façade art museum addition of 1976 at Oberlin College, are too distinctive to bear direct imitation, the firm's influence, on an ideological level, has been enormous. It has, for example, been a significant force in leading younger architects toward an appreciation of and a willingness to use vernacular architecture. And in terms of the general drift of younger architects away from a belief that the stark forms of International style modernism are an appropriate style, Venturi has been crucial.

There are a number of other architects whose work, if not directly influenced by Venturi's, has at least a certain ideological sympathy with it. Charles Moore, who followed Paul Rudolph as head of Yale's architecture school, has built a series of houses that incorporate a number of vernacular influences, from the sheds and barns of New England to the Spanish Colonial buildings of southern California. Moore's work is exuberant, far more so than Venturi's, and it is thus no surprise that it seems to have had a greater popular appeal. His Sea Ranch condominiums in northern California of 1965 are among the most imitated housing designs of modern times.

Similarly, the lively trio of architects Hugh Hardy, Malcolm Holzman, and Norman Pfeiffer, who have practiced together in New York since 1967, have created a body of work that is not as mannered or as self-conscious as Venturi's, but contains clear parallels. Hardy Holzman Pfeiffer's buildings, such as the Mount Healthy School of 1972 and the Occupational Health Center of 1974, both in Columbus, Indiana, or Orchestra Hall in Minneapolis, of 1974, tend to be brash and loud, and to use industrial imagery heavily. But they are also heavily decorative and thus take a strong stance against the austerity of modernist architecture.

Indeed, as the architecture of the 1980's begins to emerge, it is difficult to find any major practitioner who permits his work to be called austere at all. Some members of the generation now coming into prominence—those architects born in the 1930's and 1940's—have made dramatic shifts, such as that of Michael Graves, who began his career as a determined Neo-Corbusian and now designs classicizing structures with rich colors and elaborate decoration, albeit composed with a certain cubist eye. His Portland (Oregon) Public Service Build-

Michael Graves's design for the Public Service Building in Portland, Oregon, seems likely to be a milestone in postmodern architecture. Above the elaborate green base, red-brown columns are backed by a gigantic window of reflective glass that covers the center of the building. The goddess floating above the entrance symbolizes the city of Portland, while a rooftop pavilion projects the image of a temple on a mountain.

ing, due to be completed in 1982, is his first attempt to work at large scale, and it seems certain to be a building of major public impact. But even where the change is not so dramatic, it is noticeable. All of the members of the Five Architects group, of which Graves is one, have shifted somewhat in emphasis: Charles Gwathmey has put aside the white palette of early modernism in favor of buildings of color, and Richard Meier, whose work continues to have a great influence among student architects, has been designing in a style that while modernist and formal is also deeply picturesque.

Meier's ability to create a balance between the picturesque impulse and modernist discipline has thus far produced a number of buildings that seem likely to be remembered as significant works of the 1970's. His Douglas House of 1975, perched above Lake Michigan in Harbor Springs, Michigan, is a grid of solid and void, of wood and glass, that is as picturesque in its way as any Georgian revival house of the 1920's. Yet it is firmly modernist in its vocabulary, as is Meier's Atheneum, in the town of New Harmony, Indiana, completed in 1980. Here, in a visitor's center and auditorium for a restored nineteenth-century utopian village, Meier chose not to echo the style of the old, neighboring houses, but to design a modernist building, as stark and white as anything Corbusier could have created in his great period of the 1920's.

But the Atheneum is not literally Corbusian; once again, Meier's own impulse, which is heavily pictorial and compositional, makes the structure lighter and livelier than were its predecessors from the 1920's. The Atheneum recalls the utopianism of early modernism in a way that is almost poignant. For that is a moment far gone from twentieth-century architecture; the belief that a new architectural style might reform society, a belief that was at the base of the modern movement, has lost its power to sway. Meier indicates in the Atheneum not that he believes in this utopianism, but that he respects it and wishes to honor it.

The Atheneum is, thus, a building that looks backward as much as it looks ahead, and in this sense it has a kinship with most of the important architecture being made in the United States at this moment. It recalls the architecture of the past, not in the literal sense of imitation but in a sense of tribute, a sense of willing and conscious integration of certain aspects of what has come before into something that is new. It is, in that sense, eclectic—it is a mixture of many things, of many impulses. For all its modernist imagery, it is a building that is eclectic at heart, that seems to spring from the desire to symbolize a pluralist culture—a desire that has been at the root of much American architecture throughout this nation's history.

Acknowledgments

The editors wish to thank the following individuals and institutions for their help in preparing this book: Esther I. Kahn; Michael Rubenstein; Peter White; Janet Parks, Avery Library, Columbia University; Mary Jane Lightbown, The Museum of Modern Art; John Zukowsky, The Burnham Library, The Art Institute of Chicago; Sherry Burke, American Institute of Architects Foundation, Prints and Drawings Collection; City University of New York, City College Architecture Library; New York Society Library; The Mercantile Library; New York Public Library—Donnell Art Library.

The Authors

VINCENT SCULLY is the Colonel John Trumbull Professor of the History of Art at Yale. His studies include *The Shingle Style, The Shingle Style Today, Modern Architecture,* and *The Earth, the Temple, and the Gods.*

MARSHALL B. DAVIDSON is the author of numerous volumes on American history, art, and architecture, including the award-winning *Life in America,* the *American Heritage History of Notable American Houses,* and a three-volume survey of American antiques. To be published soon: his comprehensive guide to the American wing at the Metropolitan Museum of Art.

JOSEPH KASTNER was for many years the copy editor of the weekly *Life* magazine and is the author of *A Species of Eternity* (on American naturalists). He is currently working on a study of nineteenth-century diarists.

ORMONDE DE KAY, JR. is the author of several historical books, including biographies of Lewis and Clark, and of Theodore Roosevelt. He contributed to the American Heritage volumes *Mysteries of the Past* and *Mysteries of the Deep.*

JOHN RUSSELL was the art critic of the *Sunday Times* of London until 1974 and since then has been an art critic of the *New York Times.* He has written a number of books, including *The World of Matisse, Francis Bacon, Edouard Vuillard,* and *The Meanings of Modern Art.*

RICHARD F. SNOW is the managing editor of AMERICAN HERITAGE magazine. He has written extensively on many aspects of the American experience. His historical novel, *The Burning,* was published this year by Doubleday.

WAYNE ANDREWS is the Archives of American Art Professor at Wayne State University, in Michigan. He is the author of seven books on American architecture as well as four social histories. His most recent study is a biography of Voltaire (1981).

WILLIAM MARLIN was for many years the architectural and urban design critic for the *Christian Science Monitor.* He later became editor-in-chief of *Architectural Forum,* then was associate editor of *Architectural Record,* and is now the editor-in-chief of *Inland Architect.* He served as general architectural consultant for this volume.

RICHARD REINHARDT is the author of several books on the history of the Far West. He teaches journalism at the University of California at Berkeley and contributes frequently to AMERICAN HERITAGE magazine and other publications.

CARTER WISEMAN has been a senior editor of *Horizon* magazine and managing editor of *Portfolio.* He is now a senior editor of *New York* magazine, writing on architecture and urban design.

M. W. NEWMAN is a writer for the Chicago *Sun-Times* specializing in urban concerns. Previously he was an editor with the Chicago *Daily News,* then editor of *Inland Architect* magazine, 1969–80.

CHARLES L. MEE, JR. is a former editor of *Horizon* magazine. He has written several works of American History, including *Meeting at Potsdam* and *The Ohio Gang,* about President Harding's colleagues. Currently he is completing a volume on the Marshall Plan.

PAUL GOLDBERGER is the architecture critic of the *New York Times.* He has lectured widely on architecture and has been published in such prominent periodicals as *Art in America, Art News, Architectural Record, Progressive Architecture.* He is the author of *The City Observed—New York: An Architectural Guide to Manhattan* and is completing a visual history of the skyscraper. He is the 1981 recipient of a medal of the American Institute of Architects, honoring him as "one of America's most significant architectural journalists."

INDEX

References to illustrations are printed in boldface type.